THE ESSENTIAL
DEPARTMENT CHAIR

THE ESSENTIAL
DEPARTMENT CHAIR

*A Comprehensive
Desk Reference*

Second Edition

o

Jeffrey L. Buller

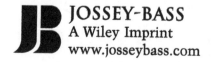

JOSSEY-BASS
A Wiley Imprint
www.josseybass.com

Jossey-Bass Resources for Department Chairs

Books

Jeffrey L. Buller, *Academic Leadership Day by Day: Small Steps That Lead to Great Success*

Jeffrey L. Buller, *The Essential Department Chair: A Comprehensive Desk Reference, Second Edition*

Don Chu, *The Department Chair Primer: What Chairs Need to Know and Do to Make a Difference, Second Edition*

Robert E. Cipriano, *Facilitating a Collegial Department in Higher Education: Strategies for Success*

Christian K. Hansen, *Time Management for Department Chairs*

Mary Lou Higgerson, *Communication Skills for Department Chairs*

Mary Lou Higgerson and Teddi A. Joyce, *Effective Leadership Communication: A Guide for Department Chairs and Deans for Managing Difficult Situations and People*

Deryl Leaming, *Academic Leadership: A Practical Guide to Chairing the Department, Second Edition*

Deryl Leaming, *Managing People: A Guide for Department Chairs and Deans*

Jon Wergin, *Departments That Work: Building and Sustaining Cultures of Excellence in Academic Programs*

N. Douglas Lees, *Chairing Academic Departments: Traditional and Emerging Expectations*

Darla J. Twale and Barbara M. De Luca, *Faculty Incivility: The Rise of the Academic Bully Culture and What to Do About It*

Daniel W. Wheeler et al., *The Department Chair's Handbook, Second Edition*

Daniel W. Wheeler, *Servant Leadership for Higher Education: Principles and Practices*

Journal

The Department Chair

Online Resources

Visit www.departmentchairs.org for information on online seminars, articles, book excerpts, and other resources tailored especially for department chairs.

Published by Jossey-Bass
A Wiley Imprint
One Montgomery Street, Suite 1200, San Francisco, CA 94104-4594
www.josseybass.com

Jossey-Bass books and products are available through most bookstores. To contact Jossey-Bass directly call our Customer Care Department within the U.S. at 800-956-7739, outside the U.S. at 317-572-3986, or fax 317-572-4002.

Wiley also publishes its books in a variety of electronic formats and by print-on-demand. Some material included with standard print versions of this book may not be included in e-books or in print-on-demand. If the version of this book that you purchased references media such as CD or DVD that was not included in your purchase, you may download this material at http://booksupport.wiley.com. For more information about Wiley products, visit www.wiley.com.

Library of Congress Cataloging-in-Publication Data

Buller, Jeffrey L.
   The essential department chair : a comprehensive desk reference /
Jeffrey L. Buller. — 2nd ed.
      p. cm.
   Includes index.
      ISBN 978-1-118-12374-4 (cloth); 978-1-118-14567-8 (ebk); 978-1-118-14568-5 (ebk);
978-1-118-14569-2 (ebk)
   1.   College department heads   2.   Universities and colleges—Administration.
I. Title.
   LB2341.B744 2012
   378.1'11—dc23   2011032348

Printed in the United States of America
FIRST EDITION
HB Printing   V10010869_060619

CONTENTS

PART THREE
The Chair's Role in Searches, Hiring, and Firing

PART FOUR
Mentoring Challenges and Opportunities for
Department Chairs

PART FIVE
The Chair's Role in Faculty Development

PART SIX
Best Practices in Evaluation and Assessment

THE AUTHOR

JEFFREY L. BULLER is dean of the Harriet L. Wilkes Honors College of Florida Atlantic University. He began his administrative career as honors director and chair of the Department of Classical Studies at Loras College in Dubuque, Iowa, before going on to assume a number of administrative appointments at Georgia Southern University and Mary Baldwin College. Buller is the author of *Academic Leadership Day by Day: Small Steps That Lead to Great Success* (Jossey-Bass, 2011), *The Essential College Professor: A Practical Guide to an Academic Career* (Jossey-Bass, 2010), *The Essential Academic Dean: A Practical Guide to College Leadership* (Jossey-Bass, 2007), and *Classically Romantic: Classical Form and Meaning in Wagner's* Ring (Xlibris, 2001). He has also written numerous articles on Greek and Latin literature, nineteenth- and twentieth-century opera, and college administration. From 2003 to 2005, Buller served as the principal English-language lecturer at the International Wagner Festival in Bayreuth, Germany. More recently, he has been active as a consultant to Sistema Universitario Ana G. Méndez in Puerto Rico and to the Ministry of Higher Education in Saudi Arabia, where he is assisting with the creation of a kingdom-wide academic leadership center.

INTRODUCTION

ONCE UPON A TIME, there was a well-known institution of higher education—a college or university located not far from where you are reading these words right now—that had an ongoing problem: people could never agree on what they should call the administrators in charge of individual disciplines. Some people at the school believed that the appropriate term was *department heads* because these people led the discipline and made important decisions about everyone else in the department. But others argued that a better term would be *department chairs* because this title would better reflect the democratic and collegial nature of the institution. During one particularly long discussion of this issue, it happened that a well-respected senior professor remarked, "You know, I think I have the answer. We shouldn't call them *heads* because I've got an uncle who served many years in the navy, and I learned from him that the expression 'going to the head' has a pretty unpleasant connotation to sailors." There was a moment of silence, and most people began nodding in agreement with the insight of this well-respected professor. But then a rather timid young instructor sitting at the back of the room spoke up: "Well, I'm not altogether sure that I'd feel comfortable working for a chair. You see, *my* uncle served many years in the state prison and, to a convict, the expression 'going to the chair' has an even *more* unpleasant connotation."

No matter whether you're a department head, department chair, division coordinator, or some other administrator who works closely with the faculty and students of particular disciplines, welcome to the often baffling world of college administration. The story just retold is probably an urban legend (at least, I've heard suspiciously similar versions of it at many colleges and universities), but the basic scenario it presents is real enough. College administration is a place where, despite our best efforts, connotations are all too often unpleasant, the disagreements over terminology are never ending, and just when you think an issue is solved, that one voice from the back of the room makes you reconsider everything. Even with all of these drawbacks, however, if you are passionate about making a difference in the world, you have chosen your career path wisely. There are probably few other opportunities in which you can affect, as significantly and as immediately as you can as chair, the way in which students are taught, scholarship is performed, and your discipline is served as you can at the departmental level. Unlike most of your institution's other senior administration, you are likely to have meaningful and ongoing contact with students, faculty members, and other department chairs. You will know them by name, be familiar with their personal and professional histories, and be asked to make decisions that will affect their livelihoods and their lives. If you were looking for challenging but important work, you're in exactly the right job.

This book contains strategies for how you can make a difference in people's lives on a daily basis. Many guides for academic administrators explore differing philosophies of administration, theoretical approaches to management and leadership, and exciting new trends in higher education administration. You probably have a shelf of such books in your office, and if you've read even a few of them, you know how useful they can be in getting you inspired to develop a major new vision for your discipline or, perhaps, your entire institution. But in order to make that vision a reality, you've probably already realized that you've got to know, on a day-to-day basis, how to excel at the many administrative tasks assigned to you. For instance, how do you cultivate a potential donor who can give you the resources you'll need to make your vision for your department a reality? How do you interview someone from outside your field if your dean assigns you to a committee searching for an administrator in a different academic area? How do you fire someone? How do you get the members of your department to work together more harmoniously? How do you keep the people who report to you motivated and capable of seeing the big picture?

This book is about the "how" of academic administration.

The chapters that follow are, for the most part, the result of a series of workshops and consultancies in faculty and administrative development that I have given over the past thirty years at colleges and universities around the world. For each topic, I have taken the essence of what administrators need to know and condensed it even further to an easily read five- to ten-page summary that focuses on the most important information you will want to have at your fingertips as you face a particular challenge or opportunity. Many of the chapters in this book first appeared as articles in the quarterly resource the *Department Chair* (one of my own favorite resources when I was a department chair), and I have adapted and updated them for this book. I have then grouped them together according to various themes and questions that you may have.

Scattered throughout the book are a number of essential principles formatted as follows:

> Essential principles are the key ideas that can help you succeed in a variety of administrative situations. These are the principles to which you'll want to give extra attention when you face your own administrative opportunities and challenges.

Essential principles are designed to be short and easily remembered, but they are not platitudes. All of them have been tested in actual administrative situations and have proven their value. Even if you end up disagreeing with a few of these guidelines, they deserve your serious and thoughtful attention. Don't ignore them.

This second edition of *The Essential Department Chair* retains all of the best features of the first edition while expanding the book to bring it more in line with its partners in this series: *The Essential College Professor: A Practical Guide to an Academic Career* and *The Essential Academic Dean: A Practical Guide to College Leadership*. The new subtitle, *A Comprehensive Desk Reference,* signifies the ambitious new scope of this volume. In addition to providing such features as the essential principles, each part of the book ends with an analysis of a scenario that builds on the ideas discussed in that part. An introduction to the concept of the scenario analysis appears at the beginning of Chapter Nine. Web sites have been updated, several new topics are included, and a number of books and articles that were not available when the first edition was published have been included in the References and Resources sections at the ends of chapters. Readers now also have access to additional content on the Web. This premium material, which deals with effective strategies for working with various groups of stakeholders, builds on the material contained in this book and provides a context for applying the solutions discussed in these pages to a wide range of administrative challenges.

Special thanks are due to Carolyn Dumore Allard, production editor for several titles of this series, for her unhesitating support and abundance of good ideas. In fact, it was her suggestion to develop *The Essential Department Chair* out of a series of articles I had written for the *Department Chair*, which she also ably edits. When I couldn't figure out a suitable way of doing that, she developed the structure for the first edition of this book that has guided the entire series. It is no exaggeration to say that Carolyn taught me how to write books for college administrators, an activity that has been one of my greatest pleasures for the past five years.

So, with that as an introduction, let me proceed immediately to the very first "How?" question you may have: How should I use this book so that it will be most beneficial to me and my ongoing administrative needs?

My suggestion is that most readers will probably not gain the most from this book by reading it straight through from cover to cover in a single sitting. (Of course, you are more than welcome to do so if you wish, and you will earn my eternal admiration and gratitude just for making the effort.) Instead, most people will benefit most by using *The Essential Department Chair* as a desk reference or an occasional guide to help address particular problems. It is intended to be what medieval authors sometimes called a *vade mecum,* a "go with me"—the sort of ready reference that you pick up and put down as you need it. You may discover, for instance, that you have a certain need or desire—perhaps you want to set up an innovative faculty development program in your discipline; the director of the institutional advancement office tells you that she wants you to meet with a prospective contributor; you find yourself exasperated by a faculty member who's using up all of your time with increasingly petty complaints—and so you turn to this book to read about precisely what you need to know about how to address your particular issue (and my hope is that you will usually read about it in ten minutes or less).

My guiding principle throughout this book has been to emphasize proven solutions over untested theories and to stress what you need to know right now at the expense of how to develop a deep and abiding philosophy of higher education administration. (You already own all the books you will ever need on how to do that.) Throughout the "Essential Series," I've tried to gather only the essential information that academic leaders need for their jobs and to provide it all in one place.

As an administrator, you have come to understand that your ultimate goal is to stop putting out fires and begin making a difference. With that in mind, think of this book as your administrative sprinkler system. Scan the Contents pages to find an issue that you're dealing with right now and see if the relevant chapter can help you turn a problem into an opportunity to make that administrative dream of yours come true.

In the meantime, good firefighting!

THE ESSENTIAL
DEPARTMENT CHAIR

PART ONE

THE CHAIR'S ROLE AND CAREER PATH

I

IN THE TRENCHES

THE JOB OF CHAIRING a department is probably the most important, least appreciated, and toughest administrative position in higher education. Because of their intimate knowledge of their disciplines, department chairs provide advocacy for the faculty, students, and curricula of their particular fields. Although the job description for department chairs varies widely from institution to institution, most people who head academic units play at least some role in scheduling classes or establishing course rotations, have budgetary responsibilities, develop long- and short-range plans for their disciplines, serve as intermediaries between the faculty and upper administration, and are involved in hiring new faculty members. They also attend meetings—lots and lots of meetings. In return, they may receive a stipend, a reduced teaching load, a twelve-month contract, or merely the satisfaction of having made an important difference to the success of their field. Most surprising, they perform all of their duties with very little training. In a study done by Robert Cipriano and Richard Riccardi (2010), a stunning 80.7 percent of the department chairs who responded to a survey had absolutely no formal training in their administrative responsibilities. Even worse, 96.2 percent had not been exposed to best practices in departmental administration during their academic course work.

We therefore work in a highly unusual profession. In most fields, you take your course work first, earn a credential, and then apply for a job. Most department chairs establish a reputation as teachers and researchers, are given an administrative position that (unless their academic field happens to be higher education administration) usually has absolutely nothing to do with their formal credentials, and only then begin to seek training in the administrative work that is now a significant part of their

3

daily responsibilities. Or they sometimes begin to seek training. In a survey conducted by Jossey-Bass (2009), 91 of 137 respondents (66.4 percent) had not bought any books or subscribed to any journals or newsletters about the role of the chair. In other words, most chairs learn their job by observing what other chairs do and by trial and error. The problem with these approaches is that the exemplars we imitate are likely to vary in consistency, and there's no guarantee that the more experienced chairs around us are all engaging in best practices. Moreover, in order to learn by trial and error, you have to commit a significant number of errors. And although mistakes can be valuable learning experiences, you don't want to commit them in situations that could damage someone's livelihood, reputation, or future career. There's got to be a better way for department chairs to learn their jobs.

The issue of the training and preparation of department chairs is particularly important because there are so many chairs at colleges and universities. Institutions may have only one chief executive officer and a handful of vice presidents and deans, but the number of department chairs tends to be large even at fairly small institutions. In addition, the turnover rate is quite high. Some institutions have formal term limits for chairs, while others rotate this administrative assignment through the members of the discipline. Cipriano and Riccardi (2010) found that the average number of years most chairs spend in their positions is six. Since at least one of those years is probably devoted to a fairly steep learning curve, the vast majority of department chairs may be relatively new to their positions.

The work that department chairs do has an immediate and lasting impact. Institutions and units can survive—perhaps even thrive—for a few years under a weak president, provost, or dean, but the actions of department chair affect the day-to-day experience of students and professors alike. In a phrase that's heard repeatedly about department chairs, these are the administrators who are "down there in the trenches." Chairs rarely, if ever, have the luxury of making a decision and then letting other people deal with the consequences. If you do something that creates a problem for someone else, you'll hear about it immediately.

The balance of this chapter explores what chairs need to do in order to take the best advantage of their unique position in the structure of the college or university.

Use Your Resources

The next chapter explores some of the steps you should take if you're a relatively new chair or a faculty member who is likely to chair your department in the future. For the moment, however, let's consider the basic things that all department chairs need to do, regardless of the size of their discipline, the mission of their institution, or the length of their tenure in office. And that topic brings us directly to the first essential principle in this book:

> Remember to use your resources. Almost every situation you will face has already been faced by other chairs at your school or elsewhere in higher education. There are precedents all around you, and although you should never feel constrained by them, it is rarely necessary to treat every challenge or opportunity as though it were occurring for the very first time. Learn from the experience (and the mistakes) of others.

This book is a good place to begin for resources. It contains a lot of basic information, and most chapters end with a list of other recommended works. But your resources are also the policies and procedures of your institution, the ever-expanding library of books and electronic materials on nearly every aspect of higher education administration, and the professional training workshops that take place online and at conferences many times throughout the academic year.

Perhaps the question should be phrased instead as, "Who are your resources?" You can learn a great deal from other chairs at your school, your supervisor, chairs of your discipline at peer and aspirational institutions, and respected members of your own faculty. Whenever you find yourself trying to work through an issue all by yourself, trying to make a decision simply on the basis of common sense and a certain amount of guesswork, stop and remember this chapter. You're not in this alone, no matter what "this" may happen to be. The following sections identify some major resources that every department chair should be familiar with.

Publications

The *Department Chair*, published quarterly by Jossey-Bass, is a thirty-two-page publication that contains ten or more articles about the practical aspects of leading an academic unit. It's an excellent way to keep up-to-date about legal issues that affect higher education administration, emerging trends and best practices in academic leadership, and the various challenges that chairs encounter routinely in their jobs. *Academic*

Leader appears more frequently than the *Department Chair*, but its issues and the articles it contains are shorter. Published monthly by Magna Publications, each issue of *Academic Leader* contains four to six concise articles on matters of current concern to academic administrators. *Change: The Magazine of Higher Learning* is published bimonthly by the Helen Dwight Reid Educational Foundation under the editorial leadership of the Carnegie Foundation for the Advancement of Teaching in Stanford, California. Distributed by Heldref Publications, *Change* is probably the premiere publication today on matters of higher education policy and emerging topics of interest for colleges and universities. Many of the concepts that we now take for granted as department chairs, such as Robert Barr and John Tagg's (1995) suggestion that higher education shift from a teaching paradigm to a learning paradigm, were first explored within the pages of *Change*. Finally, the *Chronicle of Higher Education* is a weekly resource of late-breaking academic and administrative issues. Both its printed and electronic versions include numerous advertisements for positions at colleges and universities all over the world. A good rule of thumb for any decision you are about to make is, "How would this look if it appeared on the front page of the *Chronicle*?" Letters to the editor and the *Chronicle*'s online forum (www.chronicle .com) provide an opportunity for chairs to discuss matters of policy with colleagues at other institutions worldwide.

Every department chair should be an avid reader of the publications that are most relevant to his or her specific position, but the *Department Chair, Academic Leader, Change,* and the *Chronicle of Higher Education* should be considered required reading no matter what your job description may be.

Web-Based Materials

Written materials, much of them previously disseminated through publications, are also widely available through various Web sites. These materials are often free, while others can be obtained at a nominal cost.

○ The American Council on Education (ACE) sponsors the Department Chair Online Resource Center (www.acenet.edu/ resources/chairs/), which includes resources on such topics as leadership, interacting with the faculty, and managing resources. Many of the items first appeared as articles in such publications as the *Department Chair, Academic Leader,* and the *Chronicle of Higher Education,* and materials are downloadable without cost.

- The IDEA Center, based in Manhattan, Kansas, offers a knowledge base of best practices for using its evaluation instruments, improving the quality of instruction, building on critical thinking skills, and related topics (www.theideacenter.org/category/helpful-resources/knowledge-base). IDEA papers and POD (Professional Organizational Development Notes) are free and organized by topic.
- Faculty Focus, a service of Magna Publications, is a free online newsletter (www.facultyfocus.com), and its "Free Reports" page provides access to dozens of articles that first appeared in *Academic Leader*. "Free Reports" are organized by such topics as making the transition from faculty member to administrator, assessment, faculty development, online education, and course design. Each report includes ten or more articles related to a central theme.

Workshops

A number of excellent workshops and training sessions exist that can provide chairs with information about topics of special concern to them, allow them to discuss issues of common interest, and offer them opportunities to improve their skills through exercises, case studies, and simulations. Among the many excellent conferences and workshops for department chairs are these:

- The IDEA Center's Department Leadership Seminars, offered every November and June, provide training on a wide variety of administrative issues and are conducted by experienced professionals who bring a practical perspective to their highly interactive sessions. (See www.theideacenter.org.)
- The Council of Independent Colleges (CIC) sponsors a number of annual workshops for department and division chairs that address such matters as effective faculty recruitment, tenure and promotion issues, conflict resolution, successful advocacy for the discipline, and the like. (See http://www.cic.org/conferences_events/index.asp.) The CIC also maintains a listserv for department chairs (CICCHAIR-LIST) and publishes a wide range of books and reports that will be of interest to academic leaders, particularly at private or independent institutions.
- Kansas State University conducts the K-State Academic Chairperson's Conference in Orlando, Florida, each February. The conference includes presentations, as well as full- and half-day

workshops on a wide variety of issues relating to chairing the academic department. Topics change each year, but often include such issues as budgeting, addressing concerns of uncollegiality, developing departmental identity, short- and long-term planning, and developing administrative portfolios. (See http://www.dce .k-state.edu/conf/academicchairpersons/.)

○ Harvard University's Management Development Program is an intensive two-week program that assists academic leaders with developing and maintaining leadership teams, serving their institutions as change agents, analyzing financial data, motivating members of the staff and faculty, and understanding the ethical dimension of administrative decisions. Harvard also conducts Crisis Leadership in Higher Education programs that help department chairs prepare for, act effectively during, and speed recovery from significant challenges and disasters. See http://www.gse.harvard .edu/ppe/programs/audiences/hihe/department-heads.html.

○ The Academy for Academic Leadership "is a collaborative of scholars, educational specialists, and consultants providing services that help academic leaders pursue educational excellence, the application of knowledge, the discovery of ideas, and the quest of lifelong learning" (www.didmedia.com/aal_web/AAL_faculty.cfm). It offers Webinars and CD-ROM training on such topics as improving online education, while providing consultancies on strategic planning, curriculum development, leadership enhancement, advancing scholarship, and change management. (See www.academicleaders.org.)

The Webinar—or online seminar—has become a popular alternative to in-person conferences or workshops. A number of publishers offer Webinars on many aspects of departmental governance and leadership, frequently releasing a recording of the Webinar on CD-ROM for those who were not able to participate in the original program. Administrative Webinars are available from Jossey-Bass (www.departmentchairs.org /online-training.aspx), Magna Publications (http://www.magnapubs .com/calendar/index-cat-type.html), and others, with new programs becoming available all the time.

The key considerations to make before participating in any training program, whether off-site or online:

○ Are the topics that will be covered relevant to the duties that I have now or am likely to have in the near future?

○ Are the presenters or facilitators experienced and well qualified in the issues we will be discussing?

○ Am I likely to come away from this experience with specific ideas that I can use to make my administrative efforts more effective?

Leadership Training

Sometimes department chairs underestimate their leadership role. They may assume that presidents, deans, faculty senate chairs, union officers, and senior members of the faculty are the true leaders of the institution. They themselves are just managers, organizers, or "paper pushers." But nothing could be further from the truth. Chairs are called on to solve many different kinds of problems. They're expected to be the leading advocates for their discipline and to strengthen their programs in any way they can. As a result, it's important for every department chair to develop in leadership, no matter how long he or she has served the discipline. James Macgregor Burns (1978) is famous for having begun his influential book on leadership by announcing, "Leadership is one of the most observed and least understood phenomena on earth" (p. 2). Fortunately, a lot of progress has been made in leadership training and development since Burns wrote.

The best place to begin is with Peter Northouse's *Leadership: Theory and Practice* (2010), which examines the concept of leadership from a broad range of theoretical perspectives, includes a well-designed leadership inventory or instrument at the conclusion of each chapter, skillfully melds global concepts with practical situations, and provides carefully selected case studies to illustrate the principles explored in the book. Since issues such as shared governance, collegiality, and the unique history of higher education make leadership at a college or university different from leadership in government, at a corporation, in the military, or as part of a voluntary organization, it's important to complement the ideas that Northouse addresses to those encountered in books devoted to academic leadership. Among the best places to start in this area are books by Wheeler (2008), Leaming (2006), Smith (2006), and Wergin (2006).

The chamber of commerce in your area may run a leadership training program that can introduce you to other important people in your vicinity and learn more about the area in which you live. These programs, frequently called Leadership, followed by the name of the city, county, or state in which they reside, are useful no matter whether you've lived in your community all your life or are a recent arrival. In addition to providing training in leadership and team building, the programs will expose you to aspects of the local economy, cultural life, and government that are difficult to master on your own.

Mentors

Every department chair should have a personal mentor—and every department chair who has been in the position longer than two years should also be a mentor. It's perfectly acceptable to be a mentor and have a mentor at the same time. Academic leaders learn both by the guidance they receive from others and from reflecting on their own experience in order to share it with others. A good mentor is supportive, candid, knowledgeable, available, and challenging, all at the same time. If you work with a mentor who only criticizes what you do, you'll soon get discouraged and give up working with that person. And if you work with a mentor who only tells you how wonderfully you're doing, you could start believing that you're infallible.

The best mentor is someone whom you trust enough to be absolutely straightforward, even when the situation isn't particularly flattering to you, but who isn't looking over his or her shoulder at you every moment. You may want to select a mentor from outside your discipline, perhaps even from another institution, in order to provide appropriate distance from your day-to-day decisions. It may be tempting to ask a former chair who still works in your department, but this practice entails a number of risks. You need to be able to see issues from your own perspective, not from that of the former chair, and you don't want to give your faculty members reason to wonder who's really in charge.

When you serve as a mentor, try to provide advice and an alternative point of view, but don't be insistent that your protégé do things precisely as you would have. Let the person discover his or her own strengths, even if that entails making a small mistake every now and then. After all, that person will need to learn as much as you yourself did. Because of the temptation we all face to want others to run our programs as we've been running them, it's always easier to mentor someone when we have a little bit of distance from their programs or institution.

Consultancies and Coaching

It is also possible to improve your leadership skills by taking advantage of an individually tailored consultancy or coaching. The IDEA Center maintains a Web site that lists the availability of highly experienced consultants in such areas as succeeding as a new chair, improving interpersonal skills, developing visions and plans for the department, enhancing instruction, preparing a succession plan, and so on (www.theideacenter.org/helpful-resources/consulting-general/00143-consulting-services). In addition, the center offers a coaching service that "provides personalized consultation based on the identified needs of academic department chairs to build leadership skills and maximize talent. Once chairs have completed the IDEA Feedback for Department Chairs instrument, the IDEA Center provides several coaching options to extend and enhance self-reflection and leadership development, through consultation with respected and experienced higher education leaders" (IDEA Chair Coaching Service, 1999). Consultancy and coaching services can be expensive, but they can also be a highly effective way to tailor the specific types of training that chairs receive to their own individual goals and needs.

Learn by Sharing

If it's beneficial to share your experiences with someone you're mentoring, it can be even more beneficial to share your experiences with chairs all over the world:

- Write about some aspect of what you've learned from your job for publication in the *Department Chair, Academic Leader,* or the *Chronicle of Higher Education.*
- Propose a presentation, workshop, or training session for the K-State Academic Chairperson's Conference, an administrative panel at the national organization in your discipline, or other chairs at your institution.
- Start a blog about the challenges and opportunities involved in chairing departments today.

By organizing your thoughts for an article or presentation, you'll think through your ideas in greater detail and discover possibilities you might not have thought of if you hadn't tried to articulate your advice to others. As every teacher knows, you don't master a subject until you try to teach it to others. Although you may never have thought of it in this way, administrative leadership is one of your subject areas now, and learning more about it by teaching it to others is an excellent way of growing in your position.

○

No two departments are alike, and no two chairs are alike. Because of your personality, experience, and priorities, you'll do things differently from your predecessor, and your successor will not be a clone of you. That's actually better for your department and institution because new people bring new ideas and new approaches. But regardless of how different one chair is from another, all chairs share certain challenges because they work in the trenches. It's a mistake to think that chairing a department is something people can do without preparation, planning, and training. Although the type of training that benefits you is likely to differ in many ways from that of other chairs, the important point is to obtain some sort of ongoing training and reflection in order to develop a culture of continual improvement in your work as chair.

REFERENCES

Barr, R. B., & Tagg, J. (1995). From teaching to learning: A new paradigm for undergraduate education. *Change, 27*(6), 12–25.

Burns, J. M. (1978). *Leadership*. New York: HarperCollins.

Cipriano, R. E., & Riccardi, R. (2010). What is unique about chairs? A continuing exploration. *Department Chair, 20*(4), 26–28.

IDEA Chair Coaching Service. (1999–2008). Retrieved from www.theideacenter .org/our-services/feedback-department-chairs/chair-coaching-service/00537- idea-chair-coaching-service

Jossey-Bass. (2009). *Department chair survey*. Unpublished survey data.

Leaming, D. R. (2006). *Academic leadership: A practical guide to chairing the department* (2nd ed.). San Francisco: Jossey-Bass.

Northouse, P. (2010). *Leadership: Theory and Practice* (5th ed.). Thousand Oaks, CA: Sage.

Smith, R. V. (2006). *Where you stand is where you sit: An academic administrator's handbook*. Fayetteville: University of Arkansas Press.

Wergin, J. P. (2006). *Leadership in place: How academic professionals can find their leadership voice*. San Francisco: Jossey-Bass.

Wheeler, D. W. (Ed.). (2008). *The academic chair's handbook* (2nd ed.). San Francisco: Jossey-Bass.

RESOURCES

Consulting Services: The IDEA Center. (1999–2008). Retrieved from www .theideacenter.org/helpful-resources/consulting-general/00143-consulting- services

Department Chair Online Resource Center. (2011). Retrieved from www.acenet .edu/resources/chairs/

Faculty Focus. (2001). Retrieved from www.facultyfocus.com

Gmelch, W. H., & Schuh, J. H. (2004). *The life cycle of a department chair*. San Francisco: Jossey-Bass.

Hecht, I.W.D. (1999). *The department chair as academic leader*. Phoenix, AZ: Oryx Press.

Knowledge Base: The IDEA Center. (1999–2008). Retrieved from www.theideacenter.org/category/helpful-resources/knowledge-base

Lees, N. D. (2002). *Chairing academic departments: Traditional and emerging expectations*. San Francisco: Jossey-Bass.

Lucas, A. F. (2000). *Leading academic change: Essential roles for department chairs*. San Francisco: Jossey-Bass.

Who We Are: Academy for Academic Leadership. (2010). Retrieved from http://www.academicleaders.org/who-we-are.html

2

PREPARING FOR THE CHAIR'S ROLE

PEOPLE BECOME DEPARTMENT CHAIRS for many reasons. In some programs, the position is rotated among members of the department, and the current chair is serving simply because it's his or her turn. In other cases, the person who is chair actively sought the position, seeing it as the first step toward an administrative career. Some faculty members seek to become chair because they are looking for a new challenge, while others view the position as an unwelcome intrusion into the teaching and scholarship that they consider their "real work." Regardless of the avenues that have led you to become—or even to consider the possibility of becoming—a department chair, you are bound to have questions about what you need to do to prepare, what qualities you should try to develop, and what knowledge you should try to gain. Of course, nothing ever prepares a person completely for the challenges of being a department chair (or for holding any other position, including that of full-time faculty member) because no one can predict perfectly the situations that will arise in anyone's unique situation. Nevertheless, the following ten suggestions offer good advice to keep in mind no matter whether you are actively seeking to become a chair or if you fear that, in the regular rotation of things, your turn is about to come.

1. Learn as much as possible about the technical operation of your institution.

You probably already have a fairly good idea about how curriculum proposals are approved, budgets are set, disputes are negotiated, and searches are approved within your department. (If you don't, stop reading and go find out now. This knowledge is essential.) But how do these processes work outside your department?

- ○ Which office—in fact, which specific person in which office—is contacted when there is a problem with the heating or the roof is leaking?

- ○ Aside from recording students' schedules and grades, what functions are the responsibility of your college's registrar's office?

- ○ Who is responsible for making sure that commencement runs smoothly?

- ○ If one of your alumni needs to have his or her diploma replaced because the original was damaged in a fire, how do you go about taking care of this request?

- ○ If you wish to change the number of credits required for a major in your discipline, which bodies must approve that proposal, and at what stage does it become official?

- ○ How do you go about requesting that a check be issued to reimburse someone for departmental expenses, and on what schedule are those checks issued?

Once you become chair, you will be asked questions on a daily basis that deal not only with the way in which your department functions, but about the operational processes of your institution as a whole. The more of this information you know inside and out, the more effective you will be.

2. Develop your skills at managing conflict and seeking resolutions to crises.

No matter how collegial your department may be, the occasional dispute will arise. Some departments seem torn by strife and dissent all the time. Regardless of the amount of tension there has been in your department in the past, you will need to hone your skills at conflict resolution. If your institution offers training in mediation of disputes, be sure to register for it. If this type of training is not available at your institution, local community colleges or continuing education programs frequently offer it. If neither of these options is available, at least read a book devoted to this topic, such as Dana (2001), Mayer (2000), Twale and Luca (2008), or Weeks (1994).

You will want to know in advance what approaches are most likely to lead to a satisfactory resolution of the conflict before the conflict even begins. Once an issue flairs up at a department meeting or is dropped in your lap, it's usually too late to start developing the skills you need to address the issue.

3. Develop a tentative plan for how you intend to balance your administrative duties with the rest of your workload.

Faculty members sometimes dread the possibility that they may be asked to serve as department chair because they view the position as a career killer: the job uses up all the time they need for research and to improve their courses if they wish to be promoted; it also holds a high probability of alienating other members of the faculty if tough decisions are made, yet it promises only a low probability of making friends and influencing people. Although every person who may become a department chair should carefully consider these possibilities, they are far more frightening to faculty members than they need to be. For every example you can think of where a career suffered even modestly (and even then probably not permanently) because of service as a chair, there are literally hundreds of examples of people who were able to preserve a successful balance of administration, teaching, and research and whose willingness to make difficult decisions gained them the respect of their peers.

The important thing is to be reasonable about your workload and plan accordingly. Talk to your dean if you are likely to be named chair, and see if you can gain a better sense of how the demands of this position might affect your schedule. Perhaps you can negotiate an additional course release in order to keep an important scholarly project on track. Perhaps you can make arrangements to team-teach a course or receive additional graduate support for your research project.

Almost every senior administrator has had to deal with the question of balancing priorities that you are confronting, and you will discover far more understanding and support than you may fear. In that same meeting with your dean, be candid about your worries that making certain decisions may come with a political cost in your department. Here too you are likely to receive guidance for handling such situations. At the very least, you'll have a clearer sense of how well your back is covered by those who are likely to receive appeals to overturn any tough calls that you make (and whose support you may need to count on when those future promotion decisions are made). Every department and every institution is different, of course, but by and large, you'll benefit far more (and be able to sleep better at night) when you make decisions based on what you are convinced is right than on what you believe may be expedient.

4. Brush up on parliamentary procedure.

Even if your department is very small and you tend not to have formal meetings, the more you know about parliamentary procedure, the better. This understanding will help you negotiate the complexities of the committee structure on your campus, allow you to be more effective in amending or tabling motions when necessary, and place you in a position where your own issues are more likely to help shape your institution's agenda. It is frequently the case that in the heat of a particularly intense debate, claims are made that "parliamentary procedure requires [this or that]"; since most faculty members have only a general sense of whether the claim may be true, decisions can be made that could have been more effectively challenged or debated. Get a copy of Robert's Rules of Order, which is available in many editions. For most chairs, an abridged version (Robert, 2006; Robert, Evans, Honemann, & Balch, 2004) will be sufficient. If you'd like a little more detail, try Sturgis (2001), Zimmerman and Robert (1997), or Lochrie (2003). Whichever source you prefer, your goal should be to acquire expertise in the basics of conducting meetings and the priority of various types of motions.

5. Pick your battles.

No department chair is going to fix every problem in a department or advance every initiative. Those who try to do so end up either scattering their energies too widely or making everyone in the department nervous that everything is going to change. A lesson that new chairs usually learn is a good essential principle for all administrators to remember:

> No unit of a college or university is ever ready for as much change as it claims to be.

It's far more productive for chairs to focus their attention on a very few, highly important improvements than to try to do too much. Remember that after your term as chair is over, your legacy is likely to be only one or two significant achievements anyway. Do those well, and you will have made the best contribution possible.

6. Expand your view.

It is perfectly acceptable (even appropriate) for you as a faculty member to act as an advocate for your own specialty and field of research, but as a chair, you need to view matters from the purview of your entire

discipline. At the very least, you need to start thinking of yourself no longer as a clinical psychologist but as a psychologist, no longer as a U.S.
historian but as a historian, no longer as a solid-state physicist but as a
physicist, and so on. Moreover, you must start considering issues from
the perspective of your entire college, institution, or university system.
Sometimes, in fact, it can be better to forgo a more immediate desire for
the benefit of a longer-term need. Postponing the creation of that new
line in your department in order to increase staffing in admissions or the
advancement office could alter the financial chemistry of your institution
in such a way that there are many more new faculty lines in the future.
Allowing a new position to be added in composition or statistics may
serve your majors better than staffing a new position in your own
department.

Like a chess player, an effective department chair must view the entire
board and learn to see how each individual move affects every other one.
You will be a far better advocate for your discipline if you see your role
not as that of a narrow partisan for a single group, but as a true representative of how your discipline fits into the overall needs of students,
faculty members, and other constituents at your institution.

**7. Keep repeating to yourself, "It's not personal," even when it appears to
be—or perhaps especially when it appears to be.**

If you've ever had the privilege of directing students in a play or taking
them on an extended trip abroad, you're well aware of the phenomenon
of suddenly becoming the lightning rod for others' discontent. Rehearsals
are going long into the night, the cast is tired and cranky, people are getting confused in their parts, and all at once they turn on you as the worst
director they've ever had. Or the museums are all closed due to a sudden
strike by the guards, the food has been disappointing for days on end,
everyone's getting homesick, and abruptly you become the cause of
everything that has gone wrong.

The wise director or program leader knows that this is going to happen, doesn't take it personally, and realizes that when all is said and
done, the same people who are now complaining the loudest will be
those who will later be saying, "This was the best experience *ever!*"
Somehow this lesson, so easily learned in situations when we deal with
students, is harder to recall when we're dealing with faculty members.
Nevertheless, the psychology that occurs during any experience of long,
intense work with any group will occur when you're serving as chair of a
department. Some days, one or more faculty members will treat you
coldly, and you'll be absolutely convinced that they're upset with

something that you did or said; only later will you discover that the cause of their apparent rudeness was a matter going on in one of their courses or in their personal lives that had nothing at all to do with you. On other days, faculty members in your department will blame you for everything that is going wrong, even if you had no control whatsoever over the situation.

Don't let this common occurrence distract you from the things that you need to do and want to accomplish. As a chair, you will occasionally be the object of frustration and animosity simply because these emotions require some outlet. Just remember that all of that anger is really directed at the position of the chair, not at you as a person.

8. Find a mentor.

All chairs can benefit from occasional conversations with someone who has gone through the same experiences that they are having and who knows how the system works. But if mentors are valuable for every chair, they're essential for new department chairs. If your institution does not provide you with a formal mentor, take the initiative to find one. Choose a chair or former chair in a department that has at least some similarity to your own. But it's probably better that your mentor not be a former chair of your own department. Such an individual, while wanting in most cases to be as helpful as possible, is likely still to be involved (at least tangentially) in departmental politics; carefully consider this option before you pursue it. Besides, former chairs in your own department will inevitably have their own agenda and their own way of doing things; your goal is to discover the way that works best for you, not to adopt what worked well for a different person in the past.

For all of these reasons, choose a mentor from a discipline that is not so different from yours in size, mission, or focus that the individual cannot easily understand your specific experiences but also who is not too closely tied to your own department. Remember that your mentor will provide you with advice and counsel; it is always up to you to decide whether to follow that advice.

9. Find someone that you can talk to, even vent to, when necessary.

Having a person to whom you can turn when you need to voice your frustrations is not the same thing as having a mentor. A good department chair mentor is a person who either is or recently was at your institution; this is the person who can guide you through the complexities of the system and warn you against proceeding in a manner that is likely not to be productive. In contrast, a good confidant is someone you can talk to freely without worrying that what you say is going to get back to your faculty members and upper administration.

Mentors provide advice; confidants provide support. They do this by lending an ear and restoring your confidence when you're feeling frustrated or misunderstood. For this reason, the person you choose as an outlet for your deepest concerns and annoyances should never be a member of your current institution; in fact, the farther away from your institution this person is, the better.

Certainly everyone needs someone to vent to every now and then. Remember to do so wisely and only when it is absolutely necessary. No one likes to feel that every time he or she hears from someone, it is about a new complaint or reason for whining. Moreover, even the things you say in the greatest confidence could get repeated to the wrong people. A secret, as the saying goes, is merely information we broadcast to one person at a time. So use your confidant carefully, and cherish a good one who comes your way.

10. Take advantage of every opportunity you can to gain experience.

If there's still some time before you are likely to begin your term as department chair, seek out opportunities to serve on as many departmental committees as possible. Heading a committee can help you hone your organizational skills. Serving on a committee headed by someone else exposes you to different models of leadership. Each committee you work with will educate you about another aspect of your department and how it works. Serving on collegewide or institution-wide committees can also expand your contact with the individuals and offices that can help you do your job better when you're chair. Volunteering for search committees outside your area can be particularly productive: you'll improve the skills you'll need in setting up and running searches yourself, and you'll have an opportunity to ask candidates about methods they used to solve particular problems at the institutions where they're currently working or studying.

All committee work, no matter how dreary or routine, will provide you with at least some new insights or perspectives. Don't lose the chance to take full advantage of these opportunities.

These ten suggestions will help you prepare for the chair's role or improve your knowledge and skills if you're relatively new to the position. But there also are excellent resources to which every new chair should have access. Among the works you should have on your bookshelf are Chu (2006), Gmelch and Miskin (2004), Lucas (2000), Walvoord (2000), Higgerson (1996), and Hecht, Higgerson, Gmelch, and Tucker

(1999). Many administrative conferences also host workshops for new chairs, and these can be useful opportunities to receive a great deal of information within a very short time. Also, be sure to explore the training opportunities that your own institution may provide. Many colleges and universities are realizing that effective administrators require ongoing training, and so new programs are often developed by the provost's office, center for excellence in teaching and learning, human resource department, or some other division of the institution that is devoted to leadership training.

REFERENCES

Chu, D. (2006). *The department chair primer: Leading and managing academic departments*. San Francisco: Jossey-Bass/Anker.

Dana, D. (2001). *Conflict resolution: Mediation tools for everyday worklife*. New York: McGraw-Hill.

Gmelch, W. H., & Miskin, V. D. (2004). *Chairing an academic department*. Madison, WI: Atwood.

Hecht, I.W.D., Higgerson, M. L., Gmelch, W. H., & Tucker, A. (1999). *The department chair as academic leader*. Phoenix, AZ: American Council on Education/Oryx Press.

Higgerson, M. L. (1996). *Communication skills for department chairs*. San Francisco: Jossey-Bass/Anker.

Lochrie, J. (2003). *Meeting procedures: Parliamentary law and rules of order for the 21st century*. Lanham, MD: Scarecrow Press.

Lucas, A. F. (2000). *Leading academic change: Essential roles for department chairs*. San Francisco: Jossey-Bass.

Mayer, B. S. (2000). *The dynamics of conflict resolution: A practitioner's guide*. San Francisco: Jossey-Bass.

Robert, H. M. (2006). *Robert's rules of order: Classic pocket manual of rules of order for deliberative assemblies*. [S.l.]: Filiquarian Publishing.

Robert, H. M., Evans, W. J., Honemann, D. H., & Balch, T. J. (2004). *Robert's rules of order, newly revised, in brief*. Cambridge, MA: Da Capo Press.

Sturgis, A. (2001). *The standard code of parliamentary procedure* (4th ed.). New York: McGraw-Hill.

Twale, D. J., & Luca, B.M.D. (2008). *Faculty incivility: The rise of the academic bully culture and what to do about it*. San Francisco: Jossey-Bass.

Walvoord, B.E.F. (2000). *Academic departments: How they work, how they change*. ASHE-ERIC Higher Education Report, Vol. 27, no. 8 San Francisco: Jossey-Bass.

Weeks, D. (1994). *The eight essential steps to conflict resolution: Preserving relationships at work, at home, and in the community.* New York: Tarcher/Perigee.

Zimmerman, D. P., & Robert, H. M. (1997). *Robert's Rules in plain English.* New York: HarperPerennial.

RESOURCES

Bowman, R. F. (2002). The real work of the department chair. *Clearinghouse, 75,* 158–162.

Carroll, J. B., & Wolverton, M. (2004). Who becomes a chair? In W. H. Gmelch & J. H. Schuh (Eds.), *The life cycle of a department chair* (pp. 3–10). San Francisco: Jossey-Bass.

North, J. (2008). Tips for new department chairs. *Department Chair, 19*(2), 27.

Rehnke, M. A. (2006). The life of a department chair. *Department Chair, 17*(2), 23–25.

Sorcinelli, M. D. (2000). *Principles of good practice: Supporting early-career faculty. Guidance for deans, department chairs, and other academic leaders.* Washington, DC: AAHE.

Wolverton, M., Ackerman, R., & Holt, S. (2005). Preparing for leadership: What academic department chairs need to know. *Journal of Higher Education Policy and Management, 27,* 227–238.

3

ASSESSING WHAT KIND OF DEPARTMENT CHAIR YOU ARE

DEPARTMENT CHAIRS COME IN more than one size, shape, or personality type. That degree of diversity is actually a good thing, since different departments and different institutions need different types of administrators to achieve the highly individual missions that they have set for themselves. In fact, different departments and different institutions need different types of department chairs at different times in their development. For instance, a relatively new department might need someone who is skilled as a creator. More established departments might need someone who has more expertise as a builder, sustainer, or consolidator. Departments that have grown stale might need a change agent. Units that have been through chaos or turmoil might need a calming influence or a counselor. And there are many other types of administrators, all with their proper places in different types of units at different times during their development.

As a department chair, you may take a good deal of relief from the knowledge that academic administrators do not all have to be alike. After all, it's not unusual for a chair to think that the other chairs at his or her institution are more gregarious, detail oriented, imaginative, forceful, well organized, or dynamic than he or she is. Nevertheless, despite what you may think and what all the self-appointed experts may tell you, no single type of personality or administrative style makes for a perfect department chair. Nearly any person can be a successful chair. What is required is that you know what it is you need to do and who you are.

So, Who Are You?

Each of us comes to our administrative positions with varying degrees of self-knowledge, but there are many things that you can do—that, in fact, you need to do—in order to discover your own administrative style, develop an approach to departmental management that builds on the strengths of that style, and create a departmental team in which your individual weaknesses (and we all have them) are counterbalanced by someone else's unique strengths. Begin by considering a few essential principles. This is the first:

> You can lead others only if you know where you're going.

This statement may seem absurdly self-evident. How, after all, can you lead anyone anywhere if you have only the vaguest notion of where it is you wish to lead? When we are planning a trip, we do not immediately leave the house and walk off in all directions at once. Any trip that begins without a destination ends up being merely a stroll. That kind of aimless wandering can be good exercise, and we might enjoy it as a pastime, but it is hardly the sort of intentional model for good departmental administration. As the aphorist Doug Horton has said, "If you don't know where you're going, any road will take you there." In other words, as effective chairs, we have to know our objectives. Once we do, we can map out the various ways to reach those objectives.

To return for a moment to the example of planning a trip, when we are going somewhere at some distance from home, we tend to ask ourselves various questions:

- Is time of the essence so that we should seek the most direct route possible?
- Are we more interested in scenery and adventure along the way?
- Is it likely that we will have to make detours once we have started, so it may be prudent to have several contingency plans?

These are similar to the questions that we must ask ourselves as department chairs:

- Where is it that our discipline needs to go?
- Can we get there rapidly, or will there have to be time for resources to be obtained and for people to adjust to new ideas?

○ What aspects of my plan should I delegate to others, even if that means that results will not be precisely as I envisioned it them?

○ What sort of contingency plans will I need for those inevitable situations when events do not develop as smoothly as I had intended?

Your department will benefit immeasurably from this sort of planning. In the worst of situations, if you don't have any clear-cut notion of what it is that your department can achieve in either the short term or the distant future, then you are likely to convey to your faculty members a sense of drift or indecision. They will become frustrated, and their morale will plummet. Their distress will be caused by insufficient attention paid to the next essential principle that we'll consider:

> Most faculty members would rather believe that the department is moving in the wrong direction than believe that it's not moving in any direction at all.

These first two principles probably represent thoughts you've already have had many times since you learned that you would be chairing your department. However, the corollaries to these essential principles tend to be far less self-evident:

> Corollary 1: You can tell how to get where you're going only if you know where you are now.
>
> Corollary 2: You know where you really are only if you're honest with yourself about who you are.

To resume the metaphor of the trip, just as a map will do you relatively little good unless you know where your current position is, so is it difficult to take your department anywhere unless you know its current position, that is, its budget, its status within your institution, its role in the strategic plan of your college or university, and its overall history in terms of producing majors, bringing in grants and sponsored programs, conducting research, generating student credit hours, serving other disciplines, and the like. Similarly, it is difficult to get anywhere—even with the best of maps and a thorough knowledge of your current position—if you haven't taken stock of the means of transportation available to you. Will you walk, drive, sail, or fly? If you don't know what type of vehicle you have (or don't even know if you have a vehicle available), you're not going to get very far. Again, departmental leadership is much the same. If you don't take stock of your strengths and weaknesses, your preferences and strong dislikes, you won't take your department very far, and you'll probably end up annoying both yourself and your faculty in the process.

The path to self-knowledge can involve some pretty serious business, and it has been the province of philosophers for nearly as long as philosophy has existed. For instance, in ancient Greece before the time of Socrates, the Delphic doctrine, "Know thyself," often attributed to Thales of Miletus, was usually interpreted as meaning, "Know your limits" or "Know your place." In a similar way, chapter 12, verse 4 of the Dhammapada reads, "Self is the lord of self, who else could be the lord? With oneself well trained, a person finds a master such as few can find." In other words, the difficult part is that knowledge of who one is has to include knowledge of one's imperfections, of the fact that one is *not* always the lord and master of every situation. And coming face-to-face with one's flaws can be mighty unpleasant, even if it is a time-honored tradition.

Personality Inventories

One approach to attaining this difficult and sometimes painful knowledge of who you are and what self-awareness can mean for your individual administrative style is to begin with one of the many personality-type inventories that are currently available. These prepackaged inventories have a great deal of research and literature behind them, provide results that are widely recognized, and offer a good beginning for administrators who want a candid external opinion of certain aspects of their personalities. A few of the more common personality tools and inventories include:

- The Myers-Briggs Type Indicator (MBTI) is probably the most famous and widely used of the personality assessments currently available (http://www.myersbriggs.org/). It dates back to the 1940s when Katharine Briggs and her daughter, Isabel Briggs Myers, began exploring ways of putting the central concepts of the psychologist Carl Jung (1875–1961) into a format that ordinary people—particularly employers and prospective employers—could readily understand and use. MBTI assigns each individual four letters, indicating which of two traits among four pairs a person appears to possess in greater abundance. The four pairs and their key letters (capitalized) are Introversion/Extroversion, Intuition/Sensation, Thinking/Feeling, and Judging/Perceiving. After the MBTI is scored, the person taking it receives a four-letter code (such as INTJ or ESFP) that provides a shorthand summary of his or her dominant quality in each of the four pairs. The MBTI is a registered trademark of Consulting Psychologist Press, which publishes and distributes instruments for taking and scoring the inventory.

○ The Keirsey Temperament Sorter (http://www.keirsey.com/) is an online personality inventory that classifies those taking it by four major temperaments: Rationals, Idealists, Artisans, and Guardians. These four temperaments can then be subdivided into sixteen role variants: Composer, Crafter, Performer, Promoter, Protector, Inspector, Provider, Supervisor, Healer, Counselor, Champion, Teacher, Architect, Mastermind, Inventor, and Field Marshal. A test taker then emerges with a brief identifier (such as Guardian Inspector or Idealist Counselor) that provides guidance into his or her temperament and style of relating to others.

○ The DiSC Personal Profile is based on the work of William Moulton Marston (1893–1947), a psychologist who is probably most famous for his creation of the character Wonder Woman. The DiSC inventory provides the taker with scores in four areas known as styles factors—Dominance, Influence, Steadiness, Conscientiousness—and then indicates which personality pattern the taker tends to exhibit. The sixteen personality patterns assigned by the DiSC Personal Profile are Developer, Result Oriented, Inspirational, Creative, Promoter, Persuader, Counselor, Appraiser, Specialist, Achiever, Agent, Investigator, Objective Thinker, Perfectionist, Practitioner, and Pure Style DiSC. The DiSC inventory is available online (www.discprofile.com) and in paper format, is backed by extensive research, and provides abundant information about matching one's own personality style to the needs and strengths of others.

One instrument that department chairs are sometimes tempted to use, but is really not suitable for this purpose, is the Minnesota Multiphasic Personality Inventory (MMPI). The MMPI, developed at the University of Minnesota in the 1930s and thoroughly revised in 1989, is not particularly adaptable to simple self-testing and analysis of results. As a pathology-oriented inventory, it is far more useful in detecting severe psychological aberrations than for common workplace personality issues, and its results should always be interpreted by a trained professional. (In fact, many department chairs may not be aware that the MMPI requires a clinical license for purchase.)

An important proviso to keep in mind when using personality inventories is that they indicate only where individual personality traits tend to lie along a spectrum; they do not—and never can—tell you whether you adhere to some "perfect personality type for department chairs." There simply is no such perfect type. You may hear it said that "all academic administrators need to be ENTJ leaders" or that "introverts have no business leading an academic unit" or that the "best department chairs are Idealist/Champions." All of these generalizations are nonsense. Aside from misinterpreting what the introversion/extroversion scales of personality tests actually indicate—the taker's tendency either to "think out loud" or to process information internally, to seek personal renewal in public settings or in quiet and privacy—they provide extremely little insight into the degree of one's "people skills" or whether one enjoys the company of others. Blanket statements of this kind miss the fact that all types of people are successful as administrators. Just remember that the point of taking the test is not to determine whether you can chair a department, but rather to gain a clearer image of your own personality type so as to be able to balance it better with those having other dominant traits on committees and in other working relationships. Also by knowing how you tend to approach situations, you'll find that you're more aware of the working styles of others and can adapt your strategies accordingly.

Well-established personality inventories have the advantage of relying on significant research providing widely recognized results, but they also have several major disadvantages. They are not specifically focused on the needs and duties of college administrators. Moreover, you gain more from them only if you have their results interpreted by trained professionals. Finally, even when you do go over their results with a trained (and, at times, expensive) consultant, you still may not end up with the type of information useful for improving your departmental leadership.

Personal Assessment

A second possibility for finding your administrative style is to forgo these prepackaged personality inventories by (or, at least, to supplement them with) taking a highly focused, nonscientific, individualistic inventory of your own. Begin by asking yourself a series of questions directly related to your job and its responsibilities and answering them as candidly as possible:

o What is the greatest strength that you bring to your administrative position?

o What is your greatest weakness?

o Which aspects of your position give you the greatest personal satisfaction when you do them well?

o Which aspects of your position are you willing to tolerate because they go with the territory, even though they provide you with relatively little personal satisfaction?

o If you could hand off three of your regularly occurring tasks and never do them again, what would they be?

o If you were compelled to take one aspect of your current work and do it all day long, week in and week out, which one would you choose?

To get started in making this sort of personal assessment, it might be helpful to take an informal test. To begin, look over the list of the following twenty activities that a department chair may be required to do and number them from 1 to 20 on the basis of which of them you would rather do. Let 1 indicate the activity that you find most personally interesting, satisfying, and productive. (Answer honestly, not on the basis of how you think you ought to answer or how others might want you to answer.) Let 20 indicate the activity that, all things being equal, you would do but would prefer not to. To make it easy to keep track of the twenty activities as you rank them, each has been assigned a letter. Which of the following activities would you prefer to do?

A. Speak in person with the parent of a student who is having a problem in one of the courses your department offer.

B. Write a letter to the alumni of your program, outlining some of the plans you have for your department over the next several years.

C. Speak to a group of three hundred prospective students about the courses your department offers and the career opportunities available in your field.

D. Write a report for the chief academic officer setting new learning goals based on data you've seen that indicate certain areas where students have had difficulty in your discipline for the past several years.

E. Block out several hours of quiet time in your schedule so that you can review and reconcile the expenditures made in your department over the past year.

F. Present ideas at a small faculty gathering about how the institution's new strategic plan might be implemented in your area.

G. Answer an e-mail sent to you by another department chair who is criticizing the section size that has been common in your department's courses since you have been chair.

H. Begin outlining and writing an academic article in your discipline.

I. Prepare a spreadsheet to help you improve the course rotation in your department.

J. Attend a committee meeting outside your discipline.

K. Write a position description for a new faculty line in your department, basing your description on specific curricular weaknesses cited by a discipline-specific accreditation report, alumni surveys, and departmental exit exams.

L. Meet with the dean (or the president of your institution) in response to that person's request to go over some particular issue or problem with you, even though you will not learn the nature of the issue until the meeting begins.

M. Answer a phone call from a parent who is concerned about remarks recently made by a lecturer you had invited to campus.

N. Write a survey of recent scholarship done by members of your department for publication in the newsletter of a local service group (Rotary, Kiwanis, Lions, Optimists Club, or some similar organization).

O. Polish the draft of an academic article that you have nearly completed for publication.

P. Prepare your budget proposal for the coming year.

Q. Conduct the annual in-person review session with a faculty member in your discipline.

R. Start developing a draft proposal for a new academic program in which your department will play a lead role.

S. Represent your department at a full meeting of your institution's board of regents or trustees.

T. Serve on a panel that will interpret the likely effect a new state law will have on the general education program offered by your institution.

Once you have organized your list of all twenty activities into the best order that you can determine, with the duties that you would most enjoy doing at the top and those you would really prefer not to do at the bottom, look at your top five activities and then at your bottom five. Do you notice any overall patterns in either of these groups? In other words, do you tend to favor activities in which you

- Deal more with the big picture (B, D, F, K, P, R, S) or with particular details of day-to-day academic administration (A, E, G, I, L, M, N, Q)?
- Spend time developing a plan for a new activity (B, D, H, K, P, R) or implement plans that are already made (C, F, G, I, N, Q, T)?
- Work with others through direct, face-to-face communication (A, C, F, J, L, Q, S, T) or more indirect forms of communication (B, D, G, H, I, K, M, N, O, P, R)?
- Interact with large groups (C, J, S, T) or small groups (A, D, F, G, L, M, Q)?
- Focus your attention on those to whom you report (D, L, S, T) or those who report to you (A, B, C, F, M, Q)?
- Start endeavors from the very beginning (B, D, H, I, K, P, R) or deal with matters that are already well under way (E, G, J, N, O, Q, T)?
- Take the initiative for action (B, H, R) or react to the needs of others (A, G, J, L, N, Q, T)?
- Analyze information, moving from concept to detail (D, F, H, K, P, R) or synthesize information, moving from detail to concept (B, I, T)?

Table 3.1 provides an overview of how these activities may be sorted into different categories. Keep in mind that you're unlikely to discover patterns in your responses that apply to all eight of these major differences in administrative style. Nevertheless, you should find at least two or three of these pairs in which you can begin to detect a clear administrative preference. For instance, you may discover that your style is to maintain a focus on the big picture, while you also prefer direct, face-to-face communication with smaller groups. Or you may discover that your attention tends to be directed more toward those to whom you report, while you also prefer to react to the needs of others and to move from detail to concept. As in the case of the nationally normed personality inventories, there are no right and no wrong answers to this informal personal inventory. What it will tell you is what your administrative style tends to be, not whether you are a capable administrator.

Table 3.1 Department Chair Administrative Style Inventory

	Big Picture	Details	Plan New Initiatives	Implement Existing Plans	Communicate Face-to-Face	Indirect Communication	Large Groups	Small Groups	Focus on Supervisors	Focus on Employees	Start Projects	Continue Current Projects	Initiate Actions	React to Needs	Analyze: Concept to Detail	Synthesize: Detail to Concept
A		X			X			X		X	X		X	X		X
B	X		X			X	X			X	X					
C	X	X		X	X			X	X	X						
D		X	X			X						X			X	
E	X				X					X						
F		X		X		X		X			X	X		X	X	
G			X	X		X		X			X		X		X	
H						X	X									X
I				X	X						X	X		X		
J	X		X			X									X	
K		X			X			X	X		X			X		
L		X		X		X		X		X				X		
M						X						X	X	X		
N				X		X						X				
O											X		X			
P	X	X	X	X	X	X		X		X		X		X	X	
Q			X								X		X		X	
R	X															
S	X				X		X		X							
T	X			X	X		X		X			X		X		X

Understanding Your Style

Once you know your style, you will be in a better position to balance your strengths and weaknesses when you make committee assignments, build a team to pursue a project of importance to your discipline, or appoint those with whom you will work closely such as an administrative assistant or assistant department chair. If you prefer to work on tasks that are already well under way, you may need to balance your skills with someone who prefers to be an initiator. If you are comfortable speaking before large groups but dislike small talk or interacting with others one-on-one, you may wish to delegate these responsibilities to others who have these strengths. Conversely, you may wish to pursue additional administrative training to build your skills in areas that you discover do not come to you as naturally as you might like.

---
o

Remember that there are many resources available for helping you to continue discovering and refining your individual leadership style. Among the resources every department chair should know are Leaming (2003), Diamond (2002), Glanz (2002), Kippenberger (2002), and Beck and Yeager (1994).

REFERENCES

Beck, J.D.W., & Yeager, N. M. (1994). *The leader's window: Mastering the four styles of leadership to build high-performing teams*. Hoboken, NJ: Wiley.

Diamond, R. M. (Ed). (2002). *Field guide to academic leadership: A publication of the national academy for academic leadership*. San Francisco: Jossey-Bass.

Glanz, J. (2002). *Finding your leadership style: A guide for educators*. Alexandria, VA: Association for Supervision and Curriculum Development.

Kippenberger, T. (2002). *Leadership styles*. Minneapolis, MN: Capstone.

Leaming, D. R. (2003). *Managing people: A guide for department chairs and deans*. San Francisco: Jossey-Bass/Anker.

4

SERVING AS AN UNTENURED DEPARTMENT CHAIR

UNTIL RELATIVELY RECENTLY, meeting a department chair who had not yet been granted tenure was a rare experience. For the most part, chairs were full professors who had been chosen by the upper administration, elected by their peers, or hired from the outside because they already had a distinguished record of teaching, research, and service. The department chair, by common practice, was a faculty member whose impressive achievements could serve as an example for others and who knew how to guide junior members of the faculty to their own records of success.

Increasingly at national and regional meetings of department chairs or workshops to train new chairs, a significant departure from this situation is evident: as participants are asked to "raise your hand if you have not yet received tenure," more and more hands are going up. The number of chairs who are placed in their position while still assistant professors is increasing, and that trend brings with it an entirely new series of issues, challenges, and problems for those who hold leadership positions in academic departments.

Institutional Challenges

It is one thing to argue whether untenured faculty members should be appointed as chairs. Certainly no one will deny that serving as chair can be a time-consuming enterprise, and the hours spent planning schedules and resolving thorny personnel issues are ones that cannot be spent in publishing articles, submitting grant proposals, developing new courses, and exploring new pedagogical approaches. Moreover, the department chair frequently makes unpopular decisions. Bearing the news that the discipline will not recommend someone for promotion, accept a course proposal as written, or allow a faculty member to schedule courses at his or her own convenience can create friction or resistance in a department. When the department chair must then be reviewed for promotion, tenure, or merit increases by many of the same people who might still bear a grudge from these earlier decisions, the political situation in which untenured department chairs find themselves is decidedly unfair. Yet despite all these reasons that untenured faculty members should not be chairs, more and more of them are being made chairs, and their situations need to be taken seriously. Some of the approaches that must be taken have to begin at the institutional level.

First, institutions need to modify evaluation systems in such a way that untenured faculty members are not disadvantaged by the service they perform the institution as department chairs. An evaluation system is inherently inequitable if it penalizes the very people who were willing to serve the institution as a department chair for failing to engage in those activities that their administrative duties made impossible because of time commitments. If an institution is going to have a system in which untenured faculty members are permitted to serve as chair—and even more if an institution has a situation in which it has encouraged, cajoled, or enticed even one untenured faculty member to serve as chair—then it is incumbent on that institution to guarantee that the faculty member is not placed at a disadvantage because of choices made at the institutional level.

One method of approaching this problem is for the institutional promotion and tenure committee to establish research and teach equivalencies for department chair service. The precise nature of those equivalences should be made based on the mission and expectations of the institution as a whole. Thus, for one institution, it may be excessive to establish an equivalency that says, "Each full academic year of service as a department chair shall be regarded as equivalent in weight to an article in a first-tier journal where the faculty member is first author or sole author." At another institution, that same equivalent may not be sufficient. In any case, an institution-wide discussion of exactly how much progress in teaching and research the typical chair gives up for each year of service will provide some guidance in what these equivalencies should be. Some faculty members will argue that one's service as chair can be of either high or low quality. In this case, it should be noted that even the most carefully peer-reviewed articles in first-tier journals are not always of the highest quality or significance and that, in any case, the equivalency should be somewhat generous so as to reward a faculty member for agreeing to assume a difficult responsibility at a vulnerable moment in his or her career.

Second, institutions need to provide substantive training and mentoring for all new department chairs, particularly those who have not yet been granted tenure. The rise of centers devoted to excellence in teaching and learning at universities across the country reflects the recognition that all too many graduate programs do an excellent job in preparing future faculty members to perform research but a poor job in preparing them to teach. Even less common is any concerted effort to train future faculty members for the leadership roles they will be called on to assume someday as committee chairs, department chairs, division heads, or full-time administrators.

The best solution to this problem is for colleges and universities to develop an institute for professional development and leadership that can offer this type of training to graduate students and, even more important, provide ongoing administrative training to members of the faculty, staff, and administration. An institute for professional development and leadership could exist as a unit of an existing center for excellence in teaching and learning, or it could be created as a separate entity with its own mission and focus. Just as faculty development programs have needed to expand in recent years to offer faculty members the resources they require in order to succeed at all of their complex roles, so too must institutions increase the opportunities that they provide to employees who are expected to assume administrative roles or positions of leadership. The challenges facing higher education today are simply too great to allow individuals the luxury of learning how to perform their jobs while they are doing them. Trial and error is an inadequate learning technique when the cost of those errors can be lawsuits, declining enrollments, or financial disasters.

Finally, institutions need to ensure that their appeal processes are fair when current or former department chairs are denied tenure or promotion. No matter how scrupulous an institution may be in establishing processes that are fair and equitable, human frailty can always intervene. Particularly in systems dealing with faculty evaluation and promotion, a certain degree of subjectivity is all but inevitable. Certainly you could simply count the number of refereed articles a faculty member has written, calculate average scores on student evaluations to the thousandth of a point, and list the number of committees on which the applicant has served, but few people would argue that these are the best indicators of excellence in higher education.

Despite the groundbreaking work of Arreola (2006), Seldin (2006), and others, faculty evaluation systems too often are an uneven mix of counting that which can be counted and making subjective judgments about quality, impact, and significance. For this reason, chairs who believe that they have not received adequate consideration of their contributions by departmental or collegewide committees must have access to an appeal process that can be as objective as possible about role the untenured department chair has played and its value to the institution. Many institutions have review processes that explore only whether evaluation committees at each level followed the correct procedures. This type of process can be too restrictive in the case of a chair who feels that the committee has followed procedures but some members' resentment and bias stemming from the candidate's prior decisions made a fair recommendation impossible.

Interim Solutions to the Challenges

Institutions that allow untenured faculty members to serve as department chairs have an obligation to verify that in instances where a negative committee evaluation may have been either political or personal in nature, the substance of the evaluation, not merely the procedure used, can be reviewed and appealed.

Although these institutional considerations are important whenever untenured faculty members are permitted to serve as department chairs, they can be cold comfort for junior faculty members who are already holding such positions or are about to embark on these assignments in the near future. Is there anything that individuals can do to improve their situations if they find themselves in the position of serving as untenured department chairs? In fact, there are steps to take, and they involve interim solutions to the three institutional challenges.

Address the Issue

Begin with a conversation with your dean or provost about the special challenges that untenured department chairs face. One of the easiest things you can do in response to the issues raised in this chapter is to have a candid conversation with your supervisor immediately. It may well be that he or she hasn't given much thought to the special challenges an untenured department chair faces. If you work in a highly politicized department or an area with a history of difficult tenure and promotion issues, state your concerns directly about the effects your decisions may have on those who will one day be making decisions or recommendations about you. Discuss what your options are in case you believe someday that you have been unfairly treated in the matter of tenure and promotion. Ask what allowances may be provided in your system for those who assume administrative appointments and thus may not have as comprehensive a list of achievements in teaching and research as do those who spent full time on the faculty.

This conversation may relieve your concerns completely by illustrating the ways in which the upper administration has plans to address situations like yours. At the other end of the spectrum, you may discover that your dean or provost regards your problem as a low priority and is unwilling or unable to offer any reasonable solution. The latter situation may occur if you yourself aggressively sought your administrative position, particularly if you'd been warned about its risks in advance. But this is an uncomfortable position to be in if others selected you to serve as chair or if you were the only possible candidate. In these cases, although there may be some benefit to knowing that you're on your own should problems arise in the future, you should probably press your case for greater administrative support and protection since the institution seems to be penalizing you for doing it a favor.

In the vast majority of cases, raising this issue will bring about no official changes in policy that would protect your future, just statements of endorsement for what you are doing on behalf of the institution and general promises to help if actual difficulties arise in the future. Although these vague offers may be disappointing, you have at least identified this issue with your supervisor, and you will have an opening to discuss the matter again if your situation worsens.

Seek Administrative Training

Seek a commitment from the institution that you will be provided with the administrative training you need in order to be as effective as possible in your position. Even if your institution does not provide administrative development and leadership training on your own campus, you still have many opportunities to receive training elsewhere. A number of organizations provide leadership training for department chairs at all levels of experience (see Chapter One). In addition, many individual disciplines offer workshops, conferences, and training programs, including those sponsored by the American Mathematical Society (www.ams.org/gov ernment/chrsworkshop06report.html), the American Association of Physics Teachers (www.aapt.org/Events/deptchairs.cfm), and the

Technical Symposium on Computer Science Education (www.cs.rit.edu/
~sigcse06/chairsWorkshop.shtml).

Request that as a junior member of the faculty who is chairing a department, you be allowed to attend one of these training programs each
year without impact on the travel budget of your discipline. Since the
institution should have a vested interest in seeing that its chairs have access to the tools they need in order to do their jobs, express this request as
an activity that benefits both you personally and your college or university as a whole. Offer to share what you learn in this training with other
chairs at a symposium or brown bag lunch when you return. By doing so,
you'll be developing the skills you need in order to move your department forward, at the same time that you are demonstrating your capacity
for leadership among your institution's chairs.

Make Controversial Decisions with Caution

Be cautious about making potentially controversial decisions in isolation,
particularly when you don't know whether those decisions will be supported at other institutional levels. Finally, untenured department chairs
have to be more careful than their more senior colleagues when making
decisions that are likely to be met with resistance or disappointment by
other members of your department.

Imagine the situation that arises if you make a controversial decision,
it meets with resistance in your department, and your institution's upper
administration overturns your decision. For a department chair who's
also a tenured full professor, this result is disappointing but little more
than that. In fact, more senior chairs discover that if they hold their positions long enough, this occurrence is not even particularly uncommon.
Your situation is different, however. If a senior administrator were to
overturn a major and controversial decision that you have made, you
could be placed in an extremely vulnerable position. The departmental
faculty members who will someday vote on your tenure and promotion
may be alienated by your decision, upper administration's action makes
you look weak, and you have been shown very publicly how little you
can count on the backing of your supervisor.

As a chair, you can't be afraid to make difficult decisions, but as an
untenured chair, you can't afford to be in a situation where you suffer
the consequences of having made one of these tough choices, only to
have your decision overturned. For this reason, check with your supervisor before announcing your decision in order to learn if there is broad
administrative support for it. At times you may decide that even if your

supervisor disagrees with you, it is the right thing to do anyway. More frequently, however, you will decide to give serious consideration to any decision that leaves you vulnerable and without your supervisor's backing. Not every battle is worth fighting, and you will need to consider carefully whether this is a situation that merits the considerable risks that it entails.

○

Serving as an untenured department chair brings with it a substantial number of challenges. If you are relatively new to the profession, you may just be learning much of what you need to know about being an effective teacher and researcher in an academic setting at the same time that you'll be called on to make decisions affecting the teaching and research of others. Any administrative position brings the likelihood that certain people are going to resent you simply because you have to say no to them from time to time; when these are the same people who will later be in a position to say no to your application for tenure and promotion, the risks you face become substantial. You therefore need to be aware of the challenges you will confront, your rights at your institution, and your level of support from your supervisor in order to be as effective as possible for as long as possible in your administrative and academic roles.

REFERENCES

Arreola, R. A. (2006). *Developing a comprehensive faculty evaluation system: A guide to designing, building, and operating large-scale faculty evaluation systems* (3rd ed.). San Francisco: Jossey-Bass/Anker.

Seldin, P. (2006). *Evaluating faculty performance: A practical guide to assessing teaching, research, and service.* San Francisco: Jossey-Bass/Anker.

RESOURCE

Mosto, P. (2004). *Honing the skills of department chairs at Rowan University.* ACE Department Chair Online Resource Center. Retrieved from www .acenet.edu/resources/chairs/docs/mosto_honing_skills.pdf

5

COEXISTING WITH A
FORMER CHAIR

IF YOUR DEPARTMENT IS like most others, the odds are very good that at least one former chair is serving among the faculty members in your department. At institutions where the position of chair rotates, it is even possible that all of your colleagues have been chairs at one time or another. In systems where chairs are elected by the faculty or chosen by the administration, you are more likely to find yourself in a situation where either one or a small number of your faculty members have chaired the department before you.

In the best of all situations, having former chairs in your department can be useful. They understand the difficulties of the job because they've done it. They may have advice on the best ways to negotiate your way around institutional land mines and quicksand pits and to advance the needs of your department in the unique political environment of your college or university. They can provide a sympathetic ear when you need it, serve as a mentor, and even work behind the scenes to help you when you need an unofficial departmental ambassador. These positive experiences are certainly not uncommon, and most chairs eventually work in an environment where they witness the benefit of having someone on the faculty who has been chair.

A problem arises when the reverse situation occurs: when one or more former chairs are not supportive and collaborative and instead undermine your authority as chair, work against you, or let you know in subtle but unmistakable ways that they'd handle matters quite differently, and better, if they were still running the department.

You won't find much guidance on how to handle this situation in general books on management and leadership because this situation does not occur often in the business world. In industry, when a supervisor isn't working out for whatever reason, that person is usually either terminated or reassigned in the company. He or she almost never returns to the employee ranks in the same area he or she had supervised in the same way that academic administrators regularly return to the faculty at the end of their assignment.

If you find yourself in a situation where one or more former chairs in your department are making your life miserable, what do you do? Every department and every institution has its own unique opportunities and challenges, of course, but the following advice will help you if you find yourself trying to coexist with an uncooperative former chair.

Try to determine whether some of the friction you feel with your former chair may be generational.

If you pay close attention to the work habits and expectations of college personnel, you begin to notice a few generational differences:

- More senior members of the faculty and staff sometimes feel that if meetings are not being held, work is not being done. In contrast, many younger members of the faculty and staff prefer to collaborate electronically, distributing drafts of documents by e-mail or groupware.
- Senior members of the faculty and staff sometimes intervene when they believe that someone isn't being respectful or professional in dress, informal speech, or sense of humor; sometimes younger members of the faculty and staff are resentful of "being mothered" by colleagues they regard as their peers.
- Junior members of the faculty and staff frequently want validation, even daily, to reinforce their sense that their work is of a high quality; senior members of the faculty and staff sometimes grumble that they don't see the point of "all these rewards and parties that congratulate people just for showing up and doing their jobs."

Because there exist certain generational differences in work habits and expectations, tensions with a former chair can be exacerbated when the two of you are on opposite sides of this generational line. Since you are not doing your job the way that the former chair would have done it, he or she may make you feel (and even at times tell you) that you are not doing your job at all. In these cases, your best solution may be to have an informal conversation with the former chair, perhaps over lunch, where you make clear why you make decisions, conduct meetings, and gather information in the way that you do. Explain that your operating procedure is aimed solely at doing what is best for the department, its faculty, and its students. In many cases, after the former chair understands a bit better why you do things differently from the way they were done in the past, he or she will begin to cut you more slack, and your tensions will ease.

Establish a clear new initiative.

Some former chairs may find it hard to give up their habit of running their department when they are no longer officially in charge. This habit can be exacerbated in departments where the curriculum, organizational structure, and mission have not changed since their term as chair. The way in which the department operates feels very familiar to them, and they have become so accustomed to being in charge of these matters that they act as though they still are.

If this seems to be the case in your department, you can start taking steps to make the department "your own" and to feel slightly less familiar to those who have been around for a while. The precise nature of the initiative that you take will depend on your discipline and the needs of your institution. You never want to be in a situation where you start changing things simply for the sake of leaving a legacy, shaking things up, or making a change for its own sake. But it is the rare academic department that cannot be improved in some way. Certainly there is an area of your curriculum, departmental procedures, the discipline's internal organization, or your area's academic policies that could benefit from a complete overhaul—for example:

- Has the department's mission statement been revised and updated within recent memory?
- Have syllabi been updated on the basis of what your area is learning from your institution's assessment data?
- Could you benefit from a major new lecture series, Web site, publication, award, or conference?
- Has your department been active in preparing new faculty members to teach and assume positions of leadership at your institution?
- Would an annual theme bring your department to a new level of prominence? (See Chapter Fifteen.)
- Is your current departmental committee structure fair and effective, or is it simply in place because it has always been there?

○ Has your discipline established teaching circles, scholarship networks, and service alliances as a way of promoting colleague-based support for the central responsibilities of the professorate? (See Chapter Forty-Seven.)

Your initiative can be as all-encompassing as a complete revision of the curriculum for all of your major programs or as modest as bringing your manual of policies and procedures up to date. The important thing is that it is your initiative and that you present it as an activity of substantial importance to your department. Talk about your initiative regularly at department meetings, and the message will soon become clear: the department is no longer in the same place as it was under previous chairs.

Focus only on the former chair's actual behavior and the problems that it has created.

Sometimes when we have been irritated by the treatment we receive from other people, we begin finding fault with them, even when their words or actions cause no real harm. Therefore, separate very carefully the words and behavior of the former chair that are causing you and the department genuine problems from those that, while annoying, are ultimately not interfering with the smooth operation of your program.

> Our temptation is frequently to change someone's behavior by first changing that person's attitude. Although that approach can sometimes be successful, most academic leaders find it more effective to change someone's attitude by first changing that person's behavior.

After all, you can't ask someone to have more respect for you—such a request is likely to be counterproductive at best—but you can direct a person to stop doing A and B and to begin doing C and D. Sometimes, too, when we look at a former chair's actions carefully, we discover reasons for those actions other than sheer malice or a dislike of having someone else in charge. For instance, someone who has been department chair for a long time may have gotten used to no longer needing approval for his or her course schedule, purchases, or travel plans. The former chair may resent having to go through channels when he or she is used to making decisions. In fact, a large part of this resentment may even be subconscious and have little to do with whether this faculty member thinks that you're succeeding as a department chair. In such a case, your best approach may be to have a conversation with the faculty member about how it's in the best interests of the department for everyone to submit their proposals together so that a reasonable plan can be developed. If the former chair truly cares about the strength and reputation of the department, tying the behavior that you want to the good of the program may be your most effective strategy.

Find a new outlet for the former chair's energies.

Some chairs discover that after leaving behind their administrative responsibilities, they have a great deal of experience, ideas, and talent about how to solve problems but nowhere to apply these resources. Some of the frustration the former chair may be causing you could be due to the fact that he or she is looking for something to take on as a problem to solve.

If you suspect that this may be the case in your department, see if you can find a new project at which the former chair can excel. At times, directing the person's energies inward to the department by putting him or her in charge of a curriculum revision or search committee will not solve the problem; it will merely give the former chair an official platform from which to create new difficulties. The best outlet in a situation of this type is an activity that extends beyond the confines of the department:

○ Get the former chair involved with a revision of the institution's general education program, a search committee for an upper administrator, or an interdisciplinary initiative.

○ Launch a departmental initiative to have the former chair elected to the institution's curriculum committee, faculty senate, research board, or program review committee.

○ Involve the former chair in your institution's center for excellence in teaching and learning or center for professional development and leadership.

In fact, channeling the former chair's energies externally makes good sense for both the individual and the department. Having already demonstrated success at the departmental level, the former chair is ready to assume service to the institution at a broader level of importance. With new challenges to tackle and new victories to win, he or she will also be far less likely to keep rehashing old problems at the department level, the very sorts of problems that you want the liberty to deal with untrammeled by the former chair's constant interference.

If none of the preceding strategies has worked, state your concerns directly but privately with the former chair.

Socrates held that all virtue was knowledge; all vice was ignorance. No one, Socrates believed, did wrong willingly. If people understood—truly understood on a fundamental level and not simply saying that they understood—that doing something bad was bad for them, they would cease engaging in poor behavior. After all, who would be willing do something that was not in his or her own best interests?

Certainly the Socratic approach to ethics has been criticized over the years, and we've all know people who engaged in the worst sort of behavior even after it had become abundantly clear how self-destructive they were being. Nevertheless, it remains true that some poor professional behavior occurs because people don't know any better or are unaware of how their actions are perceived. For this reason, a candid discussion with the former chair about the position he or she has placed you in, the difficulty this behavior is causing, and your expectations for the future may be highly beneficial in certain cases. Keep the conversation as constructive and forward looking as possible. Discuss past problems not in the spirit of fault finding or assigning blame but merely as indications of the sort of problems that the former chair's behavior has caused. Express, if you can honestly do so, your appreciation for what the person accomplished as chair, but make it clear that you expect the same opportunity to work unimpeded and unchallenged that the former chair had (or wished he or she had). In a private conversation, you can appeal to the former chair's understanding of the many challenges and frustrations that result from supervising a department, request some consideration for the difficult role you are playing, and seek an improved working relationship for the future. (On approaches to communicating with people like former chairs who are causing you problems, see Higgerson and Joyce, 2007.)

Admittedly the approaches we have considered so far do not always work. For one thing, they require that the former chair be a reasonable person with at least some capacity for self-awareness and generosity, prerequisites that unfortunately are all too often unmet. Nevertheless, despite how unprofessionally you may have been treated, you have a professional obligation to explore this possible solution before considering one last, more extreme measure.

Consult your dean or provost.

Perhaps the most common extreme measure you can take when you are frustrated by a former chair on your faculty is to discuss the matter with your superior either to seek support for the actions that you intend to take or to request that your superior intervene directly. Going to your boss always elevates the seriousness of the situation. For one thing, you are running the risk of appearing to be in a situation that you can't handle yourself. Depending on the personality of your dean or provost, you may receive either sympathy for being in a difficult situation or exasperation for "tattling" on another member of your department. In addition, if your supervisor intervenes, it is always possible that rather than solving the problem, you may be making it worse by giving the former chair the impression that you are forming a coalition against him or her.

For all of these reasons, if you decide that the situation is serious enough to involve your supervisor, begin the conversation by stating that you are exploring possible solutions and seeking advice, not necessarily direct action. Come to the conversation with specific instances of difficulties created by the former chair's behavior, remedies that you have attempted, and indications that your own attempts to resolve the situation have not been successful. Determine the extent to which your dean or provost seems willing to back you up in this situation, and together explore approaches that you and your supervisor can consider. Don't act as though you're giving up or leaving the problem for your supervisor to solve. Indicate your willingness to take positive action that is in the best interest of both your program and the institution. Avoid giving the impression that you expect your boss to fix the situation. Rather, suggest that you are interested in an approach that is beneficial to both someone who worked in the past to help your department and the new directions that the department must take under your leadership.

○

Few other things can undermine your authority as a department chair as completely as an uncooperative former chair. If the situation becomes severe enough, you can find yourself exasperated and unable to complete the important work of your discipline. As you try to resolve the situation by putting into effect the various strategies outlined in this chapter, it is also important to keep in mind one overarching realization: someday—perhaps in the not-too-distant future—you too will be a former chair, and you are likely to be serving as a faculty member in the same department you now supervise. When that occurs, remember to accept your new role with good humor and grace, reducing the likelihood that your successor will one day be reading this chapter and wondering what to do about *you*.

REFERENCE

Higgerson, M. L., & Joyce, T. A. (2007). *Effective leadership communication: A guide for department chairs and deans for managing difficult situations and people.* San Francisco: Jossey-Bass.

RESOURCE

Dienemann, J. (2006). *Remembrances: Bidding a fond farewell to department chair status.* ACE Department Chair Online Resource Center. Retrieved from www.acenet.edu/resources/chairs/docs/dienemann_remember.pdf

6

CREATING A CAREER PLAN

AS REWARDING A POSITION as department chair may be, one's stint doesn't last forever. Either there is a fixed term, after which you return to the faculty or seek another assignment, or the position is open-ended, with both you and the institution having the right to decide when another chair should be appointed. In either case, however, it is both natural and appropriate for you to begin considering what comes next at some point during your tenure in the position.

There are different choices that you will need to consider now as a department chair in order to keep your options open and increase the amount of success you'll have in pursuing your future plans. Let's consider several possible choices individually.

Return to the Faculty

A significant proportion of department chairs—most surveys suggest that the range is between 50 and 65 percent—eventually return to the faculty (Cipriano & Riccardi, 2010; Gmelch, 2004). They may do so immediately after completing their term as chair or may choose this option only after filling a number of other positions. Nevertheless, since serving as a rank-and-file faculty member again is a highly likely outcome for most chairs, there are several things to keep in mind during your period as chair.

As difficult as it may be, it is highly advisable to maintain an active scholarly agenda throughout your administrative appointment. With all of the pressures of time that arise as part of administrative assignments, too many chairs cut back on active scholarship as a way of freeing up their schedule. This is unfortunate because they may find that when they return to the faculty at their own or another institution, their record of scholarship is significantly smaller than that of many of their peers who continued their faculty positions all along. Even worse, scholarly activity, once it has diminished, is notoriously difficult to resume. Changes have occurred in the field that require catching up on. One's network with other scholars in the discipline may have weakened. (At times this occurs because the chair is obliged to devote limited travel funds to attend conferences for chairs and other administrators rather than participating actively in disciplinary meetings.) Nor is it likely that a chair's research, which may take several years of collecting data, will result immediately in publications or major conference presentations; one will have to gear up a research agenda again, and that can require substantial time.

For this reason, as difficult as it may be, it can be extremely important for you as department chair to remain active in scholarship, research, and creative activity in some way even during your administrative appointment. Perhaps you can join a team of scholars who are jointly working on a project, contributing time and ideas when that is possible; even being third or fourth author on an article is far preferable to a large gap in your publication record. Perhaps you can segue for a time to research on the scholarship of teaching in your discipline or curricular planning in the field. Although published works in these areas were long seen as less prestigious in many academic areas, that attitude is changing as a result of broader views of scholarship, such as those presented in Boyer (1990), Glassick, Huber, Maeroff, and Boyer (1997), and Braxton, Luckey, and Helland (2002). Work done on the scholarship of teaching can open up an entirely new field of research for chairs; it can also help you to keep your hand in until you resume your previous line of research on your return to the faculty.

The second common mistake that chairs can make before their return to the faculty is not teaching sufficiently or not teaching sufficiently broadly. Again, because of the pressures of time, chairs may frequently teach only the minimum required by their contracts. In certain large departments, the chair may not be expected to teach at all. The difficulty arises when a chair must return to teaching—sometimes after a gap of many years—and faces updated information, new teaching methods, and new means of engaging a new generation of students. Even teaching a course or two a year during the administrative tenure can be detrimental if the chair simply cherry-picks the most desirable sections: the advanced seminar for majors, the orientation course that meets only once a week, the online course for graduate students. Such selective teaching can even be counterproductive since it may provide a distorted view of the full range of students that the program is attracting. For this reason, team-teaching a course, teaching a unit within a larger course, and rotating widely the levels at which you teach (introductory, intermediate, senior-level seminar, graduate course) are all better strategies than teaching too little or too narrowly. Not only will such continued breadth of teaching help your transition back to the faculty, it will also make you a better chair by providing you with a close-up overview of your program.

The next chapter explores the opportunities and challenges of returning to the faculty in greater detail. For now, however, let's explore a few of your other options.

Obtain Another Chair Position

Some chairs enjoy the opportunities and challenges of being a chair so much that they begin to look for opportunities to make a lateral move as chair at another institution or to progress to a larger or more prestigious college or university. If this is the situation in which you find yourself, you should complement your experience as chair with a broad range of issues involving best practices, curricula, and challenges in your field. It is all too easy to fall into the practice of thinking, "Well, that's not the way we did it back at my old institution," since that tends to be our immediate frame of reference. The difficulty with such an approach is that it tends to limit one's thinking, narrowing it to what one has actually experienced. To the greatest extent possible, then, keep up with how different programs in your field are structured. How are their curricula organized? What courses are required, and what prerequisites are enforced? How do they promote scholarship in the discipline, and what do they tend to regard as the most significant contributions in the areas of scholarship, research, and creative activity? By knowing this, you will both increase your dossier of ideas to bring to a new institution and possibly even gain some new perspectives for your current department.

If you are thinking about moving to another position as chair, you will want at least one contribution that you can call your own as an example of your leadership and initiative. What courses were you instrumental in developing or revising? Have you developed any new emphases or tracks within your major? Did you inaugurate a lecture series, discussion group, or teaching circle? Did you establish a departmental office of your campus's center for excellence in teaching and learning? (See Chapter Sixteen.) Did you author a new policy manual for your discipline? Achievements such as these will help to demonstrate to your new institution that you haven't just been an effective manager of resources; you've also been responsible for the sort of initiatives that they are looking for to help their program move forward.

Seek Another Midlevel Position

Some chairs discover that they both enjoy and have talent for academic administration, but they would prefer to remain at their current institution without exposing themselves (at least not yet) to the demanding challenges of a deanship or position in upper administration. They may thus be attracted to other midlevel positions, such as an assistant or associate dean, director of a center for teaching excellence, honors program director, director of a center or institute, and the like.

To begin career planning in this area, you will need to amass skills at coping with highly detailed information and develop a thorough understanding of the office in which your new position will be. Midlevel administrative positions tend to involve managing tremendous amounts of information, completing reports, being certain that deadlines are met, keeping large numbers of people apprised of developments that are essential for them to know about, handling stress effectively, working quickly with short turnaround times, and many of the less glamorous aspects of academic administration. These positions can be solid training grounds and wonderful careers for certain people, but they tend not to be appropriate for individuals without good computer skills, organization, and attention to detail. Particularly the positions of assistant or associate dean, provost or vice president require individuals who can effectively implement someone else's initiative without feeling a need to take undue credit for the effort or to pursue their own initiatives. As a department chair, be certain that you have demonstrated not mere success in meeting deadlines and supplying information accurately, but excellence in this area.

You will also want to be fully acquainted with the needs and operation of the office to which you will move. You are unlikely to be successful in your application to serve as director of the honors program, for instance, if you have demonstrated only a modest amount of interest in honors programs and recruiting students of high ability during your term as chair. Without neglecting your primary responsibilities to your own discipline, therefore, developing a broader knowledge of campus programs and offices can be essential for any midlevel move that you are attempting to make. For this reason, try to seek opportunities that both enhance your own knowledge and benefit your department:

o What sorts of programs can you offer in conjunction with the center for teaching excellence? How can you better promote its workshops among your faculty?

o Are there opportunities for participation in the honors program that your discipline has not yet pursued? If you are already heavily involved in honors education, how can your discipline improve the experience that it is providing for these students?

○ Are you able to launch a targeted recruitment weekend for students who might be interested in your major, coordinating this activity with some office about which you would like to learn a great deal more?

Any of these initiatives will make a major contribution to your program, while also widening your network of contacts across campus and teaching you much that you need to know about the operation of other offices.

Become a Dean

Many department chairs find that the taste of academic administration that they have developed through their responsibilities as chair has given them the hunger for still greater challenges, such as serving as dean of a college. There are many right reasons for wanting to be a dean, such as a passion for making a difference in the academic program of an institution, a desire to serve as an advocate for a broad but related group of disciplines, and the belief that one's talents for motivating people and getting things done are appropriate for fulfilling the many functions of the dean's office. There are also many wrong reasons for wanting to be a dean, such as the false belief that the work involved is actually easier than teaching and research, a desire solely for the income and privileges that come with the position, and any sort of hidden agenda (a plan to promote one's own discipline at the expense of others, settle old scores, undermine senior administrators, and the like).

Seek a higher administrative role only if you truly believe that you have the skills and passion for administrative work. Too many colleges or universities have suffered from deans, provosts, and presidents who rose through the ranks simply to increase their income or because they thought it was the logical next step. If you cannot give honest and compelling answers to the questions, "Why am I attracted to administrative work, and how have I demonstrated my success at it?" then other career options are probably better for you.

Deans who assume their positions for the wrong reasons may do a disservice to their colleges and end up failing at their tasks. If money is your motivating factor, you may find it far easier (and more lucrative) to develop grant proposals, teach overloads, or write a textbook. If advancing your own discipline is your goal, there are less destructive ways of doing this than by holding back other departments. Deans need to have a sincere interest in all the fields that they are representing. They need to become intimately acquainted with how scholarship is performed in a variety of disciplines, how successful and engaged learning occurs across the college, and how to inspire others whose perspective on the world may be significantly different from their own. They also need a great deal of patience for sitting in meetings and the ability to handle even more different constituencies than they encountered while serving as chair.

If your career plans may be leading you toward a deanship, seek to develop a reputation for being able to see the big picture of your college's needs. Offer to serve on collegewide committees, such as those dealing with curriculum, tenure and promotion, and long-range planning. Gain experience in working collaboratively among disciplines, perhaps through promoting interdisciplinary approaches in your department's courses or through initiatives that gather representation from different departments. Gain as much expertise as you can in planning and defending budgets; be sure that you have a record that does not include overspending your own budget but that does include innovative approaches to bringing in grants and sponsored programs. Attend lectures, art openings, concerts, plays, and other cultural activities outside your own area; if you find that these activities are more ordeals to be endured than new tastes that you are happy to cultivate, you are unlikely to be happy in a dean's role. Offer to represent your institution at conferences and symposia that bring together faculty members from a number of disciplines. Be certain that you have not only made the hard decisions, but that you have made the right decisions and can defend them. When you make mistakes (and you will), always try to find a way of learning something positive from the experience in order to avoid making similar mistakes in the future. As a dean, you will have the opportunity to make even more mistakes than you have now, and it is highly beneficial to develop an approach to your work that allows you to grow from them.

Enter Upper Administration

Some chairs believe that their administrative careers are likely to lead them (perhaps by way of a deanship) to an upper administrative position such as provost, president, or chancellor. If this is your career path, then in addition to the other administrative experiences to amass as a chair, begin early to develop a successful record as a fundraiser. Your advancement efforts may include the successful submission of grants, the creation of new sponsored programs, the receipt of contributions from individuals or corporations, or the inclusion of your department into an individual's planned gift, such as a bequest or a trust. Increasingly, upper administrators are expected to have expertise in all of these areas, and your applications for upper administrative positions will be far stronger if you can document a solid record of achievement in at least one of them.

You may wish to start a few fairly small advancement efforts and progress from there. Offer your services to the campus phonathon or other types of solicitation efforts. Seek opportunities for applying for grants that both correspond well to your department's mission and bring indirect funding to your institution. Let your advancement office know that you are willing to accompany anyone on donor visits if the prospect has an interest in your academic field, majored in your area, or had a close connection to one of your faculty members. Once you attain some record of success in these smaller areas, you'll be able to formulate more ambitious plans for, say, an endowed chair or lecture series in your area, external funding for your facilities, or increased faculty advancement funding in your area. Just be certain to make all of these efforts in close cooperation with the advancement office. Take care not to contact donors who have already been identified for some other purpose by the institution and that your overall efforts correspond to the goals of your institution's strategic plan and its chief executive officer. In other words, if your goal is to be a president, you need to begin seeing how your activities within the department may be viewed from the presidential level. (For more ideas related to this topic, see Chapter Eight.)

Retire

One final career path for many chairs may be to retire from academic life altogether. Planning for this step in your career is rather different from those already outlined. In addition to continuing to advance the interests of your department, you will also be preparing for the new opportunities that will be awaiting you after your retirement. How closely will you want to maintain your ties with your institution, your academic discipline, and your professional organizations? Will you want, at least occasionally, to teach a section of a course as an adjunct faculty member or to serve as a consultant to a new chair who could benefit much from your expertise? Are there opportunities that you have not been able to pursue in your discipline—travel to other campuses or to parts of the world closely related to your field, offices in professional associations, or publications that you had never found time to write—that you may wish to explore now that you have time?

Although you will want to give the new department chair a chance to make his or her own name by bringing fresh perspectives to the position, it is rarely necessary to sever your relationship with your institution entirely when you retire. Offer your services to the extent that you feel comfortable and expect that the institution will take you up on your offer only to the extent that it is comfortable.

For most former chairs, retirement consists neither of complete abandonment of their discipline nor full-time service to the extent that they worked previously. As in so many other aspects of life, you can find a balance that promotes both the good of the college or university and gives you the satisfaction of making a much-needed contribution in the area of your expertise.

○

Whether they are conscious of it or not, all chairs do some sort of career planning. The more intentional you make these efforts, the more likely it is that your choices will be successful. It is never wrong to keep an eye on where you are going after your term as chair ends, as long as that is not the only focus of your attention. Properly perceived, career planning can provide many advantages to the department even as it helps bring you closer to your ultimate professional goals.

REFERENCES

Boyer, E. L. (1990). *Scholarship reconsidered: Priorities of the professoriate*. Princeton, NJ: Carnegie Foundation for the Advancement of Teaching.

Braxton, J. M., Luckey, W. T., & Helland, P. (2002). *Institutionalizing a broader view of scholarship through Boyer's four domains*. ASHE-ERIC Higher Education Report, vol. 29, no. 2 San Francisco: Jossey-Bass.

Cipriano, R. E., & Riccardi, R. (2010). What is unique about chairs? A continuing exploration. *Department Chair, 20*(4), 26–28.

Glassick, C. E., Huber, M. T., Maeroff, G. I., & Boyer, E. L. (1997). *Scholarship assessed: Evaluation of the professoriate*. San Francisco: Jossey-Bass.

Gmelch, W. H. (2004). The department chair's balancing acts. In W. H. Gmelch & J. H. Schuh (Eds.), *The life cycle of a department chair* (pp. 69–84). New Directions for Higher Education, no. 126. San Francisco: Jossey-Bass.

RESOURCES

Leaming, D. R. (1998). *Academic leadership: A practical guide to chairing the department*. San Francisco: Jossey-Bass/Anker.

Lees, N. D. (2005). The department chair position as a step in a career path. *Department Chair, 15*(3), 3–5.

Lees, N. D., Malik, D. J., & Vemuri, G. (2009). The essentials of chairing academic departments. *Department Chair, 20*(2), 1–3.

7

RETURNING TO THE FACULTY

IN CHAPTER SIX, we saw that most department chairs eventually return to the faculty after a period of administrative service, and we explored a few ideas to help ease this transition, including maintaining as active a scholarly agenda as possible throughout your administrative appointment and making an effort to teach broadly during your term as chair.

In this chapter, we consider several other strategies that can be important for chairs who are likely to return to full-time teaching and research. These suggestions are worth keeping in mind even if you've just begun your tenure as department chair and your possible resumption of faculty duties is at least a few years off.

Acceptance and Trust

Some department chairs find that as soon as they become a full-time faculty member once again, it's almost as though they had never left the professorial ranks: their colleagues immediately begin approaching them once more on equal footing, and there's an instant sense of camaraderie in the air. Others find their return to the faculty a more difficult and prolonged process. They are met with distrust, hostility, and perhaps even a bit of contempt; faculty members who had once been close friends now seem more distant; your statements about being "glad to be back at the important work of teaching and research" are treated with suspicion.

A significant part of these differences derives from the personalities of the people who happen to serve in the department. Another part is surely due to the way in which chairs are chosen at the institution and the specific duties that they're assigned. In other words, in departments where all faculty members eventually become chair as a part of a regular rotation, transition to a full-time position is likely to be rather easy. At institutions where chairs are appointed by upper administration or hired from outside primarily as administrators, this transition can be much more challenging. Particularly when the chair serves an open-ended term, faculty members are likely to be wary of statements that it was the chair's own idea to return to full-time teaching and research.

Administrators who step down because they miss working as faculty members certainly do exist, as do politicians who leave office because they want to spend more time with their families. But people have so often heard this explanation offered as a face-saving measure after someone has been demoted that their first response may be skepticism. It can be tempting, particularly after a difficult tenure as chair, to dismiss these doubts by saying, "That's *their* problem. I know the truth." But if the way that other people treat you begins to affect your morale, job satisfaction, or effectiveness, then it becomes your problem. In order to ease your reintegration into the department, it can be beneficial to follow three steps.

Step 1: Rebuild Your Bridge

Unless your term as chair was brief, your relationship with other members of the department will have changed during the time you served as chair. It's difficult to go from being someone's colleague, to being a supervisor (even nominally), to being a colleague once again without having an effect on the way in which you interact with one another. Academic departments are surprisingly complex networks of associations. Alliances arise and then dissolve; coalitions, even conspiracies, develop; and power relationships change. All of these factors become even more intense when job descriptions, administrative authority, and salary differentials are involved.

Even if you serve in the most collegial, least political department in university history, it may take some time for your colleagues to adjust their feelings about you to your new role. Go out of your way to smooth this transition. Make the first move by initiating conversations, asking colleagues to join you at lunch, and demonstrating support for the successes of others. Your bridges with the rest of your department may not be broken, but people are still adjusting to this change. Do whatever you can to make this process easy, even if your initial overtures seem unsuccessful or are rebuffed.

Step 2: Repay Your Dues

Some chairs feel that they're owed special privileges when they return to the faculty. They expect to receive the choicest classroom assignments, the most convenient class times, the best research facilities, and the brightest students. They may feel that they deserve special consideration for having served as the discipline's advocate in the trenches. But the other faculty members may view things differently. They may regard a person's term of chair, even if that position is elected or rotated, as itself a privilege that has included lighter duties of teaching, scholarship, and all the other work that faculty members see as the mainstay of higher education. In other words, while chairs may sometimes view their return to the faculty as a time to collect what they believe is owed them, faculty members can sometimes view a former chair as needing to repay some dues.

By offering to teach at unpopular times, take a fair share (or even larger than a fair share) of the least desirable courses, and assume responsibilities on the committees that other faculty members dread, you can send a message that you're willing to do your part as a faculty member and do not expect special treatment. No one will expect you to do penance forever for your sojourn in administration, but devoting the first year or two of your return to the faculty in repayment of your professorial dues can make your reintegration much easier.

Step 3: Reestablish Your Identity

For a long time now, others have probably thought of you primarily as "the chair." You may even have begun to think of yourself in these terms. As you make the transition from administrator and faculty member to full-time faculty member, be sure to ask yourself, "Who am I now?" It can be a real trap to view yourself only in terms of your professional responsibilities. People who retire sometimes find that they've so long defined their identities by their careers that they face an identity crisis once they no longer have a title after their names. So a return to faculty status can be a real threat to some people's egos, while others may discover excitement in the chance they have to reinvent themselves.

To increase the likelihood that you'll be in the latter category, give some serious consideration to what your next major role could be. You could strive for institution-wide or even national prominence as a master teacher. You could direct your efforts toward advancing a research project you never had time for when you were chair. You could serve as a mentor to the next generation of academic leaders. You could revise the entire curriculum of your discipline, making it accord more completely with the needs of today's students. Only you can determine the best fit for what your new (or reestablished) identity should be, but you're more likely to find a role that you find satisfying and stimulating if you begin preparing for it early.

Letting It Go

Once we've been assigned a position of responsibility, it can be challenging to stop ourselves from thinking, "That's not how I would've done it," once someone else is in charge. But letting it go should be one of the most important goals for a former chair who returns to the faculty. If you try to run the department from behind the scenes, you'll end up frustrating yourself and alienating the very people you believe you're trying to help. Someone else is in charge now, and the new chair is entitled to several courtesies from you:

- *The right to develop his or her own leadership style.* As we saw in Chapter Three, there's no single style of administrative leadership that works equally well for all people in all situations. The new chair has the right to do things in the way that he or she believes to be most effective: to be more hands-on or laid-back than you were, to spend more time on detailed work or developing a long-term vision, and to approach the responsibilities of the job in a manner that he or she believes to be appropriate.

- *The right to make his or her own mistakes.* A good former chair does not sit idly by when the new chair embarks on a course that will bankrupt the department, alienate students and faculty, or put the discipline's future in jeopardy. But a good former chair will also not try to intervene or provide unsolicited advice when his or her successor is simply trying out new ideas, even though all of these efforts may not be successful. The true wisdom comes in knowing the difference between mistakes that could have serious or lasting implications and those that are simply learning opportunities for the new chair. If you were like most other chairs, you probably made your share of mistakes as an administrator. Your successor has earned the right to make a few too.

- *The right to set his or her own agenda.* A good department chair does not dictate the strategic direction of the discipline, but he or she can play a vital role in helping guide the department's development and plan its growth. In this way, chairs need a certain amount of latitude in asking the questions that they feel need to be asked and pursuing the priorities that they regard as most important. Even if you felt that you were not accorded as much freedom as you would have liked to set your own agenda, it's your duty now to improve this situation for your successor. Simply because his or her goals are not the ones that you considered most important, you can't conclude that these objectives aren't worthwhile.

These were the same opportunities that you probably wanted when you first became the department chair. Even if you weren't extended these same courtesies—perhaps especially if you weren't extended them—it's your duty now to ensure that the new chair is given every chance to succeed on his or her own. Keep the following essential principle in mind at all times:

> For a surprising number of issues in academic administration, there is no clearly right and clearly wrong way of approaching the situation. In many cases, different decisions are equally acceptable, depending on such factors as the leadership style of the chair, the needs and personalities of the department members, the mission of the institution, and the current stage of the department's development. What is needed is more often a consistent and reasonable approach rather than any one specific approach.

The key test, in other words, is not whether the current chair does things exactly as you would have done them but whether his or her approach works. If it does, then you should take pride in having left the department strong enough that a new style of leadership could be as equally successful as yours. If it doesn't, then both you and the new chair have an opportunity to learn from what went wrong and how to avoid this problem in the future.

Passing Your Experience On to Others

One possibility for reestablishing your identity now that your term as chair is complete could be to act as a mentor to the new or future chairs. If this opportunity attracts you, it's best to begin pursuing it relatively soon, while your experience is still fresh in your mind and the issues you had to address are still current. Mentoring others helps both the emerging leaders, who can benefit from your knowledge, and yourself since, by reflecting on your experience, you'll become aware of patterns you might not have noticed before and make better sense of situations that may initially have seemed unconnected or random. As every classroom instructor learns, you don't really know a field until you try to teach it to others, and the art and science of academic leadership is no exception to this rule. Nevertheless, when mentoring new and potential department chairs, there are several important principles to keep in mind:

○ *It is probably best to mentor leaders in disciplines that are similar but not identical to yours.* The new chair in your department needs a great deal of freedom to pursue his or her own initiatives and develop a personal leadership style. If you act as a mentor to faculty members in your own department, people may start to consider you the power behind the throne, even if that's not at all your intention. Nevertheless, chairing an art department is different in many ways from chairing a department of management, nursing, engineering, mathematics, or criminal justice. Your experience is much more likely to be relevant if you mentor future leaders in disciplines that share a similar methodology, mission, and philosophy to your own field.

○ *Remember that you've gained experience in far more areas than simply the duties of the chair.* When most former chairs consider mentoring others, they initially think of providing advice on clearly administrative matters, such as strategic planning, developing budget proposals, conducting faculty searches, or leading curricular reform. Those areas are certainly important, and they're worth considering as topics for discussion with your protégés. But they're not the only areas in which you now have a great deal of expertise. You can assist new faculty members with creating their career plans, writing grant proposals, and preparing their applications for promotion and tenure. You can provide guidance in how instructors can use assessment as a technique for continual improvement of their courses. You can help people craft a book proposal, practice conference presentations, and become more effective advisors. The range of responsibilities of department chairs today is very broad, and you can be more effective as a mentor if you reflect on all the activities you supervised during your tenure as chair.

○ *Your mentorship role can make an important contribution to your institutional service.* Since most university administrators come to their positions with little or no formal training in their day-to-day responsibilities, you now have an opportunity to improve this situation. Work with your institution's upper administration to expand your school's center for excellence in teaching and learning into a center for teaching, learning, and leadership, where future generations of chairs and deans can learn from experience. Alternatively, propose that an independent center for administrative leadership be established by the president or provost and collaborate with other universities in your area. In this way, you can help promote your mentoring activities from informal guidance offered to a handful of potential leaders to an ongoing, expanding group of emerging administrators who truly need the benefit of your experience.

○

Perhaps the most challenging situation occurs if you were hired into an institution specifically to be the department chair but then are reassigned to a faculty position because things didn't work out in the way that everyone had hoped. While time will certainly reduce the awkwardness of this situation, you'll need to do everything you can to ease this transition by building bridges wherever possible, making sure that both your confidence and your humility remain intact and demonstrating support for your successor. As difficult as it may be, refrain from overt criticism of the new chair or voicing strong opinions in opposition to his or her policies, at least until you're certain that your transition from part-time administrator to full-time faculty member is complete. It's possible that even what you regard as mild objections to an approach taken by the chair will be read by others as resentment on your part. This situation is temporary, but it may take several years until everyone sees you fully as a colleague and not as a former supervisor. In the meantime, your own experience will be much easier if you demonstrate tact, diplomacy, and collegial support for your successor.

RESOURCES

Becker, S. J. (1999). Thanks, but I'm just looking: Or, why I don't want to be a dean. *Journal of Legal Education, 49,* 595–600.

Eckrich, J. (2010). A smooth transition for the exiting chair at small colleges: The administration's role. *Academic Leader, 26*(11), 6–7.

Engel, S. (2006). Returning to the faculty: Advice from a chair. *Department Chair, 17*(1), 28.

Gmelch, W. H., & Miskin, V. D. (2011). The chair loop: Zoom to doom—how long is long enough? *Department Chair, 21*(3), 18–19.

Griffith, J. C. (2006). Transition from faculty to administrator and transition back to the faculty. In R. J. Henry (Ed.), *Transitions between faculty and administrative careers* (pp. 67–77). New Directions for Higher Education, no. 134. San Francisco: Jossey-Bass.

Lees, N. D. (2006). *Chairing academic departments: Traditional and emerging expectations.* San Francisco: Jossey-Bass/Anker.

Marquis, L. M. (2005). Being a good FART (former administrator returned to teaching). *Department Chair, 15*(3), 8–9.

Smith, E. (2004). The end of the rein: Department chair no more. In W. H. Gmelch & J. H. Schuh (Eds.), *The life cycle of a department chair* (pp. 85–92). San Francisco: Jossey-Bass.

Strickland, R. A. (2006). Stepping down as chair and reintegrating into faculty: Chairs Anonymous, anyone? *Department Chair, 17*(2), 25–26.

8

SEEKING HIGHER
ADMINISTRATIVE POSITIONS

WHILE SOME DEPARTMENT CHAIRS are happy to remain in their positions for the remainder of their careers and others eagerly return to full-time teaching and scholarship, other chairs realize that they have an interest in, talent for, and curiosity about other administrative assignments. It may be that the challenges of solving administrative problems, planning curricular development, resolving interpersonal conflict, identifying additional sources of funding, and working cooperatively with other disciplines offer an appeal in and of themselves. Or it may be that you feel at least as capable to address significant academic issues as the deans, vice presidents, and presidents you have encountered. For whatever reason, a significant number of chairs consider the possibility of moving into a dean's role or upper administration, and there are several ways to make that transition easier. Chapter Six already addressed two considerations that it will be important to keep in mind as you proceed:

○ *While success as a department chair frequently comes to those who serve as ardent, even aggressive, advocates for their own discipline, higher administrative positions require a broader view.* Chairs who still attempt to manage activities in their disciplines—or continue to identify themselves narrowly in terms of the perspectives and methodologies of their own disciplines—are frequently not successful in higher administrative roles. A good dean or president has to take a strong interest in a broad array of activities across the institution. That's a hard goal to achieve for people whose focus remains fixed solely on the issues addressed in their own academic fields.

○ *The higher you proceed up the institutional hierarchy, the more important it will be for you to have experience in fundraising, to know its approaches and vocabulary well, and to have documented successes in this area.* While you'll find a useful overview of these concepts in Chapter Forty-Eight, you'll need to develop more advanced knowledge of institutional advancement if you're interested in a higher administrative position. Consider attending a workshop on fundamental or advanced techniques of fundraising offered by the Council for Advancement and Support of Education (CASE; see www.case.org), the Council for Resource Development (which serves administrators at community colleges; see www .crdnet.org), the Association of Fundraising Professionals (which has a much broader focus than higher education alone; see www .afpnet.org), or your own professional organization. More and more groups are offering online programs, some of which can lead to certification, so it may not even be necessary for you to travel in order to obtain the type of training you need.

Following are a few other ideas about how to begin preparing for higher administrative positions.

Identify the types of experience that administrators are expected to have.

Perhaps the first thing to do when you're considering the possibility of a higher administrative position is to scan advertisements posted for these opportunities and then ask, "What would I need to know in order to do that?" Here's a composite advertisement, assembled from the type of phrasing that commonly appears in advertisements for deans:

The dean is the chief academic officer for the college and reports directly to the provost. The dean is expected to set academic priorities for the college, work collaboratively with faculty members and other administrators, reach decisions related to such issues as budgets and personnel, and guide the college toward achieving its strategic goals. The dean is expected to promote academic excellence, recruit and develop an outstanding faculty, and serve as an advocate for all disciplines contained in the College. Applicants should hold a doctorate in an appropriate discipline, have a record of teaching and scholarship that warrants appointment at the rank of professor, and have served in a major administrative role for at least five years at the departmental level or higher. Preferred applicants will be knowledgeable about program development and assessment, possess strong communication and leadership skills, have a successful record of fundraising and grant writing, and be experienced in both regional and specialized accreditation activities. It is expected that the dean will have a strong commitment to shared governance, cultural diversity, consensus building, and the university's strategic vision.

There are two things to notice about an advertisement of this sort. First, it specifically mentions several of the areas that all good administrators need to know about: budgetary matters, making personnel decisions, assessment, program development, strategic planning, accreditation, shared governance, cultural diversity, and building consensus. Other ads might also have reference to such issues as academic freedom, higher education law, program review, general education reform, the legislative process, tenure, and posttenure review. Every administrator is expected to be knowledgeable about all of these areas and to have experience suggesting that his or her knowledge goes beyond the merely theoretical. After all, even if you work at a private college, decisions made by the state legislature have a profound effect on higher education in your area, and you at least need to know the principal players and the context in which specific bills are amended, rejected, or passed.

Second, although advertisements for administrative positions have a certain uniformity in terms of the areas of expertise they expect academic leaders to have, it's their subtle differences that you'll need to pay close attention to when you're doing a job search. For instance, the hypothetical ad has several references to working collaboratively with the faculty, building consensus, and being committed to shared governance. Anything that is mentioned several times in an advertisement is likely to have been a significant issue at that institution or in that program, so you'll want to find out as much as you can through an Internet search or conversation with a trusted mentor in order to learn whether it's a situation you feel you can handle—and sincerely want to handle. Notice, too, how the advertisement expects successful applicants to support the university's strategic vision. Institutions devote a great deal of their time and resources to developing vision statements, strategic plans, and mission summaries. Before you even apply for a position, be sure that you're familiar with these documents, can support them, and know them sufficiently well to speak about them knowledgeably. Finally, pay close attention to any language that makes the advertisement seem different from those posted by similar institutions. For example, if a university talks about *maintaining* excellence in teaching but *promoting* excellence in research, that shift in wording reveals something significant about current points of pride as opposed to areas where there's a perceived need for growth.

You'll want to go into such a position knowing that you're expected to build on established strengths in (but not make a lot of changes to) the area of instruction but be more innovative in the area of scholarship and research. The cues about priorities are sometimes very subtle in position announcements. Once you begin comparing ads from many different institutions, you'll pick up on them more easily.

Assemble a library of key resources for administrators.

Even if you don't believe you'll be ready for an opportunity in higher levels of administration for many years, it's worthwhile to begin assembling a library of resources in this area. For one thing, exposure to some of the issues that are discussed at other levels of the institutional hierarchy will improve your work as chair. You'll find that your perspective has been broadened, and you'll have better insight into what the dean, provost, and president want from you. You'll discover ways of discussing your priorities with them in terms that relate to how they make decisions and the pressures under which they're operating. Second, better understanding the issues that are dealt with at higher levels of administration will help you identify the areas of experience that you still need and the types of achievement you'll be expected to demonstrate when you apply for positions.

The precise resources you'll want to assemble will vary according to the career path you envision. Keep in mind that it's by no means guaranteed that presidents and chancellors today rose from the ranks systematically from department chair to dean to vice president, before finally reaching their current positions. Chief executive officers at colleges and universities have a wide variety of backgrounds, and there are certainly presidents who were never provosts or even deans and may not even come from academia. For this reason, keep in mind that your career plan should be as flexible as possible, since there are likely to be at least a few turns ahead that you won't be able to predict.

If you're interested in becoming a dean, I certainly can't mention a list of appropriate resources without recommending *The Essential Academic Dean: A Practical Guide to College Leadership* (Buller, 2007). This guide builds on the principles and ideas contained in this book, just as this book has been designed to complement *The Essential College Professor: A Practical Guide to an Academic Career* (Buller, 2010). Chapter Two of *The Essential Academic Dean*, "Preparing for the Dean's Role," contains specific advice on the types of experiences you should have and the areas of expertise you should develop if you're interested in college-level administration.

There are plenty of other resources that every potential dean should have. *The Academic Deanship: Individual Careers and Institutional Roles* (2001), by Mary Richards and David Bright, is particularly valuable for new or prospective deans. Gary Krahenbuhl's *Building the Academic Deanship: Strategies for Success* (2004) is an excellent guide to combining practical decision making with the important role that vision and creativity play in college-level leadership. As part of an extended review in the *Journal of Higher Education*, Mimi Wolverton (2009) contrasts Krahenbuhl's reflective approach from what she regards as the more directive approach of *The Essential Academic Dean*. In actuality, many potential deans will find both perspectives useful for different reasons: there are times when the best thing you can do is to base your decisions on your own core values and institutional situation; at other times, it's more helpful simply to consider someone's suggestion about what to do, even if you decide not to take that advice. Moreover, Wolverton's own *College Deans: Leading from Within* (2002), coauthored with Walt Gmelch, is a valuable resource that is based on an extensive survey conducted of deans from all four-year colleges and universities in the United States. Similarly, the book that Wolverton and Gmelch cowrote with Joni Montez and Charles Nies, *The Changing Nature of the Academic Deanship* (2001), provides an excellent overview of the central issues related to college administration today, including the challenges of diversity, ethical concerns, and technology. Finally, you may want to consider a subscription to *Dean and Provost,* published monthly by Wiley, as a source for current developments in legal matters, executive management, and administrative policy.

If you're considering the possibility of a vice-presidential role in higher education, the resources to have on your bookshelf become quite varied indeed. Unlike deans (and even chief executive officers), all of whom face certain issues in common regardless of the great differences among their academic disciplines and institutional missions, the job descriptions of vice presidents at colleges and universities are almost unbelievably varied. What a provost or vice president for academic affairs does frequently has very little in common with the daily responsibilities of a vice president for university advancement, research, business affairs, enrollment management, student affairs, and so on. Nevertheless, if you believe that you may be interested someday in a position at the vice-presidential level, you ought to consider the advice contained in such books as Paul Bryant's *Confessions of an Habitual Administrator: An Academic Survival Manual* (2005), Peter Seldin and Mary Lou Higgerson's *The Administrative Portfolio: A Practical Guide to Improved Administrative*

Performance and Personnel Decisions (2002), C. K. Gunsalus's *The College Administrator's Survival Guide* (2006), and James Kouzes and Barry Posner's *The Jossey-Bass Academic Administrator's Guide to Exemplary Leadership* (2003). Gunsalus provides a sensible, easy-to-read, and at times quite humorous insight into the issues and challenges of academic administration. Kouzes and Posner offer an excellent, research-based approach to sound administrative leadership practices, while Bryant achieves a similar goal from an experience-based perspective. Seldin and Higgerson offer superb advice for improving the effectiveness of administrators and documenting successes when they apply for other university positions. Finally, department chairs who are thinking of seeking positions as provosts or academic vice presidents should make sure that they have access to James Martin and James E. Samels's *First Among Equals: The Role of the Chief Academic Officer* (1997), probably the best book to date on the unique challenges of that position.

For department chairs with an aspiration to serve as president, chancellor, rector, or chief executive officer of an institution, campus, or university system, there are a number of excellent resources to consider. Arthur Padilla's *Portraits in Leadership: Six Extraordinary University Presidents* (2005) provides case studies of successful academic leaders, including the University of Notre Dame's Father Theodore Hesburgh and the University of Chicago's Hanna Holborn Gray, and identifies experiences that they shared either early in life or when their careers were already well established as a means of detecting defining moments in the development of superb administrative role models. Judith Block McLaughlin's *Leadership amid Controversy: Presidential Perspectives* (2004) offers an opportunity for prospective leaders to consider how they themselves may have handled a number of extremely challenging situations. Robert Birnbaum's *How Academic Leadership Works: Understanding Success and Failure in the College Presidency* (1992) and Francis L. Lawrence's *Leadership in Higher Education: Views from the Presidency* (2006) are valuable overviews of the issues that chief executive officers are likely to face in higher education today, while James Fisher and James Koch's *The Entrepreneurial College President* (2004) offers a perspective of the modern president as an institutional change agent and catalyst for progress. A number of works have also been written for women who are interested in leading colleges, universities, or university systems. Among the best of them are Susan Madsen's *On Becoming a Woman Leader: Learning from the Experiences of University Presidents* (2008) and Mimi Wolverton, Beverly Bower, and Adrienne Hyle's *Women at the*

Top: What Women University and College Presidents Say About Effective Leadership (2009).

Spend a year in the Fellows Program conducted by the American Council on Education.

Perhaps the best way for a department chair to gain the sort of knowledge and experience that will be necessary for a career in upper administration is to spend a year in this program. It gives emerging leaders the opportunity to embed themselves in the administrative team at another college or university and receive intense hands-on training in current issues that higher education professionals need to address. In addition to their experiential activities, ACE fellows participate in a number of seminars and meetings, increasing their knowledge of effective administrative techniques. According to the ACE's Web site,

> Since 1965, hundreds of vice presidents, deans, department chairs, faculty, and other emerging leaders have participated in the ACE Fellows Program, the nation's premier higher education leadership development program in preparing senior leaders to serve American colleges and universities. The ACE Fellows Program is unique in comparison to other leadership development programs in higher education. ACE Fellows spend an extended period of time on another campus, working directly with presidents. . . .
> The ACE Fellows Program enables participants to immerse themselves in the culture, policies, and decision-making processes of another institution. This unique program condenses years of on-the-job experience and skills development into a single year. As a result, the ACE Fellows Program is the most effective, comprehensive leadership development program in American higher education today. (American Council on Education, 2010)

A great advantage of the program is that it provides rising leaders with exposure to a broader range of administrative functions than they may otherwise experience. Academic department chairs, for instance, are frequently encouraged to become involved during their fellowship year with business offices, centers for institutional advancement, or the student life staff. In addition, both the host institution and the fellow's home institution must make certain financial commitments to the program, so it's important to work out these details before you apply. Those who participate in the program find that it offers them valuable experience, a network of contacts, and career advantages if they decide to pursue opportunities in upper administration.

○

Whereas it was once assumed that the pathway to a university presidency was to progress from faculty member to department chair to dean to academic vice president to chief executive officer, the situation is more complex today. Many presidents and chancellors are offered their positions immediately after a deanship, while others find that vice-presidential work in university advancement is better preparation for the president's responsibilities than is the traditional academic route. Still other senior administrators come to their positions following service in politics, private industry, or nonprofit organizations.

The truth of the matter is that there's no single career path that applies to even a majority of upper administrators. The best tactic therefore is likely to be to select whichever path best suits your individual interests, experience, and ultimate goals. Although the choices colleagues have made can be helpful sources of information, no two administrative careers are ever alike, and you're far better off charting your own course than trying to duplicate someone else's strategy.

REFERENCES

American Council on Education. (2010). *ACE Fellows Program*. Retrieved from http://www.acenet.edu/AM/Template.cfm?Section=Fellows_Program1

Birnbaum, R. (1992). *How academic leadership works: Understanding success and failure in the college presidency*. San Francisco: Jossey-Bass.

Bryant, P. (2005). *Confessions of an habitual administrator: An academic survival manual*. San Francisco: Jossey-Bass/Anker.

Buller, J. L. (2007). *The essential academic dean: A practical guide to college leadership*. San Francisco: Jossey-Bass.

Buller, J. L. (2010). *The essential college professor: A practical guide to an academic career*. San Francisco: Jossey-Bass.

Fisher, J. L., & Koch, J. V. (2004). *The entrepreneurial college president*. Westport, CT: American Council on Education/Praeger.

Gunsalus, C. K. (2006). *The college administrator's survival guide*. Cambridge, MA: Harvard University Press.

Kouzes, J. M., & Posner, B. Z. (2003). *The Jossey-Bass academic administrator's guide to exemplary leadership*. San Francisco: Jossey-Bass.

Krahenbuhl, G. S. (2004). *Building the academic deanship: Strategies for success*. Westport: Praeger.

Lawrence, F. L. (2006). *Leadership in higher education: Views from the presidency*. New Brunswick, NJ: Transaction Publishers.

Madsen, S. R. (2008). *On becoming a woman leader: Learning from the experiences of university presidents*. San Francisco: Jossey-Bass.

Martin, J., & Samels, J. E. (1997). *First among equals: The role of the chief academic officer*. Baltimore: Johns Hopkins University Press.

McLaughlin, J. B. (Ed.). (2004). *Leadership amid controversy: Presidential perspectives*. New Directions for Higher Education, no. 128. San Francisco: Jossey-Bass.

Padilla, A. (2005). *Portraits in leadership: Six extraordinary university presidents*. Westport, CT: Praeger.

Richards, M. P., & Bright, D. F. (2001). *The academic deanship: Individual careers and institutional roles*. San Francisco: Jossey-Bass.

Seldin, P., & Higgerson, M. L. (2002). *The administrative portfolio: A practical guide to improved administrative performance and personnel decisions*. San Francisco: Jossey-Bass/Anker.

Wolverton, M. (2009). Review of *The essential academic dean: A practical guide to college leadership* and *Building the academic deanship: Strategies for success*. *Journal of Higher Education*, 80, 354–356.

Wolverton, M., Bower, B. L., & Hyle, A. E. (2009). *Women at the top: What women university and college presidents say about effective leadership*. Sterling, VA: Stylus.

Wolverton, M., & Gmelch, W. H. (2002). *College deans: Leading from within*. Westport, CT: American Council on Education/Oryx.

Wolverton, M., Gmelch, W. H., Montez, J., & Nies, C. T. (2001). *The changing nature of the academic deanship*: San Francisco: Jossey-Bass.

9

A SCENARIO ANALYSIS ON THE CHAIR'S ROLE AND CAREER PATH

THIS CHAPTER PRESENTS THE first of the eight scenario analyses at the end of each part in this book. These exercises are useful tools to help department chairs develop and critique their skills as administrators, consider alternative ways of solving difficult problems, and prepare for challenging situations. Each scenario analysis has three complementary parts:

- ○ *Case studies.* A brief summary of two or more fictional situations that are similar to the types of challenges department chairs actually face.

- ○ *Considerations.* Questions that may cause you to see the case study in a different light or to alter how you might respond to it.

- ○ *Suggestions.* A critique of the case studies themselves, along with ideas about possible actions to take in similar situations. The case studies do not lend themselves to clear right or wrong answers or to only one solution that will be applicable to all departments and institutions. Nevertheless, the suggestions provide practical and field-tested responses to similar challenges for you to consider. The suggestions should definitely not be regarded as the only answers but rather should prompt you to consider what you might do to find the best possible solution to a difficult problem.

An excellent way to improve your administrative skills through scenario analyses is to compare your analysis with those of your peers. Critique together the suggestions given to each case study, propose your own solutions, see how the questions posed by the "Considerations" section may cause your responses to change, and reflect on how your individual approaches reveal your personal style of leadership.

Case Studies

Friends and Lovers

Your institution has developed clear policies on amorous relations between supervisors and their direct reports, as well as between faculty members and students. Nevertheless, no current policy provides you with any guidance about relationships between colleagues. This lack of direction has never been a problem in the past, but two faculty members in your department are now actively and publicly involved in a romantic relationship. Increasingly, other professors are raising concerns to you that the behavior of the two individuals, although not prohibited, is having a negative effect on your department's ability to function properly.

To begin with, what started as a relationship between two individuals has now led to something of a clique. The department has been split between those who support the burgeoning romance and find it "sweet" and those who feel that its public nature is distracting departmental attention from important and pressing academic matters. You in fact have had the impression that votes on departmental issues seem to be occurring along the lines of these two factions. As a result, you suspect that several members of the department are voting not on the basis of the issues, but on the basis of where they stand on the romance. Your formerly congenial department has suddenly become politicized. You are concerned because you know a challenging promotion and tenure decision is coming up soon, and you don't want any extraneous issues to distort that process.

To make matters worse, this is your last year in your term as chair, and one of the faculty members involved in the romance is seeking to be appointed your successor. You seriously believe that given your department's growing factionalism, such an appointment would divide your program even further. You thought that you had found a way out of this difficulty when you reminded the person who wished to be named the next chair that the university had a firm policy against amorous relationships between supervisors and employees. The inflexibility of that policy, you had hoped, might either cause the relationship to cool or dissuade the faculty member from pursuing the position as chair.

When discussing this with the faculty member, however, you learn that this couple does not perceive it as a problem: should this faculty member become department chair, the other member of the relationship would immediately request a leave of absence. You reply by saying that you're not certain anything short of a resignation would fit the policy. Besides, you suggest (still looking for an amicable solution), the department had just submitted a major grant proposal naming the other member in the relationship, who would go on leave, as principal investigator. A leave of absence might seriously jeopardize the program's ability to secure this important funding. Moreover, since chairs in your department serve for three years (or as long as six, if renewed), placing a tenured faculty member on leave for that entire period would not be in the best interests of either the department as a whole or the continuing research agenda of the person on leave.

Your observations are met with a cool and stony silence. Following that meeting, you find yourself being increasingly isolated by members of "the clique." You are outvoted several times on issues that you had thought were fairly straightforward. Issues that you hoped to have resolved before stepping down as chair now seem likely to remain undone.

How do you go about solving this problem?

Old Blindsides

Just before you enter a meeting with all the faculty members of your department, you receive a call that provides you with good news on a recent grant application: your proposal has been funded, provided that your institution can increase the amount of the guaranteed match stipulated in your original budget. Since faculty morale has been extremely poor recently—there have been no salary increases for four years, several of your faculty members have been denied promotion or tenure, and a long-awaited decrease in teaching load has been postponed by the upper administration yet again—you decide to share this bit of good news with your faculty.

Ever cautious, you make certain that everyone knows about all the challenges that still lie ahead: budgetary constraints mean that the institution may not be able to provide the increased match, you have not yet seen the amended budget figures in writing and so don't know whether the new budget will even be feasible, and any number of other problems could still arise. As a result, you remind your faculty that all of this information is still completely contingent on other factors, thank them for their excellent work in completing such a successful grant application, and adjourn your departmental meeting early so that you can inform the dean of what you have learned.

In your conversation with the dean, you are told in no uncertain terms that the proposed increase in institutional match is absolutely out of the question; the same budgetary constraints that have made salary increases impossible for the past four years will continue next year, and expenditures will need to be reduced, not increased, even in such critical areas as servicing this grant. You quickly make a phone call to the agency sponsoring the grant, and your worse suspicions are confirmed: without the increase in match, your department cannot possibly be awarded the grant.

You are still disturbed by the implications of losing such an important opportunity a short time later when you arrive at your last commitment for the afternoon: a meeting of the full faculty of your institution. You can hardly concentrate on the mostly minor business that comes up during this meeting, but one turn of events suddenly grabs your attention. A senior member of your department rises to announce to all the faculty of your college the "great news" about the new grant. Not only will this opportunity finally make possible the long-awaited reduction in teaching load, but it will also bring some welcome recognition to your department. "I tell you," the faculty member concludes, "this project is really going to put us on the map. And I think that we all ought to recognize the person whose leadership has made this all possible: the chair of our department." You find yourself receiving a loud round of applause from your institution's faculty—some faculty members have even risen to your feet—and you notice that they all turn to you expectantly. You notice too that the dean is present, but looking your way with far less delight and approval than are the others in the room. You suspect that the dean may be assuming you encouraged your faculty member to make the announcement about the grant. The room gradually quiets and you are expected to speak.

What do you say? What is the best way to demonstrate leadership in such a situation?

Considerations

1. As you reflect on the "Friends and Lovers" case study:
   a. Try to untangle the differences between the ethical issues posed and the management or personnel issues that guide your decision.

b. Is it effective to discuss the amorous relationship that everyone knows about but so far has not addressed publicly at a full meeting of the department? Is "the clique" likely to resist this tactic, dismissing it as unprofessional and simply another political maneuver?

c. Do you approach the dean about the possibility of staying on as chair for an extra year, during which time you believe the amorous relationship may unravel? Would you regard this suggestion as a good compromise or as unethical?

d. Would your views on the matter be any different if both members of the romantic relationship were the same gender?

e. Would your approach to the matter change if you yourself had had a romantic relationship with another department member (someone who was not one of the people involved in the current relationship)?

f. Does the situation become more complicated or simpler if you find that you are receiving complaints from students, saying that the behavior of the two members of your department is making them uncomfortable and likely to leave your program?

g. Would the situation become more complicated or simpler if the couple were to announce their impending marriage?

2. As you reflect on the "Old Blindsides" case study:

a. Do you embarrass your faculty member who blindsided you in the open meeting by contradicting what the rest of the faculty has just been told?

   • If you do this, do you mention that you had given your faculty advance word of the tentative approval in confidence?

   • Do you accept public responsibility for jumping the gun on your previous announcement?

   • How do you feel it would be best to deal with your faculty member's very public breach of your instructions at the department meeting earlier that day?

b. Do you try to find a way out of the predicament by saying something like the following: "Of course, we don't want to be premature. There are still many hoops that we need to go through, any one of which might make acceptance of this grant impossible. For one thing, we would need to increase our institutional match substantially, and, frankly, I doubt that that's going to be possible"?

- Would you find taking this position questionable since you already know (rather than merely think it possible) that the institution will not be able to increase its match?
- Would you be concerned that complete candor would put the dean, your direct supervisor, on the spot by encouraging the faculty to apply pressure for an increase in institutional support?

c. Would your handling of this situation be any different if any of the following were true?

- You believed that the chronic budgetary shortages at your institution were due largely or solely to the dean's inability to manage the budget?
- You were aware that substantially more than the required institutional match for your grant had tentatively been allocated for other projects that you regard as of relatively low priority?
- The faculty member who blindsided you at the faculty meeting had had a history of revealing confidential information, had been warned about this behavior in the past, and could be subject to disciplinary action for this conduct?
- The faculty member who spoke at the faculty meeting was a dearly beloved senior member of your department who probably believed in good faith that your instructions to keep the grant "purely confidential" did not apply to telling other members of the faculty?

Suggestions

Friends and Lovers

Romantic situations in the workplace create significant challenges for administrators, particularly since the guidelines vary extensively from institution to institution. Some universities place a premium on the privacy rights of the individuals in the relationship, refusing to intervene unless it is clear that there will be significant harm to the institution's ability to pursue its mission. Other universities have a much more restrictive policy on amorous relationships, treating them as inappropriate within the professional setting that is vital for the institution to function. One of the first things to do in the "Friends and Lovers" scenario is to work with your school's office of human resources to make sure that any action that you take falls within institutional guidelines and doesn't cause more problems.

Second, even if your relationship with the dean is one in which you share only major concerns and forgo elaborating on day-to-day details, this is definitely a situation in which your supervisor needs to be in the loop. As problems arise later, your boss is likely to feel that it was your duty to share information as soon as you became fully aware of the situation and to join together in formulating a collective approach. Also, if your institution has an ombudsman's office, that person might be able to work with you and the dean to address the situation in a manner that best eases tensions and promotes ongoing trust.

In some cases, an open meeting to discuss such a personal matter will be viewed as a significant betrayal of trust; in other cases, it will be the only effective way of clearing the air and far preferable to giving the appearance that you're conducting numerous secret meetings to which certain members of the department aren't invited. You can make that decision only by considering the individual personalities of the people in the department, their history together, and your own skill (or that of a mediator) in conducting such a meeting. As for your own decision about offering to continue as chair for another term, that may well be the best strategy available if you believe that you still have substantial support from the faculty, no other suitable candidate is available, and there is a strong likelihood that the problem will be resolved during your next term. If the problem cannot be dealt with during that time, an extra term will merely delay (and possibly exacerbate) a situation that you're really better off trying to address now.

Old Blindsides

In this case, you will want to follow an approach that is least embarrassing to the faculty member (even though this was the person who put you on the spot) or the dean. Mention that you had noted at the department meeting that there were many details still to be worked out and that, in a subsequent conversation with the dean, you had learned that an increase in institutional support will not be possible, given the current budgetary situation. Beginning your remarks in this way is preferable politically since it reinforces both your earlier words of caution in making the announcement and the sequence of conversations you had with the department and then the dean. (After all, even though you have been blindsided, you have nothing to gain by making the dean feel that same way.)

Although you didn't receive encouragement from the funding agency when you called about the university's inability to increase its match, you could honestly state that you still have several options to explore. You could find out, for instance, whether the funding agency would be willing to accept alternative forms of institutional match, such as increasing your department's in-kind contribution (through consumption of supplies, use of equipment and facilities, or not charging the grant for services) or negotiating a reduction in overhead costs in order to increase the proportion of total expenditures not charged to the grant. You could seek local funding from a donor willing to provide seed money in order to make it possible for your program to receive the larger grant. In other words, as challenging as the situation is, you have some options to explore, and you don't want to close the door on any of those possibilities simply because you've been blindsided at a public meeting.

PART TWO

DEPARTMENTAL MANAGEMENT AND POLITICS

UNDERSTANDING DEPARTMENTAL ETHICS AND POLITICS

ARISTOTLE VIEWED ETHICS AND politics as intimately related. Ethics, he reasoned, involved the pursuit of happiness for individuals, and politics involved the pursuit of happiness for individuals as members of societies. Too often today, however, members of academic departments appear to be better versed in Machiavelli than in Aristotle. To them, departmental politics has nothing at all to do with ethics; it has everything to do with power. Power politics is, in fact, the great bane of academic life today. Many faculty members seem to spend a distressing amount of time forming alliances, grandstanding at public meetings, cutting secret deals, and undermining the initiatives of others—not for any fundamental principles in support of academic integrity or the welfare of students, but because they are convinced that that's how the world works. Anyone who suggests that perhaps seeing everything in terms of political struggles is either not really how the world really works or how we in academic life *have* to work is likely to be dismissed as naive, ineffective, or out of touch with the harsh realities of the professoriate today.

Nevertheless, as a department chair, you are in an enviable position to depoliticize situations that can be handled in a far less adversarial manner, move your department from being politically focused to being based in collegiality and consensus building, and, most important, conduct the business of your discipline with high ethical standards.

Campus Codes

If your department already has a mission statement or code of conduct, review it to see if it is appropriately phrased to support the ethical approaches to disputes and problem solving that will serve your program's best interests in the long term. Mansfield University in northern Pennsylvania has adopted what it calls the Mansfield Creed, establishing a code of behavior rooted in the institution's fundamental principles:

The Mansfield Creed

At Mansfield University, we develop leaders. We accomplish this by focusing on the four core values that have been our tradition since 1912: Character, Scholarship, Culture, and Service.

CHARACTER

We believe in integrity. We act with honesty and respect toward others. We take responsibility for our actions and reflect on their impact on ourselves and others.

SCHOLARSHIP

We believe in learning. We use rigorous, responsible, and critical inquiry to understand existing knowledge, acquire and share new knowledge, and apply what we learn. Each of us is both student and teacher.

CULTURE

We believe in celebrating humanity. We enrich ourselves and others by sharing and exploring our similarities and differences. We honor the past as we invent the future.

SERVICE

We believe in helping others. We work with others to improve the communities in which we now live and will touch in the future. Knowledge invests us with the power to improve our world and the responsibility to act.

Source: Developed by the Leadership Committee of the Focus on Student Learning Forum; revised on May 19th, 2004. See Mansfield University (2004).

Note: For similar examples of positive conduct codes, see Gordon College (2010), University of Mississippi (2010), University of Colorado at Boulder (n.d.), and Marshall University (2007).

These campus codes provide a useful basis for an ethical approach to departmental governance (and a highly constructive approach to departmental politics) in several important ways:

1. *They are based in the core principles of the body that developed them.* Although few faculty members would state explicitly that the ends justify the means, the application of realpolitik to the academic setting necessarily places an emphasis on power rather than ideals. Developing a statement of principles that reminds everyone of why you are there in the first place—to educate students, acquire new insights, serve the community, create a community of scholars—can be an important way of breaking the cycle of viewing every choice or decision to be made as part of a political game.

2. *They are stated as positive affirmations of what people will do, not negative injunctions of what people are forbidden to do.* The honor codes and codes of conduct at many colleges and universities are largely negative documents. They include statements such as, "I will not lie, cheat, steal, plagiarize the ideas or words of others, or act in a manner that will bring dishonor to" the institution. Rarely do such statements provide positive statements of what members of the institution will do and why that behavior is important. Creating an atmosphere for your department that moves beyond political maneuvering and deal making requires a positive focus on the direction in which your program wants to go, not a negative list of rules that causes individuals to begin searching for loopholes. Positive statements are also preferable to negative commands, since negative instructions guide the individual only in what not to do, not what he or she should do, often leaving the person wondering about a proper course of action.

3. *They are inclusive and community building, not hierarchical or divisive.* Frequent use of the word *we* can be an important factor in setting a more constructive tone for your department. Too often honor codes and codes of conduct focus exclusively on the individual: they are statements of what "I" will not do. The Aristotelian approach to ethics and politics suggests, however, that social units need to be concerned with both the individual and the

individual as a member of a group. Even principles stated in a bland third-person form ("The faculty member in this department is expected to . . .") lose the advantage of creating a sense of community that is more effectively developed through the frequent use of the words *we*, *us*, and *our*.

4. *They move from general statements of principle to specific guidance that can be applied to day-to-day affairs.* Lofty declarations of belief in high moral standards are all well and good as long as they are then crystallized into a form that helps department members understand how these principles are to be applied to what they actually do. As you work to develop a statement of core beliefs for your department, ask yourself how such principles as open communication, respect for the ideas of others, commitment to scholarly integrity, and collegiality would be demonstrated in actual practice. How would meetings be different, memos and e-mail exchanges be improved, and conflicts resolved more equitably if those principles were applied in everyone's behavior?

5. *They are concise, easy to remember, and regularly incorporated into the life of the unit that created them.* A statement of principles that is simply laminated and hung on a wall ends up being yet one more political exercise. A brief set of values that everyone can remember and provides a basis for training new faculty members, opening the first meeting of the year, and celebrating successes—not merely in teaching and scholarship but in working together as a successful academic community—has the potential for effectively improving the lives of those who study, teach, and work in your department.

Developing a Statement of Principles

Some department chairs will feel that a formal statement of principles does not fit their institutional cultural. Perhaps there have been similar attempts to develop such a code in the past, and members of the department have become skeptical of such efforts. Perhaps the department is already so politicized that even the process of developing consensus about a code of shared beliefs would serve to exacerbate internal tensions. Perhaps such a notion does not suit the outlook and interests of most members of the department.

All of these possibilities exist, and a sensible department chair will be aware of them before taking on a task that is likely to be counterproductive. Nevertheless, even if it is impossible for your department to agree on a statement of shared values and principles, it is perfectly possible for you as chair to develop your own set of administrative standards that can guide your program away from unproductive political infighting and toward more constructive methods of operation.

No matter whether you are drafting a document for public discussion and consensus or for embodying your personal philosophy of administration, there are certain basic factors to consider as you proceed:

1. *Build your principles from the mission and identity of your institution, discipline, and departmental history.* If, for instance, your institution has its primary mission in the area of teaching, consider the possibility of including such principles as student-centeredness, doing whatever is necessary to enhance the learning process, responsiveness to different styles of learning, maintaining rigorous academic standards, and promoting maximum student engagement. Departments with a strong research focus may find it important to stress the integrity of scholarship, collegial respect for the contributions of others, and advocacy for the principle of free inquiry. In disciplines such as sociology, social work, and health care, where service assumes an even greater significance than it has in other academic areas, the role that service plays in advancing the work of the department may need to be given a high profile. Whom does the department intend to serve, in what ways, and to what end?

2. *Consider both the problems your department has experienced in the past and, more important, the positive directions that it can take in the future.* Just as poor policies can result from attempts to prevent the recurrence of specific (and probably) rare problems in the past, so should statements of principles not be constructed simply in response to the difficulties the department has encountered. If collegiality has been a challenge, then certainly it is appropriate to be aware of this in seeking ways for members of the department to work together in greater respect and harmony. Nevertheless, it is important also to include principles that move beyond solving this problem to taking your program where it needs to be as a community of scholars. Besides eliminating tension, what other benefits might accrue to your department if greater collegiality existed?

   • Would your program be more likely to offer a greater array of team-taught courses?

   • Would student advisement be improved?

- Would you be more likely to be successful in obtaining grants?

- Would your department's retention rate for majors increase?

By asking questions of this sort, you will begin to develop some clarity about the ultimate goals of your department—collaborative teaching, better advisement, higher levels of external funding, improved retention, and the like—for which uncollegiality and other immediate problems may serve as an obstacle.

3. *Reflect on the constituencies your department serves and the likely audience for the principles you are advocating.* It is not uncommon for institutions and departments to have codes of conduct or policies outlining "what we expect from you" designed for students. It is far less common for either institutions or departments to reflect on the principles by which all constituencies are expected to live. As you consider the set of core values that will guide the activities of either your department as a whole or you as chair, pay attention not merely to "what we expect of you" but also to "what you can expect from us." And who is the "you" served by your department? Your constituents will almost certainly consist of students and other faculty members. But who else? What expectations might you have for your interactions with former students, parents of current and prospective students, college administrators, members of the surrounding community, donors and other supporters of your program, staff members at your institution, and the many others whom you serve in the broadest possible sense? What principles should they expect you to be following, and what do you consider to be your obligations to them as members of your larger community? In the case of current students, remember that the standards you are advocating should not seek merely to guide their behavior—there are plenty of other mechanisms at your institution for that—but also to model appropriate professional activity in your own actions and in the actions of other members of your department.

Establishing appropriate and well-considered principles can be an important first step toward moving your department (and perhaps even your institution as a whole) away from viewing every situation as a political conflict and toward viewing every potential conflict as an ethical opportunity. As one of your institution's opinion leaders, you have the ability to change people's thinking from viewing curricular decisions as "non-aggression pacts" to constructive blueprints for achieving a compelling vision of the future. Ethical approaches to departmental decision making are not achieved through individual documents or single proclamations by the chair. They can be achieved, however, through continual encouragement by the chair to focus every discussion that takes place in the discipline not on how to "win," but on how to do what is right for the students, the unit's other constituents, and the institution as a whole.

REFERENCES

Gordon College. (2010). Gordon College creed. Retrieved from http://www.gdn.peachnet.edu/admissions/catalog/creed.asp

Mansfield University. (2004). Mansfield creed. Retrieved from http://www.mansfield.edu/home/mansfieldcreed.pdf

Marshall University. (2007). Marshall University creed. Retrieved from http://www.marshall.edu/president/strategic/creed.asp

University of Colorado at Boulder. (n.d.). Colorado creed. Retrieved from http://www.colorado.edu/creed/index.html

University of Mississippi. (2010). University creed. Retrieved from http://www.olemiss.edu/info/creed.html

RESOURCES

Bennett, J. B. (1998). *Collegial professionalism: The academy, individualism, and the common good.* Phoenix, AZ: Oryx.

Bennett, J. B. (2003). *Academic life: Hospitality, ethics, and spirituality.* San Francisco: Jossey-Bass/Anker.

Coffman, J. R. (2005). *Work and peace in academe: Leveraging time, money, and intellectual energy through managing conflict.* San Francisco: Jossey-Bass/Anker.

Hamilton, N. W. (2002). *Academic ethics: Problems and materials on professional conduct and shared governance.* Westport, CT: ACE/Praeger.

Hellmich, D. M. (2007). *Ethical leadership in the community college: Bridging theory and daily practice.* San Francisco: Jossey-Bass/Anker.

Lewis, M. (1997). *Poisoning the ivy: The seven deadly sins and other vices of higher education in America.* Armonk, NY: M. E. Sharpe.

Shils, E. (1997). *The calling of education: The academic ethic and other essays on higher education.* Chicago: University of Chicago Press.

Starratt, R. J. (2004). *Ethical leadership.* San Francisco: Jossey-Bass.

Wilcox, J. R., & Ebbs, S. L. (1992). *The leadership compass: Values and ethics in higher education.* Washington, DC: ERIC.

11

CHAIRING SMALL DEPARTMENTS

SERVING AS THE CHAIR of a small department brings challenges that your colleagues in larger departments or bigger institutions do not face, or do not face them to the same extent. Chairs of small departments tend to have different relationships with members of their faculty than do chairs of large departments. They may not have their own administrative support, frequently sharing a secretary with one or more other departments or having clerical help for only a few hours a day. In small departments, chairs may receive little or no release time for administrative duties; they may be expected to teach a full load while still tending to the needs of their departments, frequently receiving a stipend or release from a committee assignment as compensation. Chairs of small departments tend not to have the buffers available to their colleagues in larger programs; they are more likely to answer their own calls or receive their own visitors, which at any moment could be a dissatisfied student, an angry parent, a potential major, an alum, an administrator with a crisis, or a colleague needing some immediate guidance. Chairs of small departments may not supervise budgets as large as other chairs, but their days tend to be equally as diverse and challenging. They are simply diverse and challenging in different ways.

Issues Arising from Intradepartmental Relations

Chairs in smaller departments tend to find that in most cases, their departments are less hierarchical and more collegially organized than are large departments. The chair of a small department is less frequently the boss in a top-down manner and more frequently a colleague who is willing to provide some organizational support to the unit for a fixed period. The chair of the small department is unlikely to be the individual who evaluates members of the department and makes recommendations for salary increases. The chair may not even be the person who establishes the course rotation or schedules classes for the unit. These decisions may be made by consensus or deferred to a dean or registrar. But this relatively flat organizational structure creates its own challenges for the chair. How, for instance, do you "make" someone do something when the nature of your position provides you with extraordinarily few carrots and sticks? How do you require a faculty member to embark on a course of action when that person is unwilling (and is likely to serve as the department chair someday, perhaps in the very near future)? And, most challenging of all, how can a relatively young—and possibly untenured—chair relate to a senior member of the department who seems unwilling to accept the chair's authority and may soon be voting on the chair's promotion and tenure?

Although there are no perfect solutions to these challenges that will work in every situation, one or more of the following strategies may be effective depending on the history of your department and the personalities of the individuals involved.

Communicate One-on-One

One of the best ways that you can help improve communication within your department, particularly if you are dealing with colleagues who are senior to you in rank, is to go out of your way to communicate with them as individuals. Go to their offices, sit down, and have a frank but cordial chat about how you see things in the department and what you hope to accomplish. Be clear about explaining your hopes and visions, and be a good listener as well. One of the most valuable benefits of these conversations is a genuine understanding of the perspectives various members of the department bring to issues.

If you hold these face-to-face conversations often enough, you will begin to break down boundaries and perhaps even resistance to some of your ideas. Don't simply meet with these faculty members once a term or so as a sort of obligation. Take them out to lunch or for coffee. Get to know them, and allow them to get to know you. You may be pleasantly surprised to learn that what you had been viewing as resistance to you personally or as hostility to new ideas actually stems from other concerns. These concerns may be out of your control or, in fact, be better addressed simply by reaching out to members of the faculty as individuals.

Meet Formally

As important as these casual, unscheduled conversations may be, they should never take the place of formal meetings as a department, even if there are only two of you in the department. It is important for clear communication and the professionalism of your unit that there be a regular, recurring time for a department meeting. These sessions need not be long—many small departments can wrap up their business in no more than half an hour—but they need to be consistent. Find a pattern that works for your unit's needs and complexity: once a week, once every other week, once a month. The precise scheduling is less important than the fact that you are gathering to discuss issues in common, with a set agenda, tasks to be completed before the next meeting, and an anticipation of reports and updates on progress toward meeting your unit's goals.

Create Alliances

Creating alliances within your department should not be regarded as the same thing as collusion. In other words, you should not be working behind people's backs for the purpose of advancing a hidden agenda or overcoming another faculty member's serious resistance to an idea through keeping its continuation secret. What you should be doing is working openly to foster alliances of faculty members who might assist you in completing the essential work of the department. For instance, suppose you have a three-person department (yourself and two colleagues), and one member regards your proposal as working closely with admissions to recruit incoming students to your program as a waste of time, while the other has relatively little interest in your initiative to pursue a major new grant for your program. While perfect consensus would be highly desirable, it can sometimes not be obtained. Rather than causing progress on your initiatives to grind to a halt until there is agreement, you can form two alliances to work openly on these projects, freeing the faculty member who opposed them from direct involvement. In time, success may well encourage individuals who initially did not see the value of a proposal to jump on the bandwagon. Also if your alliance contains at least one respected opinion leader in your program, enthusiastic updates about progress in this area at department meetings might well serve to quell at least open and destructive resistance to the idea.

Seek Support

Particularly if you are a junior faculty member placed in the position of being a chair of one or some senior faculty members, you are going to want extradepartmental support for advice, counsel, and (in extreme cases) sheer gravitas. A more experienced department chair—usually in another discipline but sometimes a more senior and respected former chair in your own discipline—may be able to give you invaluable advice on how to contend with some of the personalities in your discipline. (Frequently these individuals have a long history with senior members of your department and find them a good deal less intimidating or threatening than you do.) Sharing your concerns with the person to whom you report—not in a whining or despairing way, but simply stating the objective facts—can also be extremely valuable. Your dean, provost, or academic vice president may be able to help you formulate useful strategies for interacting with these senior members of your discipline. It may even happen that this individual can set your mind at ease by explaining the protections that your institution or system has in place for you should such an individual seek to block your tenure or promotion on inappropriate grounds or because of your decisions as chair, as opposed to your contributions as a faculty member.

Offer Exchanges

Just as creating alliances is not the same thing as "creating collusion," so is offering exchanges not the same thing as "cutting deals." By offering exchanges, you are simply recognizing that every individual has different needs, interests, and ambitions at different stages of his or her career. Based on your conversations with individual faculty members, you will probably understand a good deal about the day-to-day likes and dislikes of members of the department. One faculty member will find the submission of textbook orders under your institution's system to be excessively onerous. Another will find formatting travel reimbursements particularly irksome. Still others will feel that they are never the ones who are selected for choice committee assignments or to represent the discipline at conferences.

With a bit of creativity, you will discover relatively easy ways in which you, or any clerical support you can obtain, will be able to help these faculty members find relief. Naturally the exchange you offer should never be anything that you would not, in similar situations, offer any other faculty member. You wouldn't, for instance, unilaterally reduce a faculty member's teaching load, waive the requirement for conducting student course evaluations, or excuse a person from holding required office hours. But you may well find a number of small, perfectly permissible ways of making the faculty member's life easier. Then, as part of the exchange, you might ask for participation in some project that is of great importance to you and the department. For instance, you might say, "Well, look then, if I could perhaps find a way of getting those travel reimbursements prepared for you, do you think you might at least be willing to run an eye over our grant proposal when we get it ready and give us one or two constructive suggestions on how to strengthen it?"

Issues Arising from Interdepartmental Relations

Sometimes the greatest challenges that chairs of small departments face do not come from within their own ranks. Particularly at institutions where other departments may be significantly larger, small departments may feel like the Rodney Dangerfield of the institution: they don't get no respect. While you certainly don't want to protest too much, there are several steps that you can take in order to avert the Too Small (to Be a) Department syndrome.

Use Data to Your Advantage

Regardless of a department's size, there is almost always some way in which its distinctiveness is measurable. Perhaps your discipline produces very few majors, but you have high enrollments in service courses, courses that are a critical component of the general education program, or courses that serve as prerequisites for other discipline. Perhaps your cost to produce a student credit hour is the lowest at your institution (or in your college, school, or division). Perhaps faculty members in your department score the highest in your institution on student ratings of instruction or bring in the highest amount of external funding for any unit in your institution or generate the most student credit hours with the smallest number of full-time members of the faculty.

Calculating data that demonstrate a few of the ways in which your unit's superior contribution may be measured can be important both to develop pride and esprit de corps within your department and to help it gain respect across campus. Having this information ready and updated will allow you to say such things as, "Well, yes, we're small as a discipline, but only in terms of full-time faculty lines. Don't forget that, per capita, we serve more students than any other department in our division. We also placed a higher percentage of our majors in graduate school and published more articles last year per FTE faculty member than any other undergraduate department at the university. So I think we're doing a pretty good job."

Highlight Your Unique Mission or Methodology

Your discipline is unlikely to have achieved its independence as a stand-alone department if there were not compelling reasons of mission or methods that distinguish it from other areas. It may be time to update your departmental mission statement to highlight all the ways in which what you are trying to do set you apart from other fields of study and how your methods are both unique and important. For instance, some members of your institution might not understand why your Department of Classics—or Physics or Philosophy or Germanic Languages or Art History—should not be consolidated with other disciplines they view as similar until you make the case effectively that your area possess a distinctive mission and approach to learning that sets it apart from other fields.

Even more important than serving as a defensive document, your updated mission statement can reinvigorate your department by clarifying for everyone your continued uniqueness, importance, and relevance. It will be a good starting point for your discussions with prospective students as to why they should consider taking courses in your field and possibly even completing your major. By keeping your rhetoric fresh, you will be able to tie initiatives in your department more readily to the changing needs of your student population, perhaps eventually building your small department into a unit that is not quite so small.

Become an Early Adopter

One of the great advantages that small departments have over their larger counterparts is that they can be nimble and responsive. For this reason, they can take advantage of fresh opportunities much more readily than can more cumbersome units. As new technology becomes available, as your institution is seeking programs to participate in a new pilot project, and as volunteers are sought to advance some element of the strategic plan that is dear to the heart of your president and provost, your department can quickly proceed with a proposal or offer to participate while other units are still debating the merits of the idea. If your unit is truly small, a hallway conversation—or perhaps a telephone call or two—may be all it takes to develop consensus that the opportunity ought to be pursued. The advantages of being an early adopter are that your department will soon be recognized for its entrepreneurial spirit and for its good team players.

You will increasingly look indispensable to your dean and provost since your area is always the first to step forward when a significant contribution is needed. Your department will soon discover that it has created a whole cadre of supporters (among both those who valued the project and those who didn't want their unit to have to take it on). People who matter will start saying things like, "I don't care how small they are. They're always the first ones there when we need something done for the university."

------- o -------

Chairing small departments can be an art in and of itself. Although larger units may be called on to deal with the complexities that arise from larger budgets (and there are complexities, not just benefits, that go with larger budgets) and more cumbersome course rotations, chairs of smaller departments deal more frequently with inadequate resources— both human and financial—to provide a program of the highest quality, with the struggle for recognition in the institution's priorities, and with the greater informality that tends to occur in departments of fewer than ten individuals. The chair of a small department is required to be guardian of the budget, personal mentor, solver of all problems, first resort whenever a question arises, and last to receive credit when some great achievement occurs. It is a position of great challenge and few, if any, rewards. Nevertheless, chairing a small department well can be essential to the overall academic program of any institution.

RESOURCES

Reder, M. (2010). Effective practices in the context of small colleges. In W. H. Bergquist, D. L. Robertso, & K. H. Gillespie (Eds.), *A guide to faculty development* (pp. 293–308). San Francisco: Jossey-Bass.

Schuman, S. (2005). *Old Main: Small colleges in twenty-first century America.* Baltimore: Johns Hopkins University Press.

12

CHAIRING LARGE
DEPARTMENTS

THE NATURE OF THE department chair's position changes substantially depending on the size of the department. Despite what one might initially believe, chairing a large department is not inherently more difficult than chairing a small department; it's simply different. The dynamics of interaction with members of the faculty are going to be different. The role that one plays relative to the rest of the institution is going to be different. And the nature of some of the tasks that one performs is going to be different. In addition, certain aspects of the chair's position that are not essential elements of your department's greater size are more likely to be the case if you are chairing a large department. For instance, if you are the chair of a large department, you are much more likely to have

- Line authority over the members of your department
- More of your job description devoted to administrative duties than to duties in teaching and research
- Been hired in as chair rather than as a faculty member first who was later selected to be the chair
- An open-ended rather than a fixed term for your position

Of course, there are plenty of exceptions to all of these. Sometimes in large departments, the position of chair rotates—either explicitly or informally by tradition—among all the members of the department. Sometimes, too, there is a departmental election of the chair for a fixed term; these positions are not renewable at all institutions. Sometimes even in large departments, the department chair is not given authority as an entry-level administrator, but rather serves as first among equals among the faculty in the discipline. Nevertheless, despite this great variety, certain challenges and opportunities will arise for chairs of large departments because of their unit's greater size and these common, though not universal, features of large departments.

Issues Relating to Line Authority

At one time, the presence or absence of line authority was the distinguishing difference between department heads and department chairs. Department heads were the boss:

- Faculty members in the department reported through them to the upper administration.
- They conducted performance reviews on members of the faculty, perhaps the only sort of performance review that was conducted except in cases of decisions on promotion and tenure.
- They set salaries, including allocation of merit increases.
- They assigned courses and adjudicated differences in faculty workload.
- They played a lead role, perhaps equal to or greater than that of the search committee, in all faculty hiring.
- They were usually the ones who initiated nonrenewals of probationary or adjunct faculty members.

Department chairs were considered to be much more managers of departmental resources than bosses. Like committee chairs, they were catalysts for organization and the efficient operation of departmental activities; in all important matters, however, the chair's vote carried no more weight than that of any other faculty member. The chair was regarded as the collegial solution to departmental organization. The department head smacked of top-down management and rigid, authoritarian structures.

This once-clear distinction has largely been blurred. Just as the term *university* is now commonly applied to institutions that at one time would have been regarded as colleges, so is it now common practice to refer to individuals as department chairs even though their responsibilities are far closer to those of a true department head. This tends to be the case particularly in large departments. Faculty members tend to prefer the collegial tone of the term *department chair*, even if the structure of the institution is such that the chair really does need to have line authority over his or her colleagues. The institution may be so large that annual performance reviews simply cannot be conducted in depth at the dean's or provost's level. The budgeting may be sufficiently complex that salary recommendations may need to be initiated at the chair's level—although subsequently approved or altered by the upper administration—in order for it to be completed in a timely manner. For whatever reason, regardless of the nomenclature in use at individual institutions, even chairs of large departments are far more likely to have line authority over their faculty members than are their colleagues at smaller institutions or in smaller departments.

That possession of line authority creates a special challenge for the chair. You will find that you constantly need to be changing hats. At one moment you will be acting primarily as just another member of the department, at another as the boss, at still another as your unit's mentor or coach, at others as the buffer between your department and the upper administration.

Because of this complexity, you may be at risk of sending mixed messages unless you take precautions to clarify the various capacities in which you are acting. At times, you may find it necessary to say, "I'm speaking now just as a member of this department," or, "I'm speaking now as your supervisor." If you do not take these additional steps toward clarifying your role at that moment, statements that may seem extraordinarily clear to you may end up being misinterpreted by members of your department. The statements of support that you—as a mentor and friend—made in order to create a positive atmosphere, good morale, and some much needed encouragement may well be read as an endorsement of a level of performance that you—as an administrator—believe still needs improvement. Having line authority thus complicates some of the relationships you will have with your colleagues (particularly if you are in a situation where the chair rotates and someday soon they will end up having line authority over you), and you may need to edit your comments a bit more scrupulously than you would if you were not the chair. Above all, don't let your position relative to the members of your department go to your head. It's a slight bit of eminence that you have right now—more a position of responsibility than one of grandeur—and it must always be seen as such.

Issues Relating to Delegation

Regardless of the size of your department, delegating certain responsibilities is both useful and desirable. Even in the smallest department, there is no reason that the chair should take and distribute the minutes for every departmental meeting, be solely responsible for proofreading every departmental document, or plan the four-year schedule of each student who majors or minors in the program. Delegation of certain responsibilities allows the work of the department to be conducted much more efficiently. It also helps protect the chair from burnout as a host of duties, running the full spectrum of administrative significance, fall on one set of shoulders alone. Moreover, delegation is quite beneficial to the faculty members who assume some of these responsibilities. It gives them a sense of empowerment in the activities of the department, provides them with documented evidence of service that they can use in applications for major personnel decisions, and prepares them for other administrative assignments that, by choice or necessity, may well come their way. As an added benefit, it will help increase the level of trust that faculty members place in you, since you are dealing with departmental issues in a transparent manner. For instance, delegation helps prevent the appearance that you are withholding information or "colluding with the administration." You can increase this transparency still further by sharing with the entire department summaries of meetings you hold with those to whom you have delegated responsibilities if their content is at all relevant to operation of the department as a whole.

In larger departments, delegation will be far more necessary and complex than it is in a smaller unit. The delegation will range from the very informal ("Say, can you give me a hand with this report for a second?") to the extremely formal (departmental committees that are empowered to make certain decisions, assistant department chairs, and the like). Certainly any academic department that contains twenty or more faculty members will require a significant amount of delegation. Any situation in which a person must supervise more than ten or twelve direct reports stretches the ability for careful, closely detailed management to the limit. The more people there are in a unit, the greater the likelihood is of interpersonal and intergroup conflicts; the chair is going to need time to deal with those as they arise. Larger units also tend to be responsible for larger numbers of students, bigger majors, and larger section sizes, all of which can add to the chair's challenges. By delegating day-to-day or routine matters, you are allowing yourself to focus on those issues for which only the chair can intervene, and thus you are improving the efficiency of your department.

Nevertheless, when delegating responsibilities, there are three cardinal rules to follow:

1. *Delegate responsibilities that are reasonably performed by another person or group.* Don't view delegation as merely an opportunity to

pass tasks you don't like onto others. If you do so, faculty members will become cynical about your management approach and reluctant to assume responsibilities when you offer them. Besides, it is far more efficient to delegate a set of responsibilities that can reasonably and effectively be performed by others than those that, while they may be unpleasant, are central to your position.

2. *When you delegate tasks, you surrender a certain amount of control.* The product or result that you receive may not be precisely what you had envisioned or performed precisely as you would have done it. But unless the product that you receive has serious problems with quality or the result is utterly unacceptable in some serious way, loss of having it your way goes hand-in-hand with delegation to others.

3. *Even when you delegate to others, stay in the loop.* Delegating an assignment is not the same as forfeiting responsibility. The group or individual performing the task is still doing so in your name. Therefore, without micromanaging the situation, take steps to be informed. Know the results of their process, the steps that took them there, and the reasons that they followed those steps:

Although a certain amount of delegation is required in every large, complex department, keep in mind that delegation is different from empowerment. In delegation, you assign a responsibility to someone else. When you empower someone, you also convey the authority that goes with that responsibility.

Issues Relating to Workload

The larger your department is, the more challenging your task will be in balancing your workload. The key word here is *balancing* your workload. The temptation always will be to direct more attention to situations that are critical rather than those that are important. Critical issues tend to be those with looming deadlines, faculty members or students who want answers *now*, and (in all too many cases) simply the latest predicament that has arisen. But critical issues are frequently less important in the long run than other matters; they may seem more immediately pressing because emotions are hot now, but in the long run, they may pale in comparison to improving the structure of your curriculum, putting more thought into the design of a new building, or submitting a grant proposal that will make your department's reputation for a decade or more.

Nearly every department chair has been in the situation of returning from several days away from campus to several urgent e-mail messages from a faculty member or student saying, "Please contact me at once. I have an emergency!" As soon as the chair tracks the person down, the faculty member or student says, "Oh? That? When I couldn't get a hold of you, I took care of that myself a couple of days ago." Not every crisis is like this, of course, but it does indicate how different the urgent may be from the truly essential.

In balancing your workload, be sure that you are devoting as much time as possible to the truly important and essential tasks that you face as chair. Although you may have been hired primarily as an administrator with relatively few teaching obligations, you may discover that teaching more than your required amount—and at all levels, not just the choice upper-division and graduate courses—tells you more about your department's needs and the quality of the students in its courses than can stacks of memos and reports. You may find meetings with architects excruciatingly dull, and yet they may be the most important thing that you can do to secure the facilities your program needs. The goal must always be to identify the range of truly productive activities that you can pursue for the benefit of your program (activities that may not always be your favorite academic experiences), balance those, and delegate what you can of those less significant responsibilities that remain.

Issues Resulting from Being Hired from the Outside

It is far more common in larger than in smaller departments for a chair to be hired from outside the institution. If this is the situation that has brought you to your current position, you are facing certain challenges that your colleagues who have been hired from within do not share. First, you are stepping into a set of group dynamics that every other member of your department may understand better than you do at the moment. Every department has a history, and your department members may well know far more than you do about who has quarreled with whom, who was once married to or dated whom, who is generally considered to be the brightest star or weakest link, who has a strong (but perhaps un-warranted) reputation with the upper administration, and so on. You can make all the statements you like about the past being the past and the present moment being a new beginning, but such platitudes will be only partially effective at best.

Your primary responsibility at first must be to keep your eyes and ears open, asking a few discreet questions where necessary, and learning as much as you can. Above all, avoid the temptation to take sides from the start, and don't put too much credence too soon on any one person's perspective. Inevitably there will be one or more faculty members with whom you feel a special rapport—perhaps they were even members of the search committee, so your relationship with them is of slightly longer standing than it is with other members of the department—or who impress you more at first. The temptation will be to begin to see things through this group's eyes or to put stock in the information they give you. Resist this impulse. We all have agendas, frequently not even being aware of them ourselves. Allowing yourself to be co-opted by a particular faction or member of the department can quickly destroy your credibility. Many chairs report that one of the first mistakes they made was taking the advice from someone in the department who initially seemed reliable and well respected but later turned out merely to be one more person advancing an unsubstantiated opinion.

Sometimes new chairs worry that they may appear nosy if they begin asking too many questions about past practices and events. This should not be a concern: it is the chair's obligation to learn as much as possible in order to avoid being blindsided or acting on inadequate information. Feel free to explain to anyone who asks that being a chair requires you to act on the best information possible, and you can't do that unless you ask questions sometimes. Just be certain to ask questions sufficiently broadly that you are not relying on a selective view of history. Collect different accounts, and weigh them against other facts and your own perceptions. Then rely on your own judgment.

Remember, too, that while you will be making changes to reflect your own philosophy, management style, and vision for the department, it is the rare department—particularly the rare large department—that got where it was by being incompetent. Be generous with your praise and recognition. Acknowledge publicly and often your predecessors' positive accomplishments. If you give the impression, even unintentionally, that you are there to "save the department" or have a lot of fixing to do, it is ultimately your reputation—not your predecessor's—that will suffer. Make changes quietly, and give a great deal of attention to how you are building on your program's established strengths. This approach will serve you far better in the long run.

Issues Resulting from Departmental Elections

In departments where the chair is chosen by election, larger departments are, on the sheer basis of their size, far more likely to have elections that are not unanimous than are small departments. The challenge for the chair in these cases is that, particularly when the discussions leading up to the election have been contentious or the vote was very close, there will need to be some fence mending in the department. It is important that all serious issues discussed by "the other side" be acknowledged and dealt with as openly as possible. Remember that even if you won the election by only a single vote, you are the chair of the entire department, not merely the faction that supported you. It may have been a competing vision or stance on a major policy matter that led to your election; in such a case, you will need to follow through on any commitments you made or initiatives that you advanced. But this does not mean that you cannot be sensitive to the genuine concerns on the other side of this issue. Are there any ways in which you can incorporate some of the good aspects of their position while still obtaining the goal that caused you to be elected? Even if this is not possible, it may well bring about more departmental unity—and help you achieve other goals in the future—if you acknowledge other positions rather than allowing them to be passed over in silence. Saying something like, "I know we haven't all been in agreement on this issue, but one of the things that I'm sure we can all agree on is . . . ," demonstrates that you are sensitive to other points of view, unwilling to sugarcoat constructive conflict, and yet eager to achieve consensus wherever possible.

One of the first things to do after election as a chair is to have at least a short conversation behind closed doors with every member of the department. At times, you may want to begin these meetings with an agenda, saying something like, "I'd just like to have a brief conversation with each member of the department so that I can feel up to speed on . . ." At other times, just a general "get further acquainted" conversation is sufficient. How you handle this will depend on how well you feel you know your colleagues and whether the issues that are pending for the department are already clearly defined for you. Either way, you will learn a great deal from these discussions. You will learn how much of each person's public stance was grandstanding and how much was personal conviction. You will learn how much public disagreement stemmed from different perspectives and philosophies and how much stemmed from personality conflicts. And you will learn that you probably have a great deal more support and goodwill in the department than you may originally have thought.

You may not be able to win everyone over, but you can go a long way toward understanding the motivation of the members of your department, and this knowledge will help you better address the dynamics of your unit in the future.

○

While communication is an essential quality for any department chair, superb communication skills are particularly desirable for chairs of large departments. You will need on a regular basis to share information, rally the troops, improve morale, focus the attention of diverse individuals, and lead, not merely manage, a highly complex unit within your institution. Although the size of your department may be large, so will be the degree of satisfaction you receive from leading it well.

RESOURCES

Bland, C. J., Weber-Main, A. M., Lund, S. M., & Finstad, D. A. (2005). *The research-productive department: Strategies from departments that excel.* San Francisco: Jossey-Bass/Anker.

Bryman, A. (2007). Effective leadership in higher education: A literature review. *Studies in Higher Education, 3,* 693–710.

Lees, N. D. (2006). *Chairing academic departments: Traditional and emerging expectations.* San Francisco: Jossey-Bass/Anker.

13

SETTING COURSE ROTATIONS AND SCHEDULES

FOR MANY CHAIRS, preparing each term's course schedule may seem the most mundane part of their responsibilities. Course schedules and rotations may be overly fixed at some institutions owing to history and inertia. At others, faculty members may begin to view offering certain courses at certain times almost as an entitlement. Even more often, chairs set course schedules with relatively little thought given to the overall picture of the discipline's needs and maximum benefits. As a result, certain sections end up getting canceled—or allowed to run, grudgingly, by the dean—since their enrollments are so low. Students approach graduation only to discover that they are missing essential courses that are not on the course rotation for another several semesters. Facilities are used inefficiently because little thought was given to their optimal use when course schedules were made.

The following commonplace rules are ones that every chair should keep in mind in creating the department's course schedule for an individual term and in developing a long-term course rotation for the program.

Don't compete with yourself.

One of the scheduling problems that departments inadvertently create for themselves is competing for the same students in multiple sections. This problem can arise in a number of different ways. First, it can occur when two or more courses likely to be taken by the same pool of students are offered at the same time, have overlapping course periods, or meet one after the other in buildings far apart from one another. Second, it can occur when too many options exist for the same limited pool of students during the same term, so that each option ends up enrolling too few students. The solution to this problem has partly to do with course scheduling and rotations, partly to do with curriculum development. In other words, it may be fairly easy to begin reviewing the schedule for each term or each academic year with an eye toward avoiding the most obvious sorts of scheduling conflicts, but far more difficult to deal with problems that arise from poorly considered program requirements.

Curricula that require too many specific courses, as opposed to offering several options from a list—particularly if those specific courses must be taken in a specific sequence—can end up creating course gridlock for students. You should devote one department meeting each year to consideration of the schedules planned for the next several terms, the long-term course rotation, and the general curricular requirements to determine where you may be creating problems by competing with your own courses. If such an analysis is not a required part of your institutional program review procedure, you should adopt it as part of your own departmental operating procedures.

Schedule in contingency plans when offering multiple sections of the same course.

Your department may offer several sections of the same course because student demand for this class is so great that these sections always "make." But sooner or later, whether due to a temporary enrollment decline or shifting patterns of student needs or desires, your department may be in a situation where one or more of these sections may not be needed in a given term. In these cases, it is highly desirable to have a contingency plan developed well in advance that will guide you in how sections may be collapsed and other duties assigned to the faculty members involved. One way of doing this is to schedule multiple sections of courses in pairs. In other words, instead of scheduling four sections of the same course at 9:00, 11:00, 1:00, and 3:00, you may consider scheduling two sections at 9:00 and two sections at 3:00. (This solution presumes, of course, that all sections are not taught by the same faculty member.) The advantage of this approach is that if enrollments in any one of these sections is very small, it can easily be merged with another section at the same time. Students' schedules will not have to be rewritten since they obviously have that course period free already. Nor are you competing with yourself in this way, since these are multiple sections of the same course, not similar courses taken by the same students.

If you do not wait until the end of registration to collapse the sections, you may be able to open up a section of a different course for which there is sufficient student demand and reassign one of the faculty members to that course.

Spread the day.

Departments create problems for themselves in scheduling by failing to take full advantage of every course period in the day. The popular course times with both students and faculty members may be at 10:00, 11:00, and 1:00, but overscheduling these periods does a disservice to both groups. Students find it more difficult to make schedules if many of the courses that they want to take are all offered at the same time. Faculty members may have their courses canceled for low enrollments since students are not free at that time of day to take them. Taking full advantage of the day makes better use of your facilities and avoids the waste that results from classrooms and laboratories that are heavily used only three or four hours a day and sit largely unoccupied for eight or more hours.

Review rotations with an eye toward when students may declare majors.

Different programs and different institutions have students who declare majors at different times. At some institutions, students are required to declare their majors in the second semester of their second year. In certain programs, including music and nursing, students are expected to declare a major or intention to major almost as soon as they begin college.

Regardless of the situation at your program and institution, it can be an extremely valuable exercise for you to walk through your department course rotation with the view in mind of making a tentative schedule for a student who enters your program at each possible moment. For instance, if students declare majors only at a particular time in the year, do this exercise for each year beginning at that point. If students can declare majors each term, do it for each term. Then consider these questions:

- What courses required for the major are students likely or required to bring with them at the time they enter your program officially?
- What courses will they still need before they graduate?
- Will they be able to get those courses, in the correct order and in a timely manner, within a standard four- or five-year undergraduate program?
- Where in your course rotation do you see bottlenecks forming or unmet students needs likely to occur?

○ Are there other alternatives that you may be able to offer students, such as waiving certain requirements that you are authorized to waive or recommending alternative courses from other programs at your institution, that you can begin planning for?

Develop alliances with other key departments.

Nearly every department knows of other departments with which they are in some sort of symbiotic relationship. Either that department offers service courses that are required or highly desirable for your majors or your program does that for the other department. Perhaps, too, either you or they offer a general education course that is particularly appropriate for students in the other program. Perhaps you share (or could share) facilities, equipment, or clerical support with the other program.

For these and any number of other reasons, it may be highly desirable for you to go over course rotations with one another well before you need to submit them to the registrar. There may be relatively small adjustments you can make to the times, days, or terms when certain courses are offered that can help you maximize enrollment in both departments. Reviewing schedules in common is also a good way for both programs to take the greatest advantage of shared facilities and equipment, avoid conflicts in making assignments to shared clerical staff, and foster good institutional citizenship.

Consider revising the curriculum to incorporate both pedagogical needs and likely enrollment patterns.

One of the common failings we share in academic life is the tendency to throw a course at every perceived student need. If first-year students are having difficulty adjusting to the institution, we create new Introduction to College courses. If students are perceived to be poor writers or lacking in quantitative skills, we develop new required composition courses and statistical sequences. If we feel that students need exposure to other societies or ethnic groups, we fill our curricula with international studies or multicultural studies courses. This same tendency frequently carries over into departmental programs.

Sometimes prompted by discipline-specific accreditation or certification bodies, sometimes prompted by our own desires to improve our programs, we create a host of individual courses to achieve individual pedagogical goals, even when individual courses are not really necessary. It is perfectly possible, for instance, for a student to receive an orientation to the university, improve his or her writing skills, and become exposed to other cultures all in the same course. In much the same way, it is desirable periodically to pull back from your curriculum and to ask such questions as these:

- What specific pedagogical aims are we trying to achieve in our program?
- How might those aims be achieved, not necessarily through individual courses, but through well-planned learning objectives developed for all of our courses?
- Are some pedagogical aims better achieved through cocurricular requirements (such as non-credit-bearing portfolios, lecture series, or preprofessional organizations) than through discrete courses?
- Are other pedagogical aims better achieved not through any one course but across a course cluster?
- Are some pedagogical aims that seem desirable simply not as high a priority to us that they should be required parts of the curriculum?

> Look at your schedule from the perspective that members of the upper administration, students, their parents, and various external constituents may have. Have you made the best use of the resources you've been assigned? Can students complete the program in a timely manner? Have you placed student need ahead of faculty convenience?

○

By conducting an objective review of the department's course rotations from time to time, you may be able to reorganize and simplify your curriculum in such a way that it achieves your essential aims even better than your current approach does and gives you and your students greater flexibility in course planning and selection. Approached creatively and with a strong desire to develop a program that is in your students' best interest, many seemingly insoluble scheduling problems may prove to have been mere artifacts resulting from the way in which your curriculum had been structured.

RESOURCES

Chiarandini, M., Birattari, M., Socha, K., & Rossi-Doria, O. (2006). An effective hybrid algorithm for university course timetabling. *Journal of Scheduling, 9*, 403–432.

Dinkel, J. J., Mote, J., & Venkataramanan, M. A. (1989). An efficient decision support system for academic course scheduling. *Operations Research, 37,* 853–864.

Elmohamed, M.A.S., Coddington, P., & Fox, G. (1998). A comparison of annealing techniques for academic course scheduling. *Lecture Notes in Computer Science, 1408,* 92–115.

Hertz, A. (1989). *Finding a feasible course schedule using Tabu search.* Montreal, Quebec: Université de Montréal.

Hinkin, T. R., & Thompson, G. M. (2002, January 1). SchedulExpert: Scheduling courses in the Cornell University School of Hotel Administration. *Interfaces, 32*(6), 45–57.

Murray, K., Muller, T., & Rudova, H. (2007). Modeling and solution of a complex university course timetabling problem. *Lecture Notes in Computer Science, 3867,* 189–209.

14

MAKING DECISIONS

OF ALL THE ADMINISTRATIVE duties that fall to department chairs, making decisions tends to be the area in which the fewest people seek (or believe they need) help. After all, everyone makes decisions every day, right? And isn't it true that in order to earn an advanced degree and reach your current position, you've already had a lot of experience evaluating information, weighing your options, and committing to your choice?

The fact is that we have numerous opportunities to practice the art of making decisions, and yet the types of decisions that department chairs make have a level of complexity and ambiguity that's missing from many of the choices that confront us in other areas. For one thing, department chairs make decisions in a highly volatile environment. Each year, the students in our programs change, the funding opportunities available in our disciplines change, and the needs of our institutions change. Just when we feel that we're making the best decisions we can for our disciplines, a new dean, provost, or president arrives with a new vision and priority, suddenly making it feel as though many of your right decisions were dead wrong.

Second, making decisions in a highly collegial environment with shared governance like a college or university is quite different from making decisions that affect only you, making corporate or military decisions in a very hierarchical environment, or working through various alternatives with your family or a small group of close friends. Each constituency can approach matters quite differently in higher education, and the best possible decision for the department may be the worst possible decision for the college; the choice that gives the most advantage to the students in your program may well be the one that is least acceptable to your colleagues in the program, and so on.

Finally, although everyone in higher education makes decisions, we all do it in diverse ways, depending on our academic area, core values, the stage we've reached in our careers, and our personal expectations. To cite but one example, the way in which we examine evidence and regard a certain outcome or approach as "the best" will be quite different depending on whether our academic field is accounting, English literature, psychology, civil engineering, painting, social work, organic chemistry, or military science. Yet many of the decisions that we make in one of these disciplines have an impact on what people do in several others. The result is that we may make a decision based on utility that greatly complicates the work of our colleagues who make decisions based on aesthetics, tradition, public need, economics, or several dozen other factors. It can turn out that a utilitarian decision proves to be not all that useful, an economic decision not all that cost-effective, an aesthetic decision not all that pleasing. In order to make the most effective decisions as department chairs, we need to approach the issues that confront us in a manner different from how we view the other choices of our lives.

Cost-Benefit Analysis

Let's consider the complexities of academic decision making by exploring one common basis for selecting the best choices among several options: cost-benefit analysis. Traditional cost-benefit analysis consists of weighing the negative implications of a decision (the costs) against the positive implications (the benefits). In its simplest form, this type of decision making may consist of a list of pros and cons of various decisions, similar to the process that Robinson Crusoe used following his shipwreck or the technique Benjamin Franklin advocated in his *Autobiography*. In a slightly more elaborate example, you might try to balance actual expenses involved in various choices against the benefits that will accrue from each option. We perform this type of cost-benefit analysis whenever we decide to rent versus buy a home, lease versus purchase a car, or select one model of appliance with a lower initial cost but higher upkeep versus other models that require higher initial investments but are largely maintenance free. For department chairs, cost-benefit analysis may occur when they are deciding whether to replace a full-time faculty position with numerous adjuncts, purchase various items of equipment for pedagogy or research, or build a course schedule that maximizes the use of resources.

Let's imagine the case of a department chair who works in an environment where summer terms have to pay for themselves: no department is allowed to run a summer program at a deficit. If tuition revenue does not cover salary costs, chairs are expected to cover the deficit by redirecting funding that would otherwise be spent on research, travel, supplies, and equipment during the coming year. But if the revenue gained from tuition exceeds the cost of salary, department chairs are free to allocate income any way they like. Let's further assume the following about our hypothetical university.

- A student pays $500 for each credit hour of a course.
- Of that tuition, the institution retains $350 for general expenses, passing on $150 to the department to support the professor's summer salary.
- The institution's professors are paid by a separate contract that, when salary and benefits are combined, amounts to precisely 5 percent of their base contract per credit hour.

Registration for the summer is now complete, and the chair is faced with the enrollments set out in Table 14.1. Based on this information, which courses does the chair decide to cancel? Cost-benefit analysis would proceed to answer this question in the following way. The cost of each course may be calculated with this formula:

Cost = (Faculty member's base salary × 5%) × number of credit hours

The benefit of the course may be calculated in this way:

Benefit = (Number of students enrolled × $150) × Number of credit hours

The analysis is done by subtracting the costs from the benefits in order to determine the net. After performing these calculations, the chair gets

Table 14.1 Summer Enrollment Information

	Number of Students Enrolled	Number of Credit Hours	Faculty Member's Base Salary
Course A	26	3	$ 75,000
Course B	8	4	56,000
Course C	22	3	98,000
Course D	61	3	67,000
Course E	15	4	54,000
Course F	85	3	110,000
Course G	24	3	91,000
Course H	37	3	72,000

the results in Table 14.2. Using a strict cost-benefit analysis, the chair would choose to cancel courses B, C, E, and G because they end up costing more in salary than they yield in revenue.

Table 14.2 Summer Enrollment Cost/Benefit Analysis

Course	Benefit	Cost	Net
Course A	$11,700	$11,250	$450
Course B	4,800	11,200	−6,400
Course C	9,900	14,700	−4,800
Course D	27,450	10,050	17,400
Course E	9,000	10,800	−1,800
Course F	38,250	16,500	21,750
Course G	10,800	13,650	−2,850
Course H	16,650	10,800	5,850

The Limitations of Cost-Benefit Analysis

Does any chair actually make decisions in this way? Probably not, and any who do are probably regarded by others as "bean counters," receive a large number of complaints from students about the lack of availability of certain courses, and are managing rather than leading their programs.

Measurable costs and benefits may be an important factor in academic decision making, but they do not take account of the full complexity of the environment in which department chairs work. For instance, our hypothetical example did not account for these elements:

- o Which courses the department was contractually obligated to offer in order for students to graduate in a timely manner.

- o Which courses are part of an important pilot program that isn't expected to recover its costs for several years.

- o Which courses are necessary prerequisites for students to complete in order to take the courses next summer that do generate a profit.

- o Which courses the department chair wants to keep on the schedule because the faculty member is counting on that summer salary, would leave the institution without it, and greater costs would result from the need to conduct an expensive search to replace this faculty member who has made extremely valuable contributions in other ways.

- o Which courses are the pet project of a dean, potential donor, or legislator and thus are politically advisable to keep on the schedule even if they run at a loss.

○ The entire budgetary and academic environment in which this decision is being made. For instance, if the department keeps all eight courses, it still nets a gain of $29,600 in tuition payments. Although this amount is far less than the $45,450 it would gain if four courses were canceled, that difference may not matter. The increased faculty morale, student satisfaction, accessibility to the program, and all the other factors listed above may be a benefit that far outweighs the cost of $15,850 less in profit.

In other words, cost-benefit analysis applies a particular model to academic decision making, and that model may not adequately reflect all variables of a department chair's decision. Nassim Taleb (2010) has coined the term *Platonicity* to refer to the tendency to believe (falsely) that pure models adequately capture the nuances of complex reality, "our tendency to mistake the map for the territory" (p. xv), or, in our case, the simplistic decision-making model for the far more complicated decision-making environment in which we actually work. So although cost-benefit analysis can provide department chairs with valuable insights, it's far too narrow an approach to guide every type of decision that chairs make. Even such useful and refined approaches as decision field theory, the analytic hierarchy process, and Dempster-Shafer theory, which address probability and chance in addition to factors that can be more easily controlled, ultimately rely on models that can never fully embrace the extraordinarily intricate environment in which decisions must be made in higher education. (For the three approaches to decision making just mentioned, see Golledge, 1999; Saaty, 1999; Bhushan and Rai, 2004; Yager, 2008; Terano, Asai, and Sugeno, 1992.)

The Paradox of Choice

One of the factors that makes the decisions facing department chairs so difficult is best summarized in the following essential principle:

The toughest decisions that department chairs make rarely, if ever, involve distinguishing the one good choice from numerous bad choices. They involve distinguishing what is probably the best choice from a number of excellent options or the least undesirable choice from a range of terrible options.

In other words, searches are not difficult when one candidate clearly outshines all the rest and budget cuts are not particularly challenging when you were ready to phase out a program anyway. But the vast majority of decisions that department chairs have to make require a selection of one candidate to hire from among several equally stellar applicants, how to reduce personnel costs when everyone is already working as much as they possibly can, and similar perplexing problems. While it may appear that having too many good options is far preferable than having too few, both situations can make reaching a decision quite grueling and paralyze some chairs into an inability to decide anything at all.

Barry Schwartz (2004) and Sheena Iyengar (2010) have investigated a phenomenon that Schwartz dubs the paradox of choice: the apparently inverse relationship between the number of options available to people and their ability to make an effective decision. We might intuitively believe that the more choices we have, the better our decision will be because we have the ability to select the precise alternative that best fits our circumstances. But in the course of making decisions under real work conditions, the reverse often occurs. Some people find that they can't make any decision at all. Others become overwhelmed by the number of possibilities facing them and stop paying close attention after examining several options; their decisions are actually more ineffective because they haven't thoroughly considered all of the available choices. And some people become so irritated by the number of questions asked them (Paper or plastic? Debit or credit? Cash back or not? Voluntary contribution to a worthy cause or just pay for the groceries?) that they cease evaluating the situation with a cool and rational objectivity.

Many of the decisions that department chairs have to make involve precisely this type of possibility overload. There isn't just one deserving student to whom to give the scholarship; there are more than a hundred. There aren't just two or three faculty research proposals to review; there are dozens. The paradox of choice affects administrative decisions at all levels, and department chairs must simultaneously process huge amounts of very detailed information, be able to compare apples to oranges since different options are frequently desirable for different reasons, make a decision quickly under conditions that often involve a great deal of pressure, and endure the disappointment or fervent appeals of those defending options that were not taken.

Moreover, it often seems as though when department chairs are not confronted by too many alternatives, they are dealing with situations with no satisfactory alternative. In a year where you have to implement a

10 percent budget and your supplies and expenses funding accounts for only 5 percent of your total funding, it's not possible to address the problem without layoffs. Moreover, if there's no one who's ready to retire and no one whose performance is inadequate, the people you'll be letting go are no doubt effective, valuable employees. Similarly, if you've got a maximum of fifty lab spaces because of safety or code issues, and there are fifty-three students who are counting on that lab in order to graduate this year, your decision will not be to find the best possible alternative but to identify the least destructive alternative.

The reality of academic administration is that department chairs often confront a variety of unattractive options and the unpleasant task of navigating professional minefields where success is measured not in spectacular victories but in the ability to make the best of an extremely bad situation.

So, What Are Chairs to Do?

In the end, decision-making algorithms are unreliable because they cannot possibly capture the full complexity of today's administrative environment; moreover, the majority of decisions chairs have to make involve either a paradox of superabundant choices or a scarcity of acceptable alternatives. So how do you make decisions that are in the best interests of both your own career and your disciplines as a whole? Perhaps the best advice is to approach each decision with the following three guidelines in mind.

○ *Spend nearly as much time examining your underlying assumptions and learning important lessons from past decisions as you do on gathering information and weighing alternatives* J. Edward Russo and Paul Schoemaker say that all decision-making processes—good, bad, or indifferent—have the same four stages.

1. Framing the context in which the decision will be made by understanding the perspective that you're taking and the underlying assumptions that will guide you

2. Gathering the necessary information you will need in order to make an informed decision

3. Drawing a conclusion based on your perspective, assumptions, and information

4. Learning from the experience so that you'll make even better decisions in the future

An important difference that Russo and Schoemaker (2002) have observed in leaders is that those who are unskilled in making effective decisions spend most of their time on the middle two steps (gathering information and drawing a conclusion), while more experienced leaders often devote their time more evenly to all four steps. It's difficult to make an effective decision if you're not completely clear in your own mind about the point of view you're bringing to the situation, as well as your possible limitations and biases. Understanding these matters helps you know precisely what information you need to collect and which blind spots you'll need to be on the alert for when you evaluate the data. Similarly, it's extremely profitable to spend time drawing explicit lessons from each decision, so that you'll be aware in the future of what worked well and what you'll need to improve. Failure to devote sufficient time to reflecting on the results of a decision means that each new decision tends to be made in isolation rather than as part of your continuous growth in academic leadership.

○ *As you assess the perspective that you're bringing to the decision, relate it whenever possible to your core values or fundamental principles.* A registrar I once knew approached every decision with the same question: "How will this approach help us improve student retention?" Having a central compass of this sort can be simultaneously helpful and limiting. It's limiting if your core values never allow you to see beyond the narrow confines of the single issue that you regard as most important. But it can also be extremely helpful in situations where you find yourself facing too many excellent choices or not enough acceptable alternatives. Part of the framing process of making a decision, in other words, consists of asking yourself, "What precisely is it that I'm trying to do?" which frequently can be generalized to the question, "What ultimately are my basic administrative goals as chair?" Deciding that these goals are independent of any specific decision can provide you with a much more objective perspective in the murky environment in which most administrative choices must be made. So it can be very productive to understand that your fundamental principles are increasing student learning, improving the quality of faculty research, making your department more engaged with the community, or whatever else it is that you most wish to achieve. Being clear to yourself and others exactly what your most important goals are will lead you to make fewer decisions that you regret later and establish a legacy in your department that will continue to bear fruit long after your term as chair has ended.

○ *In a large number of situations, having a decision is at least as important as making the best decision.* Department chairs are sometimes paralyzed in their decision making because they feel that unless they make the absolutely best possible decision, it's better to refrain from making any decision at all. This is not the case. There are countless administrative situations that can be handled successfully any number of ways; the important thing is for someone to commit to one approach and follow through on it. People by and large would rather be heading in a clear direction, even if they disagree with it, than to feel they're headed in no direction at all. Moreover, it is exceptionally rare in academic life for an administrator to make a decision that appeals to everyone and never receives any opposition. So it's unrealistic to expect that if you study a situation long and hard enough, the perfect solution will emerge. Higher education administration is rarely about finding perfect solutions; it's about finding workable and effective solutions in a complex and changing environment. In order to achieve that goal, it is often necessary for department chairs to make the best decision they can with the information they have available at the time, trust their instincts and experience, and make the best of the consequences.

○

Making the best decisions at the departmental level can never be reduced to a simple formula or algorithm. Decisions that would be completely proper and desirable in one environment may lead to chaos in another because the history, people, and issues are completely different there. While department chairs should base their decisions on the best possible information, they need to realize that information consists of far more than data alone. It includes not simply what you can measure based on experience or current circumstances, but also your program's vision for the future and its ability to become something far greater than what it is now. Effective decision making is, in other words, both a science and an art, and the best department chairs understand how to incorporate both of these approaches in choosing the right path for their academic programs.

REFERENCES

Bhushan, N., & Rai, K. (2004). *Strategic decision making: Applying the analytic hierarchy process.* New York: Springer.

Golledge, R. G. (1999). *Wayfinding behavior: Cognitive mapping and other spatial processes.* Baltimore: Johns Hopkins University Press.

Iyengar, S. (2010). *The art of choosing.* New York: Twelve.

Russo, J. E., & Schoemaker, P.J.H. (2002). *Winning decisions: Getting it right the first time.* New York: Currency.

Saaty, T. L. (1999). *Decision making for leaders: The analytic hierarchy process for decisions in a complex world* (3rd ed.). Pittsburgh, PA: RWS Publications.

Schwartz, B. (2004). *The paradox of choice: Why more is less.* New York: Ecco.

Taleb, N. (2010). *The black swan: The impact of the highly improbable* (2nd ed.). New York: Random House.

Terano, T., Asai, K., & Sugeno, M. (1992). *Fuzzy systems theory and its applications.* Orlando, FL: Academic Press.

Yager, R. R. (2008). *Classic works of the Dempster-Shafer theory of belief functions.* New York: Springer.

RESOURCES

Eckel, P. D. (2006). *The shifting frontiers of academic decision making: Responding to new priorities, following new pathways.* Westport, CT: ACE/Praeger.

Harvard Business Review. (2001). *Harvard Business Review on decision making.* Boston: Harvard Business School Press.

March, J. G., & Heath, C. (1994/2009). *A primer on decision making: How decisions happen.* New York: Free Press.

15

SETTING ANNUAL THEMES

AT INCREASING NUMBERS OF colleges and universities, the idea of a campuswide annual theme or special topic has been met with a great deal of success. The individual theme the college selects may be connected to its first-year experience program, may be featured in a particularly distinguished lecture series or visiting scholar program, or may simply be an attempt to provide a feeling of greater unity or focus to the academic program as a whole.

Institution-wide annual themes tend to be of great value because they can direct toward a single, significant goal much of the intellectual energy that is already present at the college or university but that would otherwise be dispersed in many different directions. In addition, a collegewide annual theme can be used to generate grant proposals or sponsored programs that the institution may not have pursued without the impetus of the theme. Administrators tend to support annual themes because they invariably provide an opportunity for the institution to receive some positive recognition in the media. As a department chair, you may discover that all the reasons for adopting annual themes for your entire college or university can also make them extremely attractive for your individual program.

If your institution already has a procedure for selecting an annual theme in place, your department is probably best served by tying into this collegewide focus in some way, a clear indication of how your discipline functions as a citizen within the larger community that will bring you some positive attention. More tangibly, participation in a broader theme might allow your program to qualify for funding from the larger institutional sources.

If your institution does not yet have a mechanism for selecting an annual theme, this is all the more reason for your department to establish its own. You will be able to use the theme as a way of making your department distinctive among its peers at your college, build on this yearly focus in order to recruit highly desirable students and faculty members, and take advantage of this annual activity to open new opportunities for departmental fundraising. If, as department chair, you plan to seek a higher administrative office, having established and successfully implemented a departmental theme program can be precisely the sort of project that allows you to demonstrate quite convincingly your creativity, entrepreneurial spirit, and strong institutional citizenship.

Annual Themes

The types of topic that your faculty members are likely to develop are limited only by their collective imaginations. Creating a discussion of this possibility in a face-to-face meeting or through an electronic forum will produce more possibilities than any one department could implement. Nevertheless, as a way of priming the pump for this discussion, this section identifies a few major sorts of annual themes that you might suggest to your colleagues. By using any of these approaches, you may be able to find an appropriate annual theme for your academic department. A topically focused theme can remind students, their parents, and your discipline's external constituents of the continued relevance of your field and its impact on their daily lives.

An Anniversary

What important development occurred in your discipline ten, twenty-five, fifty, one hundred, or two hundred years ago? Will the coming year be the anniversary of a major figure's birth or death? (The figure you choose could be someone commonly studied in your department's courses or a scholar who was responsible for a major achievement in your discipline. The anniversary of the birth or death of major authors, artists, composers, or performers frequently provides useful departmental themes.) It is not important that the anniversary you are commemorating be of a person. For instance, will next year be the anniversary of a landmark legal case of lasting importance to your field of study? Is there a major invention or discovery that has had particular significance in your field? Conceived along these lines, the anniversary theme can give your department a focus such as "The Impact of Ten Years Following

Smith v. *Jones*: A Retrospective and Assessment," "The Life, Work, and Art of Rebecca Stowers Peabody: A Centennial Appreciation," or "The Development of Verbosity Theory: A Twenty-Five-Year Legacy." Titles such as these are reminders of both the time period involved in your anniversary celebration and the important person, event, or discovery that is being examined.

A Publication

Is there a significant book or article that everyone in your discipline needs to read and discuss? If the work happens to be current, it may be possible to develop broad recognition for your discipline by bringing the author to campus and having that person discuss his or her work with a large number of faculty members and students who, because of your annual theme, have actually read the work and considered it thoughtfully. If your theme deals with an older work (a classic in your discipline, for instance), it may be possible to involve other departments in the events devoted to that year's focus, invite to campus a panel of scholars who will discuss the work from multiple perspectives, or encourage one or more members of your department to publish an update or reaction to this major work. This type of annual theme could lead your department to such titles as, "From John Henry Newman's *The Idea of the University* to an Idea for a *New* American University," "Plato's *Republic* and the Concept of 'Republic' in the Third Millennium," or "Hobbes and a Leviathan for a New Age."

A Commemoration

Is there a faculty member who is retiring during the coming year or has retired recently who could be the subject of your department's annual theme? Could you develop a year in which the students and faculty members of your department read and discuss this professor's publications, raise funds for an ongoing commemoration in honor of this faculty member's contributions, and invite back former students for a series of talks commemorating the lasting impact of this individual? Or do you have a graduate of your program who has become distinguished through important achievements in your discipline who would be the appropriate subject of a year-long study? Has a donor made a sufficiently large gift to your discipline that you could devote your department's monthly symposium or some other similar event to a discussion of topics and ideas of particular importance to this donor?

A Festival

Is it possible for your students to present their research in an annual festival that would both give them practice in summarizing their discoveries for their peers and bring desired attention to the achievements of your discipline? If so, is there a way in which you could connect their many diverse projects through the thread of a common theme? Making sure that faculty members and students alike have all read an agreed-on collection of primary sources will improve the quality of the questions that everyone asks your student presenters, lead to an even stronger set of student research projects in the future, and provide more of a shared experience for the members of your department. Alternatively, festivals can be organized around lecture series, faculty research presentations, or showcase performances or exhibits.

The important factor in each case is that the festival offers your discipline a distinct focal point that can lead to classroom discussion in the weeks or months before the festival, include the external community in significant on-campus events, and provide encouragement for intentional learning through out-of-class readings, discussion groups, or panel presentations.

A Topical Focus

What current event can provide a theme worthy of discussion for every member of your department regardless of their individual specialties? For instance, national elections occur every four years. Is there a topic of concern in the election—or might even the election process itself be considered topical for your discipline—with the result that your department's annual theme could once in every student's undergraduate career be tied to this significant activity? Has there recently been an ethical scandal or congressional inquiry that has refocused attention on the way in which professionals in your field conduct their business? Has a new discovery or a revolutionary way of approaching information in your discipline been noticed by more than just a narrow range of professionals? Is there a proposed piece of legislation that has significance in your area?

Using the Annual Theme

Once you and your departmental colleagues have selected the topic for an annual theme, the next issue is how to go about incorporating it into what you do as a discipline. The exact way in which the department decides to use the theme depends a great deal on the nature of your institution and your discipline. Nevertheless, there are some common ways in which departments use an annual theme in their activities.

Common Readings

Each member of the department, instructor and student alike, can share in a common experience related to your annual theme through reading assignments that go beyond the requirements of individual courses and provide the basis for discipline-wide discussions. Your department's common readings might range from brief articles that can be read in a single sitting to multiple books that are read one each month in an ongoing departmental book club. Lists of upcoming common readings can be distributed at the end of the spring term to be completed over the summer or can be completed as needed throughout the regular academic year.

The advantages of tying common readings to an annual theme are numerous. These experiences promote a sense of community in your department through a universally shared opportunity. They focus the attention of a large number of diverse individuals onto a single topic, providing structure and meaning to their experience. And they encourage students to draw connections among discrete courses by introducing them to a single point of significant commonality.

Lecture and Discussion Series

Departmental themes can also form the basis for conferences devoted to your discipline's annual topic, high-profile lectures delivered by nationally recognized speakers, or a series of several lectures and discussions devoted to the topic that you have selected for that year. While a primary purpose of these events will be to enrich the academic experience of your students and faculty members as a whole, a second important result of having several lectures and discussions devoted to your annual theme can be to bring the larger community to your campus, thereby reinforcing the long-term significance of work in your discipline. Series of lectures and discussions can provide valuable synergy among what the students are learning in their courses, contributions your faculty members are making in their scholarship, and public awareness of the issues that your annual theme raises.

Grant Applications

One of the most attractive features about annual themes to department chairs is that they provide built-in opportunities for seeking external funding support. Funding agencies are much more likely to provide support to a program that is fully integrated (as a properly selected annual theme would be) with a department's individual mission, strengths, and areas of distinction than they are to any number of seemingly random topics.

After establishing a successful track record with your department's annual theme, your institution may even be willing to pursue challenge grant opportunities to provide an ongoing endowment for the events associated with your program's annual theme. External support acquired in this way allows your department to be creative in planning activities in support of your annual theme without unduly drawing on your institution's internal resources. Moreover, an event that is funded through a grant or gift always seems to attract more attention and provides a department with opportunities for seeking positive media exposure.

Awards

One additional way of obtaining positive media recognition is to present a highly publicized award in conjunction with the annual theme. If your department recognizes an individual for distinguished service in your field or a lifetime of contributions to whatever topic you have selected, you will develop an automatic opportunity for positive publicity surrounding your program, create stronger ties to the individual whom you are honoring, and create an occasion in which members of your community outside your department and institution will certainly wish to participate. Other types of awards that can be offered in conjunction with your department's annual theme are scholarships for outstanding student research in this area, commendations for the best graduate student presentation on your department's topic, and recognitions of outstanding achievements by other academic programs in this area.

First-Year Experiences

Nearly every college or university has a first-year experience program designed for new students, ranging from extended orientations to comprehensive programs of courses, cocurricular experiences, and extracurricular activities that fully integrate each new student into the academic community. But what about a "First Year in Our Department" experience for new majors? Offered in conjunction with a semester-long or year-long course for new majors, cocurricular sessions devoted to your annual theme can help students understand from their first contact with your department why your discipline is unique, exciting, and relevant. Advanced students could mentor entering students, leading discussions related to that year's topic and providing the sort of guidance that will help the students succeed.

Course Clusters

One of the ways in which institutions are attempting to break down barriers between discrete courses and help students see how the experience of one discipline is related to another is through the creation of carefully designed course clusters. In this system, each cluster takes a particular theme—perhaps a historical period, a social problem, or an interdisciplinary focus—and explores that topic in two, three, or four courses that a group of students takes simultaneously. Designing one or more course clusters in which your department's annual theme is featured prominently can be an effective way of relating your discipline to others at your institution (or to relate different subdisciplines within your own department) and keeping your department's contributions fresh and topical.

Advantages to Annual Themes

Once you have begun experimenting with annual departmental themes along the lines outlined, you are likely to notice several advantages that will begin accruing to your department and to you as chair. A few of the advantages gained from having a departmental annual theme may be outlined as follows.

- *Leveraging.* By uniting what would otherwise be unrelated courses, lectures, or campus events through your annual theme, you can make each of these individual activities more significant as part of a larger, noteworthy project.
- *Publicity.* Individuals and agencies (including those that provide sources of external funding) that are unlikely to pay much attention to an occasional lecture or guest speaker are much more likely to notice the next event in what you have developed as an extended series. It will be easier for local newspapers and television or radio stations to cover "Tonight's Discussion in This Year's Ongoing

Series Devoted to . . ." than to devote scarce resources to covering a speech or panel discussion in your department that seems unrelated to a larger purpose.

○ *Interaction.* The annual theme will also prompt numerous opportunities for you to interact with other departments on your campus, other colleagues at different campuses, and interested members of the community. An annual theme is one important way that you can help your department serve external constituents more effectively and attract the interest of those constituencies in how they may better serve the ongoing needs of your department.

○

Selecting an appropriate annual theme can simultaneously provide your department with a new focus for its discussions and curriculum, an expanded set of possibilities for obtaining external funding, greater visibility, and renewed opportunities for engagement with other departments at your institution. The use of annual themes thus brings you further in your effort to move away from merely managing what currently exists in your department to leading your discipline toward new possibilities for the future.

16

CREATING DEPARTMENTAL CENTERS FOR EXCELLENCE IN TEACHING AND LEARNING

CENTERS DEDICATED TO THE improvement of teaching and learning have become common features on most college campuses. These centers, frequently bearing such titles as Center for Excellence in Teaching and Learning or Center for Innovations in Teaching and Learning, play a significant role in improving student learning, exposing faculty members to alternative forms of pedagogy, and exploring the role that technology can play in the learning process. Yet precisely because these centers have become so common, chairs may be tempted to ask: Why would I need a departmental center for excellence in teaching and learning? Hasn't that function been superseded by offices that serve the entire institution? And isn't there an economy of scale achieved by a university-wide center for pedagogy that cannot be matched even by fairly large departments?

If your institution does not yet have its own center for excellence in teaching, then your department needs one. By establishing such a center, you will be doing a favor for your own faculty and students by enhancing the learning process in your discipline and for your institution as a whole by providing a model for the advantages that could be obtained if this approach were adopted campuswide.

If your institution already has such a center, you may still want your own departmental branch to explore pedagogies that are more appropriate for your individual discipline, examine software packages that may be more useful for teaching and learning in your area than they may be in other academic departments, and inculcate the methods of scholarship suitable to your field that may not be as transferable to other fields across the institution.

If you are establishing a departmental center that will exist in addition to a center serving the entire institution, partner closely with your campuswide center in order to avoid duplication of efforts, obtain information about additional resources that may be available, and avoid giving the false impression that you are attempting to infringe on another office's territory. You may even wish to use the term "branch office" or "departmental outlet" for the larger center in order to clarify that your desire is to augment the campus center, not replace it.

Unlike larger campus centers dedicated to improving the quality of teaching, your departmental center need not occupy a great deal of geography. It may be little more than a notice board, bookshelf, or a workstation in a departmental office. In some cases, it may not be a physical entity at all, but rather something that occurs whenever and wherever there is an activity that it sponsors. For instance, your departmental center might consist of a workshop series, monthly discussion group, and electronic bulletin board rather than a physical desk, office, and specific computer. By means of your department's Web site or course management system, your department's entire "center" can be a virtual one—an idea of commitment to the importance of excellence in teaching rather than a specific location.

However you configure your departmental center, begin by developing a clear notion of the sorts of activities it might sponsor and the goals that you wish it to achieve. Many of these objectives depend on the individual discipline and institution. The ones that follow are applicable to many areas.

Methods

Each academic area has methods of instructing and engaging students in intellectual inquiry that are unique to their fields. These methods are unlikely to be addressed in large, campuswide centers for teaching and learning and lend themselves perfectly to departmental centers. For instance, in the fine arts, the critique is frequently used as a teaching tool in ways that are very different from the methods of other academic disciplines. But few opportunities exist on many campuses for art teachers to improve their skills at supervising truly outstanding critiques. In a similar manner, law schools tend to rely heavily on case studies. Nevertheless, few teachers in law programs receive formal training in how to lead case study sessions as opposed to merely participating in them. A discipline-specific center devoted to teaching excellence can assist faculty members in developing their skills at conducting this vital instructional activity.

In other cases, department chairs may find that their faculty members need to learn teaching methods that are not specific to their discipline but are being addressed by their campuswide center for excellence in teaching and learning. Moreover, departmental centers might serve other purposes not currently addressed campuswide, such as inculcating good teaching methods in the program's graduate students or even upper-level undergraduate students. Adjunct faculty members without much teaching experience might also be encouraged, or even required, to participate in some of the department's programs on instruction shortly after they begin work at the institution.

Some of the more general instructional methods your departmental center might explore are techniques for making students more active learners in the classroom, even in courses with no research component or similar contact with primary sources of information. In these instances, you may wish to explore with members of your faculty teaching strategies that are designed to promote students' more active involvement with the material of your courses. Consider these examples:

- *Inside/outside circles.* Organize the students of the course into two concentric rings, each containing the same number of students. (In very large courses, it may be helpful to use several pairs of concentric rings so that each group contains no more than about twenty students.) Assign the students a problem or topic to discuss in pairs consisting of one student from the outer circle and one from the inner circle. After a set period of time (usually only one to five minutes), have one of the circles rotate so that each pair is now different. Repeat this exercise three or four times until each student receives a variety of perspectives on the topic, different ways of solving the problem, or opportunities to explain how a task is best accomplished.

- *Send a problem.* Divide the students of the class into groups of approximately six to ten. Have each group develop a problem or discussion question based on the material covered in the unit currently under study. They should also come up with their own solution to the problem or set of key points to be discussed on that issue. Each group then sends its problem to another group, receiving a problem in return. After each group has worked on each of the problems, the entire class is reconstituted and the various solutions compared in discussion.

○ *Top ten list.* Working in groups, students are assigned the task of creating lists—in reverse priority order—of the top ten facts or observations about a particular unit. The goal is not merely to identify what students believe are the most significant observations to be made about the material but to weigh them in significance. Making the answers humorous is a desirable, though not a required, component of the assignment.

○ *Game show.* Almost every season introduces a new and television game show that becomes highly popular. Choose whichever game format is currently popular, adapt its format to your discipline, and use this structure for a unit review or to prepare for an examination. In larger courses, break the students into separate teams, have each team prepare questions in the appropriate format, and use the questions to help the students master the material or approaches covered in the course.

○ *The muddiest point.* This technique, developed by Thomas Angelo and Patricia Cross (1993), can both promote active learning and provide the instructor with midcourse feedback on where students are still having the greatest difficulty. Students complete a small form stating, "The point that is still the most unclear for me about this unit is . . . ," which they then pass to the instructor. Students may also be divided into groups to help explain to one another the points about which one or more of their members still find confusing.

Faculty members sometimes claim that such classroom techniques are merely gimmicks that are inappropriate for use in college-level courses, possibly even demeaning to good students who would benefit more from traditional lecture and discussion. In fact, students at all levels of academic ability tend to become more engaged with course material—and perform even better on classroom assignments and exams—when faculty members use a broad array of innovative teaching methods. The key is not necessarily to adopt the specific teaching methods outlined in this chapter, but rather to find an approach that fits each professor's individual teaching style and encourages students to engage actively with the material.

The advantage of the methods set out in this chapter is that they get students out of their seats, compel them to interact with one another, and engage them in teaching the material rather than just listening to it passively. As a department chair, encourage the members of your faculty to use their creativity in developing interactive teaching techniques that are appropriate to your discipline and the students who tend to enroll at your institution.

> In many cases, having a regular opportunity for faculty members to get together and focus on how they teach various aspects of the discipline contributes a great deal to the improvement of teaching and learning.

Technology

Professionals in every discipline are aware of software applications or items of technology that are perfect for their instructional mission, even if they may not be of much importance to other academic areas. Campuswide centers for teaching and learning generally conduct training sessions on hardware or software programs that have been adopted broadly throughout academic disciplines, but how do faculty members learn about individual items of technology that are unique to your field? Departmental instructional resource centers are perfect for this more specialized approach to instruction. Through your departmental center, you can pilot new applications as they become available, providing training that is adapted to your discipline's unique methodology and then trying out these approaches with small groups of students or in a select number of course sections.

Because your departmental center for teaching and learning is smaller and more nimble than your campuswide center and because it has a more focused mission, it will be able to incorporate new advances in technology much more rapidly than can your larger institutional structure. For instance, when MP3 players first became widely used by college students, departmental centers for teaching were among the early adopters of this new technology for pedagogical purposes, locating (and sometimes creating) instructional podcasts in their disciplines, providing students with access to royalty-free musical examples in their music history courses, and disseminating information to majors in a format that reached students in an accessible and timely manner.

As other new technologies appear on the market, your departmental center can serve as a leader at your institution in exploring their academic uses, incorporating them into pilot sections of courses, and using them to improve student learning.

Discussion Groups

Even a virtual departmental center for excellence in teaching can serve as a magnet for discussion groups dedicated to the consideration of student learning. Discussion groups sponsored by your departmental center might focus on a particular book, topic, or method of instruction. You might consider forming a book discussion group that deals with some aspect of teaching or learning unique to your discipline. For instance, a department in one of the natural sciences might use the National Science Teachers Association (2001), an English department might use Dinitz and Fulwiler (2000) or Showalter (2004), a math department might use Friedberg (2001) or Baldwin (2009), a theater department might use Fliotsos and Medford (2004), and an anthropology department might use Rice and McCurdy (2010). Departments of psychology have a particularly rich menu of choices for this type of discussion, including Upton and Trapp (2010), Goss and Bernstein (2005), Hebl, Brewer, and Benjamin (2000), Griggs (2002), Sternberg (1997), and Forsyth (2003). The point is that nearly every discipline has at least one major textbook exploring pedagogical approaches that are suitable at the college level. Even when your faculty members disagree vehemently with the perspectives introduced in such a text, establishing a discussion group that deals with one of these books can prompt invaluable reconsideration of how material is taught in your department, why it is taught in the manner that it is, and how instructional techniques may be improved.

Moreover, if your campuswide center for excellence in teaching isn't sponsoring discussion groups about even nonpedagogical books that may help your department in your teaching mission, you might want to consider having your departmental center assume this task. For instance, a great books discussion group, in which faculty members meet once a month to discuss a work by, for example, Sophocles, Machiavelli, Jane Austen, or Zora Neale Hurston can help them recall what it feels like to be a student again, provide sources of enrichment for their courses, and offer an opportunity for the department to get together to discuss matters other than current courses and institutional challenges.

In a similar way, taking a semester as a faculty to grapple with particularly challenging texts—Thomas Pynchon's *Gravity's Rainbow,* Oswald Spengler's *The Decline of the West,* Ludwig Wittgenstein's *Philosophical Investigations,* Martha Nussbaum's *Upheavals of Thought* (2001), or Michel Foucault's *The Archaeology of Knowledge* (1972)—can benefit teaching in your department in a number of ways. It can help promote new scholarly agendas, foster interdisciplinary approaches, and help even the most senior faculty member recall that sometimes comprehending several pages of text can be a challenging academic pursuit.

Other ongoing discussion groups might deal not with particular books but with key theories, methods, or topics that are significant in your discipline. For instance, a discussion group might be devoted to the uses of simulations or the case study technique in your discipline. Or perhaps a new perspective will emerge at the national conference in your discipline, and a discussion group can be formed to discuss its impact on the curriculum of your program. Remember too that not all of these discussions need to be face-to-face. Listservs, intranets, course management systems, and threaded discussion pages make it possible for your department to discuss these topics asynchronously and electronically.

Mentoring

Another valuable function of a departmental center for teaching and learning, particularly for a department with several junior faculty members, is a formal mentoring program. Departmental teaching mentors should be given clear guidance that their focus as a mentor must be formative, not summative. That is, the purpose of the formal mentoring program in your department must be to assist teachers in improving their skill as instructors, not to evaluate them for the purposes of contract renewal, promotion, or tenure. Departmental mentors should also be reminded that simply because a faculty member does not teach in the same way that they teach does not mean that this person is not teaching effectively; the important consideration must always be whether students in the course are engaging effectively with the material, learning information and skills at an appropriately advanced level, and progressing through the course material in an effective and timely manner. Mentors can be encouraged to sit in on courses, review tapes of class sections, go over exams and course materials, open their own classes for faculty observation, and provide any number of other constructive services that will improve the teaching of their colleagues in the department.

Clinics

Clinics are specific types of discussion groups aimed at problem solving, brainstorming, and coping with the inevitable challenges that arise in college-level teaching. Each participant in a clinic brings one or two particularly challenging situations that have arisen recently in their teaching for other faculty members to reflect on, discuss how they might have handled them differently, and develop strategies for addressing similar issues in the future.

Clinics are particularly useful departmental devices for improving teaching since they focus on a current problem, provide new insights on how it might be handled, and help develop the problem-solving skills of the faculty as a whole. Conducted on a regular basis, they serve to develop creativity in teaching strategies among the faculty and can even foster a certain esprit de corps. In some departments, virtual clinics can be created online. Blackboard Academic Suite, CourseWork, eCollege, Angel, Moodle, and other course management systems allow messages to be posted anonymously to threaded discussions. In this way, faculty members could submit problems to be discussed by the department in a way that cannot be traced back to them, allowing them to receive advice from others in a manner that protects their identity. Even in situations where teaching clinics are held face-to-face, it is often desirable to provide a mechanism whereby faculty members can submit anonymous case studies to be critiqued and discussed by the department as a whole. In that way, junior faculty members who may be reluctant to present problems they are encountering to the very colleagues who will be voting on their promotions and tenure decisions can do so in ways that protect their privacy.

Creating a departmental center for excellence in teaching and learning isn't about competing with or replacing any similar program that serves the entire university. Rather it's a recognition that certain aspects of pedagogy are specific to individual disciplines and that departmental peers are often in the best position to assist their colleagues with instructional matters of relevance primarily to their academic specialty. In addition, establishing a department center sends a clear message that as department chair, you are a strong advocate for excellence in teaching and for increasing each student's level of success. Your department center for excellence in teaching and learning can help you prevent problems in instruction, reduce the number of withdrawals from or low grades in the courses your discipline offers, and serve your faculty members well when they are reviewed for promotion, tenure, or merit increases.

REFERENCES

Angelo, T. A., & Cross, K. P. (1993). *Classroom assessment techniques: A handbook for college teachers*. San Francisco: Jossey-Bass.

Baldwin, R. G. (2009). *Improving the climate for undergraduate teaching and learning in STEM fields*. San Francisco: Jossey-Bass.

Dinitz, S., & Fulwiler, T. (2000). *The letter book: Ideas for teaching college English*. Portsmouth, NH: Boynton/Cook.

Fliotsos, A. L., & Medford, G. S. (2004). *Teaching theatre today: Pedagogical views of theatre in higher education.* New York: Palgrave Macmillan.

Forsyth, D. R. (2003). *The professor's guide to teaching: Psychological principles and practices.* Washington, DC: American Psychological Association.

Foucault, M. (1972). *The archaeology of knowledge.* New York: Pantheon Books.

Friedberg, S. (2001). *Teaching mathematics in colleges and universities: Case studies for today's classroom.* Providence, RI: American Mathematical Society.

Goss, L. S., & Bernstein, D. A. (2005). *Teaching psychology: A step by step guide.* Mahwah, NJ: Erlbaum.

Griggs, R. A. (2002). *Handbook for teaching introductory psychology: With an emphasis on assessment.* Mahwah, NJ: Erlbaum.

Hebl, M. R., Brewer, C. L., & Benjamin, L. T. (2000). *Handbook for teaching introductory psychology.* Mahwah, NJ: Erlbaum.

National Science Teachers Association. (2001). *Practicing science: The investigative approach in college science teaching.* Arlington, VA: NSTA Press.

Nussbaum, M. C. (2001). *Upheavals of thought: The intelligence of emotions.* Cambridge: Cambridge University Press.

Rice, P. C., & McCurdy, D. W. (2010). *Strategies in teaching anthropology.* Upper Saddle River, NJ: Pearson.

Showalter, E. (2004). *Teaching literature.* Malden, MA: Blackwell.

Sternberg, R. J. (1997). *Teaching introductory psychology: Survival tips from the experts.* Washington, DC: American Psychological Association.

Upton, D., & Trapp, A. (2010). *Teaching psychology in higher education.* Hoboken, NJ: BPS Wiley-Blackwell.

RESOURCES

Bain, K. (2004). *What the best college teachers do.* Cambridge, MA: Harvard University Press.

Barkley, E. F., Cross, K. P., & Major, C. H. (2005). *Collaborative learning techniques: A handbook for college faculty.* San Francisco: Jossey-Bass.

Buller, J. L. (2010). *The essential college professor: A practical guide to an academic career.* San Francisco: Jossey-Bass.

Fink, L. D. (2003). *Creating significant learning experiences: An integrated approach to designing college courses.* San Francisco: Jossey-Bass.

Johnson, G. R. (1995). *First steps to excellence in college teaching.* Madison, WI: Magna Publications.

Leamnson, R. N. (1999). *Thinking about teaching and learning: Developing habits of learning with first year college and university students.* Sterling, VA: Stylus.

Seldin, P. (1995). *Improving college teaching*. San Francisco: Jossey-Bass/Anker.

Svinicki, M. D., & McKeachie, W. J. (2011). *McKeachie's teaching tips: Strategies, research, and theory for college and university teachers*. Belmont, CA: Wadsworth/Cengage Learning.

Weimer, M. (2002). *Learner-centered teaching: Five key changes to practice*. San Francisco: Jossey-Bass.

Wulff, D. H., & Jacobson, W. H. (2005). *Aligning for learning: Strategies for teaching effectiveness*. San Francisco: Jossey-Bass/Anker.

17

A SCENARIO ANALYSIS ON DEPARTMENTAL MANAGEMENT AND POLITICS

FOR A DISCUSSION OF how scenario analyses are structured and suggestions on how to use this exercise most productively, see Chapter Nine.

Case Studies

The Dean's "Great News"

While attending a faculty meeting in your department, the dean has just announced "great news": next year, your travel budget will be increased ten thousand dollars because of the dean's long-standing commitment to faculty development. As soon as the dean leaves, however, an argument breaks out among your faculty members about how this money should be spent. Carla Marx wants all faculty members in the department to benefit equally; since your department has twenty-five members, she suggests that each faculty member be given an additional four hundred dollar travel allowance. M.N.S. Greeze rejects this idea, saying that faculty members who are more active professionally should receive more money; it doesn't make sense, he argues, for people who haven't been going to conferences or presenting papers to receive the same increase as "serious scholars" like himself who have long been nationally known. Barry Jung counters by saying that this new funding is just the thing to help junior faculty members like himself get tenured and promoted; he argues that the full amount be set aside to develop newer faculty members. May X. Plode attempts to restore peace in the department by suggesting that a new faculty committee be formed to allocate the new money on the basis of travel proposals submitted by faculty members. Secretly you wish that the dean had told you about the new money privately since faculty travel is, in your opinion, not your department's greatest need.

What do you do?

No Good Deed Goes Unpunished

During the first week of classes one semester, a student comes to see you. The student needs to complete a course offered by your department in order to graduate at the end of the current term. In fact, this single course is the only requirement remaining between the student and graduation. The problem is that the course the student needs is already vastly over-enrolled. You know that the number of students currently admitted to the course significantly exceeds the number of seats available in the class-room, and the professor told you in no uncertain terms that because of limited amounts of essential course materials, the course could not possi-bly accommodate even one additional student. You explain all of this to the student, who replies, "But that's the very professor who sent me here. I was told that all I needed to get into the course was your signature. It wasn't explained to me how there can be room in the course now, but somehow there is. Maybe someone else dropped, and so there's a seat available. Anyway, the professor knows that I need this class to graduate and told me specifically to come here to get your signature."

Not feeling particularly comfortable granting an override without talking to the professor, you try making contact by telephone and, when that is not successful, you walk down to hall to his office. Since the pro-fessor is still not available, you tell the student that you really cannot sign the form without speaking to the professor first. But the student replies with dismay, "This is the last day to add the course! The registrar told me that if I didn't get into this course today, I couldn't graduate. Besides, I've already told you: the professor told me that it's okay. All I had to do was get your signature." At this moment, another faculty member comes into your office to drop off a budget report that is due. You ask whether this professor knows anything about the situation and are told, "Yeah, I think it's okay. I heard of a couple of students who were dropping that course, so the story sounds right. If it were me, I'd go ahead and sign the form." You try one last time to contact the professor and then, taking a chance and trying to exert some proactive leadership, you sign the form admitting the student to the course.

When you arrive at your office the next Monday morning, the profes-sor of the course is waiting for you by your door and positively seething.

"Why'd you go and put that student in my course last week? You *knew* I didn't have room for the students who were already signed up for it. I specifically *told* you that I couldn't take anyone else. You said you wouldn't do it, and then I find this morning I've got one *more* student for whom I've got no materials and no space in the classroom." When you explain that you had tried to contact the professor several times and that the student was adamant that the professor was satisfied and that all that was needed was your signature, the professor responds, "What I *told* the student was that *I* couldn't let the student into the course. A couple of students have dropped it, sure, but it's still overenrolled. Adding one more student to the course would take *your* signature, and I sent that student to you *knowing* that you would have to say no because of our conversation. After all, that's what you *told* me you were going to do."

Despite your best efforts to calm your faculty member, he responds, "I don't care. This is going to be reported to the dean, and it may even result in a grievance."

What do you do?

A Textbook Example

You are chair of a department in which one faculty member has recently published a major textbook in your field. The book has received excellent reviews, and although plenty of other well-received texts are available in the area, the author has begun assigning the book as a required text in a course that all the majors in your program must complete. One day a student stops by your office and expresses a concern because this particular book is significantly more expensive than several other highly respected texts that could easily have been adopted for the course. The student is on a tight budget and worries about being able to continue in your program because of the expense. Somewhat reluctantly, the student also tells you that a number of students in the course regard it as a conflict of interest for this professor to require a textbook that results in the faculty member's own profit.

Your conversation with the student has barely finished when a faculty member approaches you with a different issue concerning the same book. It turns out that this faculty member will be teaching a different section of the same course next semester and was in the process of preparing a textbook order. This faculty member actually prefers the approach taken in a different book, and your policy does not require that identical texts be used in multiple sections of the same course. The problem is that the author in your department has been pressuring the faculty member to adopt the text that that person has written. At first, these suggestions were fairly subtle, but they quickly escalated into hints that it would be taken as a personal affront if the other faculty member rejects the new textbook. Even worse, the faculty member who is in your office now is untenured and worries about defying the wishes of an influential senior faculty member who will be voting on a future tenure decision.

What do you do?

Caught in the Middle

As a department chair, you value the ability to work with others collegially and amicably. You place a premium on having a candid exchange of views, exploring every option, and working together as a team once a decision has been made. At the moment, however, you find yourself in a situation where your commitment to this approach is being sorely tested.

As part of your institution's strategic plan, a major new proposal is under consideration that would radically change the way in which your institution assigns workload, evaluates faculty members for tenure and promotion, and reviews programs according to student credit hour production. Proponents of the new approach—which include your president, provost, and dean—argue that this extensive change is necessary for the very survival of your institution. Others, including nearly every member of the faculty, see the proposal as simply a cynical move to get them to do more work for the same pay and believe that the administration is weakly bowing to the unreasonable demands of its governing board, mostly composed of individuals who have absolutely no academic background. After much thought and due consideration, you find yourself agreeing more with the faculty position than with the administrative position.

You attend a meeting called by the administration for all deans, directors, and department chairs. There the proposal is hotly debated. You present your point of view as clearly and persuasively as you can, but are somewhat surprised to learn that you are in a very small minority. By the end of the meeting, an overwhelming majority of those present vote in a secret ballot to go ahead with the controversial plan. The president closes the meeting by saying, "I concur with this vote, and I'm glad that that's how you've decided to proceed. Now I know not everyone agrees with this idea, and we've all had plenty of opportunity to share our perspectives in this room. But now that the decision's been made, I need you all to be on board with it. I want you to sell this to the members of your faculty and staff. Some people are going to need some persuading, and I'm counting on every person here to do that. We're a team, and now we've all got to act like a team. I don't want anyone undermining this effort."

The result puts you in a really awkward situation. At your next department meeting, you discuss the decision that has been made and summarize the arguments made on its behalf. Your summary appears to please no one. You hear people mutter that you've "sold out" and comments like, "I thought you were supposed to be our advocate." You are tempted to reply by saying that you and others did present alternative perspectives but that these views did not persuade the majority; then you recall how strongly the president had insisted that once the decision was made, none of the deans or chairs do anything that could be seen as undermining the new policy.

You are attempting to play the role of the loyal opposition when one of the opinion leaders in your department says, "Look, we feel strongly about this issue and we've got to know where your loyalties lie. Either you're against the new policy, in which case you need to resign as chair since you can't enforce something you don't support, or you're in favor of the plan, in which case we don't feel that you're an effective representative for us anymore."

What do you do?

Considerations

1. As you reflect on the "The Dean's 'Great News,' " take the following questions into account:

   a. How do you go about weighing the four competing proposals suggested by members of your department? Is there a still better idea?

   b. Does any one of the four proposals make more sense than the others?

   c. In light of your own feeling that travel is not your department's greatest need (and in light of your dean's "long-standing commitment to faculty development"), has the dean left you any options for finding common ground?

   d. How can you redirect the discussion from interdepartmental politics and sniping to a focus on the fact that something truly good has just happened: your department has just been handed an additional ten thousand dollars in travel funding?

2. As you reflect on "No Good Deed Goes Unpunished," consider these questions:

   a. In retrospect, does it now appear that you did anything wrong, or was this situation one in which it was all but impossible for you to do the right thing based on the information available?

   b. How can you regain control of the situation, setting an appropriate example for both the student and the faculty member, and demonstrating good departmental leadership?

   c. Do you start seeking a solution by speaking to the student again?

      • If so, what do you say?

      • Do you include the faculty member in the conversation this time?

   d. Do you contact the registrar and have the student withdrawn from the course, even though it means that the student will not graduate this semester? If so, do you do this before or after speaking to the student?

   e. Is this a situation to which you would alert your immediate supervisor? If so, would you do so:

      • To keep that person informed?

      • To ask that person's advice?

      • To involve that person in making the decision?

      • To defer this particular decision to that person?

   f. Would your handling of this situation be any different if any of the following were true?

      • Your institution had a strict honor code to which all students were compelled to subscribe and that imposed severe sanctions for lying.

      • The father of the student in question is your institution's president.

      • Your institution is unionized.

      • You checked the registration records for this course and discovered that not just a few but a significant number of students had dropped the course during the first week and, despite the professor's claim, there is now room in the course.

      • The student has a 4.0 GPA.

      • The student has a very low GPA.

- The faculty member in question is a newly hired, untenured faculty member.

- The faculty member in question was your own mentor in the department, a distinguished and widely admired scholar who has won numerous awards for excellence in teaching.

- The faculty member teaching the course is your dean.

3. In "A Textbook Example," what would you say to the student and faculty member who came to you on this issue?

   a. Which of the issues that were brought to your attention causes you the most concern?

   b. What would you say to the author of the textbook?

   c. What role do you think it would be appropriate to assume when you met with the author? Would you see yourself more as a mentor who wished to provide constructive advice or more as a supervisor who was going to issue an instruction to a faculty member who reports to you?

   d. Does the situation become simpler or more complicated if the following information were added to the case study?
   You are just beginning to sort your way through these issues when yet another faculty member comes to see you. This faculty member has a different concern about the textbook and its author. This faculty member is concerned that the textbook in question was written on university time, using university resources, and incorporating substantial amounts of information about and research conducted by the university's students and faculty members. According to the faculty member who is in your office now, your institution's intellectual property policy requires that any royalties resulting from the textbook must be given to the university, not kept by the author. This faculty member alleges that the author may be guilty of violating your institution's code of conduct by not signing over the book's royalties to the university from the very beginning. The faculty member states that you must take action immediately and that if you don't, you'll be a party to a grievance that will be filed with the dean.

   e. Does this change in the case study from an ethical violation to a policy violation alter the way in which you will respond to this issue?

   f. Would your response be different if you knew that the author was not keeping the royalties but donating them to charity?

g. Would your response be different if you knew that the author was not keeping the royalties but donating them to the department's annual fund?

h. Would your response be different if you were the author of the textbook in question?

4. Does your response to "Caught in the Middle" change at all if

a. Your president is rather new to the position, and the new policy was a central reason that your institution's governing board hired him or her?

b. You were aware that the new policy had been widely embraced at other institutions and was regarded as a key new development in higher education by several major accrediting agencies?

c. One of your program's largest donors was bitterly opposed to the new policy?

d. You felt that the two sides in this issue were breaking not only along administrative and faculty lines but also racial, gender, or ethnic lines?

e. Several of your most highly regarded faculty members have threatened to quit if the proposed policy is adopted?

Suggestions

The Dean's "Great News"

The problem outlined in this case arises at least in part because you have been blindsided by a revelation you haven't had time to process. Regardless of how you decide to proceed, one outgrowth of this situation will be a need for you to have a conversation with your dean about ways to improve the flow of communication between the two of you so that a similar problem doesn't recur.

In dealing with the issue at hand, there are two factors that it would be wise to consider. The first is that the dean specifically tied the increase in travel funding to his or her "long-standing commitment to faculty development." So one way of approaching this issue is to ask, "Which solution has the greatest potential for improving our faculty development efforts?" From this perspective, Professors Marx, Greeze, and Plode may need to refocus their suggestions so that the faculty development emphasis of their plans becomes clearer. The second factor you may want to consider is one we encountered in Chapter Fourteen: relate a decision whenever possible to your core values or fundamental principles. In other words, what has been your fundamental focus for travel, particularly when that travel has been related to faculty development? If you have seen the primary goal of faculty development travel as positioning younger faculty members for promotion and successful tenure reviews, then Professor Jung's proposal may be your best option. But if your faculty development goals have been in a different area—such as improving your department's potential for achievements in basic research, revising and updating the curriculum, or exposing faculty members to new techniques of instructional technology—then it may well be that none of your faculty members' suggestions are the best use of this new money, at least as those ideas were initially presented.

The overriding principle at work in this case should thus be not to see this problem as a decision that can be made in isolation; it must be linked to your overall goals as chair and to the key mission of your department. By acting in this way, you'll have the best chance of depoliticizing this process and reaching a solution that most people will come to support.

No Good Deed Goes Unpunished

This case study provides an excellent example of the following essential principle:

> Any time you are asked to make a decision that involves several parties, be sure to consult with each party and refrain from taking at face value the first version you're told. There's always another side to the story.

In the situation in this case study, you wanted to act quickly because the student said that he or she had to be added into the course today and that the professor had given oral approval. In such a case, it would have been prudent to call the registrar and inquire whether it might be possible to add the student to the course in another day or two so that you have time to discuss the matter with the instructor. In most cases, internal deadlines of this sort can become flexible as long as people know there's a good reason for providing an extension and that you will conclude the matter as quickly as possible.

Since that approach was not taken, your best plan now is to apologize (sincerely!) to the professor for the misunderstanding, meet jointly with both the student (who shares culpability for misrepresenting the situation) and the professor, and try to determine the best way forward. If it is merely a matter of room size that's limiting the capacity of the course, you might take the initiative of determining whether an alternative classroom is available. If the problem is more a matter of workload, perhaps you can provide an additional teaching assistant or make some other accommodation to make the situation more palatable for the instructor. The problem is far more difficult, of course, if the course has been capped for safety reasons due to the number of laboratory spaces available, is a performance class that requires a highly specialized room, or is limited for some other similar reason. In no case should you make special accommodations simply because the student is the child of your president, the course is taught by your dean, or the faculty member is a distinguished scholar in his or her field. Once you begin altering your decisions on the basis of a stakeholder's status, there is no easy way to stop making special deals in this way, and you'll end up with a far greater problem on your hands than you have right now.

A Textbook Example

The challenge outlined in this case study is increasingly common as faculty members have opportunities to produce not merely traditional textbooks but a wide range of course enrichment materials that innovations in instructional technology make possible. This fundamental principle must be applied in the case study:

> Faculty members should never engage in any activity that causes a conflict of interest in the faculty member's primary role as teacher of and mentor to students. In particular, they should never profit at a student's expense or use their power differential to coerce a student into any activity that is not in the student's best interests.

In this case, the faculty member is in the wrong if he or she is pressuring other professors in the department to adopt the textbook against their own better judgment. Furthermore, the faculty member is at the very least in a morally questionable situation by requiring his or her own students to purchase a text that seems to be no better and far more expensive than other texts. One can argue (and the professor in this case study probably would do so) that the students do receive added value from the course by being able to say that they were taught by the very person who wrote the textbook on the topic. In addition, the professor will undoubtedly know a self-authored text far better than any other book available and be convinced of its superiority to those of its competitors; otherwise he or she would not have been motivated to write it. Many institutions have policies requiring faculty members to donate the profits received from assigning self-authored texts in their own courses, or use an honor system to make this approach more acceptable to faculty members (as well as to respect their status as professionals). If such a policy is not yet in place at your institution, the complexities of this case study provide a good reason for proposing one.

Caught in the Middle

While you may never find yourself in a situation precisely like that described in this case study almost all department chairs find themselves trapped sooner or later between the upper administration and their faculty on an issue with intense disagreement. In the best of these situations, the chairs feel free to state their own views to their supervisors, but if they are overruled, they find a way to implement the decision and communicate the reasons it was adopted to their departments.

For whatever reason, this case study implies that the department chair is in a situation where this optimal result has not been achieved. Part of your response to the challenge will depend on precisely how strongly you are committed to your views. If you truly believe that either the institution as a whole or your discipline in particular faces irreparable harm from the new policy, you have an important obligation to continue speaking up. But since you've already been given an opportunity to express your view and have been significantly outvoted, you also have an obligation to be sure you're right. After all, the case study states that you are in a very small minority. Although sometimes the tiny minority was right all along while the vast majority of the people studying the issue was wrong, this occurrence is not common and at the very least should cause you to reconsider your opposition to the plan. Moreover, there's probably no great harm in making it clear to your faculty that you did make the best possible case against the proposed policy, but since it was voted in by a significant majority, your obligation now is to try to make it work in a way that serves your department's long-term interest. Finally, in response to the faculty member who insists that you resign over this issue, remember that you're under absolutely no obligation to do so and that the speaker was making a rhetorical political point, not citing an inflexible academic law. Departmental detractors will always try to score points in this way, but unless you are ever faced with an unmistakable vote of no confidence (and sometimes even then), don't take such pontificating too seriously.

PART THREE

THE CHAIR'S ROLE IN SEARCHES, HIRING, AND FIRING

18

WRITING JOB DESCRIPTIONS AND POSITION ANNOUNCEMENTS

WHENEVER THE TOPIC OF "decisions that seemed right at the time but that are now driving me crazy" arises, many department chairs are likely to mention the search that went wrong. Advertising, recruiting, hiring, and mentoring new faculty members together constitute one of the department chair's most important responsibilities. Fulfilling these responsibilities effectively can lead to a department that is harmonious, productive, and dedicated to the success of its students. Making mistakes in even part of this process can lead to departmental turmoil, the loss of the very faculty members you would most like to keep, and an overall decline in a department's reputation within the institution and perhaps beyond. Hiring the right faculty members does not sound as though it would be particularly difficult, and yet frequently it is.

The Three Common Errors

How can you keep from making a misstep in faculty hiring and increase the odds that you will hire the best possible candidate for your department? One of the best places to begin answering this question is to consider how your department writes its job descriptions and position announcements. In many cases, the problem with an unsatisfactory hire starts at this point in the employment process, long before the first candidate has been interviewed on campus—in fact, before the first candidate has even applied. Most departments make these mistakes in writing job descriptions:

○ Not describing the type of employee really needed

○ Not including the right sort of information about the position or expectations

○ Not requesting the type of supporting materials that can help those hiring make the best decision

Each of these errors results in its own types of problems for the department, so it's important to consider each of these three common errors individually.

Not Describing the Type of Employee Really Needed

It often happens that deadlines arrive and search committees find themselves confronted with a set of applications that, in their view, does not adequately represent the amount of gender or ethnic diversity that exists in their field. At other times, problems emerge only after an employee has been hired. Perhaps the department becomes concerned when it discovers that a candidate who looked so wonderful on paper is an extremely poor teacher. Perhaps the very person who seemed extraordinarily impressive throughout the entire interview process turns out to be highly uncollegial in dealing with others. Perhaps the candidate who was the top choice of every member of the search committee now seems resistant to the idea of assuming an equitable role in committee work or advising. In a surprising number of cases where these traits were among the most important factors in the success or failure of a new faculty member, they were not even mentioned as desirable qualifications in the position announcement.

The cause of this problem is clear. As academics, we have a natural tendency to focus on credentials and areas of specialty when we create position announcements, even though interpersonal and professional qualities tend to matter most in our day-to-day relationships with colleagues. As a department chair, it is your responsibility to counterbalance a search committee's natural desire to build a position announcement around the precise disciplinary subspecialty, type of academic credential, and amount of experience your faculty may initially be drawn toward and guide the position advertisement toward describing the sort of person you really need. For instance, in diversifying your pool of candidates, it is not enough to include a cold and generic statement that "women and minorities are invited [or even 'encouraged'] to apply," particularly if the rest of the advertisement appears to emphasize precisely those qualifications and areas of specializations in which women and members of minorities are least likely to be represented. Be sure to ask repeatedly as your committee is developing its job announcement: "What's really most important here? Finding a candidate with multiple years of experience in this precise area or achieving our department's goals in the area of diversity?" If diversity is truly a valued asset in your program, then perhaps it is worth broadening the disciplinary focus of the job description to include areas where diverse candidates are most likely to be found.

> As search committees prepare position announcements and job descriptions, one of the most important responsibilities of the chair is to maintain the search committee's focus on how the new faculty member will fit in with the department's current members, long-term plans, and unmet needs.

Modifying statements like "Ph.D. in hand required at time of application" so that they are more inclusive, such as, "doctorate required by time of appointment," may expand your pool of acceptable candidates. The latter phrasing allows candidates pursuing Ed.D.s, Psy.D.s, and other types of doctorates to be considered, as well as individuals who are close to completing their degrees but have not yet defended their dissertations. An even broader phrasing, "ABD [all but dissertation] required for rank of instructor; doctorate required for rank of assistant professor," allows you to consider a superior candidate who has not yet completed his or her degree; it also emphasizes the priority your institution places on employing faculty members with terminal degrees.

Furthermore, you will be likely to improve your recruitment of minority candidates if you replace unwelcoming phrases like, "Women and minorities are encouraged to apply," with more inviting wording, such as, "Our institution actively encourages applications from women, minorities, and individuals of every sexual orientation in keeping with its policy of promoting diversity throughout the institution." You may also wish to encourage your committee to place priority on applicants who have worked in a multicultural environment, have experience with diversity issues, or have engaged in scholarship on how to teach your discipline to students from a broad range of cultural backgrounds. When you state your intention to find a candidate with this type of qualification, you send the message that your department is doing much more than giving lip-service to the importance of a highly diversified faculty. These and other suggestions about how to write position descriptions that will attract larger numbers of minority candidates may be found in a number of excellent resources, including Turner (2002), Moody (2011), Barber and Cole (2003), Jones (2001), and Wolf, Busenberg, and Smith (1996).

If issues such as collegiality, excellence in teaching, and willingness to advise or perform academic service are important matters for your department, it's important to feature them prominently in your position announcement. Writing an advertisement in this way is the most sensible way of protecting your department's interest; if you ever have to let this faculty member go, you will be on much stronger ground if you can demonstrate that the person you hired failed to demonstrate the qualities indicated as essential in your advertisement. (Conversely, imagine how weak your case would be in a lawsuit if it appeared that you were dismissing someone for not having qualifications that appeared to be secret or at least undisclosed.) In addition, advertising for what you really need, as opposed to what certain members of your department may think you need, is the easiest way to attract individuals who possess those qualities. For instance, if developing collegiality is a goal in your department, require that

- Candidates define and address interpersonal relations in their letters of application
- Interviewers focus on collegiality in the reference calls and letters made on behalf of the candidate
- Committee members include expressions like "team player," "strong departmental citizenship," and "cooperative attitude" in the description of the person you are seeking

Where space permits, discuss why collegiality is so critical to the mission of teaching, scholarship, and service of your department. If excellence in teaching is a major concern at your institution, have all applicants submit a statement outlining their philosophy of teaching, make it clear that a significant part of the interview process will be evaluating the candidate's quality of instruction in different pedagogical settings, and suggest that development of a successful teaching portfolio will be an absolute requirement during the probationary period of the candidate you hire.

If service or advising are extremely high priorities, note those concerns in the advertisement itself. Although such statements may dissuade a few individuals from applying for your position, in the long run they are unlikely to be the sort of individuals who will succeed in your environment.

In short, your basic rule as you charge your search committee should be, "We may not always get the type of person we advertise for, but we're certain not to hire that type of person if we fail to mention the most important qualifications we're looking for in our advertisement or position announcement."

Not Including the Right Kind of Information About the Position or Your Expectations

Unless a candidate already knows a great deal about your institution and department, he or she is unlikely to have a very clear idea of precisely what it would be like to hold the position that you are advertising. Candidates are likely to wonder about the following issues:

- ○ Is this primarily a teaching position, primarily a research position, or some mixture of the two?
- ○ If it is primarily a teaching position, what is the course load?
- ○ How many courses taught by the faculty member are likely to be at the introductory level?
- ○ How many are likely to be at an advanced or graduate level?
- ○ Will there be any opportunity for the individual to develop new courses?
- ○ Will there be opportunities for or expectations of interdisciplinary work?
- ○ If the position is primarily in the area of research, what are the expectations for research?
- ○ Will start-up funds be available?
- ○ Will it be expected that the individual will need to secure external funding (and, if so, will there be the support of an office of research and sponsored programs)?
- ○ If the position requires a mixture of instruction and scholarship, in what proportions are the two activities likely to occur?
- ○ Will there be an expectation that the person hired involves students in his or her research, or are duties in the areas of teaching and scholarship usually unrelated?

Your department's job announcement will be extremely ineffective if you are not clear about your expectations in any of these areas. For instance, if the advertisement states that you are seeking an assistant professor, how can an applicant tell if you'll also accept (or even be permitted to accept) applications from people whose rank is already at the associate level or higher? If you state, "Minimum of one year experience preferred," will everyone on the search committee know how they should apply this preference when selecting candidates? And what sort of experience will you consider? Does this experience have to be in a faculty position at a college or university? Does related experience in another profession count? Moreover, what precisely do you mean when you say that you "prefer" this type of experience? Does this word imply that any experienced candidate will have an automatic advantage over any inexperienced candidate or that you are simply reserving the right to give priority to experienced candidates, all other factors being equal? Without spelling these issues out, members of the search committee are likely to apply these criteria unevenly.

In the long run, it's better for the search committee to develop a compelling reason at the beginning of their discussions about the type of qualifications and experience they regard as absolutely essential for the position. A guideline such as, "Minimum of three years teaching experience at an accredited four-year college or university," may be clear, but it also means that you will not be able to consider any candidate who does not meet that criterion, no matter how desirable the candidate may be in other ways. In a similar way, you might want to warn your search committee against using meaningless phrases like, "Some teaching experience preferred," since this type of phrasing tells an applicant almost nothing. For instance, a candidate whose only teaching experience has been a first-grade Sunday school class for five minutes can be said to have "some teaching experience." So, it's far better to have hard-and-fast requirements for the qualifications that you really need and to forgo taking up advertisement space with statements that only appear to express preferences.

Not Requesting the Type of Supporting Materials That Can Assist in Making the Best Decision

The final mistake that search committees tend to make in developing position announcements is to request a lot of materials that don't give them any real help in selecting the best candidate—and at the same time fail to ask for materials that could really be important.

UNNECESSARY MATERIAL You frequently see this wording in job advertisements: "In addition to a letter of application and current curriculum vitae, applicants should submit three letters of reference, official transcripts of all college work, and samples of publications."

Several things are wrong with such a request. First, letters of recommendation almost always tell you a good deal less than you are likely to learn by simply talking to the candidates themselves. Rather than asking for letters, it's much more productive to request the names, mailing addresses, telephone numbers, and e-mail addresses of three to five references. The reason that letters are not particularly helpful is that anyone can locate three individuals who are willing to write reasonably positive, upbeat letters on his or her behalf. As you know from your own experience writing letters of recommendation, if you know something negative about a candidate, it's easy to avoid mentioning it simply by focusing on whatever positive characteristics the candidate does have.

What you really want as a member of a search committee is the opportunity to ask follow-up questions, to describe your precise position and inquire whether the candidate is a good fit, and to ask the one question that you really need to know (and will almost never learn from reference letters): "Do you know anything about this candidate that if I were aware of it, might make me hesitant to extend a job offer?" Furthermore, some—and very likely the most desirable—candidates may not apply for your position because you have asked for letters of reference up front. After all, no one likes bothering their references to prepare letters for positions until they know that there is a good chance that they will be considered a serious candidate. And the more distinguished a reference is, the less frequently a candidate will wish to occupy that person's time with a letter for a job that's only a remote possibility. Moreover, some candidates will not want current employers and colleagues to know that they are considering new positions; these candidates are likely to rule out applying for any position that requires letters of recommendation at the very start of a search.

Second, there are almost no searches in which a department needs to request official transcripts as part of an application. To be sure, accrediting agencies do require institutions to obtain official transcripts, defined as transcripts marked with an official seal and mailed directly from the registrar of the issuing institution to the institution requesting them, without ever being in the possession of the candidate, once an individual is hired. For this reason, the submission of official transcripts is often a requirement that is expressed in an initial contract of employment. But there is almost never a reason for a search committee to compel a candidate to undergo the burden and expense of requiring official transcripts at the time of application. Some candidates will choose not to apply for your position rather than supply the transcripts. If your faculty members believe that it is absolutely necessary to review an applicant's course work and grades in order for them to prepare a list of semifinalists, be sure to request unofficial transcripts or photocopies of transcripts. This phrasing will provide you with the information that you need without imposing an obstacle to the candidates you would like to have in your pool.

Third, although evaluating the scholarship of applicants is certainly an important part of every academic search process, ask yourself whether it is truly necessary to review the publications of every single person who applies for your position. It is almost always preferable to request these materials from a select group of applicants only after an initial screening has been completed. Mailing books and offprints is an expensive proposition for candidates. Returning these items at the end of a search, should a candidate request them (and the vast majority of candidates do), can be an expensive and time-consuming process for your department. Furthermore, depending on the position you are seeking, you are likely to receive between sixty and two hundred applications. Is it going to be worth the time it takes your committee to examine all of the scholarly products submitted (in fact, are they really going to examine them with any care?) and is it going to be worth the space to store these items, even temporarily? In most cases, the answer to these questions will be no. So screen applicants on the basis of the information that they provide in their cover letters and résumés; request actual samples of publications only later in the search or to be brought to the interview.

IMPORTANT MATERIALS RARELY REQUESTED Yet if many departments ask for items that they do not really need in a search, they also fail to request submission of items that could really help them: statements of a candidate's philosophy of teaching, administration, scholarship, or service; a sample syllabus or final examination; a brief description of the best student project ever submitted to that candidate; suggestions about the "one book every student [or faculty member] in our discipline should read"; or a brief faculty development plan for teaching, scholarship, and creative activity over the next five years. As a general rule, encourage search committees to refrain from asking for items simply because "that's what we always put in a job announcement." Rather, begin the search process without preconceived notions about what candidates need to submit and then ask, "What sort of things will best tell us what we really need to know?"

The Position Description

Of course, certain decisions about position descriptions can be made only in the context of individual institutions and particular positions. For instance, do you ever refer to salary level in a job advertisement; if so, do you provide a range or merely say something general along the lines of, "Salary commensurate with experience"? In making this decision, there can be no hard-and-fast rule. (Your institution may, however, have definite guidelines on this issue.) If you provide a salary range, you run the risk of losing candidates who believe that the range offered is inadequate for their current needs. You may decide that such a situation is preferable to incurring the expense of bringing a candidate to campus only to discover that the individual is out of your price range. But your institution may offer certain intangible benefits—a beautiful location, extensive cultural opportunities, a safe and congenial community, and so on—that candidates need to experience in order to appreciate.

One general guideline is to avoid stating that a salary range is "commensurate with experience" if the remuneration for this position is already largely fixed. Your statement would be inaccurate in such a case and likely to cause hard feelings or worse later in the search. In a similar way, many institutions consistently make the mistake of terming their salaries as "highly competitive" and their benefits packages as "excellent" when neither of these is actually the case.

Other aspects of the position description should always appear, regardless of the type of job you are advertising or the nature of your institution. These are the guidelines that are inflexible:

- Always clearly indicate whether the position is tenure track, temporary, or for a set term.
- Always indicate whether any required qualification applies at the time of application or the starting date for the position.
- Always provide the starting date for the position.
- Always list the documents required for the application to be complete.
- Always provide the full name and contact information of the search chair.
- Always specify whether applications are acceptable in hard copy, electronically, or both. If the search committee or institution has a preference for how the application should be submitted, state it.
- Always clarify whether dates are postmark deadlines or deadlines for receipt of material. (It is a wise idea to make sure that this date is not a weekend or postal holiday.)

As a starting point, therefore, you might adapt the following position description to meet the needs of your department. The entire sample advertisement is almost certainly too long for many publications, but it does provide a template that may be adapted to a department's individual needs:

> **DISINGENUITY STUDIES.** Tenure-track position [rank will be instructor through associate professor, depending on applicant's qualifications and amount of college-level teaching experience]. ABD required by the starting date of the position, August 1, [YEAR]; doctorate preferred. Preference *may* be given to applicants with previous experience in teaching the methods of disingenuity or the theory and practice of duplicity at the college level. Duties will include teaching the survey course Disingenuity Studies for Nonmajors, as well as other undergraduate and graduate courses in a large, interdisciplinary program. A significant commitment to research will be required for tenure and promotion. Initial screening of selected applicants will occur at the AADSP conference in San Francisco on February 3–6, [YEAR]. Send letter of application, curriculum vitae, statement of teaching philosophy, sample syllabus for Disingenuity Studies for Nonmajors, research goals, and the names, addresses, e-mail addresses, and telephone numbers of five references to Professor Harvey Dent, Chair, Search Committee #999666, Department of Disingenuity Studies, Post Office Box 666, East Central Southern University, Northfield, West Dakota, [ZIP]. (Electronic applications not accepted.) **Postmark deadline: January 15, [YEAR].** East Central Southern University actively encourages applications from women, minorities, and individuals of every sexual orientation in keeping with its long-standing policy of promoting diversity throughout the institution. Persons who require accommodation(s) in the application process under the Americans with Disabilities Act should notify the search chair.

While some colleges and universities have established guidelines for precisely how job descriptions and position announcements must be phrased, others permit a great deal of latitude to the chair of the department or search committee. By carefully constructing an effective job announcement, departments are far more likely to attract candidates who will succeed in their environments and become long-term members of the academic community. Moreover, the process of developing a position description can guide the search committee itself to reflect more carefully on what it is trying to achieve through the current hire, what its goals for the future should be, and how it can best build on its past successes.

REFERENCES

Barber, E. G., & Cole, S. (2003). *Increasing faculty diversity: The occupational choices of high-achieving minority students.* Cambridge, MA: Harvard University Press.

Jones, L. (2001). *Retaining African Americans in higher education: Challenging paradigms for retaining black students, faculty, and administrators*. Sterling, VA: Stylus.

Moody, J. (2011). *Faculty diversity: A handbook* (2nd ed.). New York: Routledge.

Turner, C.S.V. (2002). *Diversifying the faculty: A guidebook for search committees*. Washington, DC: Association of American Colleges & Universities.

Wolf, L. E., Busenberg, B. E., & Smith, D. G. (1996). *Achieving faculty diversity: Debunking the myths*. Washington, DC: Association of American Colleges and Universities.

RESOURCES

Furlong, J. S., Heiberger, M. M., & Vick, J. M. (2008). *The academic job search handbook*. Philadelphia, PA: University of Pennsylvania Press.

Wilson, C. E., & Hochel, S. (2007). *Hiring right: Conducting successful searches in higher education*. San Francisco: Jossey-Bass.

19

UNDERSTANDING THE CHAIR'S ROLE IN THE SEARCH PROCESS

WE SAW IN THE previous chapter that department chairs can play important roles in searches from the moment that a position description is developed and a search is initiated. But the responsibility of the chair in faculty searches certainly does not end once the process is under way. To be sure, the defined role that department chairs play as searches continue can vary considerably from institution to institution. For instance, at some colleges and universities, the chair is a member of every search committee that falls within his or her discipline; at times, the chair may even be appointed to head every search that takes place within the department. At other institutions, the chair may participate in searches only when there is a direct and obvious connection between his or her field of specialty and the area in which the new hire will be made. At still other institutions, the search committee operates independent of the chair, preparing a list of acceptable candidates that must then be screened by the chair, the dean, and the provost, who ultimately select the finalists or the individual who will be offered the contract. But despite this wide variety in institutional practice, there tends to be little difference in the undefined role that the chair should play in faculty searches. After all, one of the central duties of the chair when it comes to faculty searches is to serve as an advocate for the discipline as a whole, to make sure—by direct involvement with the screening committee or indirectly through mentoring and moral suasion—that institutional search procedures are being followed, and to provide guidance so that the search committee will take all the appropriate steps necessary to locate and solicit applications from the best possible pool of candidates for the department and the discipline.

No matter how many differences there may be in the way that chairs choose to perform their duties related to faculty searches, there will always be two major areas of commonality: the chair's responsibility to focus and clarify the search process for everyone involved.

The Chair's Role in Focusing the Search Process

Department chairs need to make sure that each search committee's attention is consistently directed toward the specific traits and criteria that will most effectively help the department fulfill its central missions of instruction, scholarship, and service. Accomplishing this task is not always easy. Frequently, once a search gets well under way, a committee will become distracted by certain types of qualifications that do not advance—and may even be detrimental to—the overall success of the search. For instance, when reviewing the applicants' submitted materials, a committee may notice a particularly interesting achievement cited in the materials submitted by one candidate and then begin to screen out other candidates (sometimes consciously, sometimes unconsciously) because those applicants don't have a parallel achievement—even though that criterion was never stated in the search advertisement, never discussed as desirable during the department's original planning sessions for this position, and never before regarded as relevant to the strategic plan of the institution, division, or department.

In a similar way, a search committee may at times become preoccupied with a particular type of supporting document that one candidate has submitted—a statement of research philosophy, a letter of support from a nationally prominent individual, a particularly unusual set of instructional materials, or something else of this kind—and then begin to give significantly less attention to other candidates who may be equally qualified or even superior in terms of what the department really needs—all because those candidates did not submit materials that the search committee had never requested in the first place.

Finally, it is not at all uncommon for search committees to misunderstand their proper roles and try to make decisions for the candidate. It may come to your attention that the search committee is saying such things as, "Oh, we could never really interest this candidate. We wouldn't even be close to the salary that the person is making right now," or, "We couldn't offer the rank this candidate currently has, and I'm sure this person would not accept an offer at a lower rank," or even, "Well, I can't imagine why these applicants would leave their current institutions to come here." In all of these instances, search committees have been distracted from their primary responsibility of applying the search announcement's stated criteria in order to identify a pool of highly desirable finalists who can provide what the institution and the department need.

In situations like these, the department chair can serve as an effective advocate for reminding the search committee what they really are seeking in the candidates and what its overriding responsibility must be. If the chair is a formal member of the search committee, this goal can be accomplished directly at screening meetings. The chair can say something like, "Well, let's not forget what we set out to do when we planned this position. We said that what we really needed was X, not Y. And it's not fair to the other applicants, and maybe even not legal, to apply a different set of standards. If that's what we want to do—and I'm not really convinced that it is—then what we really ought to do is to cancel this search, readvertise the position, and state that this is what we want." In other situations, the chair could say, "I'm just not comfortable making that decision for this candidate. The individual applied for our position, and I believe we need to take this application seriously. Maybe the candidate has family in the area or is interested in working in a different sort of environment, and right now that seems more important than salary [or rank or whatever other extraneous factor seems to be distracting the committee]. I suggest that we screen for the criteria we agreed on, and then, if we end up making an offer, we let the candidate decide whether to accept it." If the chair is not officially a member of the search committee, guidance of this type may have to be offered in a more indirect manner. Depending on the situation, it may be appropriate for the chair to ask to meet with the committee in order to ask for an update while the search is still in progress. Or the chair may need to consult with a trusted member of the committee to ask about the criteria that are being used in selecting finalists.

In any case, department chairs should always be on the alert for the following indications that the focus of a search committee has shifted from its original purpose:

○ In searches where the successful applicant's primary responsibilities are going to be in, for instance, instruction, a disproportionate amount of attention being paid to research, offices held in scholarly associations, and other matters not particularly relevant to the department's instructional mission. In these cases, it can be extremely useful to say something like, "Well, all of that's great, but remember the single most important thing we said we need right now is a superb teacher."

○ In searches where the department is making a genuine and significant effort to diversify the faculty, a disproportionate amount of attention is being paid to specialties unlikely to attract women or minorities or to qualifications that, although certainly desirable, are in the long run less important to the institution than a faculty that best reflects the gender and ethnicity of the student body.

○ In any search, a set of screening criteria and weights that is significantly different from those stated in the search announcement. "Secret criteria," like hidden agendas, are never desirable in a department that wishes to avoid lawsuits and earn a reputation for candor and transparency.

The Chair's Role in Clarifying the Search Process

When candidates are invited for on-campus interviews, the department chair can play a valuable role by helping the search committee clarify what specifically it is attempting to accomplish through the interview process. For instance, search committees may need to be reminded that interviews are expensive and time-consuming activities. For this reason and for the sake of increasing the likelihood that the best possible candidate will be found, the resources devoted to the on-campus interview should be used wisely. Interviews should never be seen as opportunities "just to take a closer look at" a candidate and determine whether that person is qualified; qualifications and general suitability to the position can be checked through examination of written materials, reference calls, and telephone or video interviews with the candidate off-site.

> It is never appropriate to bring in a candidate for an interview just as a courtesy or simply "to take a look." No candidate should ever be interviewed who does not have a genuine, realistic chance that he or she will be offered the position.

On-campus interviews should focus on those activities that can only be done, or at least best be done, on-site and in person. How does the candidate relate to the sort of students with whom he or she will be dealing in this position? As the candidate observes the facilities and opportunities for research, scholarship, or creative activity, is there a good fit between what the institution can offer and what the individual brings in terms of experience, interest, and talent? Is there a reasonable amount of rapport between the candidate and coworkers? Does the individual understand and support the mission of your institution and department?

The department chair can also clarify that on-campus interviews are never times for courtesy interviews of candidates whom the institution would never hire. At times, individuals having some contact with the department—such as internal candidates, adjunct faculty members, alumni, friends of current faculty members, and the like—will be given consideration by a search committee that extends far beyond their suitability for the current position. "What harm would it do just to interview them?" committee members often ask. "They're here anyway. It wouldn't cost that much. And it would make them feel good." These attempts to spare someone's feelings by including that person in an interview process without a significant chance to obtain the position frequently lead to disaster. Rather than making the person feel better, they end up making that person feel far worse by giving a false impression that he or she has a good chance of obtaining the position. Situations such as this also produce a great deal of litigation as both the insider and other candidates who were not interviewed because they were not insiders may feel that the search process was not legitimate.

To avoid these problems, department chairs may wish to consider specifically charging each search committee with its specific task and goal: to examine one or more individuals who are already considered to be extremely highly qualified for the position and likely to be good additions to the department in order to determine whether any one candidate is the best possible fit.

Avoiding Common Errors Made by Search Committees

When search committees are not clear about their purpose in conducting on-campus interviews, they are far more likely to conduct interviews poorly, possibly even alienating the very candidate whom you most want to impress. Following are some of the most common errors search committees make because they have not thought through their overall purpose sufficiently.

Overscheduling Interviews

When search committees lack a well-defined idea of what they are trying to accomplish in an interview, they tend to lapse into either planning too many activities (and thus leaving a candidate exhausted) or planning too few (and thus leaving the impression that no one was taking the candidate seriously). Overscheduling may occur when the search committee members assume that they will develop a better understanding of the candidate by planning as many individual appointments as possible; alternatively, they may actually be trying to help candidates by exposing them to everything they can about what is occurring in the department and institution. The schedule then becomes one of taking the candidate to breakfast, shuttling the candidate around to appointment after appointment throughout the morning, taking the candidate to lunch, filling the entire afternoon with another series of meetings, and then ending the day with taking the candidate to dinner, possibly followed by a social event or other campus activity.

When questioned as to why the search committee has not allowed the candidates any time to explore campus on their own, rest their voice between appointments, or even collect their thoughts, the answer frequently given is, "Well, we want them to see as much as possible, and we want to see as much of them as possible. Besides, it gives a good impression of how busy things can be around here."

As a department chair, you are in an excellent position to warn against this dangerous thinking. Overscheduling interviews gives your best candidates an extremely poor impression of your department and campus. It makes you come across as individuals who do not respect one another's time, have difficulty planning even a fairly simple schedule like an interview, and have so little respect for visitors that they grill the candidate with questions mercilessly even while he or she trying to eat. Encourage your search committee to plan an interview with at least a little bit of downtime. Do not let them plan so many events and appointments that you end up making applicants feel harried and exhausted rather than impressed.

Underscheduling Interviews

In an effort to avoid overscheduling, some search committees go to the opposite extreme and underschedule an interview. While not planning at least some free time exhausts candidates and does not allow them to perform at their best, too much free time can give the impression that you have not planned the visit well or even that the faculty members, administrators, and students do not care enough about this position to share their days with the candidate.

The key goal should be planning and deciding what the interview process can reveal that can best be learned only in person. One possibility, if you feel that an interview schedule is seriously underplanned, is to offer the candidate different options: take a walk, tour the library, chat with some students, go over a map of the campus, make use of a room to go over his or her presentation or just to regroup, get a cup of coffee, visit the art gallery, see neighborhoods in town with a realtor, and the like. These options allow you to respond with sensitivity to a candidate's needs and interests without resorting to activities that are tiring for the candidate and uninformative for you.

Misscheduling Interviews

The most effective way of being certain that the interview schedule is not too full or too empty is to develop a clear idea of what you most want to discover in the interview and how best to discover it. If teaching is the most important aspect of this position, schedule sessions where you get to observe candidates teaching the sort of students who actually enroll at your institution and interacting with them in settings similar to those of day-to-day activities on your campus. Don't expose the candidate only to honors students or your best majors; find out how well they relate to the full variety of students in your program.

If research is the primary focus of the position, have the candidate present recent research findings, critique your current facilities and library holdings, and discuss with you an anticipated research agenda for the foreseeable future. Most important, schedule these events instead of other activities that may initially sound important but give you very little information that will help you in making a decision.

Courtesy visits—opportunities to meet the president, provost, dean, and other campus officials—should be either relatively brief or even omitted unless the person whom the candidate visits will be playing an active role in selecting the candidate. The basic question you should always ask your search committee about each planned activity is, "What will we gain from this appointment or event that we are not gaining from any other activity that has already occurred?" If the committee members cannot come up with a compelling, significant answer to that question, skip that event and allow your candidate more free time to pursue the optional activities that you have offered.

Department chairs can play an important role in making sure that searches are run effectively, no matter whether they serve on the search committee or not. They can guide the committee by asking the questions that need to be addressed before the position description is written, advertisements are placed, finalists are selected, or candidates are brought to campus. Hiring the people who will become our colleagues, assist us in educating our students, and bring new research expertise to our disciplines is one of the most serious responsibilities that department chairs have. Unless you work in a department that hires rarely, you should expect search activities to occupy a significant portion of your time. Few other activities can contribute more dramatically to the success or failure of your initiatives.

RESOURCES

Furlong, J. S., Heiberger, M. M., & Vick, J. M. (2008). *The academic job search handbook*. Philadelphia: University of Pennsylvania Press.

Lawrence, J. F., & Marchese, T. J. (1988). *The search committee handbook: A guide to recruiting administrators*. Washington DC: American Association for Higher Education.

McCann, L. I., & Perlman, B. (1996). *Recruiting good college faculty: Practical advice for a successful search*. San Francisco: Jossey-Bass/Anker.

Modern Language Association. (2010). *Advice to search committees and job seekers on entry-level faculty recruitment and hiring*. Retrieved from http://www.mla.org/jil_jobseekers_caf

Royer, H. J., & Vicker, L. A. (2006). *The complete academic search manual: A systematic approach to successful and inclusive hiring*. Sterling, VA: Stylus.

Ward, K., Sanders, K., & Bensimon, E. M. (2000). *The department chair's role in developing new faculty into teachers and scholars*. San Francisco: Jossey-Bass/Anker.

Wilson, C. E., & Hochel, S. (2007). *Hiring right: Conducting successful searches in higher education*. San Francisco: Jossey-Bass.

20

INTERVIEWING CANDIDATES

THE ABILITY TO INTERVIEW candidates effectively (and then to evaluate the answers that are given) is one of the most important skills a department chair can develop. Chairs usually interview not only applicants for faculty and staff positions in the department itself, but also other potential chairs and administrators, current faculty members who are being considered for promotion and tenure, and sometimes even prospective members of advisory of governing boards. So it's important for every chair to be as effective as possible when speaking to candidates and to make the best possible use of the limited time available for an interview.

Some chairs focus more extensively on the content of an answer, believing that there are right and wrong ways to teach the material of the discipline and to develop research agendas, while others focus more on process or style. They want to know how the candidate reaches conclusions, acting according to the principle that different people may reach different but equally valid conclusions and that it's the candidate's reasoning, not the result, that needs to be explored. They become interested in matters of style too, because of the clues these answers provide as to whether the person is likely to be a collegial member of the department if hired. In truth, most department chairs evaluate content, process, and style simultaneously, giving an applicant credit for an unexpected response as long as his or her justification seems appropriate and does not suggest that that the faculty member will be a difficult colleague.

Conducting the Interview

As you conduct an interview, don't waste time asking about information that you could easily have already gleaned from the candidate's résumé.

Rather, spend your time learning, in the limited time available, what you really need to know. Since the candidate is likely to be nervous (even if that anxiety does not immediately seem apparent), start the interview with an open-ended question that he or she could take in a number of different directions but allows a few moments for the person to relax and gather his or her thoughts. Some possible opening questions include:

○ Why are you interested in this position?

○ What has been the most satisfying aspect of your current research?

○ What do you believe your greatest strength will be as a faculty member?

○ Describe for me your single most rewarding teaching experience.

○ What do you see as your career goals over the next five to ten years?

After the candidate has had a bit of time to relax, you can begin proceeding to the issues that are most important to you. For instance, if you'd like to know more about an item on the applicant's vita, ask about that next. Or describe a hypothetical situation that the person might face in teaching, research, or service, and ask the candidate to describe how he or she might handle it. Remember that the best hypothetical questions aren't those with obviously right or obviously wrong answers. These questions are most effective when they tell you something about the applicant's priorities or ways of dealing with difficult problems, not his or her ability to guess the one correct answer you're looking for.

Try whenever possible to intersperse questions about specific aspects of the job with more general questions that give the candidate an opportunity to expand on earlier responses. For instance, after asking the candidate the amount of start-up funding he or she would need in order to continue current research, you might ask something like, "In addition to the duties that we outlined in the job description, what sort of service to the department would you see yourself providing?" or "Can you give me a few examples of your ability to work effectively even with tight deadlines or under pressure?"

Applicants for jobs try to anticipate the questions they'll be asked. For this reason, their initial answers may seem rehearsed or designed primarily to tell you what they think you want to hear. Therefore, be sure to ask a lot of follow-up questions, probe more deeply, and request specific examples whenever you receive what appear to be overly general replies.

The job interview is a kind of audition: candidates shouldn't simply tell you what they'll do once they're hired; they should also show you, perhaps through opportunities to teach a sample course and the concrete examples they provide to illustrate their answers.

Interviews should not just be about the candidates themselves. They should also be about having the candidate speculate about how he or she would address the various responsibilities of the position. Ask the candidate questions related to situations and challenges that are likely to occur for a faculty member in your department, and see if you can determine how the candidate will handle each of the opportunities and challenges that are likely to come along. Since these questions are almost impossible for applicants to anticipate, they may not respond immediately, and it can be tempting to fill what will feel to you like an awkward silence. But don't fill these silences. They are the times when the candidate is thinking carefully rather than relying on a rehearsed script, and the answers that will emerge from them will probably be the most candid and informative of the entire interview.

If you have difficulty thinking of appropriate questions to ask as the interview continues, here are some suggestions:

QUESTIONS ABOUT TEACHING

- Who were the three most memorable students you ever taught? What made them memorable?

- Give me an example of what you've done to make learning in your courses active rather than passive.

- What are students likely to gain from a course you've taught that they wouldn't gain from anyone else who taught them the same course?

- What are you looking for when you're considering a particular textbook or set of course materials to adopt?

- What are some of the ways in which you've addressed the different needs of, say, auditory, visual, and experiential learners in your courses?

- How would you describe your philosophy of teaching?

- Do you have any experience in teaching students of nontraditional age? Teaching students from a diversity of social or ethnic backgrounds? Teaching graduate students?

- Have you done anything that provides evidence of support for interdisciplinary studies or for academic disciplines outside your own field?

○ If there were one book that all first-year students in college were required to read, what should it be?

QUESTIONS ABOUT RESEARCH

○ What was the most important thing you ever learned from a research project that failed?

○ If you had to rely on only three sources to keep up with the most important developments in your field, what would they be?

○ What are your three biggest research priorities over the next ten years? How do you intend to achieve those goals?

○ Describe for me the perfect research environment. Don't just focus on equipment and funding; tell me as well about the time you'd hope to have relative to your other responsibilities, the relationship you'd like to have with your colleagues, your interaction with graduate or advanced undergraduate students, and so on.

QUESTIONS ABOUT COLLEGIALITY

○ Think back on the colleague or fellow student whom you regarded as the most irritating, difficult, or frustrating. What did this person do that so annoyed you?

○ How do you define *collegiality*, and how do you attempt to exemplify it in the work that you do?

○ If I were to talk with someone who's had a conflict or disagreement with you, what is that person likely to tell me?

○ Describe the people you worked with in your last position.

○ Describe the type of person with whom you work best.

○ Describe a particularly challenging interpersonal problem you had and how you went about trying to solve it.

QUESTIONS ABOUT FIT

○ What is the greatest challenge facing college professors today?

○ What makes you unique as an individual?

○ What's the most interesting book you've read in the past six months that wasn't related to your discipline?

○ What achievement would you most like to have made by the end of your first year here?

○ What about this particular position at this particular institution makes you most suitable for it?

○ What has been your least successful work experience? Why did that situation come to mind?

○ Have you ever hand to bend a rule or policy in order to achieve a significant goal?

GENERAL QUESTIONS

○ What part of academic life gives you the most pleasure? What part do you find the least enjoyable?

○ What would you regard as the proper balance between scholarship and teaching for faculty members today?

○ What achievement would you like to look back on after your first year as a faculty member here?

○ If you could develop your knowledge or skills in any one area, what would it be?

○ What is your favorite word in the English language? Why?

○ How do you define success?

○ Based on what we've discussed here today, what do you see as the most important aspects of this position?

○ What have I forgotten to ask you?

It's a good idea to close the interview by asking the candidate if he or she has any questions to ask you. It can be a red flag if the candidate has no questions whatsoever, particularly if the conversation is occurring fairly early in the interview process; either the candidate isn't that interested in the position, hasn't done any homework, or has been preoccupied solely with rehearsing the "right" answers to interview questions instead of thinking more globally about the position you're offering. But it can also be a red flag if the questions the candidate asks are all about the benefits of the position rather than the work that is involved. This type of response tends to suggest that the candidate's focus in more on what he or she is going to receive from your department than on the contribution he or she is willing to make.

Videoconferencing, including desktop resources such as Skype and iChat, makes it possible for you to interview candidates in ways that go far beyond the in-person, on-campus interview. A laptop can be set up that allows you to see the faculty member teach one of his or her current courses, tour the faculty member's studio or laboratory, and answer many of your questions right from his or her office. The widespread use of technology can greatly reduce the cost of faculty searches, at the same time that it provides you and the other members of the search committee with a better insight into the candidate's actual strengths and weaknesses.

Evaluating the Candidate's Responses

As you evaluate a candidate's answers to your questions, consider whether they seemed of a length appropriate to the seriousness of the issue you were discussing and whether the candidate seemed to understand your department's individual needs and priorities. Was the candidate overly simplistic in the way he or she addressed complex issues? Did the person's replies seem totally out of character with the applicant's level of experience? There will be times when your instinct will tell you that although the candidate was saying the right thing in response to each question, something about the interview just didn't feel right. You'll know better than anyone else the degree to which you can trust your own gut feelings, but in most cases, if you sense that something is off during the interview process, you'll at least want to explore matters more carefully with references before offering the position to that candidate.

Areas of Caution

Search committees, particularly when they are composed of faculty members inexperienced in conducting faculty searches, may well need some guidance in the types of questions they should or should not pose to the candidates. It is all too easy, during casual conversation with an applicant, to ask questions that may inadvertently lead the committee into unacceptable areas. For this reason, you may wish to caution your search committee and the other members of your department to take special care against asking even seemingly innocent questions that could later result in a complaint against your department or the failure of a search. A few examples of these seemingly innocent questions include those dealing with these topics:

- ○ *Marital status.* "How shall I address you? As Miss or Mrs.?" "Do you have a family?" "Will your wife be accompanying you when you visit?" "What are the ages of your children?"
- ○ *Clubs, organizations, and religion.* "We have quite a number of wonderful civic and religious groups here in town. Would you be interested in hearing about any of them?"
- ○ *National origin.* "What a fascinating name! What nationality is that?" It is, however, permissible to ask, "Are you legally

authorized to work in this country?" In fact, before hiring a candidate, your institution will be required to ascertain the answer to that question.

o *Age.* "These are very impressive credentials for someone your age! How old were you when you started teaching?" or, "Why would you want to move so far away from home when you'll be retiring in a couple of years?"

o *Disability.* "How did you receive that injury?" "We have had to reschedule this interview a couple of times. Are you sick a lot?" "But we're all having wine with dinner. Why won't you?"

Remind your faculty not to ask these questions at social occasions or during formal interviews. The important thing is to ensure that all questions—regardless of where they are asked—deal solely with qualifications, experiences, and attitudes that are directly relevant to the professional position itself. A good general rule should always be to treat applicants with the same courtesy and fairness that we ourselves would wish to receive.

Interviewing Other Administrators

Another occasion on which department chairs may be asked to conduct an interview is when their institution is considering applicants for an administrative position. Sometimes this opportunity arises because there are a number of free-standing programs in the chair's own department and a search must be conducted for a new program director or, at least, for an assistant chair to help the chair with the workload. At other times, the chair may be asked to serve as an external representative on another department's search for its own chair. And quite often chairs are invited to serve on search committees for deans, academic vice presidents, or other senior administrators.

These opportunities, although usually welcome, at times pose a problem. After all, most department chairs have had experience interviewing candidates for faculty positions, but this isn't always the case when interviewing candidates for administrative positions. It's not always immediately apparent which sort of question will reveal to you what you really want to know and will do so in a way that allows the candidate to demonstrate something of his or her personality, creativity, or individual style. As a result, we all too frequently fall back on trite or unimaginative questions, such as, "What is your management style?" "Tell me about one of your faults," or "What first attracted you to higher education administration?"

Rather than reverting to overused questions, which most candidates have been asked dozens of times, it's far better for the chair to plan for an administrative interview by considering what it is that he or she needs to know about the candidate in each of the five key areas:

1. Experience
2. Knowledge
3. Point of view
4. Approach
5. Fit with this particular position and with your institution as a whole

Once you determine what you need to know in each of these areas, it will be relatively easy for you to come up with a question that allows that information to emerge, probes a bit more deeply beneath the surface, and allows the candidate to draw on his or her own experience and relate it to the new responsibilities of this particular position.

As in faculty interviews, it is better to begin by asking more general or open-ended questions, following up more precisely if needed. Just as you would probably not ask a candidate for a faculty position, "Would you be willing to teach a course in X?" (since even the most inexperienced candidate know that the only correct answer to this question is, "Yes, of course"), it is equally unproductive to ask an administrative candidate a question like, "Are you interested in helping us do Y?" A far more productive question to the prospective faculty member is, "As you examine our curriculum, what are some of the areas where you would have the greatest enthusiasm about teaching? What areas not currently in our curriculum would you be most interested in developing?" In the same way, it is more revealing to ask administrative candidates questions that do not offer them simple yes-or-no choices but allow them to elaborate and draw on their own perspectives.

Here are a few possible questions in each of the five areas outlined above. While all of these questions have been used in actual interviews, it's probably more useful for you not to ask them exactly as they're written here but to consider them as a basis for stimulating your own, more individual questions. In other words, try to develop questions with the same goals as those that follow, but more tailored to your institution, your department, and the specific position that you're searching for.

QUESTIONS ABOUT EXPERIENCE

- What would you regard as your most significant accomplishment in your current position?

○ If you were to leave your current position, what quality or aspect of your work would others at your institution miss the most?

○ Describe the biggest professional mistake you ever made and how you fixed it.

○ What was the toughest decision that you have ever had to make in your career? How did you go about making that decision? What made it so difficult?

○ What was the most unpopular decision that you've ever had to make in your career? How did you go about making that decision? What made it so unpopular?

○ Give me a specific example of a problem that you have solved. What resources did you use in solving that problem?

○ What's the most creative or innovative thing you've ever done?

○ What have you learned about managing growth in an academic setting? What have you learned about managing retrenchment or cutbacks?

○ If I had to select between you and a candidate who happened to have more experience in this area, what are some of the reasons why I should still choose you?

QUESTIONS ABOUT KNOWLEDGE

○ How do you think Boyer's four functions of scholarship might apply to faculty development and evaluation in our program? [See Boyer, 1990.]

○ What principles would you use in allocating scarce resources among compelling critical needs?

○ Which recent work about issues in higher education do you believe every member of our department might profit from reading?

○ In which professional organizations should administrators in our area maintain active memberships? Which professional organizations do you believe have the most productive and informative meetings?

QUESTIONS ABOUT POINT OF VIEW

○ If you had an opportunity to have a conversation with anyone— either a contemporary or some historical figure—who would it be? Why?

○ What do you do to relax?

○ What would you add to our institution that we'd be unlikely to get from another candidate?

○ What would you describe as your own personal core values? What, in other words, are the values or principles that you regard as nonnegotiable?

○ Where do you see yourself in five years? Ten years? Why is that particular plan, goal, or trajectory important to you?

○ What tends to give you the greatest satisfaction in your work? What tends to frustrate you the most?

QUESTIONS ABOUT APPROACH

○ What is a current trend in higher education that you believe is really a wrong direction or at least a fad that will not last very long?

○ What is the biggest challenge facing academic administrators today?

○ What specific problem or challenge would you want to address first if you were to receive this position?

○ If you were to be offered this position, how would you spend your time preparing for it in the interim before you actually started?

QUESTIONS ABOUT FIT

○ What do you like least about your current position?

○ What tends to annoy you? Describe for me a number of specific situations that, when they occur, cause you to feel there's a real problem that needs to be solved.

○ How will I know when you are angry [or being serious or just kidding]?

○ What do people who don't like you say about you?

○ If I were to speak to the people who report to you in your current position, how would they describe you?

---------------○---------------

In addition to the questions suggested in this chapter, a number of useful resources can guide you further in formulating your interview questions and steer you away from areas that may be inappropriate or legally questionable—for example:

○ DeLuca (1997), which is not intended for the academic market but is a useful source of additional interview questions. It also provides a good summary of well-thought-out answers to the various questions.

○ Falcone (1997), which also is focused more on the business market than the academic world, provides valuable help in how to phrase informative and revealing interview questions.

○ McCabe and McCabe (2000), which contains a section on searching in the academic setting and on what occurs during interviews (albeit from the candidate's perspective). This book deals primarily with the natural sciences, particularly the health sciences, although it certainly has applications in other fields as well.

Other reference works containing sources of interview questions are listed in the Resources section below. Finally, for insights into how to view the interview process from the perspective of the candidate, see Buller (2010).

REFERENCES

Boyer E. L. (1990). *Scholarship reconsidered: Priorities of the professoriate.* Princeton, NJ: Carnegie Foundation for the Advancement of Teaching.

Buller, J. L. (2010). *The essential college professor: A practical guide to an academic career.* San Francisco: Jossey-Bass.

DeLuca, M. J. (1997). *Best answers to the 201 most frequently asked interview questions.* New York: McGraw-Hill.

Falcone, P. (1997). *96 great interview questions to ask before you hire.* New York: AMACOM.

McCabe, E.R.B., & McCabe, L. L. (2000). *How to succeed in academics.* Orlando, FL: Academic Press.

RESOURCES

Cipriano, R. (2011). *Facilitating a collegial department in higher education: Strategies for success.* San Francisco: Jossey-Bass.

Cottingham, K. L. (2010). *Questions to ask (and be prepared to answer) during an academic interview.* Retrieved from http://www.dartmouth.edu/~gradstdy/careers/services/interview/acad.html

Hoevemeyer, V. A. (2006). *High-impact interview questions: 701 behavior-based questions to find the right person for every job.* New York: AMACOM.

Leeds, D. (1987). *Smart questions: A new strategy for successful managers.* New York: McGraw-Hill.

Podmoroff, D. (2005). *501+ great interview questions for employers and the best answers for prospective employees.* Ocala, FL: Atlantic Publishing.

Sies, M. C. (1998). *Questions one should be prepared to answer for job interviews.* Retrieved from http://otal.umd.edu/~sies/jobquess.html

Tips for the academic job interview. (n.d.). Retrieved from http://gradschool.unc.edu/student/profdev/documents/NegotiationsHandout_000.pdf

Veruki, P. (1999). *The 250 job interview questions you'll most likely be asked: And the answers that will get you hired!* Avon, MA: Adams Media Corp.

21

LETTING SOMEONE GO

THERE IS A COMMON image of academic administrators as individuals who relish forceful displays of their own power, enjoy wielding the stern authority that comes with their positions, and revel in their ability to refuse even the simplest request. Certainly despotic administrators do exist in academia, just as they exist in every other profession. But the vast majority of college administrators regard giving employees bad news as the absolutely worst part of their jobs. They much prefer the opportunity to say yes to people whenever they are able, dreading those days when the budget, existing policies, or other constraints make granting a request impossible. And the worst of the worst news that any department chair ever has to convey to anyone is that he or she no longer has a job.

Firing an employee has a severe and sometimes lasting effect on that person's income, career, and self-esteem. There are relatively few situations in which one can claim that a termination is "nothing personal": to the individual who will now be out of work, it is a very personal matter indeed. Probably more than any other part of their positions, firing someone is what keeps department chairs awake at night. They worry about potential lawsuits, coping with the employee's hostility (or possibly even violence), and the look in an employee's eyes just after receiving the news that his or her career at the institution has ended.

No advice will ever make this distasteful task palatable. Nevertheless, there are a number of strategies you can consider in order to protect yourself, your institution, and even the person you are terminating.

Get advice and support.
There is never any reason to go it alone when you're terminating someone. Before you take any action whatsoever, contact the

appropriate person on your institution's human resource staff. In most cases, you should also touch base with the legal affairs office or your campus attorney; we live in a litigious society, and terminations can be extremely litigious matters. Your institution's human resource staff and legal counsel will advise you on which policies must be followed, when and in what form notification needs to be given, whether witnesses must or should be present, how much of a paper trail is adequate for this dismissal, and even whether you ought to be taking this action in the first place. At the very least, consultations with capable, discreet individuals who have probably dealt with significantly more terminations than you have will provide an external scan to make sure that you have asked the right questions, followed the right procedures, and prepared yourself to be asked some potentially difficult questions.

Act sooner rather than later.

Many times department chairs delay letting someone go because the task of dismissal is unpleasant and there is always a chance that the situation may improve. This is almost always a mistake. Although there are undoubtedly a few cases somewhere of a chair who later regrets letting someone get away, nearly every seasoned chair has stories about people who should have been dismissed but were allowed to remain at an institution until it was far too late.

The faculty member who goes up for tenure, with full anticipation of being approved only to be denied, should be the rare exception in academe. If your institution does not have a systematic, formal pretenure review in a faculty member's second, third, or fourth years of service, start one in your own department. In fact, it's highly desirable to conduct some sort of formal review of tenure-track faculty members every year. Some of these reviews can be formative; these sessions can be collegial and supportive meetings with the chair and a few members of the senior faculty in which constructive advice is given and a plan for the future is developed. Some of these meetings should, however, be summative; the faculty member should be told clearly whether adequate progress is being made toward tenure and promotion, where improvements are required, and whether the individual's performance to date has met the expectations of the department and institution.

Although you will conduct some of these sessions yourself, it is inadvisable for the chair to be the only individual who reviews tenure-track faculty members annually. Tenure decisions are, after all, usually based on committee recommendations and tend to require ratification at higher administrative levels. Whenever possible, see if your own evaluation matches that of your departmental personnel review committee, the dean, and the provost. It is better to find out sooner rather than later that different levels draw different conclusions about the adequacy of an individual's progress in instruction, scholarship, and service.

In any case, it is always better not to renew a contract as soon as there is a clear consensus that the faculty member is not a good match for the institution or the duties assigned. It may seem merciful to keep giving an unsuccessful teacher or researcher numerous additional chances, but it is not. The longer an individual remains at an institution, the more difficult it is for this person to explain his or her involuntary departure to potential future employers. People may also feel that sheer length of service is itself an endorsement of their performance, sending a false or mixed message that you certainly wish to avoid.

For tenured faculty members, the difficulty of your task increases tremendously. But you should remember that despite the manner in which tenure is viewed at some institutions, it does not guarantee continued employment to faculty members who fail to perform the duties of their position, violate the law or institutional policy, or behave in a manner that is seriously detrimental to your program or your institution. What tenure provides an individual is the right to be given a reason for the dismissal and respond to that reason through some form of due process appropriate to your institution. There will certainly be specific and detailed procedures for the steps you must take in dismissing a tenured faculty member. Always consult legal counsel in these situations before you take any formal action and at each step along the way. But you should never rule out dismissing a seriously underperforming faculty member or one who has flagrantly violated a major institutional policy simply because that person is tenured.

In cases involving staff members, your institution will almost certainly have established policies and procedures outlining the notice you need to provide and on what timetable. If you work in a unionized environment, these guidelines are likely to be quite specific. If your institution is located in an at-will state (one in which employers are not required to provide a reason when firing an employee), you may not need to give the staff member whom you're terminating any explanation for your action; you may, however, be required to pay unemployment compensation to any employee you dismiss without providing a reason.

> In situations where the dismissal of a faculty member is involved, always ask yourself, "Which option does more harm for our students and for the institution as a whole: letting this person remain on the staff or letting the faculty member go?"

Have a witness present if at all possible.

Even at institutions where witnesses are not required, it is always advisable to have a third party present when you are dismissing someone. The presence of this person can be extremely useful if there is ever a question at a later date about specifically what was said, promised, and done. Particularly in cases when the chair and the employee are of different genders or sexual orientations or where there has been a history of tension and animosity, a witness can verify that the proper policies were followed and that nothing inappropriate occurred behind closed doors.

When selecting a witness, you may wish to have present someone from your institution's human resource or legal affairs office who has dealt with other terminations and can offer you guidance about what to say. Meet privately with the witness before joining the employee you will dismiss in order to plan your strategy, go over precisely who will say what, whether a written dismissal will be given to the employee, and remind one another of the importance of discretion and courtesy in matters of this sort.

Read and follow your institution's internal procedures scrupulously.

In cases of dismissals, more problems—including legal vulnerabilities—occur because of failure to follow internal institutional guidelines and procedures than from any other cause. You have come to this difficult decision after much anxiety and soul searching; you don't want it all to collapse as the result of a technicality. Be sure that all timetables for various types of notifications have occurred. If your institution requires a series of oral and written warnings before you can proceed to a dismissal, be certain that you have taken these steps. Notify all the individuals whom your institution requires you to notify. Prepare a checklist of all the steps your institution requires you to take, and be certain that all these steps have been taken.

Maintain good documentation.

You are on the safest ground if you have maintained a clear paper trail that leads up to this dismissal. In most cases, you will want a series of performance appraisals that indicated the employee was informed of improvements that needed to occur, a timetable by which to take required action, and indications that the required action has not been taken. Even if the documentation is not this clear, it is extremely useful to have documentation of conversations held in which you spoke to the employee about concerns with his or her performance, e-mail messages illustrating the problems for which the employee is being dismissed, time cards or attendance records suggesting the employee's failure to perform the full functions of the position, or other clear, written evidence that will suggest to a reasonable observer that you were justified in terminating the employee.

Don't reveal more than necessary.

When it comes to letting someone go, less is definitely more in terms of what you say. The more you tell the employee being dismissed, the more you run the risk of legal challenges, misinterpretations, and multiple appeals. For staff members, if you are living in an at-will state and your institution is willing to pay the required weeks of unemployment benefits, you are better off providing no reason for your action at all. Similarly, in the case of untenured faculty members, unless you are specifically required by your institution, it is far preferable to give no reason for a nonrenewal.

Some department chairs don't realize that there is never a legal requirement to provide a reason for dismissing an untenured faculty member at the end of a contract. In fact, some institutions and state systems forbid stating reasons for dismissing an untenured faculty member. The reason is that untenured faculty members are on annual employment contracts and have no legal right to expect their extension during their pretenure, probationary period. The difference is roughly akin to that between contracting someone to paint your house and contracting someone to deliver your daily newspaper. The house painter works for the duration of the contract and, when that period is over, has no right to expect future employment from you unless you specifically offer a new contract. The newspaper service will keep delivering a daily paper to you unless you specifically instruct it to stop (or unless you fail to pay for the service, which amounts to an instruction to cease delivery). Although the comparison is certainly not perfect, the untenured faculty member is like the house painter: after the expiration of each contract, you can part ways for no reason whatsoever. The tenured faculty member is more like the person who delivers your newspaper: there is an expectation that the relationship will continue unless you specifically give instructions to the contrary.

Even when a tenured faculty member is being terminated, it is better to say less rather than more. In these situations, there is rarely only one reason or one occurrence of an action that has led to the dismissal. (In cases where there is only one reason, the violation of policy will have been so egregious that the result is likely to seem fairly clear-cut.) The tendency of many department chairs when dismissing a tenured faculty member is to want to cite every reason in an effort to justify the termination. In many cases, this approach is a mistake. Certain reasons will be stronger and more compelling than others. By including a large number of weaker reasons in an effort at justification, department chairs can actually undermine their own case. They can open more opportunities to appeal and make even their strongest reasons seem trivial in the context of so many weak explanations. The result is that it is far better in situations where there are multiple reasons for dismissing a tenured faculty member to place your emphasis on the one indisputable reason than to attempt an approach that sacrifices the quality of your argument for the quantity of explanations you can introduce.

Be humane but honest.

No matter how difficult your relationship has been with the employee you are terminating, it is important to realize that the situation will be stressful for that person, possibly devastating to his or her career and self-esteem. Extend all the courtesy, respect, and professionalism you can possibly bring to the situation. As you review in your mind how you will approach the conversation, ask yourself how you would wish to be treated—or how you would wish your child to be treated—if you were in a similar position for whatever reason. At the same time, our tendency to want to make a painful situation more bearable can lead us to say things that we don't really mean. Because of a terminated employee's tears or look of hurt, we may start to praise aspects of the person's performance that in other situations we might not regard as of particularly high quality. It is important not to send mixed messages about the individual's performance that can end up complicating your task later. Be clear and direct in stating what you had planned to say, but do not be unnecessarily heartless in your phrasing or demeanor.

Understand that the employee will require more than one conversation on this topic.

When employees hear that they have been terminated, it is rather like hearing a death sentence. Their reaction is one of shock, and for a significant time afterward, they may not be processing everything that you are telling them. After they digest the news that you have given them and discussed it with their family and friends, they will inevitably have additional questions, concerns, and possibly even anger.

You should expect that the employee will engage you in further conversations, or at least try to do so, and you may not know when the next conversation will occur. The employee may make an appointment a day or so after the original encounter; the conversation may also occur impromptu when you are blindsided in the hallway, restroom, or off-campus. Be prepared for these follow-up conversations. Know in advance precisely what you will say and where you will draw the line in saying anything more. In truly difficult situations, you may need to say, "I've told you everything I have to say about this matter. From this point further, you'll need to direct those questions to the office of human resources or to the college attorney."

If you have decided not to provide reasons for the termination, don't allow the unexpected nature of these encounters to make you deviate from this plan. You may be tempted, for instance, in a more informal encounter with the employee to provide additional information about what he or she could have done better as a means of helping that person in the future. This type of mentoring may seem valuable, but it is fraught with peril. The informal guidance you give the employee may be construed as supplying the reason for the dismissal. So, be kind and as supportive as you can, but don't provide any information in a later conversation that you intentionally omitted from your initial meeting.

---------o---------

The essential principle set out in Chapter One remains of vital importance in any matter involving termination: remember to use your resources. There is no need to reinvent the wheel when firing someone. This is an area of administration in which there are numerous excellent sources. Among the best are Levin and Rosse (2001), Repa (2000), Weiss (2000), Fleischer (2005), Falcone (2002), Covey (2000), and Horowitz (1999). Combining the insight provided by these guides with the instructions of your institution's legal counsel and human resource office will not make this task any more pleasant, but it will help protect you, your department, and the institution as a whole.

REFERENCES

Covey, A. (2000). *The workplace law advisor: From harassment to discrimination policies to hiring and firing guidelines: What every manager and employee needs to know.* Cambridge, MA: Perseus.

Falcone, P. (2002). *The hiring and firing question and answer book.* New York: AMACOM.

Fleischer, C. H. (2005). *The complete hiring and firing handbook: Every manager's guide to working with employees legally.* Naperville, IL: Sphinx Publishing.

Horowitz, A. S. (1999). *The unofficial guide to hiring and firing people.* New York: Macmillan.

Levin, R., & Rosse, J. G. (2001). *Talent flow: A strategic approach to keeping good employees, helping them grow, and letting them go.* San Francisco: Jossey-Bass.

Repa, B. K. (2000). *Firing without fear: A legal guide for conscientious employers.* Berkeley, CA: Nolo.

Weiss, D. H. (2000). *Fair, square and legal: Safe hiring, managing & firing practices to keep you and your company out of court.* New York: AMACOM.

22

A SCENARIO ANALYSIS ON
HIRING AND FIRING

FOR A DISCUSSION OF how scenario analyses are structured and suggestions on how to use this exercise most productively, see Chapter Nine.

Case Studies

Loose Cannon Wars

You chair a department that contains four related but independent programs, each with its own director possessing signature authority over his or her own program-specific operating expenses. It's early in the fiscal year, and one of your directors has just blindsided you with what you regard as a serious problem: he has just spent a significant part of his program's annual operating budget on a single piece of equipment. According to your institution's procedure, it was within that director's prerogative to make this decision, but you believe that it was unwise to do so and are concerned that the program will not have sufficient funding for the remainder of the fiscal year. Worse yet, you discover that the order for the piece of equipment cannot be canceled.

When you call the director into your office and ask why you were not consulted about this decision, you are reminded that he was doing no more than he was authorized to do, that he was hired to make tough decisions that would improve the program, that the institution's budget officer had been duly notified of this pending purchase, and that the piece of equipment would have cost more if not purchased during a fairly narrow window of opportunity (which conveniently occurred while you were away for a week with the president doing advancement work).

When you insist that it would have been prudent to wait until later in the year to make this purchase even though the cost of the item may go up, he reminds you, "We tried doing that for the last two years running. And because of midyear budget cuts, we lost the money we had been setting aside. It was my professional judgment—the judgment I'm paid to make—that we should spend the money now rather than lose it later." When you finally ask, in exasperation, what the program will do for money if it exhausts its entire budget before the year is over, the director replies, "Well, the institution will just have to find more money somehow. After all, if you penalize us, you're really just penalizing the students."

Divide and Conquer, or Bait and Switch?

For a long time, your department has had a high service load but relatively few majors. Because your institution generally allocates new faculty lines to departments graduating the highest number of majors each year, you are increasingly understaffed. Although you conservatively estimate that you need at least two new full-time faculty members, the dean has finally agreed to allocate you one additional full-time line. You find yourself confronted with a dilemma. The easiest way to address the workload issue in your department would be to divert the funding for this new position into hiring multiple adjuncts. By doing so, however, you are afraid that you will merely be bandaging over the workload problems in your area and completely dooming your already slim chance of ever getting a second additional line. Also troubling you is the possibility that the dean will feel that you have pulled a bait and switch, requesting funding for one purpose but using it for another. Ordinarily you would simply make an appointment with the dean to discuss this matter, but you need to act at once and the dean has just left for an extended research trip.

Considerations

1. As you reflect on "Loose Cannon Wars," consider these questions:

    a. What options do you have in solving this problem? Is there a way of holding the program director accountable without penalizing the students in his program?

    b. Is it ever appropriate to address this problem by working with part of the budgets of the other three programs in your department?

What conditions would have to occur to make you willing to consider this option? How might you make this solution more palatable to your other program directors?

c. Do you replace this program director? If so, do you do so immediately or only if the program actually creates a shortfall for the year? (Remember that the director technically had the authority to make this decision.) If so, what is the issue that prompts you to make your decision: the lack of proper consultation with you, the error in judgment, or something else?

d. Is this a problem that you take to the dean, or do you try to handle it internally?

2. As you reflect on "Divide and Conquer, or Bait and Switch?" consider these questions:

a. Which takes precedence as you make your decision: the department's short-term needs or your longer-term strategy for addressing the staffing situation in your area?

b. Although you cannot consult with the dean, what steps do you need to take to make certain that your decision is fully understood at that level? Is this an appropriate instance in your institution to go over the dean's head and consult with the next highest level of administration?

c. Is there an option that gives you the greatest amount of flexibility with the new position?

d. What other information do you feel you need to know in order to make the best possible decision in this case?

Suggestions

Loose Cannon Wars

This case provides good preparation for both current department chairs and those who wish to seek higher administrative positions. The central issue is delegation and the empowerment of others. In this situation, you have authorized the program director to make certain types of decisions. The problem is that he has now implemented that authority in a manner that you regard as inappropriate or unwise. The decision you now have to make is whether the director's action is so inappropriate or unwise that it requires your intervention and, if so, how you will intervene. Among the choices you have available are to do nothing (at least for the moment), regard the situation as a teachable moment, reprimand the director, replace him, or address the issue as a funding problem, not as a personnel problem.

Let's consider each of these five possibilities. The decision not to intervene, at least initially, will largely depend on how you interpret the phrase "serious problem." After all, the program director does have some valid points to make: he was working within the sphere of authority that he had been given, the item had been purchased at the most economical moment, recent history had demonstrated that leaving too large a budget unspent caused it to be reduced before the end of the fiscal year, and the director was merely taking a calculated risk. The questions you will need to consider carefully if you decide to do nothing are how essential the piece of equipment is to the program's success and how severe the budgetary problem will be if you need to bail this area out later in the year. If you find that you can justify the director's decision and, if necessary, cover any budgetary shortfall, it may be acceptable simply to reevaluate when you wish to be consulted on large expenditures and where the sphere of authority assigned to each of your directors ends.

This type of benign neglect is less desirable, however, if you believe that the director's decision will cause an ongoing problem for your department. For example, you would be right to be concerned with the director's cavalier attitude that "the institution will just have to find more money somehow," which is symptomatic of a larger problem. If this is the first time you've heard the program director utter a statement of this sort, it may be wise to assume the role of mentor and help him see matters within the larger picture of the department's (and institution's) needs. If the statement reflects a tendency this director has had to act in ways that benefit his own program to the detriment of others, you may want to consider a more formal reprimand, particularly if you've already discussed this issue several times before. Only in the event of gross mismanagement of institutional resources—such as purchasing a wholly unnecessary piece of equipment during a budget crisis—is immediate replacement of the director probably called for at this point. A personnel change, particularly one that affects an individual's salary and workload, is a serious undertaking, and it implies that you've lost all confidence in the director's leadership. Similarly, treating the issue as a budgetary problem rather than a personnel problem is probably justified only in highly unusual circumstances. It may well be that the program is significantly underfunded. (Very few program directors will ever declare that they are fully funded at the level they need.) The real issue is how the program director responded to that lack of funding. The situation has at least the appearance of being timed for precisely the moment when both you and the president were away, and the director's nonchalant attitude toward the impact of the purchase on other programs seems inappropriate at best. For this reason, although there is probably no reason to overreact by immediately dismissing the director, there is also probably no reason to treat the matter as though he did everything that was appropriate either.

Divide and Conquer, or Bait and Switch?

In this case, you're called on to make a hiring choice that is likely to affect your department for some time to come. In many ways, the dilemma hinges on balancing short-term and long-term needs. From a short-term perspective, hiring adjuncts has a number of clear advantages:

- It gives you a larger number of sections at the same cost, thus going much further toward meeting the demand for your courses and demonstrating that you're a careful steward of resources.
- The higher number of student credit hours that will be generated in this way helps strengthen your argument that you've been understaffed and that there's clear pent-up demand in your area.
- Using adjuncts in the short term doesn't preclude the possibility that you could reallocate the funding to a full-time position in a future year (after you've had time to consult with the dean about this issue and to plan for the position more strategically). However, if you were to use the position for a tenure-track position immediately, it becomes much harder to move in the opposite direction at a later date and to replace a person holding a full-time, multiyear contract with several adjuncts. In other words, using adjuncts gives you maximum flexibility.

Nevertheless, from a long-term perspective, it probably makes better sense to opt for the full-time faculty member:

- Full-time faculty members are likely to build your department in areas such as research and service in ways that are far less likely to emerge with adjunct faculty members.
- You won't need to undergo an awkward conversion with the dean when she returns to campus about why you had argued so long for a new line but then failed to fill one when it was given to you.

○ Since a single full-time faculty member will not be sufficient to cover current demand, you're not undermining your need for a second new position.

○ Although your area has relatively few majors now, it may be able to attract others if it grows. Full-time faculty are much more likely to give your program this type of visibility and outreach than are adjuncts, who frequently have limited contact with students outside their own courses.

Some might argue that these differences are more a matter of serving students versus building your own empire rather than considering matters from a short- versus a long-term perspective, and there are ways in which such an argument is valid. Nevertheless, as the chief advocate for your own academic field, you constantly have to balance global or university-wide needs against the specific needs of your own students, faculty, staff, and discipline. In this situation, most chairs will probably decide that the long-term needs of the faculty and discipline in this case take precedence over the short-term needs of current students and thus conclude that sticking to the dean's original offer and using the funding for a full-time position is the preferable alternative.

PART FOUR

MENTORING CHALLENGES AND OPPORTUNITIES FOR DEPARTMENT CHAIRS

23

HELPING FACULTY MEMBERS
SHARPEN THEIR FOCUS

ONE OF THE MOST perplexing challenges for department chairs is how to mentor faculty members who are excellent in many ways but do not focus their energy or attention so as to achieve all that they are capable of accomplishing. Unfocused faculty members may exhibit these characteristics:

- They're always flustered, complaining about how much there is to be done and then seemingly rushing off to do it, although they rarely produce any substantive results from all of this frenzied activity. While most faculty members may tolerate (or possibly even thrive in) all the demands that academic life places on their time, the unfocused faculty member too frequently seems overwhelmed even by minor challenges.

- They give you critical information, such as self-evaluations, annual budget requests, and textbook orders only after the deadline or, at best, at the moment they are due. If on more than one occasion you find the same person's report slipped under your door late in the evening on the day you needed it or e-mailed to you only when you are printing your own summary report to the dean, this is a faculty member who could desperately use your mentoring skills.

- They receive evaluations on which students routinely say that these professors' courses did not "remain on track" or "lacked structure." Unfocused faculty members frequently carry a lack of focus or organization from their departmental behavior into their courses. When students repeatedly comment about "a general lack of organization" in someone's courses, you may find that this criticism corresponds rather well with the concerns you are sensing in other areas of this faculty member's performance.

Although it can be difficult to help habitually disorganized people achieve greater focus in their work, it's not an impossible task. The advice each faculty member needs will vary, of course, according to individual work habits and personal style, but there are some general guidelines that you should use in either a formal performance review or an informal conversation. In all cases, the faculty member may be more receptive to the advice if you mention that you have personally found these suggestions helpful as a way of better organizing your own time.

Set goals and deadlines in a timely manner.

Unfocused faculty members frequently feel compelled to work on whichever problem has just caught their attention. You can provide useful advice about how to set priorities according to the overall importance of a task and the date at which it must be complete.

Devote a certain amount of time each day to vital, ongoing work.

Guide the faculty member in setting aside a specific amount of time, perhaps an hour a day, for consistent work on his or her most important tasks. These tasks are likely to be the work that has the greatest significance for the discipline or that faculty member's professional development. Encourage the faculty member to find a time that can be devoted to work each day without interruption. The period set aside should not be during regular office hours, and the faculty member should not even answer the phone or read e-mail during that period unless it is likely to be an emergency.

Don't overcommit or underestimate the amount of time that commitments will require.

A frequent challenge of unfocused faculty members is taking on too many obligations or assuming that they can complete a task in far less time than it ends up requiring. Encourage the faculty member to say no to low-priority tasks (such as service opportunities that occupy a great deal of time with minimal benefit for either the discipline or the faculty member) and to develop the habit of budgeting worst-case schedules rather than being overly optimistic. Have the faculty member limit the number of meetings and appointments to a realistic number on any given day. Always leave room in the person's schedule for emergencies and sudden changes that cannot be anticipated. Never overfill a day.

Track your use of time.

Ask the faculty member to keep a time log that records how his or her time is being spent each day, and then group these blocks of time into various categories. Work together with the faculty member to explore ways in which certain tasks can be done more efficiently or discarded entirely in favor of more productive activities. If the faculty member's appointments and meetings tend to go overtime, ask him or her to consider why this occurs: Does the person who is conducting the meeting focus on its primary purpose immediately, or does it take some time to get to the main topic? Do people tend to linger and talk long after the main purpose for the meeting has been completed? If you observe that the faculty member frequently seems rushed when trying to keep appointments, help this person analyze his or her use of time and determine how long each appointment actually runs. Go over these results with the faculty member, and together try to develop a more realistic estimate for how long should be blocked out for these appointments in the future.

Requiring unfocused faculty members to maintain elaborate time logs can be counterproductive. The time they spend filling out the log could be better spent elsewhere. To avoid this problem, simplify the time log as much as possible. Create a spreadsheet in which the rows break the workday into ten- or fifteen-minute blocks. Label the columns according to major responsibilities, such as e-mail, teaching, appointment, committee meeting, data collection, and research writing. Then it becomes quick and easy for the faculty member to check off what he or she is doing during each block of time.

Set time limits for certain tasks.

Unfocused faculty members tend to be perfectionists at tasks that do not require perfection. Explain to the faculty member the difference between a major report to an accrediting body that should be as flawless as possible and ordinary e-mail messages that do not need to be proofread until they are free of every typographical error. Explain to the faculty member that not every e-mail message may be worth answering and that the vast majority of these messages can be answered in a sentence or two at most. Also, be sure to explain that it is perfectly acceptable to work on minor tasks for a set amount of time and move on to something else when that time is up.

Leverage your time.

Assist the faculty member in pursuing opportunities that have multiple benefits. Are there scholarly projects that can also result in curricular innovations for your department or involve students in research? Are there creative service opportunities at your institution that could be developed into conference presentations? This type of two-for-one assignment can teach the faculty member to focus by clustering his or her time into a more manageable group of projects.

Take advantage of to-do lists, but don't become overly dependent on them.

Establishing a clear list of items that need to be done can be useful for setting priorities. All too often, however, people become enslaved to their own to-do lists because the lists serve as unwelcome reminders of all the things they will never get done. Three guidelines can help make these lists truly productive:

1. *Never record any item too large to be accomplished in a single session.* Any item that is too large to be finished in one day should be broken down into multiple tasks that can be accomplished in one day each. Checking off these items as they are completed will provide the faculty member with a greater sense of accomplishment and will keep him or her from being overwhelmed by the size of the tasks on the list.

2. *An item that has remained on the to-do list for more than a few weeks should be removed from it.* Any item that gets carried over from list to list for several weeks is unlikely to be completed. Encourage the faculty member to refocus his or her priorities on tasks that can and will be accomplished rather than being tyrannized by these items.

3. *At the end of each day, spend no more than ten minutes reorganizing the list for the next day's priorities.* A small amount of time spent on setting priorities can become a useful exercise in focusing one's energy. Too much time spent on this task, however, becomes one more unnecessary distraction.

"Fake it until you make it."

Faculty members may be surprised how much more productive they can be simply by changing their attitude and approach. The next time they are tempted to complain about how much they still have to do, encourage them to speak instead about whatever it is they have just completed. After doing this a number of times, the faculty member will begin to feel that he or she is getting a lot done. Before long, he or she will have many more formerly overwhelming responsibilities well in hand.

In an initial conversation, it is frequently best to tell the faculty member that you are offering these suggestions only in a spirit of being helpful. If, in making these suggestions, you appear to be too intimidating at first, your advice may come across as simply one more thing to do rather than an approach that will ease the faculty member's workload. Be sure, too, to address one or two aspects of the faculty member's performance that seem meritorious. By acting in this way, you will be perceived as a true mentor who is trying to make good work even better, rather than as a mere supervisor who is offering criticism for its own sake.

Some mentoring challenges are best addressed in a single, highly focused session, followed by reviews of progress that occur no more frequently than once every term or even once a year. But mentoring unfocused faculty members isn't like that. The goal in these situations is to retrain an entire mind-set and a large group of daily habits, and it will require frequent intervention. You may have to touch base with the faculty member several times a day initially in order to make sure that progress is being made. Even after these initial efforts, it may be necessary to check in with the person at least once a day for many months.

Some chairs resist this idea, thinking that it seems to be nagging a colleague who is, after all, an adult and not part of the chair's official duties anyway. Nevertheless, for a department to succeed, as many members of the department as possible should be productive in their teaching, scholarship, and service. Mentoring or coaching an unfocused faculty member certainly involves a large personal commitment of time and energy, and it may well be met with resistance from the very person you're trying to help. But in the end, it is in the best interests of the faculty member, your department, and your own career as an academic leader.

RESOURCES

Crenshaw, D. (2008). *The myth of multitasking: How doing it all gets nothing done.* San Francisco: Jossey-Bass.

Crouch, C. (2007). *Getting organized: Improving focus, organization and pro-ductivity*. Memphis, TN: Dawson.

Morgenstern, J. (2004). *Time management from the inside out: The foolproof system for taking control of your schedule—and your life* (2nd ed.). New York: Holt.

Palladino, L. J. (2007). *Find your focus zone: An effective new plan to defeat dis-traction and overload*. New York: Free Press.

Sterner, T. M. (2005). *The practicing mind: Bringing discipline and focus into your life*. Wilmington, DE: Mountain Sage Publishing.

Wolff, J. M. (2010). *Focus: Use the power of targeted thinking to get more done*. Upper Saddle River, NJ: Prentice Hall.

24

COACHING FACULTY MEMBERS
TO INCREASE PRODUCTIVITY

THE VAST MAJORITY OF college professors work quite hard, devoting long hours to educating students to the full extent of their abilities, conducting research in their chosen disciplines, and serving on a wide variety of committees. Occasionally, however, a department chair will encounter a faculty member who, for whatever reason, is either unwilling or unable to match the productivity of his or her colleagues. At times, this faculty member may be relatively new to the department and appear distracted from the central mission of the discipline by personal matters or outside interests. At other times, the faculty member may be a more senior member of the department who is marking time until retirement and no longer interested in providing instruction, scholarship, and service at what may once have been a very high level. These cases of what is sometimes disparagingly called "deadwood" can pose serious problems to the department's productivity and image. The following guidelines will help department chairs determine how to mentor these individuals and attempt to increase both their own job satisfaction and the productivity of the department.

Determine the causes.

The chair first needs to attempt to ascertain the reasons for the faculty member's lack of productivity. It is rarely the case that individuals are simply lazy; even when individuals lack the work ethic of their peers, it is not usually the case that the faculty member simply does not care how he or she is perceived or takes no pride at all in the quality of the work being performed. A supportive but candid conversation, behind closed doors and in an encouraging, nonthreatening environment, may provide useful information about the origins of the behavior that concerns you. At times, even your expression of concern, coupled with the fact that you and others have noticed a decline in satisfactory productivity, may be all that is required to bring about a noticeable change of behavior. Even when this does not occur, however, you may gain insights into problems that you can solve or reasons that you can address so as to begin changing the behavior of this faculty member.

Look for possible sources of pride and motivation.

Try to determine what still motivates the faculty member. What attracted this individual to the discipline in the first place? Does that aspect of academic life still inspire his or her interest or enthusiasm? If so, what might be some of the ways in which this person could be reconnected with these vital interests? If this is not the case, are there other aspects of academic life that might be stimulating for this person?

As you explore these possibilities with the faculty member, try to determine what he or she still gets excited about. That source of motivation may be an opportunity that lies outside your department, even outside the academic affairs division of your institution. In these cases, you may wish to discuss the matter with your dean (or, if appropriate, your president) and explore together the ways in which the faculty member may be reconnected with the institution. While few of us are able to design the specific job that we want, you may be able to work out a modification in the faculty member's assignment, perhaps coupled with some development opportunities or retraining, that leads to more of the challenges that the person still enjoys.

Be certain that you have been clear about the faculty member's responsibilities and priorities.

Occasionally a faculty member's productivity has suffered because we as supervisors have not been as clear as we should have been about our expectations. If, for example, you feel that someone has not assumed his or her fair share of advisees, consider the extent to which your expectations have been outlined in plain and unmistakable language. You may wish to establish departmental guidelines about such matters as the number of office hours each week that are expected in your discipline (perhaps even mentioning that these must be on multiple days of the week), the amount of internal and collegewide committee service your department members should undertake, and your recommended practice about advising another faculty member's students in the absence of the students' own advisor. In private conversations with the faculty member you are mentoring, you may wish to provide specific observations about where he or she has not met these departmental expectations. If necessary, you may look for ways to restructure the faculty member's assignment so that there are more opportunities to address the sort of issues that you consider to be of higher priority.

Assign a peer mentor.

It is certainly your responsibility as a department chair to mentor faculty members in your area, but there are times when it is more effective for one of the faculty member's colleagues to act as a mentor. This is particularly true in the case of junior faculty members, who may see you more as an authority figure than as a colleague and find it difficult to be completely candid with you. In these cases, assign the faculty member a mentor whom he or she trusts and with whom there is already an established rapport. Discuss with the mentor the issues that need to be addressed before his or her work with the faculty member begins. Establish a plan of action, and then give both the faculty member and the mentor the freedom to make this plan work. You can easily undermine your own efforts if you hover too closely to this process or if the faculty member comes to regard the mentor simply as a conduit of privileged information to you. Nevertheless, you should expect results and feel free to measure and assess the level of progress while still providing sufficient space for those results to emerge.

Remove any obstacles that you can.

Every college or university has its own amount of bureaucracy and red tape. Some faculty members are more immobilized by these obstacles than others. Thus, if a faculty member is routinely late in submitting necessary documents—such as book orders, self-evaluations, or budget requests—see if you can determine whether the process itself is proving an impediment for this faculty member. Are there mechanisms you can provide that will simplify the process? With a bit of ingenuity and some computing skill, many cumbersome tasks of gathering and organizing data can be made almost automatic. For instance, databases of textbooks can automatically create individualized book orders for faculty members each semester based on past textbook assignments and current enrollment patterns; as new textbooks are adopted, a secretary or administrative assistant can update this information in the system so that "precompleted" textbook orders can be generated on time and as needed. In a similar way, departmental clearinghouses can be established to ease the process of preparing annual self-evaluations; whenever publications are accepted or awards are received, these achievements can be entered into a database and then produced when annual reports are due. The faculty member then merely checks and expands the departmental list each year rather than starting a self-evaluation from scratch. In this way, examining your departmental processes on a regular basis will allow you to determine where you are helping and where you are hindering the productivity of your own faculty members.

Provide public recognition.

Some faculty members cease to be productive because they feel that their contributions are never recognized or rewarded. You can reduce the likelihood of this happening by making a habit of publicly recognizing the contributions that individual members of your department have made. As little as we think it may be necessary, public praise is a powerful motivating factor. It encourages the individual being praised to try even harder and stimulates others to seek their own moment in the spotlight. In environments where budgets are tight—and for most academic institutions, this is a perennial problem—significant public recognition can make the difference between someone who wants to go the extra mile and someone who is content with a minimal amount of effort. Keep in mind, too, that public recognition does not have to be given only in formal settings. Praising the extra achievement of one faculty member to another in a private conversation, if properly done, can boost the morale of everyone. An impromptu commendation in the midst of a casual conversation can be all the more gratifying because it was unexpected.

In a study that examined more than forty years of data, management researcher Carolyn Wiley (1997) found that the top five factors that motivated employees—salary, appreciation, job security, opportunities for promotion, and interesting work—were remarkably consistent through the years regardless of the worker's age, gender, occupation, or income level. In addition to such obvious factors as good wages and job security, Wiley found that appreciation for the work one does is consistently a leading motivational factor—in some periods, *the* leading motivational factor.

Keep a paper trail.

If you have legitimate concerns about a faculty member's level of productivity, be sure to keep records documenting what you have done in your efforts to fix the problem. Maintain a log of your conversations and the advice that you have given. When you are writing a formal evaluation, be candid and precise. State clearly what your expectations were, how they were not achieved, and what should be done about this situation in the future. Although many steps can be taken to improve the productivity of your faculty members, not every problem can be fixed. In the event of a negative personnel decision, you will need clear documentation outlining precisely when you first recognized the problem, how you brought it to the faculty member's attention, what steps you took to improve the situation, and why you remain dissatisfied with that individual's productivity.

○

Faculty members sometimes bristle when administrators even use the term *productivity*. They object, and rightly so, that higher education isn't only about things that can be quantified and point out that a college professor is not a machine for producing student credit hours and refereed articles. All of that is true, even though as administrators, we need to be accountable for our use of resources—including human resources—for the public good, and many accreditation or program review processes require us to demonstrate that our departments remain viable in terms of course demand, research funding generated, and probable enrollment trends.

Department chairs have an opportunity to act as an intermediary between these two perspectives, pointing out to trustees and legislators that a program's outcomes can be viewed in terms of the effect a discipline has on the lives of its students and other stakeholders and helping faculty members understand that salaries and research funds are ultimately generated by tuition payments, external grants, legislative decisions, and donor interest. In order to promote each faculty member's productivity, it is important for department chairs to understand just how wide the definition of "being highly productive" can be.

REFERENCE

Wiley, C. (1997). What motivates employees according to over 40 years of motivation surveys. *International Journal of Manpower, 18*, 263–280.

RESOURCES

Allen, D. (2003). *Getting things done: The art of stress-free productivity.* New York: Penguin.

Bossidy, L., Charan, R., & Burck, C. (2002). *Execution: The discipline of getting things done*. New York: Crown.

Crouch, C. (2005). *Being productive: Learning how to get more done with less effort*. Memphis, TN: Dawson.

Harris, V. (2008). *The productivity epiphany: Leading edge ideas on time management, self management, communication and becoming more productive in any area of life*. Trenton, MO: Beckworth Publications.

25

PROMOTING A MORE COLLEGIAL DEPARTMENT

ALL DEPARTMENT CHAIRS UNDERSTAND the importance of promoting collegiality within their departments. Few other factors can bring the productivity of a department to a standstill and destroy its reputation as quickly as can the presence of even a single uncollegial faculty member. Continued breaches of collegiality have been known to destroy departmental morale, alienate capable students, cost the department some of its most valued faculty members, and decrease a department's competitiveness when it applies for grants and other forms of external support.

Like many other aspects of higher education law, the role that collegiality can and should play in personnel decisions is still not perfectly clear. Nevertheless, even as these legal issues continue to unfold, several precedents suggest that collegiality can be a valid factor when faculty members are reviewed. In the landmark case of *Mayberry* v. *Dees* (1981), for instance, the Fourth Circuit Court of Appeals recognized collegiality as a criterion in tenure decisions alongside such widely accepted criteria as teaching, scholarship, and service. Moreover, in the case of the *University of Baltimore* v. *Iz* (1998), the Maryland Appellate Court ruled that collegiality may be considered when personnel decisions are being made even if an institution's governance documents do not expressly cite collegiality as a distinct criterion. (On the case history of collegiality issues, see Connell, 2001; Connell and Savage, 2001; and Fogg, 2002.) To be sure, since collegiality affects the quality of a faculty member's teaching, scholarship, and service, it may well be regarded as an appropriate implicit factor—much as showing up for work on time and not plagiarizing another scholar's research are frequently unstated, implicit criteria—when personnel decisions are made.

Yet although it is in both a faculty member's own interest and in the interests of the department as a whole for coworkers to treat one another in a collegial manner, department chairs are often at a loss as to how they should mentor a faculty member whose uncollegial behavior causes problems. What, they may ask, is the best way to promote departmental collegiality and foster mutually respectful interactions among peers? Here are some guidelines.

Begin with a department-wide dialogue on collegiality.

A surprising number of faculty members do not understand what is generally meant by "collegiality." They assume that it merely means "being polite," or "getting along," or "saying hello" to their colleagues in the hallway and inviting them (or accepting their invitations) to an appropriate number of parties. What faculty members frequently do not understand is the basis of the following essential principle:

> Collegiality is not simply a matter of being nice to the people we work with. It consists of behaving in an appropriately professional manner that promotes, to the greatest extent possible, the primary functions of our institutions: teaching, scholarship, and service.

In other words, collegiality is not just "getting along with other people," and it is certainly not the same as "never criticizing anyone." Rather, collegiality is a central ingredient in academic professionalism; it is one of our obligations as academic professionals to our discipline, our departments, and our institutions. But that doesn't mean we have to like everyone or perennially be in a cheerful mood; it's perfectly possible for a "nice, cheerful person" to lack collegiality because he or she avoids a fair share of committee service, unnecessarily prolongs routine departmental processes, and squelches the free exchange of ideas during discussions. By contrast, other faculty members may offer criticism, even repeated criticism, in a perfectly collegial manner by voicing their opinions in a proper forum and using a manner that is civil, conducive to the academic mission of the institution, and professionally respectful. The real test of collegiality therefore is this: Does the behavior in question contribute to or make more difficult the central mission of the institution with regard to teaching, scholarship, and service?

Develop a departmental code of conduct.

One way of working through the issues of collegiality is for a department to define a code of acceptable behavior. Departments can even increase their reputations on campus by serving as leaders in discussions of professional civility. As a chair, you can set the goal of developing a departmental code of civility or collegiality that you will share with other departments on campus. Such a code might look something like this:

> As members of the Department of X, we undertake to communicate with others, both orally and in writing, in a manner that is polite, respectful, and courteous. Whenever we disagree with someone, we restrict our differences to the issue itself while continuing to respect the individual with whom we disagree. All of our discussion and argumentation will be conducted in a polite, courteous, and dignified manner.

Once you have established a departmental code, it then serves as a vehicle for initiating conversations with faculty members when, in your professional judgment, serious breaches of that code have occurred. Those discussions can carry particular weight if the faculty member you are addressing is one of those who voted in favor of the code or if the code was reviewed with the faculty member when that person was hired as part of the interview or orientation process.

When public breaches of collegiality occur, intervene sooner rather than later.

If discussions at a department meeting are on the verge of dissolving into rancor, it is best to step in at once. Abruptly adjourn the meeting or call a temporary recess, invite the principals into your office for a private conversation (where they can cool down or at least rephrase their concerns without grandstanding in front of other colleagues), and explain to them—calmly but firmly—the reasons that you could not allow the discussion to continue as it was. Similarly, if you encounter an uncollegial discussion or exchange of messages among members of your department, it is your duty as chair to intervene and to see if you can redirect the focus of the dispute.

Intervention does not mean that you will become involved in every faculty disagreement; many disagreements are healthy and serve to keep the department vigorous in its consideration of new ideas. Nevertheless, if it is clear that a discussion is about to become personal rather than professional or to involve matters that are inappropriate and irrelevant to the topic at hand, it is important for you to become involved.

Whenever possible, address breaches of collegiality privately rather than publicly.

In many instances, if you attempt to handle uncollegiality by openly calling the guilty party on the carpet, you will end up making that person defensive and possibly even less cooperative in the future. Handling lapses in professional demeanor privately, including such phrases as, "What I just heard was so unlike you . . ." and assuring the individual that you have his or her best professional interests at heart will make your conversation more clearly a mentoring session than a disciplinary procedure.

As you talk over the matter with the faculty member, try to determine the reasons for the breach of collegiality you observed. Was the person unaware of the impact that his or her actions might have, or was the person fully aware of what was occurring and simply indifferent to the result? Determining this will guide you in formulating your response. If the faculty member was unaware that he or she was being uncollegial, it may be useful to have that person internalize the impact of the situation. Ask, for example, "How would you feel if . . . ?" or "How do you imagine that Professor X is going to respond to you now that you . . . ?" But if you suspect that the faculty member intended to cause discomfort and was simply bullying a colleague, then it is far more productive for you to keep your focus directly on the uncollegial faculty member and the inappropriateness of his or her action; then say, for example, "Let me tell you why what you did was unprofessional," and, "Here's why your actions have been a disservice to our department."

Confront rumors and ancient history head-on.

There are few things more poisonous to departmental collegiality than rumors, innuendo, and constant reference to long-past grievances. If you have reason to believe that a faculty member has been guilty of spreading rumors or malicious gossip, speak to that person about the damaging effect of these actions. Remind the faculty member that in extreme cases, he or she might even become legally liable if someone's professional reputation or livelihood is threatened.

Whenever necessary, debunk rumors publicly in department meetings. Then, if the rumors crop up again, adopt the broken record approach: keep repeating, "As I already said in an earlier meeting, the reason that's not true is . . ." Be particularly sure to quash false rumors about members of the upper administration; being associated with misinformation of this sort can jeopardize your department on any number of levels. Similarly, if a faculty member repeatedly brings up past grievances, make it clear that you are not interested in rehashing earlier problems. Say, for example, "I think there ought to be a statute of limitations on how long we can complain about . . ." or, "We all already know about that. We can't change the past, and I'm not going to hold this department's progress hostage to something I can't do anything about. Let's move on."

Mentor faculty members in the art of constructive criticism.

Sometimes violations of collegiality occur because a faculty member does not have the proper personal skills or experience to raise objections forcefully but constructively. When this occurs, you can provide a valuable service to that person by offering instruction in collegial disputation. Start by explaining the difference between criticizing an idea and appearing to criticize the person who is advancing that idea. Offer a few verbal tips on ways in which to raise objections more positively, such as, "I think that's a great idea, but we might be able to refine it a bit by . . . ," or, "Well, I'm not sure I agree with you about that particular approach, but since we're both enthusiastic about achieving the same goal, maybe we could . . ."

Note that it is perfectly acceptable to advocate strongly for one's own ideas, but there are both appropriate and inappropriate ways of critiquing the ideas of others. Encourage the faculty member to stick to the topic at hand, making a rational and unemotional argument about why one approach is superior to another, while remaining open to and supportive of the ideas that others may have. Point out unintended subtext conveyed through posture, facial expression, body language, and the level of one's voice.

Seek common ground.

Sometimes faculty members are uncollegial in their treatment of others because of a personality conflict between them or they just got off on the wrong foot. In these situations, the chair has an opportunity to serve as a catalyst for improved professional relations by exploring areas where the faculty members share common outlooks, approaches, or aspirations. It often takes a third party to hear voices of commonality where the faculty members themselves cannot hear any agreement. Point out any areas of shared interest: "Isn't that just another way of saying this . . . And didn't I just hear you say that . . . ?" Decrease the intensity of the confrontation by using yourself as a buffer or lightning rod. Ask such questions as, "Maybe I'm not quite understanding this correctly, but haven't you both been saying essentially that . . . ?"

Maintain a focus on the benefits of collegiality.

What do you do in the case of that passive-aggressive faculty member who, while outwardly polite, is hindering the work of the discipline by avoiding a fair share of departmental service or unduly prolonging meetings with excessive questions, comments, and requests for further clarification? Be candid with this individual about the detrimental effects that these actions are having on the department. In a private conversation, state clearly why it is essential for everyone to take a turn in accepting a few more advisees, recording the minutes at a meeting, or drafting a report for a committee. Point out how everyone else has needed to take on these responsibilities, and although you understand the sacrifice that will be required, you find it necessary that he or she take on a fair share as well. Describe the time constraints that require a decision to be made without further delays caused by a discussion that may be valuable and extremely interesting but is not bringing the issue to resolution. Suggest other ways for certain questions to be asked (perhaps a departmental listserv, a bulletin board in a common area, or a threaded discussion on a faculty Web site) rather than devoting scarce meeting time to these discussions. Frequently, the lack of response to the faculty member's questions once they are posted publicly can be used to suggest tactfully to that individual that perhaps others were not as concerned about these issues as one may have thought.

o

Whenever department chairs talk about the most frustrating or unpleasant aspects of their positions, the problem of dealing with uncollegial faculty members is likely to arise. In a similar way, whenever recently appointed department chairs talk about the most surprising aspects of their positions, they frequently mention how much time they are spending mediating faculty disagreements and responding to people who feel that their colleagues have treated them uncivilly.

It's clear that higher education still has a challenge when it comes to creating an environment in which differences of perspective and temperament are celebrated, but differences of opinion can be voiced in a manner that promotes rather than stifles fully engaged discussion. Although it may not be the most pleasant or anticipated part of a department chair's responsibilities, mentoring an uncollegial faculty member can be extremely beneficial for both the success of the discipline and the continued career of the faculty member being advised.

REFERENCES

Connell, M. A. (2001). The role of collegiality in higher education tenure, promotion, and termination decisions. *Journal of College and University Law*,
27, 833–858.

Connell, M. A., & Savage, F. G. (2001). Does collegiality count? *Academe*,
87(6), 37–41.

Fogg, P. (2002, April 26). Nevada Supreme Court rules against professor who
was denied tenure. *Chronicle of Higher Education*, A14.

Mayberry v. Dees, 663 F.2d 502 (4th Cir. Ct. 1981).

University of Baltimore v. Iz, 716 A.2d 1107 (Md. Ct. App. 1998).

RESOURCES

Bennett, J. B. (1998). *Collegial professionalism: The academy, individualism, and
the common good*. Phoenix, AZ: Oryx Press.

Cipriano, R. (2011). *Facilitating a collegial department in higher education:
Strategies for success*. San Francisco: Jossey-Bass.

Cipriano, R. E. (2009). Uncivil faculty: The chair's role. *Department Chair*,
20(1), 15–18.

Clark, B. (2001). The entrepreneurial university: New foundations for collegiality, autonomy, and achievement. *Higher Education Management*, 13(2),
9–24. Retrieved from http://www.oecd.org/dataoecd/1/47/37446098.
pdf#page=8

Twale, D. J., & De Luca, B. M. (2008). *Faculty incivility: The rise of the academic
bully culture and what to do about it*. San Francisco: Jossey-Bass.

26

COPING WITH PASSIVE-AGGRESSIVE BEHAVIOR

A PARTICULARLY DIFFICULT MENTORING challenge for department chairs is a faculty member who, while possessing a number of otherwise admirable qualities, simultaneously undermines the chair, his or her own colleagues, and possibly the department as a whole through repeated passive-aggressive behavior. The passive-aggressive faculty member I am discussing here is not a pathological individual who can be clinically diagnosed as passive-aggressive. If you believe that an employee who reports to you may be passive-aggressive in this more severe clinical sense, you should consult your dean or office of human resources about whether your institution allows you the possibility of referring this individual for professional evaluation; there is probably very little that you yourself can do for such a faculty member unless you are a trained clinical psychologist. (And under such circumstances, it would be unethical and inappropriate, not to mention unwise, to confuse your clinical role with your position as department chair.) Severe passive-aggressive behavior stems from a personality disorder; those afflicted with it are often intractable and may not respond well even to therapy. In these cases, allow the problem to be handled by professionals, and turn your attention to other matters where you are more likely to make a difference.

On the positive side, it is not common to encounter a faculty member who demonstrates these extremely severe tendencies. What you are more likely to encounter is the type of individual who

- Has a history of agreeing to change behaviors that are destructive—and frequently may even express gratitude to the chair for pointing out these destructive behaviors and helping with them—but then fails to act on any of the strategies that he or she had eagerly declared to be appropriate

○ Blames others for problems and claims to be "as confused as you are" as to why he or she always seems to attract so many complaints and objections

○ When assigned responsibilities that he or she does not want to do or had resisted when they were proposed initially, performs the task very slowly or in an unsatisfactory manner, thus "proving" that the idea or assignment was a poor concept from the beginning

○ Has a highly inflated opinion of his or her contributions to the department and institution, frequently claiming to be unappreciated, even though you may find the person's performance to be weak or below standards

○ Impedes departmental work by failing to answer routine requests, memos, or e-mails in a timely manner

○ When challenged about poor performance or uncollegial behavior, routinely projects the worst of his or her own character traits onto others

Unlike other kinds of behavior problems, mild passive-aggressive tendencies often seem to give little, if any, distress to the faculty members demonstrating them. By contrast, chronic complainers may well be aware that they make themselves as miserable as they make others. Outright hostile faculty members frequently realize that their aggressive tendencies alienate those around them, even though they may be powerless to control those tendencies. Passive-aggressive faculty members, however, are often so convinced that they are trying to improve, the problems still occurring are the fault of others, and the animosity others may show them is simply the result of jealousy or that person's own problem that they remain unaware that they have a problem.

Coping Strategies

The behaviors that even mildly passive-aggressive individuals demonstrate are probably deeply ingrained. For this reason, you are unlikely to create dramatically improved behavior in this person even if you make a consistent attempt to do so. There are, however, three strategies you may wish to attempt in order to cope with someone's passive-aggressive tendencies and reduce the difficulties that are occurring in your department. (Your institution's counseling center or human resource office may be able to assist you with further techniques that could be effective in your individual situation. You may also wish to consult Lieberman, 2005, Johnson and Klee, 2007, or Topchik, 2000, for specific advice on dealing with passive-aggressive temperaments.)

Set Goals and Timetables

It is often not at all difficult to get passive-aggressive faculty members to agree that a problem exists and that they need to change. The challenge comes in prompting significant improvement in behavior without addressing the underlying causes of the difficulties. If you wish to see change, you need to establish a clear and reasonable timetable with the faculty member, monitor that timetable effectively, and adopt rewards or sanctions based on whether he or she meets the goals you have set.

At a performance appraisal meeting with the faculty member, set a specific goal that you would like the individual to achieve and impose a clear deadline. This first task you assign should, in most cases, be relatively easy, and the deadline should be relatively soon: forty-eight hours to one week. You might ask the faculty member to complete a long-overdue memo or annual report (provided that this task can reasonably be accomplished in the time that you have allowed), contact a committee in order to set the date of its next meeting, or return a graded course assignment that should have been handed back some time ago. Get progress reports, if you feel it is necessary, before the deadline arrives. Let the faculty member resent the pressure you are applying if he or she must, but take the steps that you feel are necessary to get the assignment done. In truth, the resentment may or may not subside once the task is complete. But remember that your ultimate goal is increasing your department's overall productivity and service to your students, not generating the contentment of this particular faculty member.

When the task is complete, review it with the faculty member, being generous with your approval where it is warranted but not accepting shoddy, inferior, or slovenly work. If improvements are necessary, be very clear about what you would like changed and why that is important. Set a new deadline (perhaps breaking the task into even smaller parts, each of which you must approve in turn), and begin the process again. If the faculty member successfully completes the assignment, praise him or her appropriately and begin setting new deadlines for new tasks. Start by planning various assignments perhaps six weeks out or until the end of the current semester. Establish a sufficient number of concrete steps along the way so that you will always know if the faculty member is making progress in a timely manner. Then provide frequent, candid, and constructive feedback regarding the rate of progress being made.

> Administrators have no right whatsoever to try to control what faculty members believe. Nevertheless, they do have a right to expect certain behaviors from the people who work at the institution. For this reason, whenever you're trying to work with a faculty member whose performance is unsatisfactory, limit your remarks to those directly related to the performance or specific behaviors, not the faculty member's attitude, perspectives, or beliefs.

Provide Choice and Set Standards

Allow the faculty member some flexibility and choice in work assignments when this is possible, with standards of performance in these areas set proportionately high. One of the justifications that passive-aggressive faculty members frequently make for their unsatisfactory performance is that they are asked to take on too many responsibilities, not assigned tasks that are truly worthy of their talent, or called on to work in areas where they have relatively little training, experience, and interest. One way of responding is to allow some flexibility in the faculty member's work assignment if this is possible and desirable. If the faculty member is given a chance to play an active role in selecting the assignment that he or she will take and in setting the deadline (within limits), then there can be no excuse that "this was something I really didn't want to do in the first place." It can be useful to have the faculty member provide you with a list in writing of the committee assignments, tasks, or reports that he or she is most interested in. Then if deadlines go by unmet or a pattern of excuses begins to emerge, you will have this written document to go over with the faculty member, saying, "But I'm confused as to why this isn't getting done. Back on such-and-such a date, you sent me a memo telling me that you really wanted to do this."

When allowing the faculty member some leeway in selecting responsibilities and deadlines, combining this flexibility with correspondingly higher standards of achievement is appropriate. Since you are dealing with a task that the faculty member has personally selected, poor performance or missed deadlines should not be an option. Remind the faculty member that with increased freedom comes increased responsibility and that your expectations rise proportionately with the added self-determination you are offering in this task.

Require Updates and Progress Reports

Require more frequent updates and progress reports from this faculty member than you might expect from most other employees. Although your goal is ultimately to wean the faculty member off the constant supervision and frequent deadlines that you will use at the beginning of your mentoring process, those with mild passive-aggressive tendencies will always require a higher level of guidance and supervision than other faculty members.

When you see that genuine progress is being made, reduce the number of mentoring sessions to once a month, and eventually to once or twice a semester. At those sessions, you can review progress toward goals, set new objectives, celebrate targets that have been reached, and speak candidly about any lapses or backsliding. Keep the meeting as task oriented as possible: don't reinforce the faculty member's tendencies to complain or to shift blame to others by acknowledging this behavior. You should not expect progress to be smooth or rapid. Unlike other mentoring challenges, you are far less likely to "fix" the difficulties arising from the passive-aggressive faculty member than simply to manage and reduce them.

Your Role as Chair

Whatever strategy you take, avoid the temptation of trying to solve the faculty member's problem by addressing his or her underlying issues of self-image, problems with authority figures, or past trauma. As an effective mentor for the members of your department, your role is to help them grow as professionals through your guidance and example. Being a good mentor does not mean becoming an employee's spiritual counselor, therapist, or confidante. Whatever other role you may play in other situations, you are still the faculty member's boss, and you are entitled to expect a certain amount of professionalism regardless of the problems that faculty member has had or is having.

For this reason, keep your focus on the behavior you want the faculty member to demonstrate, not on the person's underlying reasons or justifications for past actions. For instance, are there aspects of his or her performance that you can legitimately praise and cite as examples of the type of accomplishments that he or she should continue to pursue? Is the faculty member a good organizer of plans (though perhaps not as successful at carrying out those plans)? Does the faculty member tend to work effectively one-on-one with students (though perhaps less effectively in committees)? Is the faculty member a polished writer (even if it takes a very long time for his or her written works to be completed)?

As you would with all your other faculty, conduct your mentoring of the faculty member by focusing on these areas of demonstrated strength, perhaps even changing a few of his or her assignments (where appropriate) as a means of playing to that person's strength. Having established a baseline of understanding about what this person does well, you then can turn to the areas of performance that are causing problems for the department. Start with general observations about the individual's poor performance ("On the other hand, you have a tendency to miss deadlines and repeatedly to request extensions that causes a number of problems for us"). Give a few specific examples, but don't pile on so many instances of poor performance that the faculty member reverts to self-defense. If you notice a tendency toward defensiveness, ignore it. Don't let your focus deviate from the faculty member's actions, and don't give in to comforting the faculty member or discussing any justifications that he or she may give you for poor performance.

Similarly, if the faculty member keeps blaming others for his or her poor performance, routinely ignore these statements. (Either say nothing at all or rapidly return to your primary subject: "Well, that's not the issue. What we're talking about is how *you* can be even more effective.") The important impression to establish with the employee is that there are good things that he or she does, and these contributions are both recognized and appreciated by the department; but there are also some areas in which he or she can improve, and these are areas for which the individual needs to take personal responsibility, not assign blame to colleagues.

○

Coping with a passive-aggressive faculty member is likely to require a great deal of patience, and even then, the situation may well cause you repeated frustration and irritation. In the most difficult of times, it may be useful to remember that the individual's behavior is not caused by anything that you, your department, or your institution has done. Ultimately it is the individual's own problem, and although you can take steps to cope with the departmental challenges resulting from it, it is not your responsibility to solve it. Only the individual faculty member can do that.

REFERENCES

Johnson, N., & Klee, T. (2007, January). Passive-aggressive behavior and leadership styles in organizations. *Journal of Leadership and Organizational Studies, 14*(2), 130–142.

Lieberman, D. J. (2005). *How to change anybody: Proven techniques to reshape anyone's attitude, behavior, feelings, or beliefs.* New York: St. Martin's Press.

Topchik, G. S. (2000). *Managing workplace negativity.* New York: AMACOM.

RESOURCES

Cavaiola, A. A., & Lavender, N. J. (2000). *Toxic coworkers: How to deal with dysfunctional people on the job.* Oakland, CA: New Harbinger Publications.

Crookston, R. K. (2010, September). Seven steps for dealing with problem faculty. *Academic Leader, 26*(9), 7–8.

Neilson, G. L., & Pasternack, B. A. (2005). *Results: Keep what's good, fix what's wrong, and unlock great performance.* New York: Crown.

27

RESOLVING CHRONIC
COMPLAINTS

CONSTANT COMPLAINERS ARE NOT unique to academic life; they can be found throughout all professions. If you examine nearly any manual devoted to personnel management, you will find chapters exploring the whiner, the griper, or the chronic complainer and the destruction that this type of person can do to any organization. Some of the best of these general works are Bramson (1981), Lloyd (1999), Topchik (2000), and Scott (2004), with specific advice intended for academic administrators appearing in McDaniel (2002). Yet despite the pervasiveness of chronic complainers in all walks of life, department chairs soon see several important ways in which the way this type of personality displays itself in academic life that can be distinctly different from its counterparts in other professional environments. For instance, most business-oriented management guides report that chronic complainers tend to express dissatisfaction on a broad range of issues, never focusing on a single complaint for very long; the moment that you try to address one purported problem, these guides conclude, the complainer will invariably be off in pursuit of some other alleged grievance.

This pattern of behavior rarely applies to academic complainers. They are not often fickle in their objections, raising a single complaint over the course of many months or even many years, sometimes even drawing some perverse sort of satisfaction from the fact that none of their colleagues is "enlightened" enough to champion this particular cause, at least with the proper amount of vehemence and persistence. Academic complainers are less likely to be drawn to an unrelated range of issues and more likely to be drawn to one in particular (such as faculty salaries, workload, or support for scholarship) that they are willing to discuss at

length even when no one else in the department seems particularly interested, even when you may think that, as chair, you have already
addressed and solved the complainers' problems.

In a similar way, business-oriented management guides frequently discuss chronic complainers as employees who can only identify problems,
never pausing long enough to develop a plan of action that would deal
with the problem. Academic complainers regularly develop plans of
actions—even quite detailed plans of action—and while they may be
wholly impractical, excessively self-serving, or completely oblivious
to the larger needs of the institution, they are plans. Finally, books on
personnel management usually assume that chronic complainers cause
most of their difficulties for coworkers not in official meetings or formal
planning sessions but in casual conversation, around water coolers and
during coffee breaks, or in spontaneous lunchtime griping. The academic
complainer is attracted to no particular venue when wishing to voice a
concern; he or she will speak openly in faculty meetings, behind closed
doors in committees, to your face and behind your back—anywhere a
captive audience may be found for discussing a well-nursed grievance.

Perhaps it is because we academics tend to focus on problems and
problem solving for a living that the challenge of dealing with our own
breed of chronic complainer seems particularly severe. Nearly every department has, or has had at some time or another, at least one individual
who has long since ceased being merely a lovable curmudgeon and has
threatened to ruin morale, bring departmental business to a standstill,
and encouraged other members of the faculty to seek employment elsewhere, all because of the complainer's incessant carping.

As department chairs, we have both an opportunity and an obligation
to mentor these individuals who both harm our departments and render
themselves miserable in the process. Unfortunately, not every chronic
complainer wants to or can be helped—and certainly not every mentoring strategy helps in every case—but I offer some proven techniques that
may help you assist chronic complainers in the academic setting.

Model the behavior that you want the faculty member to emulate.

Sometimes complainers feel that it is acceptable to become fixated on
their objections because they observe others doing so. One of the ways in
which to break this cycle is to be a mentor to members of your department by modeling constructive behaviors and approaches to problem
solving. Monitor your own behavior to make sure that you never resort
to morale-diminishing complaining—even when you are faced with the
frustrations of dealing with chronic complainers. Try to maintain as

positive an attitude as possible about the challenges confronting your department. Attempt to suggest several possible solutions each time you are forced to address a problem. Seek to find something good to say in even the most trying of circumstances.

In a surprising number of instances, this behavior will begin to wear off on your faculty members, and they will start being more constructive and upbeat in their own approaches to you and their departmental business.

Try to determine the reason for the individual's negative attitude.

Not all complaining is alike. Some chronic complainers are seeking attention, even if it is negative attention, because they do not believe that they are being taken seriously. Some are unhappy about other aspects of their life that may have little or nothing to do with their function in your department. Some complainers may even be clinically depressed and in need of professional help. Some may simply need some guidance into more constructive ways of making suggestions for improvement. According to Michele Israel (2009),

> Dr. Mike Weber, superintendent of the Port Washington-Saukville (Wisconsin) School District, has classified three types of "complainers."
>
> ○ The "helpful complainer" has a specific gripe about an issue, but offers constructive feedback that could resolve the problem.
> ○ A "therapeutic complainer" is experiencing a temporary setback and draws out a confidante to vent frustrations, rather than liberally spreading doom and gloom.
> ○ The "malcontent complainer" is the one to watch out for, warned Weber. "They have ongoing, persistent problems with many issues, but offer no constructive suggestions. They are energy drainers," he stressed.

Since, as Israel and Weber point out, not all chronic complainers are motivated by the same need, you must determine why an individual has such a need to focus on problems in order to help that person overcome his or her own problem. You will not be able to diagnose the root cause of chronic complaining, however, unless you make a concerted effort to understand the individual who is causing the problem (as difficult as that may be in many cases) and what benefit this person perceives himself or herself as deriving from an activity that is so distressing to others.

Confront the destructive behavior head-on.

Although it is far from always the case, some chronic complainers have no idea whatsoever how their peers perceive their repeated criticisms. They may even be shocked when the reaction of others is pointed out to them. Start a conversation with the complainer—always behind closed doors—by asking, "Why is it that almost every time you speak in a meeting, you voice a complaint?" And then listen very carefully to the person's answer. When you take this approach, always keep focused throughout this discussion on what the individual is doing that is harmful to departmental progress or morale, not on the merit or contributions of the individual who has voiced the complaint. Appearing to attack chronic complainers themselves frequently makes them defensive, a situation that can even backfire on you and provide them with still one more thing about which they can complain.

It is far more useful for you, as a mentor of the faculty members in your department, to guide the chronic complainer into more productive behaviors. Are there ways in which you can guide this person into raising the points that he or she feels necessary to address but in a more positive, even morale-building manner? Are there more appropriate times or places for raising these concerns than under the conditions that are currently causing the problem? Is it possible to explain to the individual how his or her behavior comes across to individuals who have frequently heard these issues many times before and feel that other matters merit their concern?

You may be able to point out to your faculty member that raising the complaints in the manner that he or she has done is counterproductive. "It's not that your issue is unimportant," you might say, "but rather that people have stopped listening to you because you bring this up so frequently. The result is that your issue is getting lost by the way in which you discuss it."

Give the complainer an opportunity to tackle "the problem."

Channeling the complainer's energies into action rather than mere grumbling may be effective in certain cases. It sets the tone that you, as chair, value doing something about problems rather than simply whining about them. At times you can direct the complainer's energy toward the very issue that is the subject of the complaint. Ask that the details of the complaint be put in writing. Specify that concrete solutions must be recommended and that if these proposed solutions have any budgetary implications, you will also need recommendations about where this funding can be reallocated from current expenditures.

At times, complainers will reply, "That's your job, not mine. I'm supposed to identify the problems; you're supposed to fix them and figure out how to pay for them." This will give you an opportunity to explain that this is not how the department is going to work under your administration. You might say, for instance, that you see all of your colleagues as a team; for this reason, you and your faculty are jointly responsible for doing the business of the discipline. "Now, this was an issue that you brought to my attention," you might explain. "If we're going to make any progress on it, I'll need your help and the help of every other member of the department."

The complainer then has two choices: let this topic drop or write a recommendation. In situations where you receive a written recommendation, you can introduce it at a department meeting—again modeling a more positive approach to problem solving than simply griping about problems—and let the author see in person how much, or how little, support there is for the changes that he or she has recommended. In situations where the topic is dropped, don't relax too much: it is likely to emerge again later in a slightly different form. All that you have won is a reprieve.

> While chronic complainers are annoying, their complaints may actually be concerned with genuine problems and flaws in the system. In such cases, your goal should be to channel the complainer's energy toward finding positive solutions, not merely identifying difficulties.

Provide opportunities to make more constructive changes in your department.

In certain situations, it may not be possible to put the chronic complainer in charge of fixing the very problem that was the subject of the complaint. At times like this, it may be useful to direct the individual's energies to some other matter of importance to the department. This can be a particularly effective solution when you believe that the individual is complaining because he or she feels marginalized or no longer taken seriously by the other members of the department. Offering the person an opportunity to develop an important new grant, revise (or even develop for the first time) a handbook of departmental procedures, improve the advising system in the department, or take on some other administrative matter that truly needs to be done can help renew the complainer's sense of purpose in the department. Meet with the individual several times as the project is under way in order to provide mentorship in the skills needed to make this project effective:

- How can this proposal be presented to others in the department in the most positive way?
- How can the faculty member demonstrate the benefit that others will receive from this project?
- How will this undertaking strengthen the discipline or the institution as a whole?

Demonstrate that this task is important, not just busy work intended to divert energy from what the complainer sees as the "real problem."

Enlist the help of other members of the department to ensure that the disruptive behavior is not being reinforced.

Complainers frequently continue voicing their objections either because the attention that they receive in department meetings makes them feel that they are raising valid issues or because they interpret the silence that follows their remarks as tacit consent. When this happens, you may need support from other members of your department in order to make solving this problem a group effort. If even one or two other people say, in effect, "No, I really don't think that is our most important issue right now," or, "We keep hearing about this, but frankly, I think we have more urgent matters to address. Let's just move on," you may have an opportunity to say something similar to the following: "I'm hearing several of you saying that you really don't want to take up any more of our meeting time on this issue. How many of the others of you feel that way? Maybe we should just table this topic and leave it, since we have other items that need our concern."

Declare a moratorium on bringing up alleged past grievances.

One topic to which complainers frequently devote a great deal of attention is how a previous policy or decision created an inequity that is still harming the department today. Frequently these alleged past injustices resulted from actions taken by previous chairs or even previous administrations at the institution. In these cases, it may be necessary to impose a departmental statute of limitations on complaints. It may be effective to say, "I understand your concerns. I really do. But I can't change the past, and my whole attention has to be devoted to where this department needs to go in the future. So understand that rather than dealing with that, I'm going to be focused on moving us forward." At such times, it will probably be necessary to enunciate such a policy as your administrative perspective and then to keep reiterating it as the issue comes up: "As I've said before, that issue goes way beyond my statute of limitations. Now instead of going back once again to that issue, let me tell you what we're going to be addressing today."

Provide positive mentoring in more constructive ways of voicing disagreements and solving problems.

Some chronic complaining is the result of poor social skills. If you discuss with a faculty member more constructive ways of getting a point across or raising objections, you may end up both making the faculty member a more effective member of your academic community and avoiding a great deal of grief in your department.

Some chronic complainers, when you attempt to coach them out of their disruptive behavior, may accuse you of attempting to silence them or interfering with their academic freedom. Always make it clear that your goal is not to deprive the faculty member of the right to express an opinion—even if it is an opinion with which you do not agree—but rather to make him or her more effective in the vital role of a citizen of your academic community. Remind the complainer that just as you would have a duty to assist a faculty member whom you observed being ineffective in an approach to instruction, so now you have an obligation to assist this particular faculty member with a behavior that is ineffective in other ways and, in fact, becoming increasingly counterproductive. Develop a strategy with the faculty member for how the complaint will be raised, in what type of forum, and (for the greatest effectiveness) with what sort of frequency. Remind the complainer that we all cease to hear voices that are heard too often, and that now might be an appropriate time to adopt a different strategy in addressing this particular problem.

Establish clear boundaries for when complaining is acceptable.

Everyone needs to vent every now and then. The difficulty is that the chronic complainer vents so frequently and repetitively that it is causing difficulties for the other members of the department. At times, the only effective way of dealing with this problem is to create a formal griping time that occurs only occasionally.

Establish in advance a clear amount of time—usually no more than half an hour—in which complaining at a department meeting will be not only tolerated but encouraged. Use this periodic opportunity, built into the schedule perhaps once or twice a semester, for airing frustrations in the department. If the chronic complainer reverts to typical behavior at other meetings of the department, in private conversations, or when you are meeting for some other task, you can step in and insist that these complaints have to be saved for the next official griping time. The advantage of this approach is that you will have an opportunity to mentor your faculty member that there is a time for venting frustration and a time for action, and that the latter should be more common than the former. One other advantage is that by opening up griping time to the whole department, you may learn about some issues that are affecting some of your more silent and long-suffering faculty members. Finally, your chronic complainer may even learn through this process how frustrating it is to listen to the complaints of others.

Declare your department a complaint-free zone.

Work with your faculty members to develop a more positive philosophy of solving problems. Create a departmental code of conduct that includes a statement along these lines:

> As members of the Department of [name], we seek to work together positively for the solution of problems and the resolution of conflicts. Rather than complaining, we are interested in solutions. We attempt to determine a plan of action that we ourselves can take to improve a situation—and then we put that plan into effect. Rather than assuming the worst of others, we take it for granted that every member of the department and of the institution as a whole is working toward the good of our students. Rather than becoming preoccupied with the faults of others, we prefer to focus on their strengths, providing positive and constructive mentoring to the best of our abilities.

A departmental code of this sort can become an important ingredient of your orientation for new faculty, and it will give you a way of addressing the issue of excessive complaining openly and directly when it occurs.

As with many other personnel challenges, mentoring the chronic complainer requires patience and is not always successful. When you are able to make a difference, however, you will find that the atmosphere in your department will reflect a distinct improvement and the former complainer will have improved relationships with colleagues and be a more effective member of the academic community.

REFERENCES

Bramson, R. M. (1981). *Coping with difficult people.* New York: Doubleday.
Israel, M. (2009). Managing difficult people: Turning "negatives" into "positives." *Education World.* Retrieved from http://www.educationworld.com/a_admin/admin/admin313.shtml

Lloyd, K. L. (1999). *Jerks at work: How to deal with people problems and problem people.* Franklin Lakes, NJ: Career Press.

McDaniel, T. R. (2002). Dealing with department chair detractors: Strategies that succeed. *Department Chair, 12*(4), 13–15.

Scott, G. G. (2004). *A survival guide for working with humans: Dealing with whiners, back-stabbers, know-it-alls, and other difficult people.* New York: AMACOM.

Topchik, G. S. (2000). *Managing workplace negativity.* New York: AMACOM.

RESOURCES

Buller, J. L. (2008, October). How to deal with workplace negativity: A case study. *Student Affairs Leader, 36*(21), 3–4.

Carter-Scott, C. (1999). *Negaholics: How to recover from your addiction to negativity and turn your life around.* New York: Ballantine.

Klaus, P., Rohman, J. M., & Hamaker, M. (2007). *The hard truth about soft skills: Workplace lessons smart people wish they'd learned sooner.* New York: HarperCollins.

28

ADDRESSING STAFF CONFLICTS

DEPARTMENTAL STAFF MAY BE defined as all employees who are not directly engaged in the teaching and research activities of the discipline but whose services support those who do. Some departments have no staff of their own, but receive support services from other offices of the institution. Most departments have at least one staff member, usually a secretary, receptionist, or administrative assistant. Some departments, particularly at large and complex institutions, may have extensive staffs of clerical workers, computer resource personnel, budget directors, advancement officers, and communication and multimedia specialists. Lab assistants are sometimes regarded as faculty and sometimes as staff, largely depending on whether they themselves teach and conduct research or solely provide technical assistance for others.

Because of the special role of staff in the department, you are likely to find that your relationship as a supervisor to staff members takes on different dimensions from the relationship you have with faculty members. For one thing, even if you're firmly committed to the idea that everyone who works in your area has a status equal to everyone else, regardless of job description, highest degree, or salary level, the environment in which we work tends to undermine this ideal. Colleges and universities are places in which academic achievements matter. They are, after all, fundamental to the mission of what we do. For this reason, no one ever has to say that faculty members "outrank" or are more important than the staff; in ways that are sometimes subtle, sometimes more overt, staff members are often made to feel a status difference between themselves and the faculty. Indeed, the very nature of their job responsibilities—supporting and assisting the faculty—tends to reinforce this impression. If you work in a department where the position of chair is rotated, there's another way in which the staff's role is fundamentally different from that of the faculty. It's only faculty members who are ever chosen or elected to be the department chair, and at the end of his or her term, the chair always returns to the faculty, never the staff. So whether you want it to be so or not, the faculty members in your department will always be your colleagues, and the staff members will be your employees, at least in some ways. That different dynamic changes the way in which most chairs interact with the faculty and staff. They're more likely to make requests of and to use persuasion with faculty members; they're more likely to issue instruction to and to set expectations for members of the staff.

It's important to keep these differences in mind when dealing with staff conflicts because they may affect the way in which you wish to approach these issues. A conflict between a professor and a member of the staff may not be viewed by the participants as a conflict between equals, even in the most democratic of environments. Moreover, a conflict between staff members may permit you more freedom than you would have in the case of a conflict among faculty members, or it may impose greater restrictions. Let's explore why these differences may occur.

The Role of Human Resources, Employee Unions, and Institutional Policies

One resource that chairs may overlook in attempting to resolve staff conflicts is the array of services that their own institution's office of human resources provides. It isn't just snobbery or academic tradition that regards faculty and staff as somehow different; many colleges and universities have significantly different employment policies for these two groups. For instance, faculty members may earn promotion according to criteria outlined in a faculty handbook and by following procedures developed by their own colleges and departments. Staff members may earn promotion according to an entirely different system, with its own rules of reclassification and reassignment that isn't monitored at all by the division of academic affairs. Faculty and staff members may belong to separate unions, or one of these groups may be governed by a labor agreement while the other is not. And most important for the topic of this chapter, the office of human resources may offer an entire range of services for staff members that would seem irrelevant to most members of the faculty. Among the services that may be available could be mediation and conflict resolution programs that can help you directly with any problems that arise. It may not occur to a department chair to turn to a human resource professional when a conflict arises between two faculty members, but these services, when they exist, can be invaluable in helping to resolve a staff dispute. So before you attempt to handle a staff problem yourself, ask yourself the following questions:

- Are there individuals in our human resource office who are trained to mediate or negotiate in cases of employee conflicts?
- Is there an institutional ombudsman whose services could help my department in its current situation?
- Does the employee union provide any services that can help to resolve disputes among the staff or any guidance in how these disagreements should be addressed?
- Does our institution offer an employee assistance program (EAP) as one of its benefits, and, if so, is mediation or conflict resolution one of the services included in our EAP?
- Does our staff handbook impose any procedures that require me to involve specific offices outside my department or respond to this issue in any particular way?

The advantage of using these institutional resources to help resolve the issue is that they can permit you to remain neutral and eliminate even the appearance that you may be taking sides in the conflict. When you decide to intervene in the conflict (or discover that you have no other option), sometimes even a situation that you believe has been resolved amicably may continue to fester or recur. You can learn to your discomfort that one side (or even both) begins to reinterpret your efforts to resolve the conflict as an unfair alliance with the other staff member. By maintaining your status as an honest broker and allowing the union, office of human resources, or ombudsman to address the issue, you may be able to remain removed from the fray and maintain a more effective supervisory position with each side.

Guidelines for When You Must Intervene

There are times, of course, when it is impossible or unwise to rely on other offices to solve the problem. You may have to intervene yourself when the problem is so time sensitive that you can't wait for anyone else to deal with it, involves issues that are exclusively departmental in nature, or would require confidential information to be shared too broadly.

You may also need to become involved if you work at an institution where the human resource staff is not equipped to handle conflict resolution or is one of the parties in the dispute. In this type of situation, there are several factors to keep in mind:

Rather than assigning blame or focusing on who did what, begin by talking about larger principles.

If, for example, your department has developed the code of civility or collegiality that I recommended in Chapter Twenty-Five, you can start your discussion by considering these concepts. You can say something like, "Let's consider what we're talking about when we say in our departmental code that we 'communicate with others, both orally and in writing, in a manner that is polite, respectful, and courteous. Whenever we disagree with someone, we restrict our differences to the issue itself while continuing to respect the individual with whom we disagree.' Let's talk about who's meant by these terms *others* and *someone* and what we expect of ourselves in our interactions with one another."

If your department doesn't have its own civility code, you can begin a similar conversation by asking the staff to talk about good customer relations and standards of service and then broadening the discussion by saying, "But let's consider who all might be included in this term *customers* and what constituencies we're trying to serve. Is there a particular standard of service that's required when we interact with students? What about members of the community? What about our own faculty members? How about faculty members in other departments? And what about one another?" Conversations of this sort can be more constructive in the long run because they don't begin with the implication that someone has done something wrong and now has to be punished for it. Rather, they turn the situation into a teachable moment and maintain a positive focus on the future.

Take care not to end-run someone's supervisor.

So far, the assumption has been that the staff conflict you're dealing with involves people who work in your department and report to you. But that's not always the case. And even when you do act as the supervisor of all the people involved, it's important to remember that some staff members have dotted-line relationships to other administrators. Finally, if your department is sufficiently complex to include several disciplines, each with its own director or assistant chair, it will be important to include in your discussions everyone who could claim to have a legitimate reporting relationship with each staff member.

This degree of care is necessary because it can be counterproductive to try to remedy a staff conflict but inadvertently leave a key player out of the loop or provide one of the participants in the conflict a convenient way to end-run any decisions that you make. Since it's not uncommon for staff members to have multiple supervisors, formal or informal, it can be essential for all of them to establish a united front before you intervene to solve the problem. If you don't take this extra step, you will at the very least be running the risk of alienating a colleague who may feel that he or she should have been fully informed of the issue and your intention to become involved. Even worse, you may be creating a back door by which any solution you devise could quickly be undone because you neglected to explain its necessity to a key player. Like all of us, staff members often seek out supporters when they feel that their actions have been unfairly criticized. In a well-meaning attempt to help this staff member feel better, your colleague could inadvertently undermine your efforts unless you explain them and their rationale in advance.

It's often more productive to focus on what you want to achieve rather than on how you want it done.

When trying to resolve a staff conflict, it is often useful to describe what you want to occur rather than to specify precisely how the staff member is to achieve this goal. For instance, suppose your department has an outer office in which several staff members work. Faculty members and students in your area frequently complain to you of a chilly and inhospitable atmosphere when they enter the office because the staff members never greet or interact with one another. You've noticed this situation yourself and understand that due to a long series of disagreements, the staff members are no longer on speaking terms with one another. You might try to resolve the situation by saying, "Look, you've at least got to greet one another when you pass in the hallway and to speak cordially to one another whenever a student or faculty member is around." This approach, however, has two fundamental problems. First, you've attempted to deal with the symptoms of the problem, not its actual cause. Second, you've specified how you want civility exemplified. You'll probably be taken at your word: the staff members will begin uttering a curt, "Morning," when they come in each day and engage in faux cheerfulness whenever a faculty member or student is near. But the underlying issues will remain, and the staff members may not even pretend to be cordial to one another when anyone besides "a student or faculty member is around."

Your solution doesn't solve your problem if potential donors, parents of current students, and other visitors begin to notice the chilly environment. A far better tack would be to say, "Look, as your supervisor, it's creating a problem for me that the atmosphere in the outer office so frequently seems unfriendly and impersonal. No one is saying that we all have to be best friends or even to like one another to work effectively together. But part of the professional environment that we're trying to create means fostering an atmosphere that others perceive as welcoming, inviting, and pleasant. I need each of you to tell me what you yourselves are going to do in order to create the environment that I need in order to do my job effectively."

--------------- o ---------------

As much as we may feel that strict hierarchies are an outdated management structure, department chairs, as administrative faculty members, frequently interact with staff members differently than they do with the professors in their disciplines. With a faculty member, a department chair will often adopt moral suasion by asking, suggesting, and advising that certain steps be taken; only in the most extreme of circumstances will a department chair issue a direct order to a faculty member. But staff members commonly receive instructions, sometimes general but sometimes detailed and explicit, from a department chair. For this reason, chairs have additional tools at their disposal when dealing with a staff conflict. They can out-and-out forbid certain actions from occurring or certain statements from being made. They can require staff members to complete certain job-related actions as a condition of their employment. They can also take advantage of resources provided by the office of human resources, EAP, or employees' union that may not apply (at least in the very same way) to faculty members. But none of these additional resources can make staff conflicts seem any less challenging when you encounter them.

Chairs frequently begin their position believing that they'll spend most of their days dealing with high-level issues vital to the future of their discipline, but they actually end up spending much of their time trying to resolve interpersonal disputes. An effective chair is thus not always the most brilliant scholar of the discipline, but the person who can get all of the area's stakeholders to work together more harmoniously in a way that best fulfills the department's mission.

RESOURCES

Buller, J. L. (2007, October). Overcoming tension between faculty and staff. *Academic Leader*, 23(10), 1, 6.

Buller, J. L. (2008, July). How to deal with challenging staff: A case study. *Student Affairs Leader*, 36(13), 1–2, 4.

Cloke, K., & Goldsmith, J. (2005). *Resolving conflicts at work: Eight strategies for everyone on the job*. San Francisco: Jossey-Bass.

Goodwin, C., & Griffith, D. (2007). *The conflict survival kit: Tools for resolving conflict at work*. Upper Saddle River, NJ: Pearson Prentice Hall.

Katz, D. (2010). *Win at work! The everybody wins approach to conflict resolution*. Hoboken, NJ: Wiley.

Maravelas, A. (2005). *How to reduce workplace conflict and stress: How leaders and their employees can protect their sanity and productivity from tension and turf wars*. Franklin Lakes, NJ: Career Press.

29

OVERCOMING CONFLICTS

IN THE BEST OF all possible worlds, department chairs would never need to worry about personality conflicts. Every member of the department would get along amicably with every other member. The departmental faculty would all respect one another's individual contributions, value their opinions even when they disagree with them, and work harmoniously for the overall good of the department, its students, and its reputation. Unfortunately, relatively few departments function this perfectly. At least, they rarely function this perfectly at all times.

Periodically a personality conflict will arise among two or more faculty members, creating tension and affecting the department's effectiveness, either for a brief period or, in the worst situations, over quite an extended period of time. At times, too, the relationship between two faculty members will become so fractious for so long that the department chair will begin to wonder whether the individuals are not somehow deriving satisfaction from prolonging their conflict. Otherwise it would hardly seem worth all of the time, energy, and sacrifice that the individuals regularly invest in keeping their dispute going.

Resolving personality disputes is rarely as easy as determining that one of the participants is clearly at fault, while the other is a purely innocent bystander. Situations are almost never as simple—or simplistic—as those who are involved in them tend to allege.

At times, neither side in the dispute will be right, and the department chair will be placed in the awkward position of making both sides equally unhappy. (In certain situations, the result can be an ironic sort of rapprochement between the two feuding faculty members, who now find in the chair a shared focal point for their discontent.) Even more common, each of the disputants will have some justice on his or her side while at the same time being responsible for a share of the rancor, lack of collegiality, and poor judgment that has led to the impasse. As La Rochefoucauld said, "Disputes would not last long if the fault were on one side only" (*Les querelles ne dureraient pas longtemps, si le tort n'était que d'un côté*). Solving the problem (or at least improving it to the point where the functioning of the department will not be hampered unduly) will require diplomacy on your part, a special amount of sensitivity to the foibles of human behavior, and a great deal of that very precious commodity, time.

An Action Plan

In most cases, the following action plan will provide you with at least a start toward dealing with the most serious cases of personality dispute.

Step 1: Gather Information

It is almost always counterproductive to intervene in a faculty personality conflict by saying things like, "You two just need to get along better." Advice of this sort is so general that it will prove to be unhelpful in the extreme. Besides, most parties in a conflict already know that they cannot get along; what they don't know is how to improve the situation. Another inappropriate response is making a generalized announcement in a faculty meeting along the lines of, "We've been having some personality disputes in our department, and I want those who are responsible to stop it." The individuals to whom you are referring in such a statement may not realize that you are talking about them; even if they do understand you, they still are being given no help whatsoever in what to do to solve the problem.

Rather than attempting to address the problem as a general matter of intradepartmental relations, you need to learn all that you can so that you may identify the difficulty with great specificity. Determine as precisely as possible who is having conflicts with whom, which behaviors tend to be causing serious problems for your department, and what the problematic results of these behaviors have been. In other words, reflect on what has led you and others in your department to be aware of an issue needing to be addressed, the conditions under which the problem tends to arise, and the negative consequences for your department.

As you gather information in preparing to solve the problem, focus as much as possible on detrimental behaviors, not on perceived character flaws. In other words, the specific behaviors that you might observe could include directing public criticism at a person rather than at a policy or an idea, continually bringing up ancient history that most faculty members in the department would prefer to leave behind, uncollegial slights and omissions such as failure to recognize the contributions of others to a project or to apprise others of important developments in a timely manner, or blindsiding other faculty members in meetings with information or objections that could easily have been shared with colleagues in advance. The conditions under which these behaviors might be demonstrated could include formal department meetings and other large gatherings of faculty members ("grandstanding"), private confrontations with the other individual in an office or some other location where witnesses were not present ("bullying"), catching the other person off-guard in the hallway or during conversations with students ("humiliating"), or by means of excessively harsh and unprofessional communications such as memos or e-mails ("flaming").

The negative consequences of the individual's action might include preventing important departmental business from being conducted in an efficient manner, loss of potential students or majors in your program who are alienated by this unprofessional behavior, a poor reputation for the department at your institution or at national meetings of your discipline, or decreasing faculty morale that could even lead, in extreme cases, to high faculty turnover.

By giving close consideration to these issues, you will know more clearly the message that you want to provide to the faculty members embroiled in the personality conflict. You will be able to say specifically, "Here's what each of you is doing that is causing problems for yourselves and others. Here are the situations that seem to provoke these actions. And here's the difficulty that it's causing for us. Now let's discuss what we're going to do to fix this situation."

Step 2: Pick Your Battles Carefully

Resolving personality conflicts will almost inevitably require difficult, prolonged effort on your part. You can easily make a difficult task all but impossible by failing to distinguish pet peeves (annoying habits that don't really cause any lasting damage to the department) from the truly severe personality issues that can end up even destroying a program. As you examine each behavior that seems to be causing difficulty, ask your-self the following four questions about it:

- o What's the best I could hope for if I intervene to change this behavior?
- o What's the best I could hope for if I simply did nothing?
- o What's the worst-case scenario that could occur if things backfire when I intervene to change this behavior?
- o What's the worst-case scenario if I did nothing?

Only in situations where the benefits clearly outweigh the disadvantages is your direct action as department chair likely to be desirable. Like all other administrators, you need to develop a fairly thick skin against frequent but ultimately petty annoyances that occur in every management situation. Your voice will become less effective if you begin being seen as a micromanager of idiosyncrasies instead of what you want most to be: your institution's leading advocate for your discipline.

Step 3: Prepare a Clear Action Plan for Intervention

In most cases, the best start to resolving the problem is to meet privately with each of the individuals involved in the personality conflict. Scheduling this preliminary conversation will take some sensitivity: no matter which faculty member you speak with first, he or she may be perceived as the real culprit, while the second person is perceived as the innocent victim. It may therefore be desirable to offer a number of times and dates to each party and allow each to select the one that seems most suitable to him or her.

In these initial conversations, explain what you are trying to solve, why finding a solution is important, and what an acceptable outcome will be. Avoid giving the impression that you are taking sides in the dispute: your goal must always be to fix the problem, not to fix the blame. Concentrate on what your future expectations will be and state, politely but firmly, what consequences will occur if those expectations are not met. Possible consequences will depend a great deal on the situation but could include anything from out-and-out termination to placing a letter of reprimand in the person's file.

Throughout this conversation, direct your attention and that of the faculty member toward what will occur, not toward past grievances. Each faculty member may need to vent, and a little bit of griping and self-pity is acceptable, but only up to a point. If the faculty member appears unwilling after a reasonable amount of time to let go of the past, you may need to say something like, "I understand that's how you feel. But you have to understand that it's my job to make certain that the work of this department gets done. And right now, one of the things that's preventing that is all of this past history. We need a new start, and as of right now, that's what we're going to have." If the individual begins offering excuses or justification for his or her treatment of the other person, refuse to accept them. Remind this faculty member that there can be no excuse or justification for any behavior that harms the education of your students, the scholarship or creative activity for which your department is responsible, and the other essential business that your department needs to perform.

Don't end this initial meeting with each faculty member until you have outlined the clear course of action that you have determined in advance, underscored the seriousness of the issue, and summarized the next steps that all of you will be taking. Then follow up with a brief memo of understanding that summarizes and reiterates your expectations.

In the majority of cases, your next step should be to meet with both faculty members together to reinforce the new working arrangement that will be in place from this point forward, demonstrate your continued emphasis on resolving this issue, and (it is hoped) provide an opportunity for the faculty members to begin to build a sense of rapport. If one or both of the faculty members begins returning to old, destructive patterns of behavior during the course of this joint meeting, acknowledge what has occurred immediately, describe the negative impact of these actions, and reiterate—politely but very firmly—the consequences that will occur from repetitions of this activity.

Step 4: Make Your Purpose Precise and Clear

When attempting to resolve personality conflicts, chairs may be accused of trying to mandate that the members of their departments "like one another," that they socialize with and invite one another to lunch or parties, and that they must expand their working relationships into a deep and abiding friendship. These assumptions are far from the case. You should make it clear that we are all entitled as individuals to choose our own friends and to like or dislike whomever we wish. But the effectiveness of the department, not personal preferences, is the issue here.

Whenever someone's behavior interferes with the ability of the department to attract and retain students, secure its necessary resources, provide the quality of education to which it aspires, or produce the level of scholarship that your college or university expects, then your department has a problem that must be addressed. You are not seeking to control anyone's attitudes, rights, or feelings; what you are trying to do is to promote behavior that allows your department to succeed at its mission. Just as a faculty member would not wish to be pedagogically ineffective because of his or her attitudes toward a particular student, so should that faculty member not wish the discipline as a whole to be ineffective at your institution because of a relationship with a colleague.

Your purpose in speaking to faculty members about this issue is to ensure the proper operation of your department at all of its various tasks. You have absolutely no desire (and no right) to control any individual's personal likes and dislikes.

Step 5: Hold Follow-Up Sessions

If a personality conflict is severe enough to require your intervention, it is unlikely to be resolved with a single meeting. You will need to schedule a certain number of follow-up sessions with the faculty members as individuals and both together in order to monitor progress, reward steps forward, and address reversions to earlier destructive behaviors.

Do not expect the path toward resolution of the personality conflict to be one of smooth and steady improvement. There will be backsliding, particularly at those times of the academic year when stresses are high and tempers are short. These lapses should be dealt with swiftly, firmly, and (whenever possible) in private. Nevertheless, the overall trend of the relationship between the two faculty members should be one of overall improvement in collegiality and professionalism. If that is not occurring, you will need to begin again by considering what specific behaviors tend to be causing a problem for the department, under which conditions these behaviors tend to occur, and what undesirable results are occurring due to those behaviors. Make it clear to both individuals that their actions are still a long way from where they need to be and, as a result of your previous statements about the consequences for failure to improve, you will now need to take certain actions.

If instead these two faculty members are making real progress in their relationship, be generous with your praise and recognition, let them know that you understand the difficulty of the task, and congratulate them on their excellent spirit of collegiality toward one another and other members of the department.

Special Situations

Taking these actions will help improve (though perhaps not necessarily eliminate) a large number of personality conflicts in the academic setting. Two types of situations, however, require special consideration and separate attention.

More Than Two Faculty Members Seem to Be Having a Personality Conflict

The more parties there are to a departmental personality conflict, the greater the challenges will be in overcoming it and the longer your time commitment as chair will be to solving this problem. Somewhat less obvious is that the challenges in these situations can increase exponentially with each additional faculty member involved.

In fact, rarely does a personality dispute involve three or more faculty members, each having equivalent grievances about all of the others. Far more common in these complex disputes is the development of factions, blocs, or cabals in which several faculty members join forces against another, at times creating a shifting pattern of alliances and counteralliances that may remind you of George Orwell's *Nineteen Eighty-Four*. Moreover, the sheer number of issues that will need to be worked through in these more complex personality conflicts is likely to be greater than in cases where you are dealing with only two individuals. Although the basic method of approaching the problem (individual meetings with the various faculty members, followed by a group meeting of all those involved in the dispute) will probably remain the same, you may wish to supplement this tactic with one or more of the following, depending on the details of the situation and the severity of the departmental rift:

○ *Mediation.* Someone from outside the department who has training and experience in mediating workplace conflicts can bring a fresh perspective to a situation that members of your department (including yourself) may only be able to see from the inside. External mediators can free you from appearing to take a partisan interest in the conflict, work behind the scenes in ways that you cannot, and draw the participants' attention to the genuine seriousness of their problem.

○ *Training.* While general training in workplace relations or collegiality is likely to be of only limited value in complex personality conflicts, a more focused departmental retreat on techniques that will help your faculty move beyond departmental tension, foster teamwork, and achieve greater professionalism in their relationships with colleagues can be one useful step in particularly large departmental conflicts. Constructing a half-day workshop around a work such as Masters and Albright (2002), Coffman (2005), Van Slyke (1999), Schmidt, Gallagher, and Weiss (2001), Weeks (1994), or VanSant (2003) can provide an ongoing context for resolving personality disputes in your department.

○ *Receivership.* In the most extreme cases of personality conflict, you may wish to consider the desirability of some form of receivership. Is there some shared project, facility, or enterprise that appears to be provoking repeated outbreaks of the conflict? If so, then assigning that responsibility to a neutral party—with a clear understanding of what changes in behavior will be required for reconsideration of this assignment at some future date—may be necessary to underscore the severity of the problem. Receivership is not always a possible or desirable option, but if no other solution seems possible, it may be your last hope when other attempted solutions have failed.

You as Chair Are One of the Parties in the Personality Conflict

Your awareness that one of the challenges facing your department is a personality conflict involving you and at least one of your faculty members means that you either have a remarkable degree of self-understanding or an unusually candid colleague who has confided in you. In either case, congratulations! We rarely see disputes involving ourselves as personality conflicts, preferring to characterize them as simply the other person's fault. If, however, you have good reason to believe that you are a contributing party to a personality conflict that is affecting your department's function, you should consider taking at least one of the following steps:

○ *Clear the air.* Sit down and talk to the other person with whom you seem to be in conflict, openly admitting that your differences are hampering your department's work and stating your dissatisfaction with this result. Try to formulate a working arrangement that will minimize differences and avoid situations that tend to aggravate your conflict.

○ *Consult a neutral party.* Just as you may sometimes have a better view of the causes of conflict between faculty members than the faculty members themselves may have, an impartial third party (another department chair, a trusted senior faculty member, or an unbiased party from elsewhere in the institution) may be able to provide you with insight that you cannot gain from other sources. If your institution employs trained mediators, these individuals may be able to assist you with reducing departmental tensions in an objective manner that is not possible within the department itself. In all such cases, it will be important for the neutral party to be fully aware of the confidentiality that will be required in this situation. While trained mediators will already be fully aware of the need for confidentiality and discretion, more informal mentors may well need some guidance—or at least a polite reminder—in this area.

○ *Delegate appropriate responsibilities.* If certain departmental decisions seem to be exacerbating the conflict you have with another faculty member, try to seek processes that remove as much personal tension as possible from the situation. A committee that reviews departmental travel requests, an assistant chair who must also sign off on departmental course rotations, or a process that bases certain decisions on seniority or other nonsubjective factors can help reduce the number of situations that lead to tense encounters and perceptions that decisions are based on personal likes and dislikes.

In every case involving a personality conflict between yourself and another faculty member, remember that there may be at least a perception of a power differential. Whether you see it or not, the other faculty member may view you as "the boss" and, particularly in cases of junior faculty members for whom promotion and tenure decisions are in the future, that person's perceptions may not be that the issue is merely a dispute among equals. Always go out of your way to be sensitive to how you may be perceived by faculty members simply because of your title, position, and authority. Issues that may not even occur to you as being stumbling blocks in your relationship with another faculty member may be the very reasons that your personality conflict appears so difficult to resolve.

○

New department chairs are frequently surprised by the number of personality conflicts they're expected to resolve. It can sometimes seem as though interpersonal behavior that wouldn't be tolerated in any other profession is merely par for the course in higher education. Obtaining specialized training in conflict resolution, keeping a cool head when tempers flare, and intervening quickly before problems become truly serious are all approaches that every chair will find useful when encountering the personality conflicts that seem to besiege a great number of academic departments.

REFERENCES

Coffman, J. R. (2005). *Work and peace in academe: Leveraging time, money, and intellectual energy through managing conflict.* San Francisco: Jossey-Bass/Anker.

Masters, M. F., & Albright, R. R. (2002). *The complete guide to conflict resolution in the workplace.* New York: AMACOM.

Schmidt, W. H., Gallagher, B. J., & Weiss, S. (2001). *Is it always right to be right? A tale of transforming workplace conflict into creativity and collaboration.* New York: AMACOM.

VanSant, S. (2003). *Wired for conflict: The role of personality in resolving differences.* Gainesville, FL: Center for Applications of Psychological Type.

Van Slyke, E. J. (1999). *Listening to conflict: Finding constructive solutions to workplace disputes.* New York: AMACOM.

Weeks, D. (1994). *The eight essential steps to conflict resolution: Preserving relationships at work, at home, and in the community.* New York: Tarcher.

RESOURCES

Coffman, J. R. (2009). Conflict management for chairs. *Department Chair,* *20*(1), 18–21.

Furlong, G. T. (2005). *The conflict resolution toolbox: Models and maps for analyzing, diagnosing, and resolving conflict.* Hoboken, NJ: Wiley.

Maravelas, A. (2005). *How to reduce workplace conflict and stress: How leaders and their employees can protect their sanity and productivity from tension and turf wars.* Franklin Lakes, NJ: Career Press.

30

A SCENARIO ANALYSIS ON MENTORING CHALLENGES

FOR A DISCUSSION OF how scenario analyses are structured and suggestions on how to use this exercise most productively, see Chapter Nine.

Case Studies

The Office Dilemma

There has been a substantial amount of new construction at your university, and as a result, your department has just inherited a corner office that abuts a small workroom. You are pleased to be assigned this new office for the department since the space is better than any existing faculty office. Perhaps more important, your department is acquiring this office just in time to accommodate a new faculty member who will be joining your department in the fall.

This is the first time your department has obtained a new office in anyone's memory, so you have no established policy on how to allocate the space. The dean wants you to take responsibility for making this decision. Because the dean has arrived at your institution only within the past several months, how you handle this decision will be one of the first opportunities to show your new boss your leadership style. Almost immediately after the news is out about the extra office, you begin receiving advice:

○ Faculty member A says that the faculty member who currently occupies the largest office now should be given the new office and explains: "That way, all of us can move up a notch, and everybody gets something. The new faculty member will receive the smallest of the old offices, and that's fair in terms of seniority."

- ○ Faculty member B pleads with you not to force everyone to move, which would be disruptive. Letting the new person have the new office would be the easiest solution.
- ○ Faculty member C says that choice of offices should be done on the basis of seniority. This will require some wholesale reassignment of office space since some more senior faculty members may want to swap offices with those who arrived at the institution more recently.
- ○ Faculty member D agrees with faculty member C but insists that seniority should mean "years in the profession, not just years at the institution," and this interpretation would require a different ranking of preferences.
- ○ Faculty member E disagrees with faculty member D, saying that rank is a more effective reflection of "true merit than mere seniority" and "I don't want some unproductive associate professor having first choice over me in office space just because that person's been here longer."
- ○ Faculty member F says that the attached workroom makes the new space suitable for the journal she is editing, and "appropriateness of function simply has to be a more important consideration than anything else."
- ○ Faculty member G insists that "a lottery is the only fair way to decide this."
- ○ And faculty member H recommends using the same principle in assigning office space that the college uses in setting the line of march for commencement—"whatever that principle is."

After discussing this matter in a department meeting for some time, you realize that a consensus is simply not possible.

What factors do you consider as you make your decision?

Allegations Con Brio

One morning, Professor Tattler enters your office, closes your door, and tells you there is a certain "very serious matter" the two of you must discuss. Then, for the third time this month, Tattler begins to outline the shortcomings of Professor Weiner, another member of your faculty. The first time Tattler came to see you, he complained that Weiner was spending too much time conducting personal business on the phone or over the Internet, frequently requiring Tattler to assist Weiner's own students. Next, Tattler accused Weiner of begging off a departmental committee, citing an excessive workload, even though "everyone knows that Weiner has the fewest students in the department and is not the discipline's most productive scholar." Now, in little more than a week, your department will be participating in an institutionally mandated diversity awareness workshop, an activity about which Weiner has been skeptical in the past. Your dean has told you that because of a grievance that caused the institution some bad national publicity, everyone in your department must attend the workshop and only severe illness will be regarded as an excused absence. Tattler tells you that Weiner has scheduled a job interview at another institution on the very day of the workshop. "I can't tell you how I know this," "Tattler says, "and you can't use me as a source. But you can count on this: Weiner's going to call you the morning of the workshop and claim a sudden illness."

You suspect that there may be some truth to Tattler's allegations, but you also know that Tattler resents Weiner for a negative promotion recommendation given several years ago and would like nothing better than for Weiner to get into trouble.

What do you do?

Considerations

1. As you reflect on "The Office Dilemma," consider these questions:

   a. Do any of the positions advanced by members of your faculty appear to have particular merit? Can you rule out any of these positions immediately?

   b. Are there possible solutions that the members of your department have not yet suggested?

   c. What, in the end, is your decision in this matter? On what basis did you make that decision? How do you go about selling it to the members of your department?

   d. Is there a way in which you can make use of this problem as an opportunity to mentor your faculty into appropriate strategies for achieving consensus and resolving conflicts?

2. As you reflect on "Allegations Con Brio," consider these questions:

   a. Do you suggest to Tattler that supervising members of the department is your business and that this sort of gossip is inappropriate?

b. Do you confront Weiner in order to learn if the allegation has any merit? If so, how do you respond if Weiner says to you, "You heard this from Tattler, didn't you? Well, let me tell you Tattler's no saint either because . . ."

c. Is your response any different if you found no corroborating evidence for any of Tattler's earlier allegations?

d. Is your response any different if Weiner really is an underperformer whom you would be happy to see leave the institution?

e. Where do you draw the line between due diligence in being informed about what is going on in your department and mere gossiping that harms morale?

Suggestions

The Office Dilemma

This case study provides a good opportunity to assess your leadership style. For instance, if your initial impulse was that instead of having a series of private conversations, your department really needs to hold a meeting to discuss all of these alternative approaches, it's obvious that you put a priority on consensus building and collective decision making. If your initial impulse was to assign the office to faculty member F because she was the only person whose case was based on how the space would be used for the good of the discipline, then you seem to take a utilitarian view when making decisions. Finding other solutions may indicate that you value long-term goals over temporary inconvenience, place a priority on either merit or seniority, or prefer that the choice ultimately be in someone else's hands (as in the case of relying on a lottery or the system used to determine the line of march for commencement). Ultimately this case presents two issues:

○ How do you view a material asset like a new office? Is it primarily an opportunity to reward for someone for past service or a means by which you could obtain some future goal?

○ Since there are such divergent opinions about the best course of action, how will you keep this issue from becoming divisive in the department? How will you mentor those who disagree with whatever decision you make?

The first issue is best addressed in terms of your overall goal as department chair. If you're working in an environment where morale is extremely low, salary increases have been minimal or nonexistent for several years, and other opportunities to acknowledge people's contributions have been limited, then seeing the office as a way to reward your faculty may be your best alternative. But if alternative means of compensation exist, this is a good situation to fall back on your core principles.

It's always beneficial to have a clear criterion to use as the starting point for making any difficult decision. One such criterion might be, "How will this action serve to improve student learning?" or, "How will this choice increase the research potential of my program?" If you have a guiding principle of this sort, use that question to evaluate each of the faculty members' suggestions to see which of them is strongest according to the standard you've adopted. If, by using this test, you find that none of your faculty's suggestions seems sufficiently strong, then you should develop your own alternative that best achieves the goals you regard as most important.

The more difficult challenge will probably be bringing about unity in the department if each person seems entrenched in his or her position. It's at this point that, no matter whether you've adopted one of the alternatives suggested or developed your own solution, it will be important for you to present and defend your rationale. If you've acted according to principles that you've long articulated, your ultimate decision will come as no surprise. For instance, you might say something like this:

> As you know, I've always said that although one of us chairs the department, we all have an equal voice in making decisions. So we're not going to take any action that doesn't receive widespread departmental support. Right now, we've eight possibilities on the table. We're going to discuss the merits of each of them and then, in a secret ballot, everyone will vote for seven of the eight alternatives. We'll eliminate the solution that receives the least support, talk about them again, if you wish, and then vote for your six top choices. After another elimination, we'll vote for five, then four, and so on until one alternative gets at least a majority of votes in the department. That way, we'll make sure that every voice is heard and considered, but that ultimately we act in a way that suits most, if not all, of us.

As a procedural note, this sort of incremental voting almost never takes as much balloting as you might expect. People tend to gravitate rather quickly to two or three preferred options, and these become the focus of discussion almost immediately after the first ballot.

If no consensus emerges and you haven't yet articulated a consistent guiding principle, it is often still preferable for you to explain your choice within the context of larger objectives. For example, you can say something like, "This has really been a difficult decision. The good thing is that we have so many excellent options to consider. But since we can choose only one of them, the issue finally came down to this for me: How can we raise the visibility of our discipline nationally without creating the kind of upheaval we'd have to go through if everyone had to change offices? Since our journal will be able to be produced more efficiently with the workroom that we're getting and the journal acts as the front door through which many people first meet our department, I've decided to allocate the space to faculty member F and our publication needs."

If there is still resistance to this decision despite the care you've taken in explaining your reasons, this may be a good opportunity for you to mentor the faculty member involved (and there may be more than one) and see if you can learn any underlying issues for this reaction. For instance, is the person feeling underappreciated for his or her achievements, simply waging a turf war, or assuming that bigger space is always better? Once you better understand the reasons for the person's reactions—and they frequently are not the reasons that seem most obvious—you'll be able to mentor that person more effectively, perhaps offering an alternative or finding a different solution, and demonstrating that it wasn't out of a lack of personal support that you decided not to select that faculty member's proposal.

Allegations Con Brio

This case presents two challenges—one by Tattler and the other by Weiner. Mentoring challenges frequently come to department chairs in exactly this way. In a conflict between two faculty members, your solution is relatively easy when one of them is clearly in the wrong and the other is clearly in the right. But actual administrative situations are generally filled with gray areas, and there will be a combination of both right and wrong on each side.

In this situation, it may be useful to mentor Tattler on the differences between a faculty member's responsibilities as a colleague and your responsibilities as supervisor. While you certainly want to be notified of anything that constitutes a severe violation of university regulations or the law, as well as anything that is potentially dangerous or significantly opposed to the good of the program, it's counterproductive for one colleague to snitch on everything another employee does simply because he or she doesn't agree with it. Assure Tattler that if you're concerned about another faculty member's level of committee service or use of a university telephone for personal calls, you'll deal with it. Moreover, right now Tattler doesn't have any evidence that Weiner will miss the required training session, merely a suspicion that he may. As a result, it may be appropriate in your role as mentor to caution Tattler about making accusations that he can't substantiate, and you'd be ill advised to intervene too aggressively with Weiner on the basis of Tattler's conjecture.

If we adopt a standard of proactive intervention in the case of issues that involve a violation of the law, are potentially dangerous, or threaten the long-term well-being of the program, it's clear that Weiner's absence from the training session does not meet this criterion. Your best strategy may be to remind all department members that in light of the dean's requirement that everyone must attend the diversity awareness workshop unless prevented by severe illness, you'll expect anyone who is absent to provide the dean's office with a suitable medical excuse. (In view of the fact that the workshop was called in response to a grievance, some documentation of either attendance or legitimate reasons for absence will probably be required anyway.) In that case, if Weiner does miss the training in order to participate in a job interview, you'll have done your part to underscore the importance of the workshop without singling anyone out but placed the responsibility clearly on each person's own shoulders. Moreover, in practical terms, if Weiner has actually caused at least some of the challenges that Tattler alleges, you may not want to stand too firmly in the way of this faculty member's exit strategy. This seems to be a situation is which a more indirect strategy serves everyone's best interests, including Tattler's.

PART FIVE

THE CHAIR'S ROLE IN FACULTY DEVELOPMENT

31

FACILITATING A POSITIVE FIRST-YEAR FACULTY EXPERIENCE

THE VALUE THAT FIRST-YEAR experience programs play in the academic success of students has been established by numerous studies. As a result, campuses across the country are putting into place programs—at times quite elaborate ones—designed to integrate first-year students more fully into the campus community, expose them to the institution's cherished traditions, and provide them with the resources they will need in order to succeed in a type of work that may be altogether different from any they have done before.

But what about faculty members? Frequently new faculty members arrive at a college or university with only the most tentative idea of the institution's fundamental values, the role that they will be expected to play on campus, how they will find the information they need to succeed, and the expectations by which they will be judged throughout their professional careers.

Too frequently institutions try to address these needs and concerns through a short orientation program in which everything that newcomers to the college or university could possibly want to know is covered in one or two days, at times even in a half-day session. Yet the question that is too infrequently asked is: If short, intense orientation programs don't work for students, why do we expect them to work for faculty members? Instructors are frequently making transitions that are at least as dramatic as those of first-year students. They may be emerging from a graduate program at a research university to begin a position in which they will be teaching mostly undergraduates in the environment of a liberal arts college. They may be arriving from situations in which they were surrounded by advanced majors and graduate students with an inherent love for their discipline, only to find themselves teaching required courses for students who want only to get that particular class out of the way. At the very least, they will have left an institution where they knew the basic values and rules for success, had a well-developed core of colleagues, and were highly successful at what they did (otherwise you would not have hired them) for a new institution where they don't know what the ground rules are, have few if any friends, and need to prove themselves all over again. To help new faculty members succeed in such an environment, you don't need an orientation; you need a faculty first-year experience program.

Faculty first-year experience programs are structured in such a way that information is offered to new faculty members in a timely manner but at a pace at which they can absorb it. They recognize the anxieties inherent in operating in a new environment. They provide advice, access to information, and support. And then, like any good first-year experience program for students, they wean the individual away from the program itself, allowing the new faculty member to succeed on his or her own.

Faculty first-year experience programs are frequently run out of faculty development offices or centers for excellence in teaching and learning. If the institution does not offer such opportunities, department chairs can create their own departmentally based programs. In fact, in situations where no institution-wide faculty first-year experience program exists, it is incumbent on department chairs to help fill that gap. If you are thinking about designing and implementing your own program, here are a few best practices for you to keep in mind.

Be certain to distinguish the formative aspects of your faculty development efforts from any summative decisions you may need to make.

In other words, you will need, as department chair, to have several types of meetings or sessions with newer faculty members. Some of these sessions will be formative: you will be working through issues with the faculty member because you want to improve the quality of that person's instruction, bring the faculty member into a more constructive relationship with his or her peers, and nurture the quality of his or her scholarship or creative activity. At other times, you will be meeting for summative purposes: you will be making or announcing a decision, probably on such matters as contract renewal and a possible salary.

If you do not specifically and clearly distinguish those activities, new faculty members are likely to confuse them. They are less likely to share with you challenges that they are having in their teaching if they think that you are merely collecting this information to "use against them" when it comes to allocating a raise or offering another year's contract. For this reason, make an effort to go out of your way to clarify the purpose of a meeting from the very beginning—for example:

> What I'd like to do today is to have each of us talk about a challenge that we're having in the classroom, and then we're all going to offer specific suggestions or insights into how we might try meeting that challenge. No matter how good any of us is as a teacher, after all, we can all do better, and there are always some new difficulties to face in teaching a class. So the point is not to judge here, but rather to work together to get better.
>
> I'll go first. Here's a challenge that came up in one of my classes the other day, and I'm still working my way through what I could have done better. What happened was . . .

An introduction like that makes the purpose of the session absolutely clear to the new faculty members: you are there to help them, not evaluate them. By candidly offering examples of how you yourself are still making progress toward improving your instruction, you will help your faculty members open up to one another, see the faculty first-year experience program as a useful opportunity for professional growth, and begin making real progress. Alternatively, in a session where you really are evaluating the faculty member, you can begin by saying, "Today we're going to switch roles a little bit, and I'm going to shift somewhat from mentoring and faculty development to playing more of my supervisory role. It's kind of like when you change roles from offering students advice on drafts of their papers to actually assigning them grades. So you can think of today as rather like the day that a grade on an assignment comes in. And here's where I think that your strengths and weaknesses have been this year . . ."

Organize sessions with new faculty members along the lines of what they need to know now rather than what seems to make the best self-contained topic.

As academics, we frequently like to organize the information that we present in ways that seem to make the best sense to us, forgetting that individuals who are learning this information may have entirely different needs or abilities to absorb what we are presenting. In other words, it may initially seem to make sense to organize a group of faculty development sessions topically around such general topics as "Campus Traditions," "Employee Benefits," "Institutional Exam Policies," "Teaching

Introductory Courses," and the like. But these thematic groupings are unlikely to reflect the needs of first-year faculty members. If they hear all of the college traditions at once, they are almost certainly not going to remember the nuanced distinctions among "Fall Homecoming," "Spring Fling," and "Summer Alumni Weekend." In much the same way, a general overview of everything they need to know about teaching introductory courses is likely to cause them to become frustrated (because they are now learning how they should have constructed that syllabus that has been in place for six weeks) or to experience sensory overload (because they are hearing about the best ways of constructing final exams when what they really need now is free time to write their midterm exams).

Rather, you will develop a much more useful session with faculty members by looking only a short distance into the future and asking yourself, "If I were a newcomer, what would I need to know now?" Perhaps one of your special campus traditions will be taking place within the next two to three weeks; that is the time to talk about the meaning of Founder's Day or Family Weekend or Community Appreciation Week. Spending five or ten minutes talking about this activity in a session that also includes other equally timely information—how to submit the campus book orders that are due within a month, the best way to pass budget requests to you in time to incorporate them into your annual proposal, your institution's expectations about reporting students whose midcourse progress is unsatisfactory or who are amassing an excessive number of absences, and so on—will acclimate your newer faculty members much more quickly than will a set of workshops tailored to your needs and schedule, not theirs.

A well-organized faculty first-year experience program has both group and individual activities.

Newer faculty members tend to have two not wholly compatible needs. On the one hand, they need peers; they need to know that they are not alone as a newcomer, that others are experiencing similar challenges and frustrations, and that there is a social environment in which they can fit and play a part. On the other hand, they need guidance; they need to vent, ask questions that they may be embarrassed to ask in front of others, and feel comfortable letting their guard down.

These different needs can best be addressed by constructing your program so that newer faculty members have an opportunity both to meet with a mentor (you or some other experienced faculty member, within or outside your department) and in a group of others who are like them. The size of your department may determine how to organize these activities. Your department may be small enough that a critical mass can be obtained only by offering your faculty first-year experience program to everyone in their first three years at the institution or even everyone who has not yet been reviewed for tenure. Other departments may be large enough that you will have a critical mass for discussions by including only teachers who are actually in their first year on the faculty. The important thing is rarely the specific amount of service that individual faculty members have provided, but rather getting enough people together to have meaningful exchange, offer a support group to others when they need it, and provide a diversity of opinions. In a similar way, there is no perfect frequency for first-year faculty members to meet one-on-one with you in your office, even if for nothing more than an informal update on their progress and sense of how they're fitting in. At some institutions, regularly scheduled meetings once a week will not be too often; at others, setting time for a formal meeting only once a month will not be too rare. Use your own best judgment to determine a proper rhythm for these meetings based on your own administrative style, the amount of support your newer faculty require, and the individual personality of your college or university.

Use a connected topic as a theme to guide your program.

Building a faculty first-year experience program around a specific topic or book helps connect your different sessions, even if the topic itself occupies no more than five or ten minutes of each session. Useful books around which to build an effective semester-long or year-long series include Bain (2004), Walvoord and Anderson (1998), Bean (2001), Baiocco and DeWaters (1998), and McKeachie and Svinicki (2005). A more topic-oriented approach might be built around ideas like student learning styles, tying scholarship to teaching, active learning and maximum student engagement, addressing the needs of the whole student, social, intellectual, and developmental learning, as well as other subjects that seem particularly appropriate for your individual institutional culture. In some ways, the book or topic of the program provides the excuse for the meeting, session, or workshop; the real progress will be made as faculty members build outward from the expressed purpose of the program to deal with their own needs as new faculty members and the situations they are encountering in their classes.

Including information from other offices both shares your burden and begins building a network for your faculty members.

There are important contacts that your faculty members will need to have in the business office, the registrar's office, student life, the computer and information resource center, and other departments. By including individuals from these other offices in your program, you relieve yourself of the necessity of answering every question and leading each discussion; at the same time, you help make your new faculty members true citizens of your college or university. You teach them not only the resources that are available but also whom to call in different offices on campus when they have needs in particular areas.

> A major component in what we might call institutional literacy comes from knowing not merely which offices are responsible for which functions, but specifically who in which office can most effectively address any particular issue.

By introducing newer faculty members to a broader range of people than they are likely to encounter in your department or building, you are playing an important role in their overall socialization to the campus. Experienced department chairs understand the very real possibility of losing a valued new faculty member because he or she never quite feels at home in a new environment or is unsuccessful in finding a circle of friends. By helping your newcomers make contacts within the larger academic community, you are taking a positive step toward making them happier, more productive, and less likely to leave the institution too soon for other opportunities.

Whenever possible, try to make your program highly participatory and an opportunity that leads toward the production of a useful product.

Conducting sections on the importance of active learning by lecturing to those in attendance sends the wrong message. So does taking up the time of extremely busy junior faculty members with a series of discussions that, while perhaps presenting useful theories and general concepts, seem to have little practical bearing on their immediate needs.

As a result, it can be valuable to focus at least part of your faculty first-year experience program on the practical creation of some tangible product that the faculty members will need. At some institutions, the most appropriate product to use as the focus for the program will be the annual report or portfolio of teaching, scholarship, and service that each faculty member is expected to compile. At other institutions, faculty members may spend part of their second semester critiquing their own and their colleagues' first-semester syllabi, examinations, and course materials to discover how these items may be improved, how the course may be better structured so as to achieve the department's learning goals, and ways of better evaluating student achievement. In still other cases, each faculty member may be asked to develop a conference presentation and practice presenting it before the other new faculty members, who will assess it for ways in which it may be improved; the faculty member will then rehearse until it reaches the level that both he or she and the chair are satisfied. By using workshop time to create these products, faculty members are less likely to view the faculty first-year experience program as yet another requirement to be endured and more likely to appreciate its positive value from the very beginning.

o

However you organize your department's development program for new faculty members, it will be most successful when you try to anticipate the needs of the faculty members themselves, pay due attention to your institution's individual culture and expectations, and provide the same sort of varied opportunities that we as instructors try to provide in the courses where the greatest amount of learning occurs.

REFERENCES

Bain, K. (2004). *What the best college teachers do*. Cambridge, MA: Harvard University Press.

Baiocco, S. A., & DeWaters, J. N. (1998). *Successful college teaching: Problem-solving strategies of distinguished professors*. Needham Heights, MA: Allyn and Bacon.

Bean, J. C. (2001). *Engaging ideas: The professor's guide to integrating writing, critical thinking, and active learning in the classroom*. San Francisco: Jossey-Bass.

McKeachie, W. J., & Svinicki, M. (2005). *McKeachie's teaching tips: Strategies, research and theory for college and university teachers*. Boston: Houghton Mifflin.

Walvoord, B.E.F., & Anderson, V. J. (1998). *Effective grading: A tool for learning and assessment*. San Francisco: Jossey-Bass.

RESOURCE

Provitera-McGlynn, A. (2001). *Successful beginnings for college teaching: Engaging your students from the first day*. Madison, WI: Atwood.

32

COACHING FACULTY IN WRITING EFFECTIVE RÉSUMÉS

IT SEEMS AS THOUGH department chairs are always being asked to review someone's résumé. Either there is a new person to hire or the chair must submit a recommendation about some other major personnel decisions (promotion, tenure, merit increase, performance appraisal, and the like). Or the chair may be asked to assist some member of the department with improving the format of a résumé that will be submitted with a grant proposal, award application, or request for a publication contract. Most of us are only too glad to help, but what is the most useful advice that department chairs can give a faculty member, particularly one who simply needs a few well chosen hints that will restructure a perfectly good curriculum vitae so as to make it truly spectacular?

Here are a few suggestions, some of them all too frequently overlooked but all of them important, that you can give to your faculty.

Don't assume that you can have only one form of your curriculum vitae that must be submitted for all purposes.

Computers make it easy to maintain a résumé file that contains all of the pertinent professional and biographical information you can pull together for a specific purpose quickly. While your curriculum vitae is a factual document (absolutely everything in it must be accurate, clear, and verifiable), it is also a rhetorical document (you are submitting it because you are trying to persuade someone of something). For this reason, every time you are about to create a version of your curriculum vitae, ask yourself two questions.

The first question to ask is, "What will someone who examines this document need to know and to conclude in order to say yes to me?"

Once you have a clear answer to that question, you will know immediately how to structure your résumé. In other words, depending on the purpose you are trying to achieve, you need to highlight certain aspects of your achievement and minimize or omit other material. In applications for promotion and tenure, for instance, most institutions require documentation in three essential categories of performance—teaching, scholarship, and service (although the terminology used may differ from institution to institution)—in addition to certain supporting materials, in order to evaluate applicants. But faculty members frequently do not structure their résumés in such a way as to make evaluation of all three areas easy for reviewers to conduct.

In this case, it may be useful to have three clearly labeled sections of your résumé—"Teaching," "Scholarship," and "Service"—with roughly similar sections under each heading. If, for example, it seems appropriate to include a brief "Philosophy of Teaching" section, include "Philosophy of Scholarship" and "Philosophy of Service" sections too. Reviewers are likely to care about more than just the number of courses you've taught, articles you've published, and committees you've served on, so include some information on the quality of these achievements as well:

- Do you have median scores for student evaluations that can be compared to others in your unit?

- Do you have information on the number of your students who have gone on to graduate school or to success in their upper-level courses?

- Can you discover the acceptance rates of the journals in which you publish or the general qualifications of the referees?

- Did your service contribution result in any new course of action, award, or lasting product?

In a different situation, if you are applying for an administrative appointment, restructure your curriculum vitae so that it highlights the opportunities you have had for managerial or leadership roles. Too frequently applicants for administrative roles submit résumés that make a clear case for numerous scholarly and instructional accomplishments, while leaving their administrative success in the background. It is always important to structure a curriculum vitae so that it makes the case you wish to make clearly and convincingly.

The second question to ask is, "Who will be reviewing this résumé? What can I be certain that they will know? What are they not likely to understand?" Consider a number of aspects of your résumé.

For example, if you use abbreviations for the journals in which your publications appear, will everyone who reviews your material know what those abbreviations mean? Will they know whether a journal is highly competitive and thus evaluate your accomplishment appropriately? If reviewers are unlikely to be aware of this information, you may need to assist them. Provide the full titles of journals where necessary. Then group your publications where appropriate into "Highly Competitive Journals," "Second-Tier Journals," and "Essays and Other Publications" sections. If one of your teaching accomplishments is that you were asked eight times to guest-lecture for Dr. Smith in her INT 577 course, be certain that all of your reviewers will understand what course you are referring to, that INT in this case means "International Studies" rather than "Interdisciplinary Studies," and that Dr. Smith is the president of your college and a highly acclaimed scholar in her own right. Don't just assume that a reviewer will understand what might be a confusing entry: when in doubt, spell it out.

Format your résumé so that it conveys as much information about you as possible quickly and easily.

- Always number the pages of your curriculum vitae. Whenever possible use the structure "page [number] of [total]" in your header or footer. By doing this, you'll have created a structure that can be reassembled quickly and easily if (when!) the reviewer happens to drop your résumé.

- Number the entries in each section rather than using a bulleted list. This conveys information quickly—"Wow, 48 refereed articles!"—without forcing your reviewers to count every item in a list. And make no mistake about it: most reviewers are going to count entries like publications and conference presentations anyway, so why not make it easier and do it for them?

- Include dates not just for publications and presentations, but for all activities. List the years you served on committees, held offices, or joined professional and service organizations. In a résumé that you submit for an annual performance evaluation or merit increase, make it clear which accomplishments occurred during the period under review. For promotion evaluations, indicate your achievements since your most recent promotion or your date of hire. You can separate these achievements from earlier accomplishments with a dotted line or note that "accomplishments completed in the period under review are in boldface type."

○ Be consistent in listing all items in reverse chronological order. Reviewers will automatically assume that all of your publications, conference presentations, awards, and so on will be listed in this order, with the most recent entry first. If you structure your listings in any other way (for instance, if your publications are listed in alphabetical order), a reviewer may simply look at the first listing and assume that it is your most recent achievement, even if you wrote it ten or more years ago.

○ Include the date on which your résumé was printed at the end of the document or in a header or footer. This will inform your reviewers the date at which the information they are examining was current. And always be sure to submit the most current version you have. Never submit a résumé that has not been updated for six or more months.

Plan your curriculum vitae with the assumption that it will be photocopied.

In almost every process that requires review of a faculty member's résumé, a committee will be involved at some point. That means that the document will need to be photocopied for all the reviewers. If you plan your curriculum vitae with this likelihood in mind, you'll avoid certain mistakes that will complicate the committee's task:

○ Unless specifically asked to do so, never slip the pages into plastic page protectors. This will make it at best difficult to photocopy—requiring each page to be painstakingly pulled from your static-laden plastic covers before the copies can be made—and, at worst, smudged and illegible.

○ Use sturdy plain white paper. Sturdy paper holds up better when you are making multiple copies. Colored paper and paper bearing a prominent watermark or design will pose a challenge on copies and may end up making your text difficult to read.

○ Avoid cramped, hard-to-read, or minute type. As a general rule of thumb, always use a type size no smaller than 12 point and no larger than 14 point.

○

One of the ways in which department chairs are judged is the extent to which their faculty members excel in teaching, scholarship, service, and collegiality. Certainly many of these components are beyond your control. You can establish a wonderfully rich and supportive environment, but not everyone will take advantage of it or act in their best professional interests. You can't earn a record of success for individual members of your faculty. But you can give them the tools by which they can make their strongest cases when they apply for promotion, seek external grants, or are nominated for major recognitions. A surprising number of faculty members structure their résumés in ways that don't make as strong a case as they could. Assist them by discussing the points raised in this chapter, and provide them with access to such sources as Anthony and Roe (1998), Buller (2010), Jackson and Geckeis (2003), or McDaniels and Knobloch (1997).

REFERENCES

Anthony, R., & Roe, G. (1998). *The curriculum vitae handbook: How to present and promote your academic career.* San Francisco: Rudi Publishing.

Buller, J. L. (2010). *Creating an effective curriculum vitae. The essential college professor: A practical guide to an academic career.* San Francisco: Jossey-Bass.

Jackson, A. L., & Geckeis, C. K. (2003). *How to prepare your curriculum vitae.* Chicago: VGM Career.

McDaniels, C., & Knobloch, M. A. (1997). *Developing a professional vita or résumé.* Chicago: J. G. Ferguson Publishing.

RESOURCES

Corfield, R. (2007). *Preparing the perfect CV: How to make a great impression and get the job you want.* London: Kogan Page.

Eggert, M. (2007). *Perfect CV.* New York: Random House.

MacGee, P. (2007). *How to write a great CV: Discover what interviewers are looking for, focus on your strengths and perfect your presentation.* Oxford: How To Books.

33

CREATING AN EFFECTIVE PROFESSIONAL DEVELOPMENT PLAN

THE EVALUATION SYSTEMS IN place at most institutions are rather inflexible when it comes to individual differences. Some colleges and universities provide a certain amount of flexibility by allowing the faculty member to decide whether that year's evaluation is to be conducted according to teaching track or research track standards. Some institutions offer still more flexibility by permitting the faculty member to weigh the amount of emphasis given to instruction, scholarship, and service, within certain preset ranges. Sometimes slightly different sets of standards may be adopted in different colleges or for different programs. But by and large, the standards imposed at most institutions are fairly monolithic. Assistant professors are expected to have done X, associate professors Y, and full professors Z. The rigidity of these systems may even be seen as an advantage. "In our system," administrators might say with great pride, "we have the same high standards for all of our faculty members. It doesn't matter what your field is. It doesn't matter what else is going on in your life. We expect no less than excellence from everyone, and we get it."

The fact of the matter is, however, that faculties tend to contain extremely diverse individuals. Not only are members of the professoriate at different stages of their careers and scholarly agendas, but they also have extremely different needs, talents, and backgrounds. Interests shift over the course of a career: a faculty member who may have had a burst of creativity in research at one point may find it attractive at a different point to explore opportunities in administration or teaching interdisciplinary courses or taking on more responsibilities as an advisor. A great deal of attention has been given to the different learning styles of our students—and how those styles may change over the course of the student's education—but relatively less attention has been paid to the different styles and needs of faculty members or to how those styles and needs may vary over the course of a professional career. If your faculty evaluation system gives you fairly limited abilities to reflect the diversity of your faculty, how can you in your faculty development role help the members of your department find an appropriate balance between their own needs and your institution's expectations?

Junior Faculty: Creating a Tenure and Promotion Plan

Part of your responsibility as chair is to help your faculty members grow into both the type of faculty members your institution demands and the sort of individuals who fulfill their own potentials. One way to do this is to work out with them each year a personal development plan that can then be used to set goals, evaluate progress, and tailor individual skills to institutional needs. A faculty member who is relatively new to the profession, for instance, will require a substantial amount of time to learn how to be effective in various instructional settings and establish a record of scholarly productivity that will already have begun to bear fruit when he or she is considered for tenure.

Each new faculty member is different, of course, but it is common for those who have just started their first teaching positions to seek out too many course overloads (because their salaries tend to be lower and they may have student loans to pay off), volunteer for too many committees (because this puts them in contact with individuals from other parts of the institution and because they are frequently grateful to the institution that hired them and thus want to help), and try to take on too many new assignments (such as forming student clubs, leading field trips, and developing multiple course proposals). The energy that stands behind these efforts is commendable, and you will certainly be tempted to take full advantage of it. Nevertheless, that same energy that causes these faculty members to want to do so much may end up distracting them from other activities that may better serve both the department and the faculty members themselves in the long run.

In most cases, the most important type of development plan you can create with a new faculty member is a tenure and promotion plan. In its simplest form, this plan consists of a timetable listing the dates when various personnel decisions will be made about the faculty member, a summary of recommended products of professional activity that are typically expected in cases where positive decisions are made, and guidance about when each of those should be completed. You can begin to develop this type of plan in the following way:

1. Open a new document in your word processor and create as many blank pages as there are years until a final tenure or promotion decision for a specific faculty member will be made. For instance, if you work at an institution at which tenure is typically granted at the start of the seventh year, create seven pages in your document.

2. Head each page "Year One," "Year Two," and so on. Clarify this information by adding the dates of the actual academic year this page refers to for the faculty member whose plan you're developing.

3. Under the appropriate years, enter the date and requirement for each deadline related to a professional decision. In other words, if your institution requires that a tenure application be submitted to the departmental review committee by October 15 of a faculty member's sixth year, record the deadline on the Year 6 page. Remember to include deadlines for each level when an application must be reviewed at more than one point in your institutional structure. Include due dates for annual review materials, notification dates for contract renewals, dates for major preliminary reviews (such as a second- or third-year review), and any other dates that are appropriate for your institutional processes.

4. If you find it would be helpful to review an application before it is formally submitted, include those dates as well, allowing enough time for you to review the application carefully and for the faculty member to make any changes that you recommend.

5. Include time for any process that may require letters from an external reviewer. When should those reviewers be selected and approved? When should they be contacted? When should their letters be expected to arrive?

6. Examine the criteria for promotion at the department, college, and university level; identify specific products of professional activity that successful applicants tend to submit; and divide those products appropriately and reasonably among the years that you have listed.

For the teaching, scholarship, and service categories, there are some further guidelines.

For teaching, what items that document success in teaching should the candidate prepare in specific years? For instance, some faculty members may not understand that they need to maintain copies of the reports resulting from their student evaluations, and they discover several years later that they cannot find this material when it's required. If peer reports are required or expected, when should the faculty member invite colleagues to observe his or her teaching? Which items in support of instruction are usually included in the application binder or teaching portfolio (see Chapter Thirty-Four) and when should the faculty member set these aside?

How many products of scholarship do successful applicants for tenure or promotion in your discipline usually have by the time they're reviewed? How should these products be allocated among the years that are available before the application must be complete? In other words, if you work in a discipline in which successful applicants usually have six refereed articles accepted for publication before the candidate comes up for review in the sixth year, equal distribution would suggest that the faculty member must complete one refereed article per year. But it may not be reasonable to expect this level of production in a person's first year when new courses must be prepared and other types of transition completed. So what's the fairest way to allocate this expectation within the time available? When would each paper need to be researched, started, completed, submitted, reviewed by the editorial committee, revised, and resubmitted? Make a similar allocation in the case of other appropriate products of scholarship in your discipline, such as books published, grants received, patents awarded, recitals held, and so on.

Regarding service, what level of committee work and other types of service do successful applicants usually have? When should the faculty member try to complete these assignments? How are they best allocated in light of the other expectations you've outlined for teaching and scholarship?

The tenure and promotion plan guides faculty members by making sure that they're not caught unaware of the different expectations that your discipline or institution will have and the dates when these activities should begin. The plan will also help you by alerting you to years when you may wish to advocate for a reduced load in teaching or service for the faculty member because the scholarship demand will be quite high, and so on. Be sure to meet with the faculty member several times each year to gauge progress being made and to provide an early warning if one seems needed.

Establishing a clear development plan with the faculty member also allows you to suggest what activities you believe are of highest priority for the faculty member now and which are better postponed. In some ways, your faculty development role is similar to what you do when advising students: you don't want to dictate every aspect of what the person does or experiences, but you can provide sound guidance that can help the person in making some appropriate choices. For example, if a faculty member isn't demonstrating success in teaching through the information that you're receiving on course evaluations, peer appraisals, and your own review of course materials and what you see occurring in class, you can suggest appropriate sessions at your campus's center for excellence in teaching and learning. Offer to set up a formal mentoring relationship with someone who will not be involved in evaluating the faculty member and begin researching conferences where training in pedagogy occurs. These activities, you can suggest to the faculty member, are ultimately more important than teaching one more overload or serving on one more committee.

Together you might explore achieving a suitable balance:

- ○ Which committee will be most likely to give the faculty member adequate exposure to the way your campus works, represent a solid service contribution, and not consume too much time that is better spent in other pursuits?
- ○ During which term might it be possible for the person to teach that financially lucrative overload while not proving a distraction from scholarship?
- ○ Is it better to take an overload now and forgo summer teaching so that concentrated time can be devoted to scholarship at that time? Or is the person's scholarship the sort that requires small but frequent intervals of work, suggesting that overloads should be sacrificed altogether, with the possibility of additional teaching duties in the summer?
- ○ Are funding opportunities available that can both provide the additional income the faculty member needs and result in a tangible product of scholarship?

Issues like these are best explored early in a faculty member's career when it is still possible to make choices and midcourse corrections. Your sense of how important the relative weighting of teaching, scholarship, and service is at your institution can be one of the best contributions you make to the faculty member in your faculty development role. Just be sure that that when you give advice to junior faculty members, you keep in mind the following essential principle:

> Promotion is a decision made about a faculty member's achievements; tenure is a decision made about someone's potential. Although many institutions bind the granting of tenure with a promotion to the rank of associate professor, review committees are actually looking for two very different things when they make these decisions. A successful promotion application must demonstrate that the faculty member has fulfilled in the past all the criteria that are required for the new rank. A successful tenure application must demonstrate that the faculty member is likely to perform in the future at a level that will serve the institution well for many years to come.

Finally, another important contribution you might make as chair is to propose the development of an institutional tenure stop-clock policy if your institution does not already have one. These policies allow junior faculty members to apply for extension of their individual tenure timetable under certain conditions. The policy might be written to apply to

- New parents who are faced with child care responsibilities
- Individuals who must care for an aged parent
- Faculty members whose illnesses are not severe enough for them to go on disability leave but whose workday is frequently interrupted by treatments, low energy, or recurrence of symptoms

The development of such a policy can help your institution retain highly qualified and desirable faculty members whose lives become complicated by one or more occurrences beyond their control.

Professional Development Plans for Midcareer Faculty Members

We usually think of a tenure and promotion plan primarily as a tool for those who have recently been hired. But similar types of development plans are suitable throughout a faculty member's professional life. For instance, when someone is in midcareer—tenured and established in your program but with at least one more promotion to receive—the nature and focus of your advice is likely to be quite different from what you'd recommend to a person just starting out. This individual has probably already demonstrated a record of success in teaching; otherwise he or she would not have been granted tenure. Evaluations of courses by students and peers are probably solid, and all the person will need to do is to keep amassing evidence each year of continued strong performance in this area. (If it is not the case that the midcareer faculty member is seen as a successful teacher, then you have some serious remediation to do. Be candid with your advice and establish a clear plan for the individual to receive guidance through either your campus resources or pedagogical opportunities that may be available through professional organizations.) For the midcareer faculty member, your advice will thus most likely focus on service and research rather than achievements in instruction. A person at this point in professional life will need continual, probably increasing scholarly activity. The evaluation systems at most institutions require those who are being considered for promotion to the rank of full professor to have demonstrated substantial, significant scholarship that goes well beyond what was required at their previous promotion. Mentor these individuals to put their efforts into the scholarly activities that matter at your institution, not those that occupy time without producing results that carry sufficient weight. In most cases, this may mean cautioning faculty members away from proposing too many conference presentations and poster sessions and urging instead production of books, monographs, and major grant proposals.

At the same time, most institutions require that full professors demonstrate that they have been solid citizens at the college or university, making serious contributions on major committees, having their voices heard in public discussions, and taking part in events that benefit the community as a whole. This may be the time to plan how best to elect the faculty member to the faculty senate, an institution-wide curricular committee, a search committee for an upper administrator, a major task force, or a body that reports to the institution's governing board. Explore with the faculty member which of these opportunities might be most obtainable and in which the person has expertise to contribute. In cases where elections are held for these positions, you might wish to discuss the possibility of block voting by members of your department to increase the likelihood that those colleagues who need these service contributions for promotion will be successful in their campaigns.

You should also do some serious long-range planning with faculty members who have reached the midpoint in their careers. How would they like to spend the rest of their professional life? If they are thinking that they eventually might like to seek employment elsewhere, you may wish to discuss with them the desirability of making this move sooner rather than later. Only in rare cases do institutions hire in faculty members at the rank of full professor; people quickly discover they their credentials are much more portable before they undergo that final promotion to the rank of full professor. For this reason, faculty members who believe that they may wish someday to relocate might be encouraged not to seek promotion at the earliest possible time. They may believe that higher rank will make them more attractive to other institutions, when it may actually disqualify them from consideration for the very position they'd most like to have. Don't take it personally if a faculty member tells you candidly that he or she would prefer to move on in a few years. There are likely to be many factors that went into this decision, and it is far better to lose a good faculty member than to persuade someone to remain reluctantly. Besides, at least some turnover is probably desirable in most departments: it is frequently better to have a star on your faculty for a few years than not to have had the benefit of that person's work at all. A certain amount of fresh blood brings new insights and can prevent a department from becoming stale.

Faculty members may also be experiencing something of a midcareer crisis as they consider whether their current professional course will remain meaningful to them in the future. Sometimes people find that they've attained all of the important goals that they had originally set for themselves—the book that they had always wanted to write is now out, they've won an award for outstanding teaching, and their idea for a major grant application has been funded—and they begin to ask themselves, "Now what?" At other times, people in midcareer begin to feel that all of their grandiose hopes and dreams are not likely to occur, and they are wondering whether they've chosen the appropriate path in life after all.

At this point in their lives, it becomes apparent which faculty members have set their aspirations either too high or too low, and many of them start to lose their way. The chair's faculty development role can help a person rediscover what it was that made the field seem exciting in the first place or to search out new goals and new possibilities. Some may be encouraged to try their hands in various administrative roles. Others may be guided toward looking for grants capable of buying out their time for a year or two, during which they can refocus their energy and develop a new sense of direction. Some can retrain in different specialties that will bring back their sense of discovery. In extreme cases, you may want to explore an unpaid leave of absence to allow time for the individual to work out certain issues. And some faculty members may benefit from formally exploring other career opportunities, either to discover that the grass is not always greener or to find an environment that will bring them the next challenge. Your job as chair may be to help each individual decide which of these many options is the best for that person's individual situation.

Professional Development Plans for Senior Faculty Members

Just as midcareer crises are not uncommon, so you may find that some faculty members in your department are undergoing something of a crisis late in their professional careers. One of the great failings of American higher education is that all major opportunities for peers to recognize one another's achievements in a formal manner tend to occur relatively early in a person's career. The decision to grant tenure and promotion to the rank of associate professor usually occurs after six or seven years of full-time teaching. Promotion to full professor rank frequently occurs between twelve and fifteen years of professional service. Most academic careers, however, extend over thirty to thirty-five years. This means that for roughly half of each successful faculty member's career, peers do relatively little to acknowledge the important contributions that person has made. Posttenure review can fill this gap somewhat, but too many systems of posttenure review are negative in nature; they are constructed to weed out deadwood or remediate problems, not to celebrate the superb accomplishments of the vast majority of faculty members. Titles of "Distinguished Professor" or "University Professor" and named, endowed chairs can also be of great value, but they are not found at every institution, and many endowed positions are limited to certain fields. (In fact, one of the most lasting contributions you could make as a department chair is to work with your advancement office to secure funds for one or more titled positions in your department. These are naming opportunities for colleges and universities. Unlike buildings and programs, they are not finite in number; in fact, the more named, endowed positions an institution has, the better. If you are seeking a significant project for which to secure outside funding for your department, increasing the number of endowed chairs may well be the best thing you can do for your program.)

Many department chairs are surprised to discover that their senior faculty members may require even more mentoring and guidance than their newly hired faculty. These are frequently the individuals who have given their lives to the institution but have lost that initial energy. In some cases, they may be willing but simply unable to find what their next focus should be. Now is the time for you to work out with them their important set of new goals in each area: teaching, research, and service. In teaching, explore the option of providing opportunities for the faculty member to teach a few special topics or directed inquiry courses into material that is not currently part of your core curriculum. Seek some funding to increase the faculty member's use of technology in the classroom. Secure the assistance of the faculty member to serve as a mentor to a newer instructor who could benefit from years of experience gained from teaching several generations of students.

In research, try to map out the next big project or question that will occupy the faculty member for at least several years. Encourage consideration not just of traditional research and refereed publication, but the full range of scholarship, including integration, application, and pedagogy. Nominate the faculty member for a Fulbright or other international opportunity that will allow new insights to be gained from exposure to different cultures and ideas.

In service, think of creative contributions that may be possible apart from committee work. Do policies and procedures in your department need to be updated and improved? Do you need help from an unofficial assistant department chair who can assist you in implementing your faculty development efforts or draft grant proposals? Does your department's approach to advising and student mentoring need to be reexamined? Nearly every department has some important work that remains undone because no existing committee sees it as its responsibility. Appointing an ad hoc czar of advising (or faculty development, grant writing, or something else) can both accomplish these long-overdue tasks and help provide a renewed sense of purpose for an individual who has many valuable insights to contribute.

In providing development advice to senior faculty members, you can also assist them in focusing on activities that are likely to have the biggest impact for them as individuals and for the department as a whole. For instance, you can assist them in directing their energies toward activities that matter to the institution's mission and strategic plan. Sometimes too there are activities that faculty members do not present in the most effective way in their annual reports or on their résumés. You can help them describe those community service projects in such a way that the benefit to the institution is made clear, and you can provide guidance about which innovations in teaching make an important contribution to the scholarship of teaching.

――――――― o ―――――――

Even varying your advice to faculty members based on their seniority only begins to suggest the diversity of their needs. Each member of a department will have a career with its own rhythm, its own highs and lows, and its own unique opportunities. One of the best services that you can provide in your faculty development role is to recognize that this variation exists and to help your faculty see beyond the rather monolithic performance standards that most institutions have to an approach that better suits the range of needs and talent existing in every department.

RESOURCES

Arreola, R. A. (2000). *Developing a comprehensive faculty evaluation system: A handbook for college faculty and administrators on designing and operating a comprehensive faculty evaluation system.* San Francisco: Jossey-Bass/Anker.

Austin, A. E. (2010). Supporting faculty members across their careers. In W. H. Bergquist, D. L. Robertson, & K. H. Gillespie (Eds.), *A guide to faculty development* (pp. 363–378). San Francisco: Jossey-Bass.

Braskamp, L. A., & Ory, J. C. (1994). *Assessing faculty work: Enhancing individual and institutional performance.* San Francisco: Jossey-Bass.

Centra, J. A. (1993). *Reflective faculty evaluation: Enhancing teaching and determining faculty effectiveness.* San Francisco: Jossey-Bass.

Glassick, C. E., Huber, M. T., Maeroff, G. I., & Boyer, E. L. (1997). *Scholarship assessed: Evaluation of the professoriate.* San Francisco: Jossey-Bass.

Luna, G., & Cullen, D. L. (1996). *Empowering the faculty: Mentoring redirected and renewed.* Washington, DC: ERIC Clearinghouse on Higher Education: Association for the Study of Higher Education.

Rice, R. E., & O'Meara, K. A. (2005). *Faculty priorities reconsidered: Rewarding multiple forms of scholarship.* San Francisco: Jossey-Bass.

Rocque, B., & Laursen, S. (2009, January 1). Faculty development for institutional change: Lessons from an ADVANCE project. *Change, 18.*

Sorcinelli, M. D., Austin, A. E., Eddy, P. L., & Beach, A. L. (2006). *Creating the future of faculty development: Learning from the past, understanding the present.* San Francisco: Jossey-Bass/Anker.

Zhao, Y., Mishra, P., & Koehler, M. J. (2007). *Faculty development by design: Integrating technology in higher education.* Charlotte, NC: Information Age.

34

CREATING AN EFFECTIVE
TEACHING PORTFOLIO

OF THE THREE ASPECTS of professional activity commonly evaluated at colleges and universities—teaching, scholarship, and service—assessing the quality of a faculty member's teaching frequently poses the greatest difficulty for the department chair. When individuals are being reviewed for tenure or promotion, applying for a grant, being nominated for an award, or under consideration for another position, documenting their success in scholarship may seem relatively easy to do. We are all used to evaluating lists of refereed and nonrefereed scholarship. We know the publications that are highly regarded in our disciples, as well as those that are given less professional regard. We can tell from the number of successful grant awards whether that person's research has been recognized as important in the field. We can count the number of presentations each faculty member has made at national conferences, as well as the number of patents received, consultancies given, citations of their research, and similar items that regularly fall into neat categories on the résumé. In a similar way, it may not seem very difficult to evaluate the quality of a faculty member's service when examining a list of professional offices held, committees served, projects completed, and other contributions to the department, institution, or discipline as a whole. We can, in other words, quantify the quantifiable.

But how can we objectively evaluate and document excellence in teaching? To be sure, many faculty members consider themselves to be excellent, even distinguished instructors within their chosen fields, even if they can present little documentation of this achievement aside from stacks of student course evaluations. Perhaps for this reason, many personnel review processes end up putting an undue emphasis on these evaluations.

Since many institutions use forms for student ratings of instruction that yield quantitative scores, these scores often become the sole markers of success or failure as a teacher. Numbers, however, can provide a false impression of reliability. For instance, it is not uncommon in personnel evaluations to encounter such meaningless statements as, "This candidate has demonstrated excellence in teaching, as indicated by an overall average of 4.89 on last semester's student ratings of instruction." There are plenty of reasons that such a statement is without value. First, it overlooks every single one of the questions we would need to ask in order to conclude anything informative from this average score. For instance, how was the average calculated? Was it an average of the responses to every question on the evaluation form, or were questions included only if they specifically related to this instructor's teaching in this particular course? If all the questions were included, were the questions dealing with the professor's individual performance given any greater weight than those dealing with textbooks, course scheduling, and other matters over which the professor may have had relatively little control? If only some of the questions were used, were any comparative data for other faculty members calculated in the same way? Other important considerations should be included too—for example, how many students were in each in class and what percentage of the enrolled students answered each question. This information can be important because very high or very low ratings with only a small percentage of students replying are highly suspect.

Moreover, in developing an overall score, were the different responses of the students truly averaged, or is the overall score only an average of the averages for different courses? (In the latter scenario, a course that enrolls 6 and a course that enrolls 350 count as the same in the average.) In developing an average score, was the institution using means or medians, and, in either case, why was that particular statistical measure selected? Is the resulting figure statistically significant to the decimal place cited? How do the resulting scores compare to others who have been assigned the same course (either currently or in the past), the rest of the department, and all the faculty members of the institution in general?

Lacking clear answers to these questions, we cannot hope to draw any useful conclusions from that impressive-sounding "overall average of 4.89." Nevertheless, in the absence of other compelling indications of teaching excellence, presidents, deans, and committees frequently misuse or overinterpret student evaluation scores just because they are some evidence of instructional quality. They conclude that a faculty member receiving an overall student evaluation average of 4.56 is "better" than a faculty member receiving a score of 4.53, even when there is no statistically significant difference between the two numbers and even when the methodology used to generate those numbers is highly questionable.

For all of these reasons, department chairs are confronted with both an opportunity and an obligation to help faculty members make an appropriate case about the quality of their instruction whenever this is an important factor in that individual's evaluation. One of the best solutions is to encourage faculty members to develop a teaching portfolio, a device used to illustrate achievements and growth in the area of instruction. Unlike traditional methods for documenting success in teaching, the teaching portfolio combines quantitative measures of success (such as student ratings of instruction, pass rates for students on standardized tests in the discipline, and peer evaluation scores) with qualitative indicators (such as annotated revisions of syllabi or course materials, illustrations of how the faculty member implements a philosophy of teaching, and electronic materials that demonstrate innovation or effectiveness of instruction). Most important of all, the teaching portfolio is not merely a binder in which a faculty member provides every course syllabus, student rating, alumni letter, or examination, but a carefully chosen representative sample of materials that the faculty member proffers as illustrating his or her best work. The leading figure in promoting the use of teaching portfolios to improve and evaluate instruction in higher education has long been Peter Seldin, Distinguished Professor of Management at Pace University (see Seldin, 2004). In order to assist your faculty in developing the most effective teaching portfolios, there are several suggestions you might consider making.

Encourage your faculty members to develop brief statements detailing their philosophy of teaching.

A statement that reveals why an instructor has made certain choices in the classroom can go a long way toward documenting how that instructor has been effective. At times, these short philosophy statements can be included as part of the supporting materials in applications for tenure, promotion, and other types of personnel decisions. At other times, the statement can be fully integrated into the curriculum vitae itself, perhaps heading a section outlining that faculty member's contributions to instruction. For instance, you might encourage your faculty members to include a section of their résumé constructed in the following way:

Teaching

PHILOSOPHY OF TEACHING

The highest form of learning occurs when students are actively engaged in applying what they encounter in their courses to their own lives, truly making a discipline their own. College-level learning does not merely involve the transfer of information from professor to student. It also involves discovery of how to acquire information and new skills on one's own, how to work with colleagues toward the successful completion of a goal, and how to make a difference in the lives of those around one. All learning should be active, highly engaged, and inquiry based. The professor's most important purpose must be not only to develop successful professionals in the discipline but also to develop the best possible members of society.

TEACHING EXPERIENCE

[There then begins a list of teaching appointments, in reverse chronological order.]

By using this type of structure for his or her résumé, the instructor is indicating that he or she has carefully considered what effective teaching is and how it may be used to help students learn. One of the great advantages of this approach is that the faculty member must reflect on the values that he or she embraces as a teacher in order to create this statement, and there is likely to be a genuine improvement in the faculty member's instruction as a result. For this reason, after formulating a statement of teaching philosophy, the faculty member should be encouraged to define what specifically is done in his or her courses—and how it is done—in order to achieve these goals.

When faculty members include data from student ratings of instruction in their teaching portfolios, suggest that they indicate how they calculated this information and provide an appropriate context for their results.

Despite all of their obvious flaws, numerical summaries of student ratings of instruction are widely used throughout academia to document success in instruction. And they do have value. Student evaluations correlate rather closely with other measures of teaching effectiveness, including peer evaluations and appraisals by supervisors. Nevertheless, "averages" of student ratings of instructions are often cited rather carelessly at many institutions, presenting an ambiguous picture of a faculty member's strengths and weaknesses or, worse, leaving these colleges and universities open to legal challenge when their decisions are questioned. So if you either wish or are required to provide summarized data from student ratings of instruction, encourage your faculty members to do the following if it is possible at your institution:

○ *Supply medians and modes, as well as arithmetic means, when providing average ratings.* Most institutions either calculate for you or require you to calculate some sort of average score for student ratings of instruction. Generally these averages are determined by calculating simple arithmetic means; in other words, the numerical scores are tabulated for each response in the evaluation, and the resulting number is divided by the number of responses received. But this type of averaging can produce misleading results, particularly in small classes where single responses can skew the calculation. Moreover, a mean is not a suitable form of averaging responses when students must provide discrete rather than continuous numbers on an evaluation form. For instance, many institutions use paper or electronic forms that require students to rate their professors according to a Likert scale, with integers ranging from 1 to 5. Even when this numerical scale is not used on the form itself, the answers that students are asked to provide to each item—Excellent, Very Good, Good, Satisfactory, or Poor—are then converted to these whole numbers for averaging. Both of these systems involve discrete numbers since any response that falls between the integers, such as 2.5 or 3.674, is not allowed. Only in rare cases where this type of fractional answer is permitted does the institution gather continuous numbers from its student evaluation forms. There's an essential principle at work here:

Medians and modes are far more accurate indications of the "average response" when you've collected discrete data. Arithmetic means are reliable only when your responses consist of continuous data.

As we've already seen, means are notoriously susceptible to outliers: one or two students who really love or hate a middling professor can distort an entire set of results. So if you start making judgments based on misleading information, you're likely to end up making decisions that are not in your program's best interest. The median is the middle-most score whenever there is an odd number of responses or the average of the two middle-most scores whenever there is an even number of responses. The mode is the most commonly chosen response, and it tends to be particularly informative in data sets consisting of discrete numbers. As you will discover if you try all three of these types of calculations (particularly in a course enrolling fewer than thirty students), medians and modes prove to be much less susceptible to the effects of outliers than are arithmetic means and provide better portraits of the average response when students are filling in bubble forms or selecting responses from a drop-down menu. Remember too that you don't have to calculate these statistics by yourself; there are formulas built in to whichever electronic spreadsheet you may already be using.

o *Calculate true per class and per student averages.* All too frequently, the methods that institutions or individuals adopt to calculate per student averages result in incorrect or misleading figures. Many chairs calculate an average score per class and then simply average all the averages, calling the result they receive the "overall average score." The problem is that this method doesn't really result in a per student or per response figure. It treats all classes as equivalent, regardless of the number of students enrolled in the course. The only way to derive a true per student average is to add all the scores reported for a question in all sections of the faculty member's courses and then to divide that total by the total number of responses. That will give you an average response for that question. The real danger comes when institutions summarize results for all of the questions on the rating instrument and then generate one comprehensive score. The reason this approach is highly unreliable is that student evaluation forms frequently have questions that evaluate more than just the individual professor's effectiveness in teaching, such as those that deal with the effectiveness of the course design itself, and the suitability of the textbook, the structure of the lab sections, and the helpfulness of other course materials. If all of these scores are simply averaged together, you end up combining so many different variables that it's impossible to learn anything significant about that professor. It is far better for you as chair (even if it is not the custom at your institution) to select a few specific key questions—questions that get to the heart of this professor's ability to engage his or her students—and then to focus on those questions in your evaluation of the faculty member.

○ *Individual averages are meaningless unless you provide a context.* Some department chairs may feel that statements such as the following are extremely clear and detailed: "In last fall's three sections of Dr. Indiana Jones's EGYP 101 (Introduction to Egyptology) course, students responded to the central question on 'the overall excellence of this faculty member's instruction' with a mean score of 4.33 (median: 4.0; mode 4.0) on the standard 1–5 scale, thus attesting to the high quality of instruction in Dr. Jones's introductory courses." As detailed as this statement may appear initially to be, it lacks at least one important element that it needs to be effective: a context for the figures cited. In other words, how does Dr. Jones's score relate to other members of the department and the college? How does this figure compare to that seen in other introductory courses within the department and across the institution? Without more information, the reader cannot tell whether the score cited is good, adequate, or highly inadequate. For this reason, you should encourage your faculty member to follow the statement above with specific grounds for comparison, such as, "Excluding Dr. Jones's own scores, the department's overall rating on this same question results in a mean of 3.21 (median 3.0; mode 3.0), while that of the college a whole is 3.77 (median 3.5; mode 3.0). Similarly, comparable scores for all introductory courses across the college are . . ."

○ *To place the scores from student evaluations into an even clearer context, calculate standard deviations if the institution does not automatically provide them.* Standard deviations, which any spreadsheet program can calculate automatically, provide an indication of how much variation occurred in the students' answers to each question. If the standard deviation is low, most students tended to answer that question in the same way. If the standard deviation is high, there was widespread disagreement among students on that issue. Even more than average scores, standard deviations can be useful indicators for faculty members of where they need to direct their efforts at improving instruction.

Encourage the faculty member to combine student ratings with other evidence for success in teaching, such as indications that enrollments in the department have been growing as a result of his or her quality of instruction.

Student ratings of instruction—which, for all of their apparent sophistication, are essentially customer satisfaction surveys—are not the only measures of a faculty member's teaching ability, even though they're the only ones that some institutions recognize. In many cases, the true merit of a professor's instruction may be realized by students only years later. Although it is certainly possible to document some of the faculty member's strengths with alumni surveys and letters received years after a course is completed, for certain personnel decisions (such as annual contract renewal or initial tenure decisions), department chairs do not always have the luxury of waiting that long. Therefore, they should encourage faculty members to compile indicators of their quality of instruction that go beyond standard student evaluations and alumni surveys. One means of doing this might be to provide data indicating that enrollments in the department have increased (or at least have stabilized after a period of decline) since the faculty member was hired or some other major event in the faculty member's career. For instance, the department chair might encourage the faculty member to include a section similar to the following on a résumé or an application for promotion:

Enrollment Growth

Average number of students in Dr. Jones's courses at time of hiring	11
Average number of students in Dr. Jones's courses at last promotion	23
Average number of students in Dr. Jones's courses currently	48

Development of Majors

Number of Egyptology majors at time of hiring	4
Number of Egyptology majors at last promotion	7
Number of Egyptology majors currently	12

It is certainly no guarantee that these improvements occurred only because Dr. Jones was hired and promoted, but it does appear to make the case that with this faculty member teaching in the department, the program is growing. Certain faculty members, particularly at the junior ranks, may be reluctant to introduce this type of information on their own behalf. In these cases, you have an excellent opportunity to use your authority as chair to encourage them to do so or even to introduce the information for them.

Recommend that the faculty member supply information indicating that students have been succeeding in their other courses as a result of his or her quality of instruction.

A brief but compelling section of a vita or promotion application might include a simple tabulation of how students who have been prepared by this instructor fared in their upper-level courses or in graduate school. One way of presenting this type of information would be as follows:

Academic Preparation of Dr. Jones's Students

Number of students advancing from Jones's EH I to Smith's EH II	89
Average grade of these students in Smith's EH II	B—
Number of students advancing from Jones's EH I to Jones's EH II	53
Average grade of these students in Jones's EH II	B
Number of students advancing from Jones's EH I to Smith's EH II since last promotion	21
Average grade of these students in Smith's EH II	B
Number of students advancing from Jones's EH I to Jones's EH II since last promotion	6
Average grade of these students in Jones's EH II	B+

Encourage faculty members to provide data that indicate their students are succeeding after they leave the institution as a result of their high level of instruction.

Another brief but effective way of demonstrating a faculty member's effectiveness is to provide information about advisees or students who took multiple courses from that instructor and then went on to graduate school in the discipline or received attractive offers of employment in the field. Statements of this sort might be phrased as follows: "Nine Egyptology graduates who were Dr. Jones's advisees advanced to graduate programs in the discipline (Jane Richardson and Mark Howard, Penn State; Tasha Reese, Brittany Pierce, and Lloyd Maxwell, Johns Hopkins; Marvelle Edwards, University of Chicago; Robert Elder and Jamal Roberston, University of Michigan; Jei Li, University of

Wisconsin) compared to only four such graduates in the entire five-year period before Dr. Jones's arrival."

When quoting comments made by students or peer evaluators, suggest that the faculty member select only those comments that indicate why he or she is an effective instructor.

A few carefully selected comments from unsolicited student letters or standardized ratings of instruction can provide a much clearer impression of what makes a faculty member successful as a teacher than can pages of numerical summaries. Nevertheless, it is far more compelling to include three to five comments that clearly state the reasons behind a faculty member's success—even if some of these comments are less than glowing—than to include numerous remarks that say merely, "Terrific professor!" or, "Best class I've ever had!"

As you know if you've served on many promotion committees, any professor can locate at least a fair number of positive comments on student course evaluations. The truly informative comments are those that give the reader a sense of what precisely the professor is doing to engage students so deeply with the material. Consider, for example, the following student comment:

> I hated Egyptology long before I registered for this class, and I wouldn't have taken this course if any other offering in the Humanities had been open this semester. And now that it's over, I can't really say that I've come to enjoy the material at all. But I will admit that Dr. Jones made me *think* in a way that no other professor has. This was a hard class. We had to write something nearly every day and then turn it in. We had to critique one another's ideas and compositions. And then we wrote fresh drafts based on what we learned from one another. Okay, so I may never be an Egyptologist (thank heavens!), but maybe I'm a better writer because of Dr. Jones.

A comment such as this one is certainly not the most flattering remark any of us will ever receive on a student course evaluation, but to reviewers and selection committees, it provides far stronger evidence of what makes this particular instructor effective than could pages of "Great prof!!!!!!!!" comments.

Remind your faculty members that successful instruction also occurs outside the classroom.

Sometimes faculty members become so fixated on demonstrating their excellence as classroom teachers that they forget all of the other ways that their instruction occurs. How successful were they as advisors and mentors to students? Did they provide guest presentations (including lectures, recitals, exhibits, online discussions, Web pages, and other formats in which ideas may be exchanged) that could be considered an extension of their teaching mission? Did they demonstrate excellence in teaching by updating curricula and syllabi for the department, thoroughly revising courses or recommending more pedagogically effective course rotations, proposing new courses in critical areas, or teaching students by giving them a significant role in their research? Has the faculty member been an effective coach in studios, lab experiences, or private lessons? Did he or she participate in workshops sponsored by a center for excellence in teaching and learning or undergo special pedagogical training as part of a national conference in your discipline? Has this person directed theses or supervised interns in a way that significantly enhanced the students' learning?

As a department chair, consider situations that you were in a position to observe but that students, peers, and other observers may have overlooked.

You may be in the best position to know all of the ways in which the faculty member has effectively incorporated new technologies into his or her teaching. You may have observed the teaching that goes on outside class as this person meets with students during office hours or discusses ideas with them in the dining hall. You may be aware that the faculty member has chosen a specific textbook, Web site, or set of course materials that is significantly more effective than those in use earlier. You may be in a better position than anyone else to document that the faculty member has met or exceeded the professional standards of your discipline in terms of remaining current with advances in your field, incorporating appropriate inter- or cross-disciplinary perspectives into courses, adhering to the regulations of your institution and department, and evaluating students according to the accepted standards of your field.

○

A carefully designed teaching portfolio gives you, as well as any review committee that examines it, far better insight into a faculty member's quality of instruction than can the huge binders of materials submitted at many institutions. Examining a syllabus in isolation can give you a great deal of information, but the context in which that document is examined in a teaching portfolio—"Here's the syllabus I used in this course five years ago. And here's the syllabus I use now. And these are the reasons why I implemented those changes"—can tell you far more. Moreover, in collaboration with Elizabeth Miller, Peter Seldin (2009) has explored how a teaching portfolio can best be incorporated into a comprehensive academic portfolio that addresses scholarship and service, as well as quality of instruction, as a means of most effectively documenting the full contribution of faculty members today.

REFERENCES

Seldin, P. (2004). *The teaching portfolio: A practical guide to improved performance and promotion/tenure decisions* (3rd ed.). San Francisco: Jossey-Bass/ Anker.

Seldin, P., & Miller, J. E. (2009). *The academic portfolio: A practical guide to documenting teaching, research, and service.* San Francisco: Jossey-Bass.

RESOURCES

Buller, J. L. (2007, November). Improving documentation for promotion and tenure. *Academic Leader,* 23(11), 8–9.

Devlin, M., & Samarawickrema, G. (2010, January 1). The criteria of effective teaching in a changing higher education context. *Higher Education Research and Development,* 29(2), 111–124.

Van Note Chism, N., & Stanley, C. A. (1999). *Peer review of teaching: A sourcebook.* San Francisco: Jossey-Bass/Anker.

Ryan, K. (Ed.). (2000). *Evaluating teaching in higher education: A vision for the future.* San Francisco: Jossey-Bass.

Seldin, P. (1999). *Changing practices in evaluating teaching: A practical guide to improved faculty performance and promotion/tenure decisions.* San Francisco: Jossey-Bass/Anker.

Seldin, P. (2006). *Evaluating faculty performance: A practical guide to assessing teaching, research, and service.* San Francisco: Jossey-Bass/Anker.

Stronge, J. H. (1997). *Evaluating teaching: A guide to current thinking and best practice.* Thousand Oaks, CA: Corwin.

35

CREATING AN EFFECTIVE COURSE SYLLABUS

EVERY COURSE TAUGHT ON a college or university campus requires a syllabus. Many accrediting agencies mandate them. Faculty members rely on them in order to approve, revise, or evaluate courses. Students turn to them for essential information about an instructor's objectives and requirements. And yet only rarely do we teach faculty members how to write an effective syllabus. Although many institutions provide lists of items that must be included in course syllabi, it is relatively uncommon for faculty members to be shown how to communicate this information effectively or how to construct a syllabus that will improve their students' performance in their course. Department chairs who are committed to excellence in teaching may thus find it useful to provide faculty development to members of their disciplines in the art of good syllabus construction. Faculty development of this sort includes the following principles of best practices.

A well-constructed syllabus conveys the right tone and includes the right information.

Every course syllabus includes information about the rules and expectations that will be in effect throughout the class. Too often, however, the need to establish clear policies and procedures results in course syllabi that look like little more than long lists of don'ts and thou shalt nots. This negative tone can alienate students from the instructor at the beginning of a course; students see the instructor more as a warden interested in rules than as a mentor who wants them to succeed at their educational goals.

As a department chair, you can help your faculty members avoid this problem by critiquing their syllabi for tone as well as for content.

An undesirable tone may be conveyed through devices as simple as the sheer amount of boldface type, underlined type, or capitalization that appears in instructions. Similarly, too many exclamation points create a tone of suspicion or condescension that impedes rather than assists the learning process. Avoiding unnecessarily strict language does not mean that a professor should not set boundaries or state specific expectations. What it does mean, however, is that it is preferable to convey high standards through a supportive, constructive tone than through a style that puts students on the defensive. Consider the following sections from two hypothetical course syllabi:

Attendance Policy

Each student is expected to be in class, on time for every class period. **DO NOT** miss class more than **three** times during the semester. **DO NOT** arrive in class late or after the door is closed. **DO NOT** expect exams to be given as makeups. **NO EXCEPTIONS WILL BE GIVEN!!!!!!!** Students who miss class more than three times may have their final grade reduced by at least a full letter grade; doing so will be completely my option. **THERE WILL BE NO APPEALS TO THIS POLICY!!!!!!**

Contrast this tone to that in the following passage:

Attendance Policy

Since this course involves active and participatory learning, many of the activities we'll be engaging in cannot occur outside class. For this reason, I'll take attendance every day and base part of your grade on your rate of class participation. When you are unable to attend a particular class session for any reason, please try to find out from your fellow students what you missed that day. If you stop by my office during regular office hours, I'll be happy to give you any handouts or other materials that you may have missed. Do remember, though, that while I'm here to help, ultimately I can't do the learning for you. So please make every effort to be in class on time for each session and prepared to learn what we will cover that day.

What conclusions can we draw from these two approaches?

○ As a student, which of these two courses would you rather take?

○ As a faculty member, which instructor do you think is more effective at teaching?

○ As a department chair, which instructor do you believe is more likely to develop the sort of rapport with students that leads to better learning?

Notice that in addition to phrasing what is essentially the same attendance policy in a manner more respectful of the students and more helpful to them than the first example, the second passage also explains why the instructor has required class attendance. Students are willing to work under many different systems as long as they understand the rationale for the rules being enforced. Too often in course syllabi, however, instructors establish an unnecessarily hostile tone by outlining policies that seem necessary to the instructor but appear arbitrary to the students in the course. A tone of unapproachability can be avoided with a bit of explanation and softer phrasing.

A well-constructed syllabus does not bury essential information under dense portions of text.
Syllabi communicate ineffectively if they consist of nothing more than page after page of fine print. Greater impact is obtained with course outlines that present material in an uncrowded, user-friendly manner. For instance, the presence of a few well-chosen pictures or diagrams can make an entire document seem more readable and understandable. While even a certain amount of white space can make a syllabus communicate more effectively, some carefully planned graphic design can take effective communication to an even higher level. It illustrates that the instructor has taken great care in planning the course and has considered how students are likely to best receive and understand information. While in larger classes it may be necessary to reproduce syllabi in black-and-white, in smaller classes it is not difficult to use the techniques of desktop publishing to create attractive full-color course syllabi. Moreover, even if they are printed in only black-and-white, full-color syllabi can be posted in a variety of formats to the department's Web site, where they can be downloaded by both current students (who invariably misplace copies of paper syllabi) and prospective students. So faculty members may ask, How can I be graphically innovative if I have no skill or experience in design? Here are six easy steps you can take:

1. Begin by using the templates available for your word processing programs. Although your word processor may already include a template specifically labeled "syllabus," you will also find plenty of attractive templates for newsletters, catalogues, calendars, flyers, planners, and brochures. Take one of those templates, experiment with it, and modify it to include your own course information.

2. Even simple graphics can create an impressive result. Most word processing programs allow you to create basic geometric shapes automatically. Several perpendicular rectangles, filled with light or pastel colors that do not interfere with reading the text, can be placed behind your course information to give your syllabus a published look.

3. Choose a font for the title of the course that effectively conveys some aspect of the course material. For instance, if you are teaching medieval history, use a gothic font in your header. Find a technical font for a computer science class, a "playbill" font (or record your name on an image of a marquee) for a theater class, a cartoon font for a course in popular culture, and so on.

4. Add scanned or digital photographs. Images of students on a field trip or working in the lab during previous semesters can instantly explain what it will be like for students to take your course. When the text wraps around these photographs, which is not particularly difficult to create, the result can be graphically striking. Experiment with a few photo placements, and see what you like best. Students will probably be attracted to that design as well.

5. Include charts or tables. Many students understand information better when it is portrayed graphically. Clear, simple charts or tables make grade weighting and assignment due dates easier to understand.

6. Make your syllabus look like something other than a syllabus. In certain courses, it might be effective to design your syllabus as a menu. What is the appetizer to the course? What is dessert? Where are there options among various "entrees"? Is your course prix fixe or à la carte? Or should your syllabus be more like a concert program with a prelude, several main features, an intermission, and a coda? Is the course an investigation that lends itself to a syllabus designed as a detective's file? Choose a creative metaphor for your course, and design the syllabus accordingly.

A well-constructed syllabus need not be a single document.

If instructors put into their syllabi all of the information required by their institutions and all of the information that they themselves would like to include, the result can be an unwieldy document. For instance, a list of recommended or required items for a syllabus might include

- Your full name
- How you wish to be addressed
- Your title
- The location of your office
- Your office phone number and the best times to call you
- Your office hours
- Your e-mail address
- Instructions about calling you at home
- The course title, prefix, number, and number of credits
- The basic goals of your course
- The topics you will cover
- Essential dates and deadlines for your institution (such as the last date to drop a course or to take the course pass/fail)
- Your course's requirements, assignments, and deadlines
- Information about your final examination (its date, time, and location if this is different from the last day of the class)
- Your attendance policy
- How the student's final grade will be calculated (weighting, the number of grades, and any additional factors to be considered)
- Any general criteria you will use in evaluating all assignments
- Information about how best to succeed on your exams
- Your policy on retaking an exam
- Your policy on offering extra credit assignments

If you try to include all of these items, plus any others that are important to you personally, your syllabus is likely to be so long that students may never read it in any detail. Then if you seek to incorporate white space or illustrations, the entire document will become hopelessly bulky. One solution to this problem is to divide the syllabus into a variety of syllabus documents—for example:

- Course calendar
- Course goals and philosophy
- Assignment guide

○ Exam guide

○ Study guide

○ Your own profile

These syllabus documents can be distributed one at a time over the first several weeks of the course. They will receive more attention then since you are introducing information to your students gradually and can take a few moments at the start of each class to explain them. Several short syllabus documents will not be as intimidating as a single huge syllabus and will not require the entire first session of the class just to review it. This will give you time on the first day for introducing yourself and your subject, learning about the students and their interests, discovering what the students already know about the material, and the like. Also, if you distribute these documents on paper that has already been three-hole-punched, you will be silently instructing your students about one way to keep track of this information.

A well-constructed syllabus conveys something of the instructor's personality.

A brief quotation that summarizes an essential point to be covered in the course makes an excellent epigraph or conclusion to a syllabus. For example, a course in folklore might open with this line from *Zorba the Greek*: "If only I could never open my mouth, I thought, until the abstract idea had reached its highest point—and had become a story! But only the great poets reach a point like that, or a people, after centuries of silent effort" (Kazantzakis, 1952, p. 279). A course on Wagner might follow Wagner's claim, "I write music with an exclamation point!" with Mark Twain's observation that "Wagner's music is not as bad as it sounds." A history course might feature the Sappho fragment: "But I claim there will be some who will remember us when we are gone" (Diels, 1970, fragment 59). Alternatively, an instructor might personalize a syllabus with a statement of personal philosophy, a brief reminiscence about his or her own experience taking a similar course, or two parallel sections: "What I Expect from You" and "What You Can Expect from Me."

A syllabus needs to provide a great deal of course information to students. It also conveys, intentionally or not, something of the instructor's personality and teaching philosophy. If you were an external reviewer examining one of your syllabi for the first time, what conclusions might you draw about the author's values and priorities?

———————— o ————————

Many centers for teaching and learning conduct periodic workshops on syllabus design and construction. Moreover, your own institution may have specific policies on what syllabi must contain and how they should be formatted. If neither of these situations is true for your institution, consider offering your own departmental work in effective syllabus design. Encourage one of your faculty members whose course documents are always clear, attractive, and well constructed to share a few models with his or her colleagues. Finally, keep in mind that what some colleges and universities require for a course syllabus (the student learning outcomes, basic methodologies, and course goals that do not change regardless of who is teaching that particular course) may be different from what regularly appears in a section syllabus (the specific assignments, textbooks, and exam dates that are unique to a single offering of the course). By distinguishing these two types of document, faculty members can develop a clearer sense of the difference between that which is vital for, say, Organic Chemistry I to be Organic Chemistry I and that for which they have broader academic freedom to plan and execute according to their best professional judgment.

REFERENCES

Diels, H. (1970). *Die Fragmente der Vorsokratiker*. Berlin: Weidmann.

Kazantzakis, N. (1952). *Zorba the Greek* (C. Wildman, Trans.). New York: Ballantine.

RESOURCES

Buller, J. L. (2010). *Writing an effective course syllabus. The essential college professor: A practical guide to an academic career*. San Francisco: Jossey-Bass.

Diamond, R. M. (1998). *Designing and assessing courses and curricula: A practical guide*. San Francisco: Jossey-Bass.

Grunert O'Brien, J., Millis, B. J., & Cohen, M. W. (2008). *The course syllabus: A learning-centered approach* (2nd ed.). San Francisco: Jossey-Bass.

Lowther, M. A., Stark, J. S., & Martens, G. G. (1989). *Preparing course syllabi for improved communication*. Ann Arbor, MI: National Center for Research to Improve Postsecondary Teaching and Learning.

University of Minnesota Center for Teaching and Learning. (2009). *Syllabus development*. Retrieved from http://www1.umn.edu/ohr/teachlearn/tutorials/syllabus/index.html

36

PROMOTING CREATIVITY IN TEACHING AND LEARNING

DEPARTMENT CHAIRS IN EVERY academic field are interested in exploring ways of promoting more creative teaching by their faculty members and more creative learning by their students. Creativity, long regarded as the domain of the arts, is now widely understood to be an essential part of every discipline. Regardless of the programs included in our departments, we all want our students to

- Approach problems in new ways
- Develop original questions about the material in our courses
- Discover new applications for existing knowledge
- Form interesting conclusions that can lead to better understanding
- Question established interpretations
- Assist their fellow students in fostering their own creativity

In a similar way, we as department chairs want the faculty members in our disciplines to be creative in designing their courses, original in their approaches to scholarship, and adaptable in their instructional methods. And yet despite this importance, creativity is often regarded as unteachable. We may therefore ask whether there are any ways in which we can help the members of our departments develop greater creativity in their courses.

A departmental workshop on creativity is an excellent way to begin addressing this issue. Such a workshop might include the study of a text, such as Cropley (2001), Csikszentmihalyi (1996), or De Bono (1973), which can then be followed by a discussion of how the book's ideas might be incorporated into various courses. Faculty members rarely object to learning more about what they can do to foster more creative ideas in their own work and in that of their students. Too often, however, they discover that an approach that worked well for one of their colleagues is not particularly transferable to what they do in their own courses or to their own style of teaching. As a department chair, you can assist these faculty members by exploring with them the following ten classroom-tested approaches that promote creative learning at the college level:

1. Model creativity for your students in your own course design.

Students are not likely to adopt creative approaches in a course that itself seems hidebound, restrictive, or sterile. If the organization of a course is inventive—if students are frequently caught off guard by being offered new ways of seeing or doing things—they are more likely to consider even familiar concepts in unfamiliar ways.

Faculty members can encourage student creativity by exercising a little instructional creativity themselves. They should ask themselves: To what extent does the methodology that I use in this course fall into the typical lecture and discussion, laboratory, or studio framework? To what extent is that particular structure essential to what I'm doing? In other words, are there ways in which I can stimulate creative thinking by having my students enter an environment that helps expand their comfort zones? For instance, how might a student view a history course differently if it were structured, described, and presented as a laboratory? How might the dynamics of a chemistry course change if instructors presented their roles as "personal trainers" rather than as lab instructors? What might a psychology "studio" be like?

> We can't expect students to be creative and innovative in their approaches to our disciplines if we continue to design courses, teach classes, and evaluate students in an uncreative or old-fashioned manner.

2. Revise one course totally each year.

By reorganizing a course completely—new textbook, new syllabus, new set of assignments, new structure, new everything else—faculty members are encouraged to look at their own teaching methods in different ways. For one course each year, each faculty member should try not merely to improve the syllabus but to recreate the syllabus from top to bottom. The faculty member might explore what occurs, for instance, when a course is designed not from the top down (that is, chronologically from the first day of the course to the end or the front of the book to the back), but from the bottom up (from the last day of class or from the final exam backward). Have the instructors ask themselves: In a perfect world, what final exam or final project would I like my students to be able to complete? Then, setting that perfect project as a goal, have the faculty member design the course backward so that this goal can actually be attained. What intermediary assignments or steps along the way would get the students to reach this goal? Plan each class period or unit not by the material that appears in a chapter of your textbook, but by the essential steps that will lead the students to the best possible final project you can imagine.

3. Select an appropriate metaphor, image, or structural principle for each course.

Ask the members of your department to come up with an image that best describes each of their classes. Is the course most similar to a play, a pilgrimage, a banquet or feast, an excavation, an investigation, a conversation, an experiment, a session of psychoanalysis, a saga, Marine basic training, or something else? The more your department engages in this activity, the more creative and revealing these images will become. A faculty member may find that different metaphors are more appropriate for different courses; this is perfectly acceptable. As a department chair, you should then explore why a particular metaphor was chosen for a course and consider how the image that the faculty member selected could be used to shape individual course assignments and requirements. Even more important, how might a metaphor for a course affect how the faculty member spends time in class? If, for example, the course is "an investigation," is teaching with lectures the most appropriate technique to be used?

4. Adopt methods of evaluation that encourage students to take risks.

Students are less likely to take risks and be creative in their answers if they believe that their entire grade, or even a significant portion of it, will be determined by one assignment. In cases where much is at stake, students tend to err on the side of conservatism; they attempt to give you what they think you want rather than what they really believe. Teachers can minimize this reluctance to be honest and take risks by allowing revisions of assignments, adopting portfolio or progress-based projects rather than by using one-time, discrete-task-based assignments, and developing learning opportunities that are either not graded at all or graded in such a way that they can only help one's final grade.

5. Consider assignments that include a creativity component.

Some students will try to be imaginative or innovative only if it is clear that the instructor expects, values, and rewards creativity. In these cases, it can be extremely valuable for an instructor to explain how he or she intends to acknowledge a particular assignment that has been innovative, elegant, or effective in its approach to some problem. The professor might then address these issues: What are some examples of solutions that would be deemed suitably creative? What are some examples of approaches that might seem lacking in creativity? What are the qualities that the creative approaches tend to have that are missing from their non-creative counterparts?

If the creativity component of the assignment is to be graded, the instructor has options in assigning an appropriate and minimally subjective score. The instructor can develop a rubric that clearly outlines the qualities and expectations for this creativity component and how these qualities and expectations will be graded. Alternatively, he or she could assign the creativity component enough value to make it worth taking seriously, but not enough to threaten or intimidate students who are particularly challenged by having to think in new ways. A weight of 5 percent or less of the project's total grade is probably appropriate. The instructor can also have these creativity scores set by a group or even by the class as a whole, an approach that will be fairer and will expose students to other examples of creativity. When using group grading, the instructor may wish to calculate the median score of the group so as to minimize the effect of outliers.

6. Reflect seriously on which aspects of a course must be in an instructor's control and which can be left flexible.

Students get excellent experience in creative problem solving when they are given an opportunity to design or organize certain parts of the course themselves. Students may be permitted (within certain limits) to choose the relative weighting of various course components, the specific focus of individual units or subunits, or the method of evaluation to be used at the end of one or more units. By giving students this opportunity, faculty members encourage them to become active participants in the course rather than passive recipients of instruction. They also provide a practical lesson in how creativity can often involve imagination, negotiation, and the inventive use of scarce resources such as time.

7. Consider structuring each course around a specific problem or inquiry.

With the inquiry method of instruction, students are asked not simply to learn a set of disparate facts but to solve a mystery. The mystery they set out to solve might be a puzzle (a problem having only one solution) or a conundrum (a problem that has several possible answers but no single solution). For example, in a course on Roman civilization, the instructor might begin with the following conundrum:

> During the reign of the emperor Trajan (who ruled A.D. 98–117), the Roman Empire was at its greatest size and strength. In fact, the opening line of Gibbon's *Decline and Fall of the Roman Empire* states, "In the second century of the Christian era, the Empire of Rome comprehended the fairest part of the earth, and the most civilized portion of mankind." Almost immediately after the reign of Trajan, however, the Roman Empire began to shrink in size, and, before the medieval period was over, cattle were grazing on the site of what once had been the Roman Forum. Your goal in this course will be to figure out *what went wrong*.

8. Adopt collaborative learning techniques such as jigsaw groups.

Jigsaw groups were developed by the American psychologist and teacher Elliot Aronson as a means of promoting collaborative learning and helping students break issues down into manageable parts, master those parts, and then synthesize small pieces of information into a larger picture (see Montana State University, 2006). Like a classic jigsaw puzzle, jigsaw groups involve a number of interlocking units. For example, in a college-level history course, each student might be assigned

- A specific city, region, or nation
- A specific era
- A specific topic (art, literature, warfare, politics, or architecture)
- A specific resource (a book, Web site, collection of essays, or CD-ROM)

When subgroups are needed for discussions or to critique each other's assignments, they are then organized according to one of these preestablished categories. The instructor can say, for instance, "All right. Let's have all the Paris people over here, Beijing over there, Kinshasa in that corner, and Caracas across from them. The issue that I want you to talk about today is . . ." After twenty minutes or so of this discussion, the students might be asked to leave their city groups and reorganize according to their era groups; they would then address the same issue from a different perspective and with a different group of classmates.

The advantage of this approach is that students tend to be more creative when given frequent opportunities to work with other students, modifying and improving their ideas based on the suggestions of their classmates. The usual disadvantages to these team-based approaches are that groups all too often move no faster than the level of the least productive member, share work assignments inequitably, and receive grades that are not reflective of individual effort or learning. Instructors can minimize the effect of these disadvantages by constant reconfiguration of groups according to the jigsaw method and then encouraging group critique and improvement of assignments that are ultimately the responsibility of each individual student.

9. Develop what-if assignments.

In what-if assignments, students are asked to consider what the world would be like if we could waive a certain historical event, natural law, or social constraint. They may be asked, for instance: What would have been the consequences if the French rather than the English had made extensive use of the long bow at the Battle of Agincourt, or if there were no second law of thermodynamics, or if the verification principle of the logical positivists were to be regarded as invalid? Such exercises not only encourage students to engage in creative speculation but also reinforce for them what the actual consequences of the given event, law, or constraint proved to be. (For excellent historical examples of this approach, see Cowley and Ambrose, 1999; Cowley and Bradley, 2001; and Cowley, 2003.) In courses dealing with history, world civilization, or government, the Reacting to the Past series, developed at Barnard College (2009), provides a creative set of opportunities for students to assume specific historical roles, work with primary sources, and consider what they might have done in certain situations based on the cultural perspectives of their characters.

10. Encourage students to remain physically active.

As early as the mid-1980s, Joan Gondola, a physical education professor at Baruch College, conducted several studies that indicated that the creativity of students is enhanced—at least as measured by several standard measures—when they engage in physical exercise. (See Gondola and Tuckman, 1985; Gondola, 1986, 1987.) Although this effect tended to be most pronounced among students who adhered to a regular program of physical exercise, certain differences could be measured after even a single session of strenuous physical exercise. Such findings indicate that instructors would be well served to encourage activity by their students or, at least, to get them out of their seats and moving around the classroom on a regular basis. By so doing, students are likely to be more creative in their solutions to problems and in their approaches to unfamiliar ideas. (See also Steinberg et al., 1997.) Professors can thus encourage classroom activities that get students out of their seats, assign projects that require an apropriate level of physical exertion, and address (when possible) the academic benefits that can accrue from making time for physical fitness.

○

Creativity and innovation across the curriculum are as significant for the development of student learning as are writing, critical thinking, leadership, and quantitative skills, which are also often not regarded as the private domain of any single discipline. As part of their commitment to faculty development, chairs who provide an environment in which professors feel empowered to teach creatively, and thus students are encouraged to develop their own creativity, are making a significant contribution toward improving the quality of instruction in the departments they lead.

REFERENCES

Barnard College. (2009). *Reacting to the past*. Retrieved from http://www.barnard.edu/reacting/

Cowley, R. (2003). *More what if? Eminent historians imagine what might have been*. London: Pan.

Cowley, R., & Ambrose, S. E. (Eds.). (1999). *What if? The world's foremost military historians imagine what might have been*. New York: Putnam.

Cowley, R., & Bradley, J. (2001). *What if? 2: Eminent historians imagine what might have been*. New York: Putnam.

Cropley, A. J. (2001). *Creativity in education and learning: A guide for teachers and educators*. London: Kogan Page.

Csikszentmihalyi, M. (1996). *Creativity: Flow and the psychology of discovery and invention*. New York: HarperCollins.

De Bono, E. (1973). *Lateral thinking: Creativity step by step*. New York: HarperCollins.

Gondola, J. C. (1986). The enhancement of creativity through long and short term exercise programs. *Journal of Social Behavior and Personality, 1,* 77–82.

Gondola, J. C. (1987). The effects of a single bout of aerobic dancing on selected tests of creativity. *Journal of Social Behavior and Personality, 2,* 275–278.

Gondola, J. C., & Tuckman, B. W. (1985). Effects of a systematic program of exercise on selected measures of creativity. *Perceptual and Motor Skills, 60,* 53–54.

Montana State University. (2006). *Active learning.* Retrieved from http://www .montana.edu/teachlearn/PageFrames/ActLearn2.html

Steinberg, H., Sykes, E. A., Moss, T., Lowery, S., LeBoutillier, N., & Dewey, A. (1997). Exercise enhances creativity independently of mood. *British Journal of Sports Medicine, 31,* 240–245.

RESOURCES

Kaufman, J. C., Plucker, J. A., & Baer, J. (2008). *Essentials of creativity assessment.* Hoboken, NJ: Wiley.

Treffinger, D. (2009). Myth 5: Creativity is too difficult to measure. *Gifted Child Quarterly, 53,* 245–247.

37

A SCENARIO ANALYSIS ON FACULTY DEVELOPMENT

FOR A DISCUSSION OF how scenario analyses are structured and suggestions on how to use this exercise most productively, see Chapter Nine.

Case Studies

The Great Compression

You have just been hired from outside the university to serve as a department chair, joining your new institution after an extensive national search. Because starting salaries in your department have increased faster than salaries for continuing faculty members, you have inherited a department with extremely severe faculty salary compression and inversion problems. You have already noticed since you started your term as chair that this salary situation is having a detrimental effect on faculty morale. When March comes, the dean assigns you a 4.5 percent salary pool to use for raises (cost-of-living adjustments, merit increases, inequity adjustments, or whatever else you like). You are tempted to apply some of this funding to address the inequity problems in your department, but you notice that your predecessor as department chair never decided to pursue this option. Because of your strong commitment to both the principles of equity and comprehensive faculty development, how do you proceed?

Bound by Past Practice

Your department is fortunate to have received every year a substantial faculty development fund that supports a broad array of activities.

Because of the generosity of a donor who makes this contribution, you have the luxury of allowing faculty members to participate in a large number of conferences, workshops, advanced course work, certifications, research projects, and other activities that fall broadly into the category of faculty development. Although you have the nominal right to accept or reject each faculty development proposal that is submitted, the practice has been for the chair to approve whatever a faculty member desires. The generosity of the fund has not made a selection process necessary. One advantage to this approach has always been that it allows faculty members to be as innovative as they like. In fact, several new directions in your program began as a result of some rather unusual projects that the chair may not have approved if budgets had been tighter.

Increasingly, however, one member of your department has been causing difficulties related to this fund. This individual has been receiving monetary support for a number of years to develop expertise in a field that you and many of your colleagues do not regard as particularly necessary for your program. Whenever you raise your concerns about this matter, the faculty member in question is openly hostile. Many people in the past, he or she repeatedly tells you, have used that fund to support projects in areas that others didn't like at first, but those are now some of the discipline's most important initiatives. "It's not appropriate for you to single out this project just because you don't support it," she says. "I have the same rights as anyone else."

Nevertheless, the real problem, in your opinion, is that this faculty member was hired into the department because of her existing expertise and recently has felt entitled to replace those courses with others in the area of the new subdiscipline. You are worried that if you continue to fund her proposals, you would be viewed as endorsing a change of teaching assignment that the department has not accepted. It might also leave your program without courses it needs in that faculty member's original area. You try to discuss your concerns with her, but she says, "You can't tell me not to complete this training now. If it were true that the department doesn't need me to teach courses in this new field, I should've been informed of that years ago. I wouldn't have wasted all my time with this new training. As you well know, I was given encouragement by previous chairs to do work in this area, and now you're just going to have to live with it." Privately you suspect that previous chairs did not so much support the faculty member's retraining as avoid the issue in order to forestall conflicts like the one you've just had.

As an added concern, you suspect that the faculty member is using the excuse of ongoing faculty development work to shirk other duties in your department. She has missed committee meetings. You are aware of several students who have complained that she is never around when needed. The faculty member has replaced refereed publications and presentations at major conferences with poster sessions at meetings that experts in your field regard as relatively insignificant.

Because of her repeated claims that your lack of support is a personal vendetta, you decide to see if others share your views by discussing the matter openly at a department meeting. The result is a disaster. Several department members echo your concerns, leading to a tirade by the faculty member who accuses them of misconduct with the fund: "You've been using this money for years for junkets and vacations and other non-academic purposes. When you do fund retraining, you only do it so as to position yourself for paid consultancies. You're the ones who are unethical here. I'm the only one left in the department who has any standards!" The meeting is so uncomfortable that some of the junior faculty who will soon be up for tenure and promotion become cowed and recommend that the faculty member's funding be continued. Despite your best efforts, your department now seems more divided and the atmosphere more poisoned than ever before.

Considerations

1. As you reflect on "The Great Compression," consider these questions:

   a. Is it a wise idea to use part of this year's salary pool as an equity adjustment? What risks do you run if you adopt this plan?

   b. If you decide to go ahead with the idea, is it better to attempt a radical fix all at once (at least to the extent that is possible within a 4.5 percent salary pool) or seek an incremental solution over several years?

   c. If you decide to address the inequity problems with this year's raise money, how do you make the most compelling case to your dean?

   d. How do you make the most compelling case to your faculty members?

   e. After announcing your decision, a newer faculty member shows up in your office outraged that you are "balancing the budget on the back of the junior faculty" and shifting her "hard-earned money yet again to the good old boys." How do you reply to this accusation?

f. Would your decision be any different if you know that the majority of the faculty members who are suffering from salary compression and inversion will be retiring in a year or two?

g. Would your decision be any different if the salary pool were higher or lower than 4.5 percent? What might you do, for instance, in a particularly lean year when you had only 0.5 percent to allocate? Is it wiser to "raise all boats" or to address a few of the most critical cases while others receive little or no increase? In a very different year, what might you do if you were given a one-time-only salary increase pool of 10 percent in an environment where the raise pool usually varied between 3 and 5 percent?

2. As you reflect on "Bound by Past Practice," consider these questions:

a. The angry faculty member was right about at least one thing: several other projects that did not originally have much departmental support did eventually prove to be important new directions for your department. How do you know that she is not correct in her own case?

b. How do you deal with the faculty member's demands to teach in a subdiscipline that the department has not voted to pursue?

c. Would it affect the way in which you approached this matter if you suspected that the donor might discontinue the large annual contribution should allegations of impropriety become public? Could you live with the reputation of being "the one who cost us all that money"? Is such a large sacrifice proportionate to the problem you are trying to solve?

d. If you were audited and had to explain the expenditures that occurred during your tenure as chair, would you feel comfortable doing so in the light of how this situation has developed?

e. Do you feel any obligation to previous chairs in your department whose past support of the faculty member's project created this situation? Does their precedent have any factor in your decision? Are you influenced by the fact that no previous chair ever vetoed a faculty member's proposal for use of this fund?

f. Do you now feel required to investigate the faculty member's sudden claims of inappropriate behavior by other members of your department? Can you safely dismiss these claims as due to the anger of the moment?

g. Was the open discussion a poor decision, or were you right to discuss your concerns openly, even if the result was not what you had hoped?

h. How do you deal with the faculty member's attempts to hold the department hostage through intimidation?

i. Would your course of action be any different if

- You were stepping down as chair within a few months?

- You were retiring within a few months?

- The faculty member is someone with whom you have had a long personality conflict?

- The faculty member is the spouse of your institution's president?

- The faculty member is the child of someone on your institution's governing board?

Suggestions

The Great Compression

One of the keys to how you approach the situation represented in this case may be found through the way in which you view this challenge as a faculty development opportunity. Certainly it's perfectly acceptable to regard the problem as merely one of gross inequity—and if you have clearly established yourself, during the interview process and since your arrival, as a strong proponent of salary equity, that may be the best possible approach. But it may also be possible to combine the solution to this problem with advancing your faculty development goals. To do so, you'll need to make clear precisely what those goals are, such as submission of grant proposals over a certain amount, the use of new technologies for pedagogical purposes, the publication of refereed works of research, and the presentation of papers at major national or international conferences. Then a departmental merit structure can be developed that couples achievement of these goals with seniority, rank, or any other clear and objective measure that helps you deal with your equity concerns. In this way, you're not simply rewarding people for their longevity alone; you're recognizing the substantial service that certain members of the department have given, but also making sure that genuine achievement plays a significant role in your decision.

Of course, the larger a salary pool is, the easier it can be to address severe problems of inequity. For example, if you have only a 2 percent pool to work with, it is difficult in most years to provide raises even to your best performers that match the current increase in the cost of living. With small salary pools, across-the-board increases usually cause least damage to faculty morale. It may be tempting, therefore, in the alternative scenario in which the increase pool was only 0.5 percent, to target the most egregious cases of inequity and to hold everyone else level. "It's almost impossible to notice an increase as small as .5 percent," you may think, "but by pooling these resources, I can give one or two people 4 or 5 percent where it'll make a real difference." While that may well be the most rational approach to the challenges you're facing, it is likely to be met with strong resistance from most faculty members unless they see themselves as full participants in the process. If you attempt to make the hard decisions and follow this path on your own, you may well encounter declining morale or even overt opposition to your leadership.

Bound by Past Practice

The situation described in this case presents a genuine dilemma: since you cannot find support for what you'd like to do in either the precedents set by early chairs or a clear consensus of your department, you have to approach this problem by saying, "What good am I really trying to accomplish here? What harm am I trying to avoid?" In other words, how sure are you that the type of development activities the faculty member is engaging in won't be for the long-term benefit of your program? If your soundest professional judgment tells you that the funds are being wasted and that the faculty member is moving further and further away from the specialty you need this person to pursue, you may have to fall back on the position description that was used to hire her and the official syllabi that have been approved. In other words, although the principles of academic freedom give an instructor a great deal of latitude to teach course material in a manner that he or she believes to be best, professors are contractually bound to teach the courses they are assigned with the content that is indicated in the catalogue and on the approved syllabus. Although you can certainly sympathize with someone who feels that she was given tacit encouragement to pursue a new area by the failure of previous chairs to intervene, an important principle comes into play in this situation:

Errors made by our predecessors need to be corrected at the earliest possible opportunity, not continued merely because a precedent was set.

You may well want to bring your dean into these discussions before you act. If your dean supports your decision, you'll have powerful backing for what you intend to do. If your dean doesn't support you, you may well want to reconsider whether to proceed at all. In the latter case, you'll have the decisions made by previous chairs, the feelings of many members of your department, and your direct supervisor all aligned against you. That's a difficult struggle to win, and it may well be an indication that you haven't explored the matter from every possible perspective.

PART SIX

BEST PRACTICES IN EVALUATION AND ASSESSMENT

38

CREATING WRITTEN EVALUATIONS

AT MOST COLLEGES AND UNIVERSITIES, the department chair plays an important role—frequently the most important role—in preparing each faculty member's annual performance evaluation. Often the result of this evaluation directly affects the amount of an instructor's annual merit increase or salary adjustment. Sometimes, however, the chair submits an evaluation to a dean or another administrator, who in turn is responsible for allocating an increase from a faculty salary pool. At other times, evaluation systems have been devised that are completely separate from the process of setting salaries, either because the institution is unionized or because the evaluative process is considered to be formative and mentoring rather than summative and judgmental.

No matter how central or peripheral a role the chair may play in conducting faculty evaluations, however, writing effective performance appraisals is an activity that all chairs must take seriously. Few other processes are subject to the sort of repeated and vigorous challenge that tends to be associated with annual faculty evaluations. Few other processes are as daunting for department chairs because so much of the professional development—even the very livelihoods—of faculty members depends on each chair's ability to exercise skill and judgment properly when writing annual performance evaluations. Certain institutions have made the evaluation process much more consistent by adopting a standardized evaluation form (or at least a standardized evaluation format) that must be used in all performance reviews. At many institutions, however, the chair's evaluation is either free form or subject to a great degree of flexibility and personal discretion. In you're in the latter situation, you're probably quite eager to receive some guidance in how to write and structure the evaluations of the faculty members you supervise.

Surprisingly, even positive evaluations can be extremely difficult to write. We want to praise the people who report to us without being either tepid or excessive, and positive remarks often become repetitive through the excessive use of a few overused superlatives such as *excellent, outstanding,* and *exceptional.* At the other extreme, writing an evaluation in which a faculty member is criticized is a challenge because these evaluations are likely to be the very documents that will be given the greatest scrutiny and at times must even be defended in grievance hearings or legal challenges. Furthermore, good administrators always want to offer advice in a positive manner so that the criticism they feel obliged to make does not cause discouragement or reduce morale; at the same time, they understand the reason for providing a clear paper trail in case the improvement they are recommending does not occur in a timely manner.

The department chair's goal is to create a set of annual evaluations that are as useful as possible to both faculty members and the department's own growth, professionalism, and service to its students. The chair needs to record, candidly and fairly, all of the areas in which each faculty member is expected to improve. Weaknesses should be documented in an appropriate manner so that the individual can continue to work toward progress. Strengths should be celebrated enthusiastically so that these activities are more likely to be continued in the future. Most important of all, in order to write first-rate faculty evaluations, it is necessary for the chair to ask the right questions at every stage of the process.

This chapter addresses a number of questions related to the evaluation process, beginning with those you should ask before beginning to prepare any set of written evaluations for annual review, promotion or tenure consideration, merit increases, or any other personnel process. By asking these questions at each stage of your evaluation process, you'll have a clear idea of the message you wish to convey to each faculty member, how to convey the message, and how you'll be able to guide your department forward through the advice that you offer.

Questions to Set the Stage for the Evaluation

What is my purpose in writing this set of evaluations?

Some faculty evaluation processes are formative and concerned with mentoring or improving a faculty member's performance. Other processes are more summative and are concerned with reaching a conclusion based on the faculty member's past performance—for instance, the amount of a salary increase, whether promotion should be granted, or the terms under which a contract should be renewed. Most common are evaluation processes that seek to be both formative and summative simultaneously, although this type of evaluation is the most difficult to complete effectively since offering any type of advice about how a faculty member can improve in the future may be read by the recipient as implying that he or she has a future at the institution. It is therefore important for chairs always to consider what purpose they are trying to achieve in the evaluation process itself. For instance, in a formative evaluation, you should use the individual's past performance as the basis for suggestions about future goals and needed changes. In a summative evaluation, you should include numerous evaluative remarks specifically categorizing each aspect of the instructor's performance as "sufficient," "appropriate," "exceptional," "inadequate," "not up to our standards," "meeting our departmental expectations," and the like. In an evaluation that must be both formative and summative, your goal is to achieve a careful balance of both of these ingredients, citing areas where the faculty member needs improvement without causing him or her to lose morale (unless, of course, the situation is so dire that drastic improvement is urgently needed or the faculty member is likely to be terminated).

What are my institution's established criteria for this evaluation?

One of the problems that chairs inadvertently cause themselves in writing faculty evaluations is discussing matters that turn out to be irrelevant to the stated criteria of the institution for faculty evaluation. To avoid this problem, chairs may wish to structure their evaluations around the specifically stated criteria of their institutions. For instance, if a college states that annual evaluations are to be based 50 percent on teaching, 30 percent on scholarship, and 20 percent on service, it may be useful to create a template for each evaluation that contains three separate headings, clearly designating the three major criteria with underlining or boldface type. Where these criteria are defined or illustrated in the institution's evaluation procedures or a faculty handbook, it may be valuable to cite those definitions in the evaluation template itself. Then, as you are writing each faculty member's evaluation, ask yourself repeatedly, "Are these statements germane to both the criteria I'm supposed to be using and the specific definitions that have been established at my institution?"

What resources do I have available?

As with many other administrative matters, there is no need to reinvent the wheel when doing faculty evaluations. Numerous books, Web sites, and software packages deal with performance reviews or employee appraisals, and although the vast majority of these resources were designed for a business environment, their advice is easily tailored to an academic setting. Books that are particularly useful in this regard include Heathfield (2011), Armstrong (2010), Max and Bacal (2003), Terk and Willis (2009), Swan and Margulies (1991), and Neal (2001). Informative Web sites to examine when preparing for annual faculty reviews are Jacksonville State University (n.d.), Austin Community College (2009), and University of Nebraska-Lincoln (1989/2001). A number of software packages can also assist chairs with the evaluation process, such as Performance Now by HRTools, Performance Appraisal Solutions by CareerTrack, and eAppriasal by Halogen Software. In addition, Falcone (2010) and Lyster and Arthur (2007) contain the best of both worlds: a book on the employee evaluation process and a CD-ROM with all examples provided in electronic form for you to cut and paste.

Questions to Ask Before Writing the Evaluation

Now that we've considered the questions every chair should ask before tackling any set of evaluations, let's consider what you should ask before beginning the written evaluation of any particular faculty member.

What is the overall message that I wish to convey in this written evaluation?

The National Council for the Accreditation of Teacher Education requires that all of the teacher education programs it accredits have a clear conceptual framework underlying the entire program. This framework serves as a unifying structure that gives a program both its meaning and its direction. (For more information on the idea of the conceptual framework, see Rasch and Gollnick, 2005.) In a similar way, the chair's evaluation of each faculty member should be based on a clear conceptual framework of the message and advice that this particular faculty member most needs to receive from you as chair. For this reason, if you are unable to summarize each evaluation you have written in a sentence of fifteen words or less, then you have not made your overall message clear enough for the faculty member to understand it. (In fact, include that single sentence in boldface type prominently somewhere in the evaluation itself.) The philosopher G. E. Moore was famous for challenging the statements made by others with the refrain, "What exactly do you *mean*?" (Edmonds and Eidinow, 2001, p. 60). If you are not able to answer Moore's question easily about a given evaluation, then you have not yet refined your thoughts thoroughly enough to convey them to someone else.

How can I be specific enough in my appraisal, citing clear examples where appropriate?

The most frustrating criticism we ever receive is that which is vague since we can neither challenge it nor be improved by it. Whenever you make a criticism, be sure that you have based your remarks on something that you have observed or on some data that have been reported to you. Don't keep these observations secret. Make it clear why you have concerns about certain aspects of the individual's performance. If you believe that a faculty member's teaching has not been up to departmental standards, state how you have developed this belief—for example:

- ○ Student ratings of instruction for this individual are consistently low.
- ○ The faculty member's peers have expressed concerns directly to you.
- ○ Students have consistently stated their concerns to you in your office.
- ○ You are basing this observation on something that you witnessed.
- ○ The materials for the instructor's courses are outdated or the exams too reliant on multiple-choice questions.

Similarly, if there have been problems with a faculty member's scholarship, be specific as to what those problems are—for example:

- ○ The faculty member is not submitting articles to the right sort of journals or not making presentations at the appropriate type of conferences.
- ○ The faculty member needs to bring more projects to fruition. If this is the case, provide information on how many projects, articles, reviews, or other publications would have been appropriate, and explain how you arrived at that number.
- ○ The faculty member's research agenda is veering so far from the discipline that it is difficult for you to assess it effectively.

By determining these matters, you will be able to give clear, specific guidance to the faculty member rather than make vague statements such as, "Your quality of instruction has not been sufficient," or, "We need to see further growth in scholarship."

How can I be positive and constructive in my criticism, even when I have to point out some genuine weaknesses?

Particularly in evaluations that contain both a formative and a summative component, it is important to give criticism that preserves a faculty member's morale and supports his or her willingness to take whatever steps are necessary in order to make improvements. In most cases, achieving this goal is a matter of adopting a tone that conveys recommendations for improvement in an overtly helpful and positive manner. Read over each sentence that you write and ask yourself, "How would I feel if a superior wrote this to me? If I had to be given this advice, how would I want it to be phrased?" In many cases, you can include some phrase that makes the appropriate point without causing any unnecessary blow to the person's ego or implication that the individual has failed in some irremediable manner. For instance, you can often achieve a constructive tone through phrases such as, "Of course, I understand that this incident is out of character with your usual high level of achievement in this area . . . ," or, "Since we all have aspects of our performance in which we'd like to do even better next year, I'd like to suggest that . . . ," or, "One topic that I may be able to offer you some help on is . . ." Don't belabor a minor point to such an extent that it takes the bloom off what would otherwise be a highly favorable evaluation. Always ask yourself, "Does this criticism really need to be given?" and, "What do I hope to accomplish by pointing out this particular weakness?"

Questions to Ask After Drafting an Evaluation

Finally, let's explore a few questions to ask after drafting the evaluation and now editing it before sharing it with the faculty member under review.

Have I been forward looking enough, setting clear goals for the future?

Frequently we are so focused on past achievement in evaluations that we neglect planning for the future. To avoid this problem, use the evaluation process to recommend some specific goals for the coming year. (This will be useful to you when you write next year's evaluation because you will be able to refer to progress, or lack thereof, in attaining those goals.)

In particular, you should never give a criticism to a faculty member without including two additional items: (1) the specific observations you made that led you to give this criticism and (2) clear advice about what the faculty member should do in the future in order to improve. To make these goals as clear as possible, outline them with numbers or bullets so that they stand out to anyone reading the evaluation.

> Although we tend to think of evaluation solely as a retrospective process, it also is a good time to set future goals. At the very least, goals can be developed that seek to remediate any weaknesses uncovered by the retrospective aspects of the evaluation.

Have I made my overall conclusion clear?

Never send an evaluation on the day that you write it. Always let at least a day go by (and holding an evaluation for a week or a month is even better if your evaluation timetable is sufficiently flexible) between your writing of an evaluation and sending it to the faculty member. In every case, before you send an evaluation, read it over carefully. Are all your points clear? Do they really seem necessary? Can you still summarize your conceptual framework for this evaluation simply when rereading it? One useful technique is to score each evaluation on a scale of 1 (extremely poor overall performance) to 10 (extremely good overall performance) immediately after you write the evaluation. Repeat this scoring when you reread the evaluation later. Has your score changed significantly for any evaluation? If so, try to determine whether the language you used in the evaluation was as clear as you would like it to be. Also, be sure that you have evaluated everything. A statement such as, "Your scholarly activity for the year consisted of three presentations at regional conferences," does not make it clear whether you consider this to be an adequate level of activity. As you reread your evaluation, make sure that you have assessed all achievements, not merely listed them.

What aspects of this evaluation are most likely to be challenged? Why? What will be my response in such a challenge? Do I have evidence to support my position?

Finally, it is an all-too-real aspect of academic administration that evaluations are sometimes challenged. Often these challenges will be informal, as faculty members want to meet with you to have you explain why you criticized them as you did. Less frequently, but more seriously, evaluations can lead to grievances or even legal challenges. For this reason, ask yourself how you would respond if any sentence that you wrote in a faculty evaluation were challenged in a court of law, read publicly at a faculty meeting, or quoted in the local paper. Can you defend and give examples of every statement that you make? If you can, then you are probably on firm ground. If not, then you may wish to go back and refine or omit the passage in question. In truly serious cases, always run the phrasing in question by your institution's counsel before you send it to the faculty member or submit it to the next level of evaluation.

By asking these questions at each stage of your evaluation process, you'll have a clear idea of what message you wish to convey to each faculty member, how to convey the message, and how to guide your department through the advice that you offer.

○

Standardized course evaluation systems, such as that offered through the IDEA Center, can provide chairs with nationally normed data against which to interpret an individual faculty member's student ratings of instruction within a broader context (www.theideacenter.org). That wider framework makes it easier to determine how particular instructors are performing while controlling for such factors as class size, the nature of the discipline being taught, and demographic issues. Furthermore, no discussion about written evaluations would be complete without reference to the growing literature that is critical of the entire performance appraisal process. Although most colleges and universities require written evaluations of all faculty members—and these requirements are intensifying because of cries for accountability—many experts in human resources believe that traditional evaluation procedures are deeply flawed, ineffective, and often even counterproductive. For further insights into this perspective, see Coens and Jenkins (2000), Culbert and Rout (2010), and Markle (2000).

REFERENCES

Armstrong, S. (2010). *The essential performance review handbook: A quick and handy resource for any manager or HR professional*. Franklin Lakes, NJ: Career Press.

Austin Community College. (2009). *Faculty evaluation procedures*. Retrieved from http://www.austincc.edu/hr/eval/documents/ProceduresManual9-09_001.pdf

Coens, T., & Jenkins, M. (2000). *Abolishing performance appraisals: Why they backfire and what to do instead*. San Francisco: Berrett-Koehler.

Culbert, S. A., & Rout, L. (2010). *Get rid of the performance review: How companies can stop intimidating, start managing—and focus on what really matters.* New York: Business Plus.

Edmonds, D., & Eidinow, J. (2001). *Wittgenstein's poker: The story of a ten-minute argument between two great philosophers.* New York: Ecco.

Falcone, P. (2010). *101 sample write-ups for documenting employee performance problems: A guide to progressive discipline and termination* (2nd ed.). New York: AMACOM.

Heathfield, S. (2011). *Win-win performance appraisals: Get the best results for yourself and your employees: What to do before, during and after the review.* New York: McGraw-Hill.

Jacksonville State University. (n.d.). *Guidelines for faculty evaluations.* Retrieved from http://www.jsu.edu/cas/guidelines.html

Lyster, S., & Arthur, A. (2007). *199 pre-written employee performance appraisals: The complete guide to successful employee evaluations and documentation.* Ocala, FL: Atlantic Publishing Group.

Markle, G. L. (2000). *Catalytic coaching: The end of the performance review.* Westport, CT: Quorum Books.

Max, D., & Bacal, R. (2003). *Perfect phrases for performance reviews: Hundreds of ready-to-use phrases that describe your employees' performance.* New York: McGraw-Hill.

Neal, J. E. (2001). *The #1 guide to performance appraisals: Doing it right!* Perrysburg, OH: Neal Publications.

Rasch, K., & Gollnick, D. M. (2005). *Conceptual framework: What it is and how it works.* Retrieved from www.ncate.org/documents/IOFall05/introframework.ppt

Swan, W. S., & Margulies, P. (1991). *How to do a superior performance appraisal.* Hoboken, NJ: Wiley.

Terk, N., & Willis, M. (2009). *Writing performance reviews: How to write performance objectives, reviews, appraisals, and other performance documentation that is clear, descriptive, objective, and acceptable in today's workplace.* Oakland, CA: Write It Well.

University of Nebraska-Lincoln. (1989/2001). *Guidelines for the evaluation of faculty: Annual evaluations, promotion and tenure.* Retrieved from http://www.unl.edu/svcaa/hr/tenure/tenureguide.html

RESOURCES

Bruce, A. (2005). *Perfect phrases for documenting employee performance problems.* New York: McGraw-Hill.

Dalager, J. K. (2011, Winter). Legal issues in faculty evaluation: Avoiding problems. *Department Chair, 21*(3), 9–11.

Neal, J. E. (2003). *Effective phrases for performance appraisals: A guide to successful evaluations.* Perrysburg, OH: Neal Publications.

Swan, W. S., & Wilson, L. E. (2007). *Ready-to-use performance appraisals: Downloadable, customizable tools for better, faster reviews!* Hoboken, NJ: Wiley.

39

CONDUCTING ORAL
EVALUATION SESSIONS

AT MOST COLLEGES AND UNIVERSITIES, the chair's written evaluation of a faculty member's performance is accompanied by a face-to-face discussion in which key issues arising from the evaluation process may be addressed and follow-up questions may be asked. An oral evaluation plays a key role in the department chair's responsibilities for faculty development and mentoring, in addition to making certain that each faculty member is performing at the level anticipated for his or her specific rank. Despite the great significance attached to this duty, many department chairs receive little or no training in the basic techniques of how to conduct oral performance appraisals, and as a result, they feel uncomfortable in evaluation sessions. Some institutions have specific requirements for how oral evaluation sessions are to be conducted, but many offer little guidance, leaving chairs largely to figure out the procedure on their own. In this chapter, we'll consider standard good practice for effective oral evaluation sessions, covering most of the basic principles that all department chairs should know.

Keep good and timely records.
The day to start planning a faculty evaluation session is not the day of the session; it's the day after the session. That's when you begin planning the faculty member's evaluation for next year. Use a word processing file, a spreadsheet, a database, or a legal pad to which you can add notes concerning every faculty member under your supervision over the coming year. Whichever method you choose, be sure to prepare a backup copy and keep both the original and the backup in safe, confidential locations.

Organize your notes into the sections you will need for the evaluation itself: teaching, scholarship, service, overall, or the specific categories that your institution uses. Throughout the year, whenever the faculty member does something significant—whether good or bad—make a clear, dated record in your notes. Be specific. If the faculty member did something that you regard as worthy of criticism, specifically note the problem and the result of the faculty member's action. What could the faculty member have done differently? If you wish to offer praise, explain why the faculty member's action was so successful. How did it benefit the department, the students, and the academic community? How can the faculty member have similar successes in the future? Be sure to record positive accomplishments as well as specific suggestions for improvement; you'll be glad that you have a list of commendations to make when you are preparing for your next evaluation session.

Prepare carefully for each evaluation session.

You are preparing for your face-to-face meeting while you're creating the written evaluation that you will send to the faculty member and place in his or her personnel file. In addition, just before your meeting occurs, give yourself at least fifteen minutes to clarify in your mind precisely what message you want to convey. Decide in a single sentence what the message of the meeting will be. In most cases, that one sentence will be all that the faculty member will take away from the session. Because of this, be sure that this sentence—what I'll refer to as your central message—is clear in your mind. As a general rule of thumb, adhere to this principle: if you can't summarize a faculty member's evaluation to yourself in one sentence, then you haven't refined your thoughts clearly enough. Never permit yourself to go into an evaluation session cold. If you don't have enough time to prepare, try to reschedule the meeting. Evaluation sessions are far too important to be done carelessly or impromptu.

After greeting the faculty member, begin the evaluation session by clearly stating the result.

Don't keep the faculty member waiting as to what the outcome of the session might be. Here are some examples of what you might say to a faculty member, although you should rephrase each message in your own words:

○ *Completely positive evaluation.* "The one thing that I want you to take away from today's meeting is that this has been an absolutely first-rate year for you. What we're going to be doing is taking a look at a lot of successes, and I think you should be congratulated for that."

○ *Positive evaluation with suggestions for minor improvement.* "The most important thing I want you to remember about today's session is that this has been a very, very good year. I want you to be proud of what you've done; it's really been extremely good. Now, we're also going to talk about one or two areas where I think we can work to make some improvements. But I don't want any of that to overshadow the central message I'm going to try to convey: this has been a really wonderful year."

○ *Negative evaluation with suggestions for improvement.* "What I'd like to focus on today are a number of areas where I think we've seen some problems during the past year. Basically, what I'm going to tell you is that I think you could've done better. And I want to help you do that over the coming year."

○ *Negative evaluation with specific warning.* "I don't want to sugarcoat this. I think this has been a year where your performance wasn't what it should've been. I'm going to give you some specific examples of that, and I'm going to try to explain how I think you could have done better. The message that I want you to take away from this meeting is that we're going to have to see some changes, and see them soon. If I don't see the improvements I suggest by [date], then what's going to happen is this: [state likely outcome]."

When you give extremely bad news, you've got to remember that to the faculty member being evaluated, what you say will be like hearing a death sentence from the doctor: the faculty member is going to stop absorbing what you say for a while. Don't expect all of the details to be remembered; you'll need to follow up with a thorough written report, constructed according to the requirements set down by your institution and the principles explored in the previous chapter.

Take your time in conducting the face-to-face meeting.

A repeated criticism from faculty members is that evaluation sessions with their chairs tend to be perfunctory. The reason for this is that we, as supervisors, don't feel comfortable in conducting these sessions. Giving both public praise and candid criticism tends to embarrass us. Nevertheless, remember that when you're being praised, you want to take some time to revel in it. If you're being critiqued, you want information about what you've done wrong and how you might improve. Faculty members feel precisely the same way. Don't speed through your sessions with them. Plan on spending a half-hour or more with each person you evaluate.

Don't mix meetings.

One of the ways in which supervisors send mixed messages is by holding multipurpose meetings. Talking about a curriculum proposal for the future makes the faculty member assume that he or she will be part of that future. Discussion of departmental successes implies that the faculty member has contributed to those successes. If you feel you must cover several agenda items in a single session with a faculty member, schedule a separate time for the formal evaluation session itself. Make it clear that this is a special meeting conducted simply for the purposes of evaluation. Don't allow a general conversation to segue into a performance appraisal.

Give specific examples.

Telling a faculty member, "You did a great job," is not helpful; it gives the faculty member absolutely nothing to go on in order to repeat the success. In much the same way, saying, "Next year teach better," is of little use. Instead offer specific advice. If quality of instruction is an issue during an evaluation session, offer the faculty member suggestions on how to improve. Is there a center for excellence in teaching on your campus? Are there faculty development workshops that deal with pedagogy? Can faculty development funding be used for off-campus improvement of instruction? Is there a formal or informal mentoring program that you can suggest? Also, make it clear to the faculty member on what basis you are making this criticism. Was a repeated concern raised in student ratings of instruction? Were problems noted in peer evaluations? Have you received student complaints? Rather than issuing a general complaint or concern, try to deal with the specific behavior that you would like to see improved.

Set specific standards.

If you are concerned that a faculty member's level of scholarship has not been sufficient, what would it have taken for you to feel that adequate progress has been made? What were you looking for in the faculty member's performance that you didn't see? If the faculty member provides that level of achievement next year, will you be satisfied, or are standards increasing each year? For example, you might say something like, "For next year, I want to work with you to choose at least three sessions that you'll attend at the Center for Excellence in Teaching, and then we'll discuss the best ways in which to apply what you learn in those classes to your specific courses. In addition, you should submit at least two articles to the journals that our promotion committee regards as first tier for our discipline, and I'll expect at least one of those to be accepted for publication without further revision by the time the department reviews your portfolio for tenure."

After you have conveyed your message once, stop to repeat and clarify it.

In what is essentially a positive evaluation, be sure to follow criticism with some specific praise. But take care not to do this when you want the overall message to be negative. Tempering bad news with praise in order to make the faculty member feel good may send a confusing message. As uncomfortable as it may be, staying on message as much as possible throughout the session is better.

Be aware of subtext.

As you conduct your session with the faculty member, be alert to any signals you may inadvertently be sending. What are your facial expressions? What is your body language? Are you undermining your words by nonverbal communication?

Make sure that the central message of the session is clearly recorded in writing.

There should be a clear connection between the overall focus of the oral and written evaluations conducted for each faculty member. In fact, if at all possible, have your one-sentence summary of your central message stated verbatim in the overall section of each evaluation, oral and written.

Be forward looking in addition to reviewing past performance.

Set goals for the coming year with the faculty member. Discuss with him or her possibilities that might lead to a more positive evaluation next year.

End by reiterating your central message.

Evaluation sessions should sandwich the central message. In your notes, you may wish to outline your plan for the performance appraisal in this way:

1. State the central message.

2. Provide details.

3. Make other comments that the faculty member needs to hear.

4. Allow the faculty member to ask questions and make observations.

5. Restate your central message.

6. Be certain that the faculty member understands your central message. Ask the faculty member to repeat the primary thrust of your meeting, and if it differs from your intention, try clarifying your main points by expressing them in a different way.

---

o

Oral evaluations are particularly uncomfortable for new chairs. Many people dislike situations where there may be confrontation or where they have to provide bad news face-to-face. At times, it can even be awkward giving someone good news if we're unused to paying people compliments or tend to feel ill at ease in situations that can quickly become emotional. Conducting face-to-face performance reviews requires a set of skills that develops over time, and if you're new to your position as department chair, you may find these sessions among the toughest parts of your job. Therefore, prepare thoroughly and practice some of the phrases that you'll use by saying them out loud in front of a mirror until you begin to feel a bit more comfortable with them. Remember a truth that is easy to forget in the pressure of the moment: no matter how nervous you feel, the person who's being evaluated is even more nervous, and the best thing you can do for both of you is to convey an air of calm, confidence, and clarity.

RESOURCES

Arthur, D. (2008). *The first-time manager's guide to performance appraisals.* New York: AMACOM.

Deblieux, M. (2003). *Performance appraisal source book: A collection of practical samples.* Alexandria, VA: Society for Human Resource Management.

Grote, D. (2002). *The performance appraisal question and answer book: A survival guide for managers.* New York: AMACOM.

Malouff, J., & Beebe, S. (1994). Performance appraisal meetings: Strategies for the person being evaluated. *Journal of College Student Development, 35,* 354–358.

Runion, M., & Brittain, J. (2006). *How to say it performance reviews: Phrases and strategies for painless and productive performance reviews.* New York: Prentice Hall Press/Penguin Group.

40

WRITING LETTERS OF
RECOMMENDATION

THERE IS ONE FACT of life that all department chairs must learn to accept sooner or later: if you don't like writing letters of recommendation, you're going to have a very tough time on the job. Every department chair ends up with an almost unbelievable number of requests for letters of recommendation. Students need them for employment or for admission to graduate school. Faculty members need them when they are submitting grant applications, applying for promotion, and even when seeking positions at other institutions. And your obligations in this area do not end even with the boundaries of your department itself. Your chair colleagues in other departments may ask for letters of recommendation when they undergo performance evaluations or seek new opportunities in college administration.

Since writing letters of recommendation will be such an important aspect of your position, is there any way in which you can make this task easier? And at the same time that you are making the task easier, is there any way in which the letters that you produce can be more informative to the person who is reading them, truly outstanding from all the other letters that may receive little more than a cursory glance?

The letters of recommendation that you write will be more effective—and less of a burden for you to produce—if you systematically ask yourself each of the following questions before you actually begin to draft the letter:

1. How strong a recommendation do I wish to write?

2. On what basis am I making this recommendation?

3. Which three central points do I wish to make?

4. What examples can I provide for each of these three points?

5. What insights can I provide that the reader can gain nowhere else?

Spending just two or three minutes reviewing these five questions will instantly give you insight into what you need to say, how to organize your letter, and how to keep it focused enough for it to be effective. Let's examine each of these in turn.

Determining the Strength of the Recommendation

The first thing that you should do when beginning a letter of recommendation is decide in advance what overall impression you wish to create. In other words, where along the overall spectrum of "recommendability" would you place this candidate? Do you wish to leave the reader with the impression that the person about whom you are writing is one of the very best individuals with whom you have ever worked? Is this a candidate about whom you have absolutely no reservations whatsoever, someone on whom you would stake your reputation? We all have students and colleagues we might place in that category, and when these individuals are requesting a letter, you will not need to hold back the superlatives in your praise. Usually, however, a person who is asking for a letter of recommendation is not a denizen of these exalted regions, but rather someone not unlike the vast majority of us: good—perhaps even extremely good—at certain things, less capable at others. In these cases, try to develop a clear picture of precisely how you would rank the person. Is he or she in the top 2 percent of all the people you might recommend for this position? Perhaps the top 5 percent? The upper quarter? The best third? The top half? Or is this an individual who, for whatever reason, you do not feel you can give a particularly strong recommendation, at least for this opportunity?

It is important at the start to have a clear impression of the degree of support you wish to convey. If you are not certain yourself, there is no way in which your reader will be certain after reading your letter. Deciding in advance on the strength of your recommendation calls for far more than simply determining how emphatic your adjectives will be; it requires knowing what one thing you want the reader to know most of all. Try to state that one overall impression to yourself in twenty words or less. If you are unable to frame your basic message that concisely, your reader will not be able to interpret your message no matter how carefully you craft your prose or select the anecdotes that you will relate.

The Basis for This Recommendation

Once you have decided the overall strength and tone that your recommendation will take, your next step is to decide the basis on which you are writing this letter. This question is a little more complicated than simply knowing that you are writing the letter as the person's colleague, mentor, or advisor. It is a matter of developing a clear image in your mind of the reason that you feel that you can serve as a reference for this candidate's suitability to this opportunity. In most cases, your letter will be based on several factors.

Experience

A letter based on experience argues that the candidate has already had prior success in programs or positions extremely similar to the one about which you are now writing and therefore would be an excellent choice for the position at hand. Because the candidate is likely to have amassed experience in situations relevant to this opportunity, your letter will be filled with more examples of obstacles overcome and opportunities seized than is usually the case in other types of letters. The best cases that you can cite are those that help clarify for the reader how the person approached the challenges that arose, made effective decisions, and grew in responsibility over the time that you had direct observation of him or her. Try to cite situations in which you directly observed the candidate's strengths or that go beyond information that is probably contained in the person's letter of application and curriculum vitae.

Potential

A letter based on the candidate's potential or promise is appropriate when that person is seeking an opportunity that goes significantly beyond or is substantially different from his or her experience—for instance, an undergraduate who is applying to graduate school or for a first job, a teaching colleague who is seeking a first deanship, or a graduate student who is trying to find an initial appointment on the full-time faculty of another institution. Although they may not have held a position identical to the one for which they are currently applying, you might cite examples of somewhat similar activities that the person has successfully accomplished. Has he or she been a teaching assistant in a course, demonstrated leadership on a committee, or excelled at course work at all similar to what will be involved in this new opportunity? In a letter based on promise, you build your case around experiences that are similar, though obviously not identical, to the proposed position and extrapolate the candidate's likely success from these other situations.

Intelligence

A letter based on the candidate's innate intelligence is most suitable when you are asked to write a recommendation for someone who is applying for a position far outside his or her prior experience. Since you may not even know of appropriate comparable achievements, you might discuss how quickly this individual learns to succeed in unfamiliar situations, masters challenges quickly, and demonstrates unusual insight into the root causes of various problems. Your central point should be that although the person has not yet had the opportunity to demonstrate success in this or truly similar areas, he or she is bright enough to adapt to any sort of challenge that may come along. You are arguing that the person is a quick study (and providing a number of specific examples to back up your claim), even if that talent has not yet been applied in an area similar to the current opportunity.

Character

Letters of reference based primarily on a person's strength of character should be used only in certain situations, and then only advisedly. Although it is always appropriate in any letter of recommendation to describe the candidate as principled, having a strong sense of values, and trustworthy (providing that you believe such claims to be true), most letters that overemphasize an applicant's personal qualities strike reviewers as rather weak. They appear to be saying that the applicant is unqualified for this opportunity, that you recognize this lack of qualifications, and that you are intentionally avoiding making reference to the central criteria on which this decision will be made.

In most cases, you should focus your letter on the applicant's character only if that is the type of letter specifically requested by the institution (as may be the case, for instance, with an applicant to law school or seminary) or if that is the primary capacity in which you know the individual (if, for instance, you are writing a letter not primarily as the applicant's chair but as his or her spiritual advisor or colleague in a religious education course).

The Three Central Points to Convey

Having now decided on the strength of your recommendation and the basis on which you will be framing your letter, your next task is to decide how to be as helpful as possible to the person or committee receiving your letter. Be concise. Long letters of recommendation simply are not read. Although you may feel that your pages of eloquence are serving the candidate's best interests, your efforts may actually be counter-productive. A five- or six-page letter will be set aside and ignored, along with all of your arguments on behalf of this candidate. Other candidates, potentially less qualified, may end up getting more attention because the letters of recommendation written on their behalf were concise and easily digested.

For the most part, fit letters of recommendation on one side of a single sheet of paper. In certain rare instances (for example, that truly special advisee who will undoubtedly go on to a distinguished career in your discipline), you may allow yourself to extend onto a second page for perhaps a paragraph. But under no circumstances should you ever write a letter of recommendation that is longer than two pages. The task facing you is to make your point as clearly, crisply, and directly as possible. Don't allow valuable information to become lost in excess verbiage.

The best way to do this is to ask yourself what three things are most important for the reader to know about this candidate's potential (or experience or intelligence or character). Make each of those three points the topic sentence of a brief paragraph, and your letter will largely structure itself. For instance, when writing a letter on behalf of a student who is applying to graduate school, you may decide that the most important information the reader can receive is that the student was highly original in selecting research topics, is a good self-starter and independent worker, and recovers easily from unexpected setbacks in his or her academic work. For a faculty member applying for promotion, you might decide that your three observations will be that the faculty member has introduced classroom techniques that greatly engaged his or her students, this person's research is highly respected in your discipline, and his or her collegewide service commitments, while few in number, have made a tremendous impact on the good of your community. For a colleague who is applying for a senior administrative position, you might note that this individual takes a highly collegial approach to problem solving, sees the central issue of a problem quickly, and strives to ensure that every side of an issue is examined.

Examples of the Three Points

Once it is clear to you which three observations will provide the central structure of your letter, support each point with one or two clear, specific examples. Try to focus on a substantive instance where the individual has demonstrated the positive quality that you are describing. Use concrete action words (*developed, recruited, founded, increased, advised, transformed*) rather than abstractions, too many adverbs, and weaker, less action-oriented verbs (*supported, approved, served*). In each paragraph, be sure that you have stated not merely that the person is good, but why the person is good and the specific behavior or accomplishment that led you to this observation.

> A tightly constructed, one-page letter of recommendation, listing several clear and compelling examples of the achievement you are describing, is far more effective than a multipage letter filled with positive but ultimately vague descriptors.

New Insights for the Reader

Finally, ask yourself if you have provided the reader with insights or observation that could not be gained (or, at least, not easily gained) from another source. One of the mistakes that many writers of reference letters make is simply to repeat information that the recipient already knows from a transcript, curriculum vitae, or the applicant's own letter. In a letter written on behalf of a student, for instance, it makes very little sense simply to state the individual's cumulative grade point average (GPA). At best, this statement will merely repeat information that the reader already knows from other sources and will make it look as though you are padding your letter because you don't have anything else positive to say. At worst, either your information or the transcript mailed by the student may be out of date, and the recipient will end up giving undue attention to why the student's cumulative GPA is listed as 3.83 in one place and 3.77 in another. If you believe that the student's GPA could be particularly important to the reader of your letter, place that information in a context that only you can provide. Say something like, "While this student's cumulative GPA was an impressive 3.43 at the end of fall semester [year], it should be noted that in advanced practica and seminars—where students are competing against the most accomplished of their peers in the most rigorous of conditions—the student's average reached a perfect 4.0, the only such example I have known in my twenty-two years of teaching."

In all cases, try to select specific examples of achievement that are unlikely to be documented in standard sources such as résumés and transcripts. Since the individual selected you to be a reference, what opportunities have you had to experience this person's work that other observers are unlikely to have shared? Which examples provide the most informative picture of the candidate as a person, even if the reader of your letter has not yet met the person about whom you are writing?

The more you can tie your examples to your own observations and the more you can bring the person about whom you are writing to life for your readers, the more effective your letter will be.

Two Final Principles

Keep in mind two other principles while writing letters of recommendation.

First, make your task as easy as possible for the reader. Recipients of letters of recommendation are frequently dealing with dozens of letters at once. Keep their needs and interest in mind. The first time that you mention the subject's name, place it in boldface type. Open your letter, for instance, with language similar to the following: "**Jennifer G. Student** has asked me to write to you in support of her application to the [program]. I am delighted to do so because . . ." You thus keep the reader from having to sift through the entire letter trying to discover about whom you are writing. (It also helps the person sorting the mail know how to file your letter.) When addressing a letter to someone outside your department or institution, try to consider what they will know and what you will need to explain to them. Will it be clear to your reader that the "APA" you feature prominently in your letter is the American Philological Association and not the American Psychological Association, the American Psychiatric Association, the American Payroll Association, the Audio Publishers Association, the Allied Pilots Association, or the American Planning Association? (All of these are real organizations, and they are all widely known as APA among certain groups of academics.) Will your reader know whether the "ENG 101" that you mention is a literature course or a composition course? Will it be obvious that GR 300 is a German rather than a Greek course and that IN 411 is an independent study course rather than an international studies course? (As a general rule of thumb, always use course names rather than course numbers.

They tend to be more easily understood.) Proofread your letter to be sure that every reference—including references to people who may be known locally in your department but not in wider academic circles—is either obvious or explained.

Second, be judicious about writing negative letters. There are very few instances when you should write a letter of reference that is not, on balance, far more positive than negative. If you are asked for a letter by the individual himself or herself and do not feel that you can write a positive letter, the kindest suggestion that you can make is for the person to seek someone else to serve as reference. (In most cases, merely making this suggestion is all that you will have to do. Certain people will press you, however, in order to learn the reasons that you are reluctant to write a letter on their behalf. In these cases, it is far preferable to provide one or two concrete reasons face-to-face—as uncomfortable as that may be—than to give the false impression that you are submitting a positive letter.)

In all letters of recommendation, be 100 percent certain of what you state, and make sure you can document everything. This rule is even more important in the case of less than completely positive letters of reference. Even letters for which the subjects waive their rights to see cannot be guaranteed to remain confidential. The subject may well see your letter at some point in the future and could begin a legal challenge that could have been avoided. As a general rule, write nothing in a letter of recommendation that you would not want the subject to read and to be quoted in a large-circulation newspaper. In a worst-case scenario, both of those contingencies could occur.

o

There are a number of useful sources to consult in developing additional insights about writing outstanding letters or recommendation. These sources include Bodine (2010), Whalley (2000), Bly and Kelly (2009), Fawcett (2008), Mamchak and Mamchak (1998), and Bell (2004). While most of these resources are written for the corporate world or K–12 education, by combining their suggestions with your own insights and style, you'll develop letters of recommendation that are easier to write and more effective in achieving their goals.

REFERENCES

Bell, A. H. (2004). *Writing effective letters, memos, and e-mail: A business success guide.* Hauppauge, NY: Barron's.

Bly, R. W., & Kelly, R. A. (2009). *The encyclopedia of business letters, faxes, and e-mail: Features hundreds of model letters, faxes, and e-mail to give your business writing the attention it deserves*. Franklin Lakes, NJ: Career Press.

Bodine, P. (2010). *Perfect phrases for letters of recommendation*. New York: McGraw-Hill.

Fawcett, S. (2008). *Instant recommendation letter kit: How to write winning letters of recommendation* (3rd ed.). Montreal, CA: Final Draft Publications.

Mamchak, P. S., & Mamchak, S. R. (1998). *Educator's lifetime encyclopedia of letters*. West Nyack, NY: Center for Applied Research in Education.

Whalley, S. (2000). *How to write powerful letters of recommendation*. Minneapolis, MN: Education Media.

41

DOING ASSESSMENT
EFFECTIVELY

ASSESSMENT AT YOUR INSTITUTION is likely to affect nearly every office on campus. As a department chair, your direct involvement in assessment is much more likely to be concerned with your discipline's own academic program than with other issues. In other words, even nonacademic programs at your college and university are being assessed. The business office, residence life, student affairs, advancement, college relations—any unit at your school is doing a form of assessment that is appropriate to its structure, function, and mission. In a similar way, multidepartmental academic programs—the first-year experience, the honors program, the general education program, and the others—will be assessed in a manner that is appropriate for them. If you are asked to participate in any of these types of assessment that move beyond your individual department or discipline, you will almost certainly receive a great deal of guidance on what is expected from you by your institution's assessment office or whoever supervises these campuswide efforts. Where you will probably be given a good deal more autonomy (and thus may feel that you may need more guidance) is in the area of assessing the effectiveness of your department and its proprietary academic programs (your major and minor programs, for instance).

In order for department chairs to play an effective role in leading the assessment process for their disciplines, they must start by knowing what assessment is and what it is not. Faculty members may sometimes tell you, "I don't know why we have to jump through all of these hoops on assessment. We're doing assessment all the time. We're assessing students in our courses by means of assignments, examinations, and final projects, and those assessment measures tell us that we're doing just fine." This perspective, however, confuses evaluation with assessment and tries to draw a conclusion more appropriate for one of these activities from the means developed to accomplish the other.

> Evaluation measures the success of individuals, such as students and faculty members, and individual sections of courses by determining whether these reach a defined standard. Assessment measures the effectiveness of larger or collective entities—such as programs, offices, or units within an institution—by determining whether those groups are achieving defined outcomes.

Evaluation is summative and results oriented. It involves a decision as to whether the individual has met the standard. Should this particular faculty member be promoted? Was this specific section of the course well taught? These are appropriate questions for evaluation. Assessment, in contrast, is formative and process oriented. Is the writing program achieving the goals that we've set for it? If not, how might we improve the program in order to achieve more satisfactory results? These are the types of questions to ask in assessment. Thus, the grading of students—one of the types of "assessment" cited by the imaginary faculty member above—is actually a quite appropriate means of evaluation but a completely inadequate form of assessment.

Consider this scenario. As an administrator, I tell a faculty member, "Eight of thirty students failed your introductory course last semester. From this observation, I'm concluding that your department is not successful, particularly since there's another department where no one failed the introductory course." In such a situation, the faculty member would certainly respond that my conclusion doesn't make any sense. It wasn't the department that failed or even the specific course that failed, I would be told, but rather those eight students. Perhaps they didn't study sufficiently or come to class. Perhaps they weren't strong enough academically to be admitted to the college in the first place. Perhaps this is just a fluke, since most students have done well in the course in the past. All of these points would be valid. The final exam in that course evaluated those particular students' progress in the course; it doesn't assess the effectiveness of the program at all, at least not in any useful way.

In a similar manner, your evaluations of individual faculty members indicate whether you believe that each individual has met the standard that you and the department have developed; they don't tell you anything useful about the success or effectiveness of your program as a whole. To learn this, we must rely on the procedure of assessment.

Mission, Goals, and Outcomes

Assessment is the process of determining whether academic programs (or other units of the institution) are meeting their stated objectives. For academic programs, those stated objectives are placed in the form of student learning outcomes. In order to determine appropriate student learning outcomes for the individual programs in your department, begin with your departmental mission statement. To the greatest extent possible, you want there to be as much logical flow as possible from your departmental mission statement to your goals, to your student learning outcomes, to your assessment measures, to the action plan you develop based on the results from those measures.

Let's start with your mission statement. While your departmental mission statement may be inspired in part by that of your institution as a whole and the larger units of which you are a part, your departmental mission statement should reflect more specifically how that larger institutional philosophy is being interpreted in light of your discipline's approaches, methodology, and resources—for example:

> As a service department within a public research university, the mission of the Department of X-ology is to contribute to the general education program of all students, provide support courses to other disciplines, and produce a small but consistent number of highly accomplished majors. Secondary missions of the Department of X-ology are to assist the university in fulfilling its research mission by producing original scholarship within the discipline, supporting interdisciplinary courses in conjunction with other campus programs, and offering outreach to local schools in X-ology and related disciplines.

Rather than a generic mission statement that provides no guidance for making decisions, this mission statement specifies what the department is seeking to do, for whom, and why. It would be phrased completely differently if the mission of the department included a large major program, a highly popular minor, or a graduate program. It would also have been phrased quite differently if the department were serving a liberal arts college, a professional school, or a teachers' college.

One of the great advantages of developing a well-crafted departmental mission statement is that it makes it quite easy then to enumerate the goals of the department. Department goals are broadly conceived general statements about what the program is trying to accomplish so as to carry out its mission in the future. A program goal answers the question, "What purpose are we trying to serve?" Unlike student learning outcomes, goals need not be directly accessible or measurable. In fact, they need not even be particularly attainable, at least in the sense of providing indisputable evidence that you have attained them. In other words, goals are the sorts of things that your program will continue seeking year after year. Perfection is a goal: although it's something no program will ever completely achieve, that does not mean that it's not something worth striving for.

One excellent illustration of how this principle might be applied in your department may be found in the very useful assessment planning guide developed at California Polytechnic State University (2006a). Departments are urged to begin designing their goals by considering the following generic example:

Example: The Department of _____ will produce graduates who:

    I. Understand and can apply fundamental concepts of the discipline.

    II. Communicate effectively, both orally and in writing.

    III. Conduct sound research.

    IV. Address issues critically and reflectively.

    V. Create solutions to problems.

    VI. Work well with others.

    VII. Respect persons from diverse cultures and backgrounds.

    VIII. Are committed to open-minded inquiry and lifelong learning.

Your first response is likely to be that these are worthwhile goals for any department. Your second response, however, may be more along the lines of, "But how could I demonstrate to anyone that my students in our program really do respect persons from diverse cultures and backgrounds? And how could I prove that our graduates are committed to open-minded inquiry and lifelong learning?" The answer is that it is not important for you to assess your goals either easily or effectively. These are aims that your program is striving for, not targets that you expect to hit every time.

The ability to prove the attainment of an objective becomes much more important at the next level, when you make concrete the general goals of your program by phrasing them as student learning outcomes. A student learning outcome is a concise statement of precisely what a student is expected to know, understand, or be able to do as a result of the goals that your program has adopted. In other words, each learning outcome answers the question, "What will a student be able to accomplish after a particular unit, course, or program has been completed?" Because it deals not with general aims for the future but with specific tasks to be accomplished, each outcome must be assessable: the program must be able to demonstrate whether all students (or a specified percentage of them) are able to perform the task in question.

As you move from your department's mission statement to its overarching goals, to developing assessable student learning outcomes, it is probably useful for you to proceed by discussing the following questions with your colleagues in the discipline:

1. What specifically do we want our students to know by the time they complete our program?

2. What specifically do we want students to be able to do with this knowledge by the time they complete our program?

3. What information, content, or skills do we want our students to retain long after they have completed our program?

4. What should our students be able to do with that information, content, or set of skills?

5. What competencies do we want students in our program to learn or develop?

6. What observable behaviors will indicate to us that those competencies have been developed?

7. Where—in which specific courses or through what specific experiences—do we expect students in our program to develop these competencies?

8. Is there a certain acceptable level or threshold of achievement beneath which we will not permit a student to graduate from our program? If so, what is that threshold, and how do we determine whether it has been crossed?

9. Is there a certain percentage of students who, if they develop certain skills or competencies to a specified level, we would feel that our program is successful? (Remember that the goal may be perfection, but how close to perfect mastery do you realistically expect to achieve?) What might we decide to do if our program failed to produce that desired percentage?

10. In what kinds of higher-level thinking do we want our students to engage?

11. Besides completing exams at the end of discrete courses, how do we expect students to demonstrate what they have learned in our program and how well they have learned it?

12. If an employer or the dean of a graduate school were to ask the students in our program what have they learned, how would we like them to answer this question?

By the time you and your colleagues answer these twelve questions, you should have a fairly clear image of what specific objectives your program is trying to attain and how someone would recognize whether students attain those objectives.

Your next step is to phrase your department's specific objectives in terms of measurable learning outcomes by using concrete and observable action verbs, such as *express, critique,* and *examine.* An excellent list of suggested action words to get you started in phrasing your learning outcomes may be found in *Verbs for Learning Outcomes* (Abilene Christian University, 2010). For instance, you might consider a structure for your student learning outcomes based on the following template:

> By [specific point in the program], [all or an acceptable percentage of] students majoring in [program] will be able to [general action phrase] by [performing specific observable activity].

Admittedly, this template may look quite awkward initially. But once you begin to use it in developing outcomes for your program, you'll see how flexible and useful this structure is. Consider the following examples based on this template:

> On completion of ITAL 350, 355, and 365, all Italian majors will be able to demonstrate mastery of intermediate language skills by having read an approved work in Italian of no fewer than one hundred pages, discussing that work in Italian for no less than half an hour with no more than five grammatical errors, and writing a critical response to the work in Italian (entirely free of grammatical or spelling errors) of no fewer than ten pages in length.

> On completion of any 100-level mathematics course, at least 90 percent of nonmajors will have demonstrated basic quantitative competency by being able to:
>
> a. Interpret core mathematical models such as formulas, graphs, tables, and schematics
> b. Draw proper inferences from these core mathematical models

   c. Represent sufficiently complex mathematical information symbolically, visually, numerically, and verbally

   d. Use arithmetical, algebraic, geometric, and statistical methods to solve problems

   e. Estimate and check answers to mathematical problems in order to determine their reasonableness, identify alternatives, and select optimal results

By the time they are ready to begin the senior seminar, all history majors will be prepared to conduct independent and original research by having demonstrated that they can formulate appropriate and significant historical questions, use appropriate primary and secondary sources to determine information relevant to answering historical questions, organize historical information so as to formulate and defend a thesis, and present that thesis and its defense in an effective written form.

Students who complete the minor in music performance will be able to communicate musical ideas effectively by demonstrating that they are able to perform on at least one instrument with a substantial level of understanding; provide a satisfactory oral summary about the nature of a performance career; demonstrate satisfactory acquaintance with a variety of music, styles, and cultural sources; understand basic compositional processes and styles; and both develop and defend musical judgments convincingly.

As these examples make clear, the general action phrase allows you to tie each outcome to a particular statement in your department's goals; "specific observable activity" allows you to indicate how that more general goal will be made operational in a student's academic development. The most important thing is that these learning outcomes, unlike goals, are always stated in ways that are measurable, at least measurable in the sense that one can readily determine whether students are achieving the outcomes that you have specified. Once your discipline has agreed on appropriate outcomes that are congruent with your mission and goals, you are ready to plan your strategy for assessment.

Assessing Student Learning Outcomes

The means that you will use to assess whether students are achieving the outcomes you have set for your program will vary according to your discipline, its pedagogical methods, and the specific outcomes that you have set. For instance, in the case of the outcomes for the programs in Italian and history presented in the previous section, final projects or examinations might be constructed to include the activities required by the outcome.

You might now ask, "Earlier you said that examinations were techniques used to evaluate individual students. Why are they now suitable forms of assessment?" The difference comes in how an examination is constructed and in the use that is made with data resulting from the exam. For example, in the case of the Italian outcome, the curriculum might be organized so that each student takes ITAL 365 last in the 300-level sequence. Then the activities specified by the outcome can be included as part of the final project for this course. This does not mean that the instructor of ITAL 365 cannot also include other questions on the final exam or additional requirements for the final project. All of those elements—those required for assessment and those required by the specific material of that course—would then be used to evaluate the progress of each student. It is only the aggregate data—were all the majors in the course able to perform all the activities specified in the outcome?—that are used to assess the program. What the outcome says, in other words, is, "We will consider our program to be fulfilling its objectives if all of our majors can do this by that point in the program. If they can't, then we have to determine how we can improve the program so that they can." In this way, individual course grades still evaluate the performance of each student; parts of the exam and final project are used to assess the program itself.

In other situations, different types of assessment measures—portfolios, surveys, exit interviews, employer questionnaires, and the like—may be more suitable for collecting the data you need. For instance, in the case of the history outcome cited above, students might be required to accumulate a portfolio throughout their course work indicating that they have fulfilled all of the criteria before being permitted to enroll for the senior seminar. In the case of the outcome for the music minor, a jury hearing might be structured in such a way that the elements of the outcome are required components. In each case, however, the important questions for your discipline to come to some agreement on are these:

○ What are the specific thresholds or trigger points that would indicate whether the outcomes we have established are being achieved?

○ What would our discipline's course of action be if the data suggested that one or more of our learning outcomes are not being achieved?

○ How might we then document any improvement resulting from this course of action?

These questions will help your department use the insights gained from your assessment to improve your program continually.

It could be that, based on what your assessment reveals to you, you modify course content, alter the pedagogical methods used to cover certain material, alter course prerequisites or the order in which certain types of material are covered, introduce a peer mentor program for majors, spend longer teaching skills that are regarded as higher priorities, provide supplementary materials to students on your Web site, or introduce additional checks for competencies in lower-level courses. In certain circumstances, you may conclude that your outcomes need to be revised because you had established objectives for your program that are impossible for your department to achieve. However the members of your discipline decide to improve your program, you will be doing so now on the basis of clear and demonstrable data rather than gut impressions or hunches.

Remember that unlike evaluation, there is no way to "fail" an assessment. If your assessment demonstrates that your program is fulfilling completely all of its objectives, you win: you now have data to demonstrate that you are accomplishing the very things that you set out to do. And if your assessment demonstrates that your program is not accomplishing all of its anticipated outcomes, you still win: you now have the information you need concerning how improvements can be made, and you may even have the proof you need to support a budget increase in an area of critical concern.

Assessment has now been in place for so long at so many institutions that there are a wide variety of resources available to draw on. For instance, excellent examples of program goals include those developed at Central Washington University, Wartburg College, and George Mason University. To see examples in a specific discipline, go to the institution's Web site and enter "program goals" or "learning goals" into the school's search engine. For a more precise search, add the name of the academic discipline that you'd like to explore, as well as any other key words (such as *undergraduate, graduate, general education,* or *upper division*) that can better focus the results. A number of Web sites provide information on how to develop appropriate student learning outcomes. Among the resources you may wish to consider are these:

- ○ The University of Western Australia's guidelines for statements of learning outcomes, developed by that school's Centre for the Advancement of Teaching and Learning: *A Basic Guide to Writing Student Learning Outcome Statements* (2005)

- ○ San Jose State University's *Guide to Outcomes Assessment of Student Learning* (2007)

- ○ Kansas State University's Web site on how to write learning outcomes, developed by that school's Office of Assessment: *How to Write Student Learning Outcomes* (2008)

- ○ The *Learning Outcomes Assessment Planning Guide* developed by California Polytechnic University (2006b)

- ○ A survey of what learning outcomes are, how to write them, action verbs to include, and a bibliography of some basic resources provided by the National Center for Geographic Information and Analysis in its *Writing Learning Outcomes for the Core Curriculum* (1996)

---------------- ○ ----------------

Assessment is such an important topic in higher education that there are more books devoted to this issue than any department chair has time to read. Among the works you may wish to consider are Walvoord (2004), Banta (2004), Angelo and Cross (1993), Allen (2004), Suskie (2004), and Huba and Freed (2000). Few other areas of further study repay the department chair's time as much as assessment does. You will use this information for continuous improvement of instruction, program development and review, progress reports on strategic initiatives, accreditation reviews, and many other administrative tasks. For this reason, every department chair should maintain a good library of assessment materials and should seek frequent opportunities to expand his or her understanding of this important topic.

REFERENCES

Abilene Christian University Adams Center. (2010). *Verbs for learning outcomes.* Retrieved from http://www.acu.edu/academics/adamscenter/course_design/syllabus/verbs.html

Allen, M. J. (2004). *Assessing academic programs in higher education.* San Francisco: Jossey-Bass/Anker.

Angelo, T. A., & Cross, K. P. (1993). *Classroom assessment techniques: A handbook for college teachers* (2nd ed.). San Francisco: Jossey-Bass.

Banta, T. W. (Ed.). (2004). *Hallmarks of effective outcomes assessment.* San Francisco: Jossey-Bass.

California Polytechnic State University, San Luis Obispo. (2006a). *Assessment planning guide.* Retrieved from http://www.academicprograms.calpoly. edu/assessment/assessplanguide.htm

California Polytechnic State University. (2006b). *Learning outcomes assessment planning guide.* Retrieved from http://www.academicprograms.calpoly. edu/assessment/assessplanguide.htm

Huba, M. E., & Freed, J. E. (2000). *Learner-centered assessment on college campuses: Shifting the focus from teaching to learning.* Needham Heights, MA: Allyn and Bacon.

Kansas State University. (2008). *How to write student learning outcomes.* Retrieved from http://www.k-state.edu/assessment/slo/instructions.htm

National Center for Geographic Information and Analysis. (1996). *Writing learning outcomes for the core curriculum.* Retrieved from http://www .ncgia.ucsb.edu/education/curricula/giscc/units/format/outcomes.html

San Jose State University. (2007). *Guide to outcomes assessment of student learning.* Retrieved from http://www.sjsu.edu/ugs/docs/assess_tools/Guide_to_ Assessment_-_SJSU_-_2007–10–25.pdf

Suskie, L. A. (2004). *Assessing student learning: A common sense guide.* San Francisco: Jossey-Bass/Anker.

University of Western Australia. (2005). *A basic guide to writing student learning outcome statements.* Retrieved from www.catl.uwa.edu.au/current_initiatives/ obe/outcomes

Walvoord, B.E.F. (2004). *Assessment clear and simple: A practical guide for institutions, departments, and general education.* San Francisco: Jossey-Bass.

RESOURCES

Banta, T. W. (2002). *Building a scholarship of assessment.* San Francisco: Jossey-Bass.

Diamond, R. M. (2008). *Designing and assessing courses and curricula: A practical guide* (3rd ed.). San Francisco: Jossey-Bass.

Dugan, R. E., & Hernon, P. (2004). *Outcomes assessment in higher education: Views and perspectives.* Westport, CT: Libraries Unlimited.

McKeachie, W. J., & Svinicki, M. (2006). *McKeachie's teaching tips: Strategies, research and theory for college and university teachers* (12th ed., pp. 74–86). Boston: Houghton Mifflin.

Mezeske, R. J., & Mezeske, B. A. (Eds.). (2008). *Beyond tests and quizzes: Creative assessments in the college classroom.* San Francisco: Jossey-Bass.

Wehlburg, C. M. (2008). *Promoting integrated and transformative assessment: A deeper focus on student learning.* San Francisco: Jossey-Bass.

42

CONDUCTING PROGRAM REVIEWS

THE TERMS *EVALUATION, ASSESSMENT,* AND *PROGRAM REVIEW* refer to three fundamentally different, though at times overlapping, methods of collecting and analyzing information. As we saw in the previous chapter, *evaluation* is a summative and results-oriented activity that measures the effectiveness of individual people, courses, or programs; it helps the evaluator decide whether the person or thing being evaluated is making the grade and bases a judgment on that decision. *Assessment* is a formative and process-oriented activity that determines whether entire programs are achieving an established set of goals and outcomes; when these objectives are not being met, assessment helps clarify how the program (not the performance of individual students, faculty members, or administrators) should be modified.

Program review is a far broader process that raises questions not addressed by either evaluation or assessment. For instance, these other two processes examine only the quality of the person or program being considered: Did this individual perform up to expected standards, or did that entire program achieve its stated outcomes? What they don't reveal is whether the program itself is viable in terms of student enrollments, the size of its budget, or likely demands for graduates in the future. Nor do they indicate how important the program is to the institution's overall mission and strategic plan. To provide this more comprehensive look at an institution's programs, the techniques of program review come into play.

A solid program review process includes data obtained from both evaluation and assessment, but it also requires additional sources of information. For instance, in determining the quality of instruction, some institutions require departments to provide aggregate scores on student course evaluations in order to compare these overall averages to median scores in other related disciplines and to those of all disciplines at the institution. They may also require submission of external reviews developed by accrediting agencies or peer programs. Almost certainly, institutions will require that departments either provide or respond to data about enrollment trends, numbers of majors, graduation rates in the discipline, the size of externally funded grants received, placement of students in graduate school or professions closely related to the major, and trends in faculty scholarship, research, and creative activity.

Let's explore in greater detail how program review functions by looking separately at the internal and external aspects of this process.

Internal Program Review

A well-designed program review process examines far more than just academic programs. Nevertheless, most department chairs play a limited role at best in the review of such offices as physical plant, the business office, and residence life. Also, while most program reviews address an institution's general education requirements, department chairs have far greater responsibilities in the processes that examine their own disciplines. This discussion of internal program review therefore focuses largely on the way in which your majors or degree programs are likely to fit into this process. In the discussion, I'll use the term *program* as equivalent to "departmental program" or, in other words, the curriculum offered by an individual academic department that in most cases leads to an academic degree.

What Information to Gather

If your institution already has a clearly established program review process in place, it should be fairly easy to determine what type of data you need to collect and in what form your institution wants that information reported. If your discipline has not yet had to submit a program review, ask to see examples of successful documentation submitted by departments as similar to yours as possible. Then use these other reports as a model for your own collection of data. If your institution is relatively new to program review or if your reports are allowed to be more free form, the task that you face will be more challenging, since you need to determine both what you should report and how you should present this information in such a way that it makes your department's strongest case. One good place to begin is to ask yourself such questions as these:

- ○ What are my department's strongest assets—the features that make it both distinctive from other departments at my own institution and from departments similar to mine at other institutions?

- ○ What weaknesses might others see in our program, and how can I account for these areas of vulnerability in such a way that even someone not familiar with our field will see the larger picture?

- ○ If I were examining a program that I didn't know very well, what information would demonstrate to me that students were learning what they needed to know, that faculty members were producing scholarship or creative activity of the appropriate quality, that the program was sustainable for the future, and that the program as a whole was an essential part of what we do as an institution?

The answers that you provide to these questions will tell you a great deal about what type of information you may wish to collect and how you might wish to present it.

If your institution permits some flexibility in the program review process, you may wish to assemble data in any or all of the following categories.

QUANTITATIVE INDICATORS These indicators consist of data that are countable, or at least measurable, in some consistent, reproducible manner. They may be raw numbers, percentiles, rankings, averages, or other similar types of information. The most useful types of quantitative indicators at most institutions tend to be ratios, since they place a raw figure into at least a partial context. For instance, you might provide a raw figure such as, "Over the last five years, an average of eight graduates each year were admitted to their first-choice postbaccalaureate program." But while this may be interesting information, ultimately it is meaningless for review purposes. Is eight a high figure or a low one? The number alone gives the reader no way of making this judgment.

Presented as a ratio, the figure begins to take on meaning and to be incorporated into a larger context: "Over the past five years, an average of eight out of eleven (72.7 percent) graduates each year were admitted to their first-choice postbaccalaureate program, while our overall institutional placement rate is only 53.1 percent and the rate within our closest peer disciplines is 65.5 percent." In a similar way, presenting raw numbers of student credit hours generated per term or per academic year may be requested at some institutions, but this information becomes useful only when it is calculated in terms of some other relevant factor, such as the number of full-time-equivalent (FTE) faculty members who produced those credit hours.

QUALITATIVE INDICATORS These indicators include sources of information that are not specifically measurable but are nonetheless helpful in providing a more comprehensive picture of a program. Because they tend not to result in specific scores, qualitative indicators almost always require more interpretation than do quantitative indicators. Nevertheless, they can demonstrate aspects of a department's success, viability, or unique mission in a manner that proves to be far more compelling than sheer numbers.

Perhaps the most commonly used type of qualitative indicator for program review purposes is the portfolio. Representative portfolios of student work provide a valuable impression of the level of work students achieved and their rate of growth during the program. In much the same way, faculty portfolios of teaching, scholarship, service, and administrative contributions can provide a much more balanced view of the faculty than can mere scores on student evaluations or the number of refereed articles published. For information on best practices in using qualitative indicators, see Seldin (2004), Seldin and Miller (2009), and Murray (1997).

INDICATORS OF QUALITY As their name implies, indicators of quality are factors that suggest to an observer how good a program is or the level of success that the program has had in achieving its goals. These indicators may be quantitative or qualitative and may draw on data dealing with students (five-year graduation rates, placement rates for graduates, alumni portfolios of scholarship in the discipline, and so on), faculty (percentage holding a terminal degree, number of refereed publications per FTE faculty member each year, teaching and administrative portfolios, and the like), support staff, access to information resources, and other elements that contribute to the overall quality of an academic program.

INDICATORS OF VIABILITY Indicators of viability are factors that indicate whether a program is likely to be sustainable. Quantitative indicators of viability include, for example, enrollment trends, estimates of probable demand for graduates in the discipline over the next five to ten years, additional sources of program revenue such as grants and sponsored programs, and ratios of tuition generated by the program to expenditures made in such areas as salaries, benefits, and operating expenses. Qualitative indicators of viability might include a discussion of factors that are likely to affect demand for graduates within the foreseeable future, a listing of honors or achievements that alumni have attained, a statement of the advantages accruing to your program from your institution's location or the uniqueness of your curriculum, and so on.

One quantitative indicator of viability that disciplines occasionally overlook is the correlation between enrollment in one or more of the department's courses and retention at the institution. Frequently courses that have a clear mentoring or experiential component—for instance, studio art, lab science, or applied music courses—produce students who are more likely to persist at the institution because they develop a closer bond with a faculty member. By demonstrating a differential between the retention rates of students who have enrolled in your department's courses and the retention rate of the institution as a whole, you can provide a perspective on viability that your college or university may find particularly compelling.

INDICATORS OF CENTRALITY TO MISSION These indicators are the types of information that suggest the degree to which your department is essential to your school's fundamental purpose, strategic plan, and vision for the future. For instance, at a research university, the ratio of books and articles, grants received, patents obtained, or academic recognitions won per FTE faculty member helps to suggest the vital role your department is playing in advancing your institution's mission. At a liberal arts college, the connection you can make between your discipline and the traditional liberal arts goals of developing critical thinking, improved communication, and aesthetic appreciation is likely to assume greater significance. Church-related schools, professional schools, community colleges, comprehensive institutions, and schools adhering to the model of the "New American College" are each likely to have distinctive missions and goals for the future to which you will need to relate your mission as a discipline. (For a discussion of the New American College model, see http://www.anac.org/aboutus.html.) In each case, however, it is likely to be outcomes—what students and, under certain conditions, faculty members produce—that will be important, not faculty credentials, SAT or ACT scores of incoming students, or the number of volumes relating to your discipline in your institution's library that will be most compelling as sources of evidence.

How to Make Your Case

Every institution's program review process is based on its own individual set of core values and assumptions. As a department chair, you need to determine what those underlying values and assumptions have been in order to know how you can make the strongest case for your discipline. For instance, does the program review process at your institution primarily focus on the number of majors in each program or on your discipline's overall production of student credit hours? If you find that most of your school's questions tend to deal with the number of majors in your department, then it is clear that what your institution values most is recruiting students to your program, graduating them on time, and placing them in graduate school or employment closely related to your field. Departments that do not generate a large number of majors will then need to put this information in its proper context: Can you demonstrate that although your major itself may be small, you provide a vital role in supplying service courses to other majors and offer a number of important courses in the general education program? If most of your institution's questions tend to deal with student credit hour production, then the overall focus appears to be on general productivity and efficiency rather than the size of the major. Programs such as business administration, which may be required by their accrediting agencies to have majors take a substantial amount of course work outside the department, may need to clarify this situation for reviewers who may not understand the context in which your discipline is compelled to operate.

Similarly, are you ever asked in your institution's system to differentiate your student credit hour production into upper-level as opposed to lower-level courses or according to courses that satisfy the institution's general education requirements as opposed to courses that are usually taken to satisfy major requirements? If not, and this distinction is integral to your department's mission, try to find a way in which you can make this distinction, clarifying the data for the individual or the committee that will be reading your review. Also, at many institutions, the revenue produced by a department is calculated by a formula similar to this one:

$$\text{Department revenue} = \text{Discounted tuition generated} - (\text{salaries} + \text{benefits} + \text{operating expenses})$$

If your discipline is also contributing to your institution's overhead through significant grant activity or sponsored programs, and this is not reflected in your college or university's revenue formula, be sure to cite this added resource as an important factor in your department's ongoing viability.

Above all, be sure to consider assets of your program that are not easily quantifiable or do not lend themselves to the reporting format that your institution requires:

- Are your faculty members or the students who take courses from your department demonstrably more diverse than elsewhere in the institution? If so, then this may be an asset in enhancing your college or university's diversity plan that may not be visible from the data required by your institution's program review process.

- Consider whether a larger percentage of your faculty members or students have had a significant international experience compared to their peers across the institution.

- Do your faculty members or students help improve your institution's diversity in terms of gender or socioeconomic background? Either of these factors can add value to your discipline in a way that may not otherwise be clear from the review format that your institution requires.

- It may also be that your discipline is attracting an exceptionally large number of first-generation college students to your institution, a factor that you can present as contributing to the school's mission to reach out to traditionally underrepresented groups.

- If your faculty's scholarly output appears low in terms of the number of refereed publications or the total number of pages appearing in books and journals, can you document that these works have been commonly cited by other scholars in your field or that your department's scholarship tended to appear in highly selective journals? If so, you will need to introduce this information in a discussion of quality versus quantity even if your review format does not specifically request this information.

Finally, remember that a score or ratio alone, without the benefit of interpretation, rarely tells the entire story. For instance, the incoming SAT or ACT scores of your majors may be significantly higher or lower than those of students in other disciplines. Either one of these results may be an asset to your institution depending on the interpretation that is made of it. High standardized test scores may indicate that your department's recognized level of academic excellence is attracting exceptionally strong students. Low standardized test scores may nevertheless result in high rates of student success after graduation, demonstrating the life-transforming nature of your program.

By making your case in this manner, you will be much more likely to create a review of your program that casts your achievements in the best possible light, places vulnerable areas within a more comprehensive context, and guides your department as it continues to make progress.

External Program Review

As part of the program review process at many institutions, departments may be encouraged—or even required—to obtain an external evaluation. In many cases, this external review may be conducted by an accrediting agency specific to that individual discipline. At other times, it may follow a process set forth by the institution itself. Or it may be left up to the individual department to propose the most appropriate form for this review to assume. In the last of these cases, the department will find itself having great flexibility, but the chair may also be left wondering how best to conduct this external program review, what should be included in the review, and how the information should be collected and analyzed. At times, chairs may not be sure which questions they should ask or even where they should begin. To assist in these cases, it is frequently helpful to have a general framework for what the chair's role is likely to be in the most common type of external program review, what information will be most beneficial for the chair to obtain, and how to make the strongest possible case for the department undergoing external review.

If you are scheduled to participate in an external review of your department, you may be asked to select (or at least to recommend) your own partner institution for an external paired assessment. In these cases, recommend an institution that has a program reasonably comparable to your own, is not located so far away as to make visiting the other campus needlessly expensive or time-consuming, and stands to benefit as much from the external review project as will your own institution. When looking for a comparable institution with which to share program reviews, try to consider not only such matters as the size of your specific programs and the overall similarity of the two institutions' mission, but also such factors as entering student SAT and GPA scores, size of endowment, and the condition of the physical plant the departments use. Failure to consider variables of this sort can result in a forced comparison of two departments that are in reality so different that meaningful results will end up being all but impossible to obtain.

Even while you are still seeking a comparable program with which to conduct this review, you should begin thinking about what instruction you will give faculty members who themselves may never have participated in such a review before. What types of observations are they likely to find most useful? What sort of information should each team examine in order to develop a realistic assessment of and worthwhile advice for the other program?

Areas for Review

When institutions themselves do not provide any standard set of guidelines or templates for external program reviews, their department chairs might begin by instructing faculty members on each review team to examine nine areas.

LEARNING GOALS Try to determine the adequacy of the learning goals adopted by the department that you are reviewing. Have goals been written at the appropriate level for each of the following types of students: majors (where the department offers its own major), minors (again where this is an appropriate question), and nonmajors and nonminors? Where specifically in the curriculum is each of these learning goals addressed? How does the department assess its effectiveness in attaining these goals? What has this assessment process suggested about the program's effectiveness to date? What improvements has the department made on the basis of the results of its assessment plan?

CURRICULUM Using these learning goals as your guide, assess the adequacy of the program's curriculum as a whole. Consider its overall structure. Does it flow in a logical sequence? After examining catalogue offerings and syllabi, members of each review team should consider whether, in their professional judgment, there are noticeable holes in curricula, course offerings, or course content. Conversely, are there areas of exceptional strength, distinction, or innovation? What recommendations can you give your peers in terms of improving their course offerings, content, and rotation?

STUDENT ACHIEVEMENT Looking beyond the program's formal program of assessment, try to gauge a sense of how effective the department has been in helping students develop their knowledge and skills in the discipline. One of the best ways to do this is by examining a representative sample of student projects. For instance, Barbara Wright, Peter Ewell, and Jerry Gaff write:

> There should be periodic evaluation by external reviewers of the goals, the proficiency standards, and work samples submitted by students to meet standards. Such external reviews provide validation of both the goals and standards. A representative sample of student performances in different fields will provide sufficient evidence for external feedback. (Association of American Colleges and Universities, 2004, p. 12)

In performance-based disciplines such as art, music, and theater, ask to attend an actual jury, performance, or exhibition. In more research-oriented disciplines, try to review a selection of senior projects or at least of significant course work done for upper-level courses. In your professional judgment, is the discipline taking students to the level they need to be? If not, what suggested improvements can you recommend? Ask to see examples of what the department considers to be its best student products. Then ask to see the same number of examples of minimally acceptable (and even unacceptable) student projects. The difference between these two sets of course work should indicate the expected standards of the department and provide you with a touchstone by which to compare student achievement at your own institution.

FACULTY Consider the number, credentials, and achievements of the faculty members in both departments. Adjusting for FTE, calculate how many full-time and how many part-time faculty members are serving how many students. To get a more accurate sense of comparison, you may need to calculate this figure several ways. For instance, first compare FTE faculty to the total number of students enrolled in any of the department's courses, then to the number of majors (where applicable), then to the number of students in introductory courses, and finally to the total number of student credit hours generated by the department (or in some disciplines, such as the natural sciences, to student contact hours).

If the total number of student credit hours changes significantly from year to year, you may find it useful to develop a three- or five-year rolling average. How do the two institutions compare in terms of teaching load, average number of students in a discipline's courses, the maximum number of students allowed to enroll in a course, the number of advisees per faculty member, and the average number of students served by each faculty member? Where there are striking differences, see if you can determine why those differences exist:

- ○ How do the two institutions compare in terms of expectations for scholarship and service by faculty members?
- ○ In which professional organizations are the faculty members of the two institutions active? Are these at all comparable?
- ○ Over the past five years, how many publications have the faculty members of each program produced on a per capita basis and how many conference presentations?

In cases where there are reviews or referee reports related to these publications, try to gauge how successfully the scholarship of the two faculties was received by the academic community. Did the publications of each program tend to occur at the highly competitive publishers and most selective journals in the field or in less distinguished venues? At institutions where there are aggregate data on student ratings of instruction, how did the department fare relative to the rest of the institution? How did it fare relative to other disciplines that are similar to it (say, in the same college or division or that logically seem comparable to one another)? Aside from retirements, what has been the rate of faculty turnover during the past ten years? If it appears to be high, ask for possible reasons that this turnover may have occurred.

STAFF Evaluate the adequacy of support staff in fulfilling the department's mission. Again adjusting for FTE, calculate how many full-time and how many part-time staff members are being called on to serve how many students. Think of support staff in the broadest possible sense: in addition to departmental secretaries and administrative assistants assigned to each area, be sure to include laboratory assistants, audiovisual technicians, staff accompanists, costumers, curators, editorial assistants, and others. What is the breakdown of administrative staff—chair, cochair, and assistant chair—per FTE student and student credit hour generated? Compare the ratio of administrative to teaching assignment of all members of the administrative staff, and then relate this figure to the number of FTE students and student credit hours generated by each department.

DEPARTMENTAL MISSION AND VISION Examine any internal documents generated by the institution's own planning and review processes:

o What do these items reveal to you about points of similarity and contrast between the department that you are reviewing and your own?

o How has the department that you are reviewing attempted to develop a distinctive mission and identity?

o In your professional judgment, are the mission and identity appropriate for the number and level of students that the institution is enrolling, the expectations for teaching and scholarship of its faculty, and the resources that the department has available?

o Are there constructive suggestions you might make as to how that department's individual mission or vision for the future might be clarified?

o Are there ways in which each department may want to revise its mission or goals after learning from the other?

PROGRAM SUPPORT Examine the operating budget of the program, prorated by FTE faculty member and then prorated by the total number of student credit hours generated. Compare travel funding and other sorts of faculty development support at the two institutions. What resources are available for faculty members who wish to present a paper at a national conference, hold an office in a professional organization, or complete additional course work to advance their knowledge? Take a look at the professional organizations in which faculty members serve and where they actively participate. In your professional judgment, are the faculty members active in the appropriate organizations and at the most suitable conferences for their individual mission?

FACILITIES Do the classrooms, office space, laboratories, practice rooms, gallery space, rehearsal rooms, and so on appear to be meeting the needs of each department in terms of its size, mission, and focus? Do instructional spaces have a level of technology that allows them to achieve their pedagogical mission, or are they hampered by facilities that are obsolete or in a poor state of repair? If you can obtain the information, try to gain a sense of the cost of deferred maintenance for the facilities most used by the department and determine how this figure compares with the amount of deferred maintenance of the institution as a whole.

OVERALL As you review all of these areas, where are the noticeable strengths? Where are any weaknesses? If you were a prospective student or faculty member being recruited by the program, what would most attract you to it? What would concern you? What are the three to five greatest successes of the department that it should be featuring in all of its contacts with prospective students, donors, and administrators? What are the three to five things that ought to be improved if resources were available?

As you review the information you have received, remember that the most important factors to consider are always the results: What has the department done with the human, physical, and monetary resources that it has? Those resources will be interesting in offering points of comparison for discovering where the two programs are similar and where they are different, but they cannot tell the whole—or most useful—story alone.

Results of the Review

By examining the information in these nine categories, you will begin to learn several important things about the department that you are reviewing and its areas of success and weakness relative to your own program.

First, you should gain a clear sense of how the department you are reviewing is similar to your own and how it operates in ways that are not comparable to the practices of your department. Understanding these similarities and differences is an important part of the external review process for one important reason:

> The fact that two programs are different in some way does not mean that one of the two departments is flawed, inadequately funded, or poorly designed.

You may discover, for instance, that the department you are reviewing has a much larger budget in some area—or even in many areas—than your own. You cannot immediately assume that your department is underfunded. It is possible, of course, that the other department is overfunded; but it is even more likely that you will learn this difference in funding exists because of an underlying difference in mission, size, or focus between the two programs. Therefore, use the distinctions between your department and the program you are reviewing to begin asking why those distinctions exist. Don't immediately assume that they indicate a problem.

Second, you should develop a good sense of what the expectations for or standards of the department have been. You know the prestigious journals in your field. You know the conferences where it is difficult to get an abstract accepted and those where virtually everyone who applies to be on the program is successful. You know the level at which students should be performing by the time that they complete upper-level course work in your discipline. Are faculty members and students at the institution you are reviewing performing at those high levels? If not, should they be doing so in light of the department's size and stated mission?

Finally, you should be receiving a clear sense of whether the department is meeting its own stated goals. Do the learning goals expressed by the department have any real meaning—for instance, are they reflected in the design of the curriculum—or have they been suggested as a mere exercise? Is any systematic assessment being conducted of these goals? Can the department point to anything that it is doing differently now than it was five or ten years ago because it has gathered data about its effectiveness, given serious consideration to those data, and made a deliberate attempt to improve in areas where it has not been as successful as it would like? Is the department intentional about the learning that occurs under its supervision, or does it appear not to have much insight into how it is achieving success?

Common Mistakes Made in External Reviews

Faculty members who do not have much experience with external program reviews must take care not to make two common mistakes if the review is to be valuable.

One of them is referred to as "log-rolling," which develops when the express or tacit operating principle of each review team is, "You tell us we're wonderful, and we'll tell you you're wonderful." At the other extreme, log-rolling can occur when the operating principle is, "You tell us that we desperately need what we say we want, and we'll do the same for you." This type of providing mutual favors between the review teams is unethical and degrades the reviewing process. Moreover, as a strategy, it never works. There is no ploy easier for an upper administrator to see through than this type of mutual back-scratching. After all, if an external review does not contain candid and substantive reporting of both programmatic strengths and weaknesses, it will end up being dismissed out of hand, and the department that did not push for more objective analysis could easily suffer as a result.

The second mistake is excessive fault finding. External reviews that are nothing more than long lists of extra faculty positions wanted, facility improvements needed, reductions in workload required, and budget increases sought are unlikely to be given serious attention by anyone outside the department. Whenever needs or recommended changes are included in a report, they should always be carefully prioritized, not simply dumped as a laundry list of requests. Ask instead:

○ What needs to be done immediately, and what is likely to happen if this action is not taken?

○ How does that priority rank compare to the other competing needs of the department: scholarship support, salary increases for faculty and staff, technology improvements, renovations in facilities, and the like?

○ If a recommendation is regarded as extremely urgent, what expenditures ought the department to defer or what reductions in its budget are permissible in order to make this recommendation possible?

○

By helping your faculty members understand the guidelines discussed in this chapter, you will be taking an important step toward developing a valuable internal review of your program and of receiving a more useful external review from those who visit your campus. By reviewing the suggestions in this chapter with your faculty members and (where possible) the team that will conduct your review, you are more likely to receive a final report that contains accurate, reliable observations with clear guidance about how you can improve your program.

REFERENCES

Association of American Colleges and Universities. (2004). *Our students' best work: A framework for accountability worthy of our mission.* Washington, DC: Author.

Murray, J. P. (1997). *Successful faculty development and evaluation: The complete teaching portfolio.* San Francisco: Jossey-Bass.

Seldin, P. (2004). *The teaching portfolio: A practical guide to improved performance and promotion/tenure decisions* (3rd ed.). San Francisco: Jossey-Bass/Anker.

Seldin, P., & Miller, J. E. (2009). *The academic portfolio: A practical guide to documenting teaching, research, and service.* San Francisco: Jossey-Bass.

RESOURCES

Barak, R. J., & Mets, L. A. (1995). *Using academic program review.* San Francisco: Jossey-Bass.

Bogue, E. G., & Hall, K. B. (2003). *Quality and accountability in higher education: Improving policy, enhancing performance.* Westport, CT: Praeger.

Bresciani, M. J. (2006). *Outcomes-based academic and co-curricular program review: A compilation of institutional good practices.* Sterling, VA: Stylus.

Martin, M., & Stella, A. (2007). *External quality assurance in higher education: Making choices.* Paris: UNESCO.

43

CONDUCTING POSTTENURE REVIEWS

INSTITUTIONS DIFFER WIDELY IN their approach to posttenure review. At some institutions, people say that there is no posttenure review process at all. (Even at these institutions, however, tenured faculty members almost always receive at least some sort of review, even if it is only an annual performance appraisal or consideration for a merit increase.) At the other end of the spectrum, some institutions have elaborate, multilayered systems in place for posttenure review with special committees that conduct these evaluations and reports made to various members of the senior administration. Depending on where along this spectrum your institution falls, your precise contribution as chair to a faculty member's posttenure review may well be specified by an official policy manual or set of operating procedures. Nevertheless, no matter what your institutional procedure may be, issues will inevitably arise as to how you might mentor the faculty members who are undergoing this process, how you can make this procedure as constructive as possible for your program, and how you can provide more useful advice to senior faculty members than blanket, uncritical praise or bland and unhelpful statements that "some improvement is needed."

Preliminary Review of Materials

Unless your system requires you to be the sole individual responsible for deciding the outcome of a faculty member's posttenure review, you might begin the process by meeting with each faculty member who is scheduled to undergo the process and discuss, well before the deadline for submitting official materials, where the person stands relative to your own evaluation of his or her performance and what some of the likely conclusions of the process could be. Help the faculty member assemble the following materials, even if not all of these are required for your institution's official posttenure review process:

- A draft of the application or cover letter that the faculty member intends to submit
- An updated curriculum vitae
- All official evaluations of the faculty member's performance that you or any other authorized groups and individuals on campus have written about the faculty member for the past five years
- Summaries of student ratings of instruction for all courses
- Representative student comments taken from evaluation instruments used in all courses
- Results of any peer evaluations that may have been conducted in your department or at your institution
- Sample course materials (syllabi, exams, and other items used in courses, including links to electronic materials)
- Representative publications
- Photographs, recordings, or summaries of creative works, if applicable
- A set of goals to be accomplished during the next five-year period
- A self-assessment of progress toward completing goals in teaching, scholarship, and service over the past five years

With these materials at hand, you can sit down with the faculty member and reflect candidly on areas of strength that emerge from your review of these documents, areas of weakness that are likely to be noted, and (most important) areas in which the faculty member has made significant contributions that are not made clear or are not sufficiently highlighted by the materials you have seen.

By reviewing these materials early, you still have time to help the faculty member reformat a curriculum vitae that is out of date, idiosyncratically presented, or organized in such a way that it does not highlight the faculty member's true strength. You will also have an opportunity to review syllabi and course materials with a new lens, seeing them not merely in terms of how they might be effective in communicating with students, but also in terms of what they may suggest to the administrator or review committee about this faculty member's philosophy of teaching and methods of instruction.

Your goal at this point should be to be as candid in your assessment of weaknesses that you perceive as possible. It is far better to identify a problem area now and try to remediate it before these same weaknesses may be noted by others who are acting in a more official capacity. Even in cases where a faculty member's weakness in an area is chronic and impossible to alter in the time that remains before the posttenure review begins—if, for example, a scholarly record is so weak that there is no hope of improving it in the six months to a year that you have before the formal review begins—it is a kindness to point out in advance criticism that is likely to emerge, rather than allowing the faculty member to undergo the process with little inkling of problems ahead.

As you review the faculty member's materials, try to do so with fresh eyes, and consider solely the picture that emerges from the written documentation. Do those documents present a fairly accurate assessment of this individual's strengths and weaknesses? If there are aspects of his or her performance that are strong but don't appear to be adequately reflected in the materials that you are reviewing, what additional information will it be necessary for the faculty member—or for you as chair—to provide to those who are conducting the formal review? If there are problems with the faculty member's professional contributions that are glossed over or distorted by the written materials, how can you, as the faculty member's supervisor, fulfill your obligations to the institution by providing a corrective?

Try, as you are examining the packet of materials prepared by the faculty member, to determine if you can draw one of the following four conclusions from your review:

1. The faculty member is fully meeting the institution's expectations for performance by a tenured faculty member, and no specific recommendations for improvement are necessary.

2. The faculty member is meeting the institution's expectations for performance by a tenured faculty member but could make several improvements.

3. The faculty member is not meeting the institution's expectations for performance by a tenured faculty member, and several improvements need to be made.

4. The faculty member is performing at a level severely lower than the institution's expectations for performance by a tenured faculty

member, and it is in the institution's best interest that this faculty member leave the institution.

Faculty members placed in the first category are those you regard as completely fulfilling your institution's expectations in all categories. Their teaching is engaging, conducted at an appropriate level in each course, and designed to prepare students for success in later course work or in their lives. They have remained active as scholars—not merely keeping up-to-date with your field but contributing to the discipline at a level appropriate for the mission of your institution. In service, they are team players, assuming their fair share of the business that is necessary for the efficient operation of your department and institution, making positive contributions at a level equivalent to their tenured status, and participating actively in the essential functions of your discipline. The percentage of your faculty members for whom you believe this category is appropriate will vary according to your institutional expectations and the personnel of your department. Nevertheless, it is the rare department for which more than approximately one out of every five or ten senior faculty members has absolutely no areas of weakness. While it may appear to be the easy option for a chair to conclude that nearly every member of his or her faculty falls into this first category, using this designation a bit more restrictively can be in the best interest of both your department and the faculty members themselves.

The second category is where most chairs will probably discover that a majority of their faculty members belong. This designation indicates that although the faculty member is performing his or her duties according to the institution's expectations, there are one or two areas in which you would like to see some further development. Perhaps the faculty member has not been as aggressive as you would have liked in incorporating technology into certain courses or in updating his or her instructional techniques. Perhaps the burst of scholarship that led this faculty member to promotion and tenure has decreased beyond the level at which many departmental peers are performing. Perhaps both teaching and scholarship are superb, but the faculty member is proving to be obstructionist in departmental meetings or reluctant to assume a suitable load of advisees.

Since you are reviewing the faculty member's materials before the official posttenure review, there may be time to address some of these concerns or, at least, to develop an improvement plan that can be submitted along with the faculty member's other materials. Your advice to faculty members whom you believe belong in this category should always be constructive and forward looking. Remember that these are individuals whom you value and on whom the department depends. Your effort in making recommendations should be clearly depicted as an effort to improve an already strong record of performance, not to discourage a respected faculty member who probably already believes that he or she is performing at an extremely high level. Remind these faculty members that everyone, including you, has areas of performance in which improvement is desirable; you would be failing in your role as mentor if you did not work with them to obtain these improvements wherever possible.

For most departments, the chair will probably find relatively few faculty members who fall into the third category. Nevertheless, these are the individuals for whom most institutions or systems adopted their posttenure review process. They are the faculty members who—sometimes gradually over a number of years, sometimes precipitously as soon as tenure was granted—ceased making the effort that led to their initial success. Perhaps their courses have not been updated in a number of years or their instructional methods are badly out of date. Students are feeling disengaged in the faculty member's courses because of an excessive reliance on lectures, films, and other passive methods of instruction. Examinations are not gauged at an appropriate level for the material or consist almost exclusively of multiple-choice and matching questions even in smaller sections where essays, portfolios, and more complex projects are far more suitable. Scholarship has dwindled to a trickle at best, and there is little or no evidence that the faculty member has continued to grow in your field. Contributions to service are either refused or made only with great reluctance. Lack of collegiality is hampering the smooth operation of your department. Reports are submitted late or in a format that makes them unusable.

In these cases, as difficult as it may be to do so, you may well need to set out these concerns frankly and objectively to the faculty member following your initial review of his or her material. Wherever possible, try not to rely on mere impressions or anecdotal evidence. Provide clear data on, for example, the average number of advisees, committee assignments, publications, conference presentations, or student projects assigned per tenured faculty member elsewhere in your department or across the institution. How does this faculty member compare to others in terms of updating and improving course material, participating in sessions to improve pedagogy, or volunteering for substantive service projects? In most cases, the improvements you will expect from faculty members in this category are sufficiently substantive that it will not be possible to complete them by the time of the faculty member's formal posttenure review.

Nevertheless, it will still be important for you to describe the areas in which you believe that serious weaknesses exist in order to prevent the faculty member from being blindsided later in the process and to allow time for him or her to develop an adequate plan for remediation. It does no one a favor for demonstrable limitations of a faculty member's performance to be ignored at the departmental level. As a chair, you are failing in your obligation to do everything you can to improve performance in your department. As a mentor, you have spared a faculty member some discomfort in the short term only to set that person up for a major disappointment in the future. And you will have squandered the time that you have available to plan for appropriate actions that may be taken.

The fourth category should be reserved for only the most severe cases of failure to perform one's professional duties and for those individuals who, for whatever reason, are now proving seriously detrimental to your department's mission of instruction, scholarship, and service. Although many people in higher education believe the contrary, it is simply not the case that tenured faculty members can never be removed from their positions against their will. Nearly every institution has a procedure for the removal of tenure in extreme cases, and certain posttenure review policies are connected to this procedure. These procedures, when invoked, can cause a great deal of turmoil in the departments and institutions where they occur, resulting in negative publicity, misunderstandings by outside parties, and legal challenges. For this reason, they should be reserved for situations in which no other outcome has proved to be possible.

If you regard termination as at all within the realm of possibilities for a faculty member undergoing posttenure review, it is far better to discuss alternative exit strategies at the earliest possible date. A reassignment of duties might be possible. Your institution might have a phased or early retirement plan that the faculty member can pursue. If these are not options, a willing departure from the institution to take a position elsewhere or to "pursue other opportunities" may preserve the individual's career in a way that outright dismissal would not. For faculty members with enough self-awareness to understand both the nature and severity of the problem, these alternatives to being removed from their positions may well be attractive face-saving options. Unfortunately, all too often the very reason that these faculty members are now in such extreme difficulty is that they lack the sort of self-awareness that would have caused them to modify their behavior before the problem became insoluble. In such cases, the dismissal of the faculty member will be one of the tensest challenges you may face as a department chair. However, you are unlikely to face these challenges more than once or twice in your career, you are making your decision only for the good of your program and institution, and you will not be alone in recognizing that the faculty member's continued presence at your institution could well be disastrous.

Another bit of good news is that the entire posttenure review process, while occasionally revealing areas of weakness where improvement is needed, is far more likely to be a highly positive one for you and for the faculty member. It will reinforce for you just what a strong faculty you have, remind you of numerous important contributions they have made, and give you an opportunity to congratulate the faculty member formally on his or her continued record of excellence in instruction, scholarship, and service. Particularly for faculty members who have already reached the rank of full professor, these opportunities for public reinforcement of their positive contributions tend to be relatively rare. By making the post-tenure review process a means to accentuate the positive and plan for continued growth in the future, you will go a long way toward maintaining high morale in your program and expanding its reputation across your campus.

Many institutions have procedures in place for awards and recognitions that arise from highly positive posttenure reviews. If your institution does not yet have such a recognition campuswide, it may be highly desirable to explore the possibility of a departmental recognition for those who successfully complete their formal posttenure reviews.

Formal Posttenure Review

Once a faculty member's formal posttenure review begins, your role in the process as chair is likely to change. You will shift from being a mentor and advisor to the faculty member (providing constructive, formative criticism) to being an evaluator of the faculty member (providing decisive, summative criticism). In some institutional processes, your role may be set out in great detail. You may be asked to submit a report that must contain certain types of information or be structured in a particular way. At other institutions, you may be asked to submit letters on behalf of your faculty members only in certain situations or if you desire to do so.

In all of these cases, you should remember the gravity of your written report for, and the impact on, the faculty member's career. Your formal evaluation is now no longer a matter of informal advice and observations made behind closed doors; it is part of the public record and a document on which certain decisions will be made. At some institutions, your letter may even be the formal document that declares the outcome of the post-tenure review. For that reason, you must weigh your statements carefully, recording only observations about which you are certain and for which you have data to support your conclusions. Avoid repeating innuendo or third-hand observations. Tie all of your remarks to specific indicators that can be verified. If the faculty member missed deadlines, what were those deadlines, and what were the consequences of this failure to meet them? If you have concerns about the faculty member's teaching, what were the student complaints, peer observations, or unsatisfactory course materials that gave rise to these concerns? If scholarship is an issue, how does the faculty member's scholarly productivity compare to those of colleagues in the department or in similar disciplines? Be as specific and data oriented as you can. It serves the interest of neither the institution nor the faculty member for you to render a decision of "not good enough" without specifying your standard, the reason for it, and some targets for suitable attainment.

The best posttenure review processes are those that not only penalize ineffective faculty members for poor performance but, even more important, significantly reward successful faculty members for superior performance.

If you work in a system where the entire focus of posttenure review appears to be on what isn't working, you can play an important leadership role by advocating for a more constructive, balanced system. With many faculty members reaching the rank of full professor with twenty years or more of their careers still ahead of them, there's an increasing need for institutions to develop processes that recognize, reward, and celebrate those who excel as faculty members. Even if it proves impossible to effect this change across your entire college or university, you may be able to initiate an approach in your department that causes posttenure review to become a powerful force for positive change and increasing morale.

RESOURCES

Alstete, J. W. (2000). *Post-tenure faculty development: Building a system of faculty improvement and appreciation.* San Francisco: Jossey-Bass.

Licata, C. M., & Brown, B. E. (2004). *Post-tenure faculty review and renewal: Reporting results and shaping policy*. San Francisco: Jossey-Bass/Anker.

Licata, C. M., & Morreale, J. C. (2002). *Post-tenure faculty review and renewal: Experienced voices*. Washington, DC: American Association for Higher Education.

Licata, C. M., Morreale, J. C., & Bensimon, E. M. (2006). *Post-tenure faculty review and renewal III: Outcomes and impact*. San Francisco: Jossey-Bass/Anker.

Neal, A. D. (2008, January 1). Reviewing post-tenure review: Trustees should guarantee the integrity of tenure. *Academe: Bulletin of the AAUP, 94*(5), 27.

Neumann, A. (2009). *Professing to learn: Creating tenured lives and careers in the American research university*. Baltimore: Johns Hopkins University Press.

Sorcinelli, M. D., Shih, M.-Y., Ouellett, M. L., & Stewart M. (2007). How post-tenure review can support the teaching development of senior faculty. In D. R. Robertson & L. B. Nilson (Eds.), *To improve the academy: Resources for faculty, instructional, and organizational development* (Vol. 25, pp. 280–297). San Francisco: Jossey-Bass/Anker.

Wood, M., & Jarlais, C. D. (2006). When post-tenure review policy and practice diverge: Making the case for congruence. *Journal of Higher Education, 77*, 561–588.

44

A SCENARIO ANALYSIS ON EVALUATION AND ASSESSMENT

FOR A DISCUSSION OF how scenario analyses are structured and suggestions on how to use this exercise most productively, see Chapter Nine.

Case Studies

All for One or One for All?

For whatever reason, the number of students choosing to major in your department has declined in recent years, and enrollments in your upper-division courses have suffered occasionally. You've done all the right things: worked closely with the office of admissions to try to attract students interested in your program, promoted your program to students already enrolled at your institution, and encouraged your strongest students to serve as ambassadors for the discipline. But you've seen little, if any, fruit from these labors. You're convinced that the situation represents just a temporary setback and that numbers will pick up again in the next few years. Your dean is not so sure. You've been feeling a lot of pressure lately over enrollments, and you're beginning to worry that unless something is done soon, you could lose at least one faculty line. In a worst-case scenario, your program might even be dissolved.

At the moment, your biggest concern is one of your upper-division courses that you are desperately trying to enroll to the point that it can be offered. The dean has told you in no uncertain terms that it will not be allowed to remain on this term's schedule unless you can get at least six students to take the course. The problem is that only five students are currently enrolled, all of whom will be able to graduate on schedule this year only if the course is offered. You've looked for other options—having the students take the course as an independent study, rearranging the course schedule to cancel another class, voluntarily teaching the course yourself as an unpaid overload—but none of these options is possible. The course requires a great deal of experiential activity, discussion, and group work that cannot be replicated in an independent study. Canceling another class will either prevent these same students from graduating or deprive you of the essential feeder courses you need to keep your major going. You can't teach the course yourself because it's far enough out of your area to raise a concern for accreditation and conflicts with another obligation that you cannot reschedule.

Just when you are thinking that there is no way out, a possible solution appears in your office. A student comes to you to be advised from a program on campus that is not in your department but for which you provide service courses. As you review the student's schedule, several issues become clear. Among several other options, this student could take the course for which you need one more person. However, that would prevent the student from taking another course this semester that is absolutely required for graduation. So if you advise the student to take the course that is in jeopardy in your department, you would be giving that student one of several options for filling a requirement, allowing the course to run and your five majors to graduate on time, preventing your program from possible elimination for at least this year, but compelling this one student from a different department to postpone graduation for another term or possibly a year. If instead you advise the student into a different course that fulfills the requirement, you would be allowing this student to graduate on time but compelling five of your majors to postpone graduation for another term or possibly a year and placing your entire program in immediate jeopardy.

Do you sacrifice one student to save the many?

Rewarding the Guilty

You have recently become the chair of the department in which you have served as a faculty member for a number of years. Most aspects of the department appear to be in excellent shape, with one glaring exception. A senior member of your department is extremely unproductive, engaging in almost no scholarly activity whatsoever since last being evaluated for promotion, receiving very poor student evaluations, and having low enrollments in courses at all levels since students tend to drop this faculty member's courses within the first week of the term.

The previous department chair was a close friend of this faculty member, and you suspect that their personal relationship resulted in annual evaluations that ignored the extent of the problem. While you fully intend to reflect the faculty member's poor performance more accurately now that you are responsible for these annual reports, your first opportunity to do so is many months away. You also intend to take more forceful action three years from now when the faculty member will again be up for posttenure review. Because of the previous chair's positive evaluations, there is no paper trail permitting you to take action more quickly, and you are committed to both doing the right thing and acting according to your institution's written policies. Once the opportunity comes for posttenure review, you intend to recommend that either serious remediation occur within a very short time or that the institution's regular procedures for revocation of tenure and dismissal be undertaken.

Since you are new to the chair, the faculty member does not have a clear understanding of your views. Perhaps for this reason, the faculty member stops by your office and surprises you with a proposal. The faculty member wishes to submit an application for a paid sabbatical for the coming academic year. In the course of this conversation, the faculty member mentions plans to retire early, provided that this sabbatical application is approved. Your institution requires faculty members to remain at the institution for at least one full year after the end of a sabbatical, so the faculty member proposes a plan to teach this year, go on paid sabbatical for the coming year, remain at the institution the minimum one more year after that, and then retire. You quickly realize that the plan would mean you'd be free of the faculty member one year earlier than the soonest you had envisioned and that the person wouldn't be around for one of the years before then.

The problem as you see it is as follows. On the one hand, what the faculty member proposes permits you to attain your goal of making a permanent replacement more quickly and without the potentially divisive necessity of a public hearing for the removal of tenure. Your institution has a fund that will permit you to hire a full-time temporary replacement for the faculty member during the year of sabbatical, and you are extremely likely to secure a better teacher and scholar than your current faculty member even if the person is hired only for a single year. On the other hand, you feel reluctant to reward poor performance with a positive recommendation for sabbatical. You know that even if the faculty member signs a document committing to early retirement at the date indicated, your institution has allowed these statements to be rescinded in the past when faculty members have changed their mind. Should that occur, you are also concerned that your positive recommendation of the sabbatical application may undermine your subsequent negative annual evaluations and your recommendation for dismissal at the time of the posttenure review.

Do you keep to your original plan—rejecting the sabbatical application, further alienating the faculty member, and guaranteeing that you have at least several more years of substandard performance in your department—or do you approve the sabbatical request in spite of your misgivings?

Publish and Perish

You chair an extremely small department that has had to fight for its continued existence under your institution's program review process. Enrollments in your program tend to be low. You have very few majors, and you don't provide service courses to any other discipline. Your institution has just adopted a new strategic plan, and you feel that you are being bombarded with requests to appoint members of your department to this committee or that task force, all of them charged with implementing the goals of the plan. Every faculty member of the department, including you, is already fully committed on several of these committees in addition to your institution's high workload in the areas of teaching and scholarship.

You have, however, protected one of your faculty members from over-commitment to the onslaught of new committees and task forces. This person is a junior faculty member who is rapidly completing a scholarly project that will make all the difference in her upcoming tenure process. If the publication is completed in a timely manner, you know that the granting of tenure is all but assured. Without this publication, you stand to lose an outstanding member of your department. Your plan to protect the faculty member's time has been very successful, but one day all of that changes. Your chief academic officer calls you with a request—more of a demand, actually. As you fear, there will be yet another new task force, involving substantial commitment of time every week, and you are being asked to nominate a member of your staff. You reply that you are a very small department, that you are already well more than represented on all of the other committees that have recently been formed, and that everyone in your department has more than his or her share of responsibilities even without this new assignment. You are then asked about the junior member of your department whom you've been protecting. "What about Dr. Ross?" you are asked. "I was going through the list of all our strategic planning bodies, and Ross isn't on a single one of them."

You mention the important scholarly project that is near completion, the upcoming tenure process, and the inability for the publication to be completed if the faculty member is placed on this time-consuming new committee. "I don't see that as relevant," you're told. "It's sort of like a student who's let a big research paper go until the deadline is looming and then gets the flu. I'm sorry, but poor planning on Dr. Ross's part is no reason for us not to fulfill our strategic plan. I've just about had it with your department anyway. We don't get any majors from you. Your student credit hour production is inexcusably low. I personally don't see your area as really all that essential to our institutional mission. And now you're telling me that you don't want to be good community citizens. Let me put it to you this way: either put Ross on the committee, or I'll recommend to the program review board that we phase out your department. Those of you who are tenured maybe we can reassign to other disciplines, but this is Ross's last chance to have a tenure-track position available anyway."

You feel caught between a rock and a hard place. You feel strongly that Dr. Ross will not be granted tenure if the current scholarly project is not completed on time and that service on the task force will delay publication beyond the tenure deadline. You also feel strongly that your chief academic officer is serious and that you risk losing both your autonomy as a department and the position of your junior faculty member.

How do you proceed?

Considerations

1. As you reflect on "All for One or One for All?" is your decision any different if

   a. One of your current faculty members is likely to lose his or her job unless the upper-division course "makes"?

   b. The student who comes to you is the child of your institution's president or the chair of the governing board?

   c. You yourself are not fully convinced that the upper-division course is pedagogically sound or essential for majors in your discipline?

   d. You have repeatedly had unpleasant encounters with the parent of one of the five students currently enrolled in the upper-division course, and you know that this parent is likely to be extremely upset if his or her child cannot graduate on time?

e. There has recently been a scandal at your institution, and the local newspaper is paying close scrutiny to the basis on which administrative decisions are made?

2. With regard to "Rewarding the Guilty," consider these questions:

a. Do you respond any differently if the faculty member belongs a protected class?

b. Would you handle the situation in a different way if the faculty member has a history of filing grievances and lawsuits whenever receiving a negative decision?

c. The case study states that you've been a member of this department for many years. Would you approach the situation any differently if you had been hired in as a chair from outside the institution?

d. How might it complicate this situation if you and the faculty member had had a long-standing relationship of hostility to one another as faculty members?

3. As you read "Publish and Perish," consider these questions:

a. Is there ever an occasion for you to go over your supervisor's head and speak directly to the president or chancellor?

b. Do you share the chief academic officer's comments with Dr. Ross, or do you attempt to address the situation in another way?

c. How can you position your program so that it can make a stronger case in the pending program review process?

d. Do you handle the situation any differently if you happen to agree with your supervisor that Dr. Ross did not get an early enough start on preparing for tenure?

e. Is there any way to disentangle the challenges facing your program from those facing Dr. Ross?

f. Is there any way that you can actually use the upcoming program review process to your advantage in this situation?

Suggestions

All for One or One for All?

The situation described in this case initially may appear to be an unsolvable dilemma, but in actuality it is a case of whether the end justifies the means. For this reason, it may be important to consider the following essential principle:

> The ends never justify the means.

In other words, even in situations in which you may believe that you're serving the greater good by sacrificing the rights of an individual student, faculty member, program, or colleague, the harm that will result from that choice will never be in the long-term best interests of your institution. You simply cannot place the student into the course without full disclosure of the impact that action is likely to have on his or her progress toward graduation.

This situation is one in which the efforts that you'll have invested in maintaining good relationships with offices all across campus will pay handsome dividends. For instance, if you call the person who is in charge of that student's degree program and explore ways in which the course that you're offering could substitute for more than one of the student's degree requirements, thus keeping the student on-track for graduation, you have an opportunity to transform an apparent dilemma into a situation where everyone benefits. Such a compromise may not be possible, but your counterparts elsewhere at the institution will be far more willing to propose alternative solutions if you've established good relationships with them than if you've never acted as a team player yourself.

This situation is also one that could have been avoided with a well-designed program review process in place. Since program reviews consider not only the quality of a program but also its viability and centrality to mission, the information arising from this process would have given you precisely the ammunition you would have needed in your conversation with the dean. For instance, the data gathered about the program's continued viability could be used to assuage the concerns of the dean who's "not so sure" that enrollments are likely to pick up again. Alternatively, you could argue that although enrollments are not as robust as you might like, the program is so central to the institution's mission that it must be sustained, perhaps even enhanced through additional funding. If, however, your most recent program review demonstrated that the problems of viability would be ongoing and that the program was not critical to the mission of the institution, you may well need to reconsider how strongly you can reasonably support it. We all feel passionate about the disciplines that we represent, but this battle may well be one that you can't win.

Rewarding the Guilty

This case study may also seem to involve a situation where the department chair is trying to make the ends justify the means, but this time the context is quite different. Unlike the previous case study, no one is likely to be harmed if you agree to the sabbatical. In fact, your professional judgment is that the experience of students in your program will improve during the year the faculty member is freed from instructional duties and from his or her early retirement.

You are probably best advised to bring your dean and provost fully into the discussion with you. Clarify to them why you're supporting the sabbatical application, why you would like their support if the faculty member does try to rescind the agreement to retire, and how you believe this decision is in the institution's best interests. No matter how principled we try to be as academic leaders, there are going to be times when a greater good is served by allowing someone a benefit that person didn't really earn. There is no harm of any kind resulting from this decision for the institution, your program, or your stakeholders, so the best choice is to grant the sabbatical, provide realistic evaluations during the years when the faculty member is on active duty, restrict (if possible) the instructor's course load to classes where he or she appears to be least ineffective, and move on as quickly as possible.

Publish and Perish

Unlike the previous two cases, the situation described in this case puts you in a genuine dilemma. Although we may regard it as inappropriate and unprofessional for the chief academic officer to use the program review process as a threat unrelated to the issue at hand (staffing the new task force), inappropriate and unprofessional actions create genuine problems for academic administrators all the time. While we can protest that it "isn't right" and "shouldn't happen," part of effective academic leadership is dealing with the problem, regardless of how it was created.

The challenge in this case may well call for creative solutions. Since course enrollments are small anyway, you may be able to cancel one of Dr. Ross's courses, reassign the students to another class, and make either the research project or the service activity part of this faculty member's official load. It is also possible that your president or chancellor may be a valuable ally in these discussions. But this option should not be chosen lightly. Just as you'd be disturbed by a faculty member's attempt to perform an end run around you by taking a matter directly to your supervisor, you could end up exacerbating an already difficult situation by going over the head of your chief academic officer. This action may well be regarded by your boss as a mutiny, and you could end up losing your position as chair and possibly your entire program. There's an old adage (and an essential principle) that goes:

When you strike a king, you must kill the king.

The idea is that you can't take on the chief academic officer unless you're absolutely sure that you have the full support of the president or chancellor. If there have been a number of other problems with your supervisor, you know that he or she is going to be forced to step down soon, and you have the commitment of his or her boss to defend you in this situation, then it may be wise to proceed with your end run. Otherwise you're in too weak a position because of recent enrollments and your department's limited role in the institution's essential mission. Seek other solutions. Weigh the overall benefit of Dr. Ross and her research program to your department's continued viability, try to find a compromise where you can, and understand that in case studies as in real life, perfect solutions are rarely, if ever, found.

PART SEVEN

ESSENTIALS OF BUDGETING AND PLANNING

45

STRATEGIC PLANNING

STRATEGIC PLANNING MAY BE defined as an institution's process of identifying specific transformative goals for the future and then aligning its budget, priorities, and policies so as to achieve those goals according to the timetable desired. It differs from other types of planning in three ways.

First, it seeks to fulfill transformative goals. In other words, strategic planning starts by asking, "What are we now, and what should we become in the future?" Its operating assumption is that colleges and universities need to reinvent themselves continually in order to respond to an ever-changing world, the evolving nature of research in higher education, and the different needs of new generations of students. To remain effective, institutions must always be aware of what they are capable of becoming and how to transform themselves in such a way that they remain relevant or even increase their relevance in the years to come. Thus, desiring to build a new student union within five years is a goal; desiring to progress from a master's-level college to a doctoral institution is a transformative goal, and strategic planning will tend to focus on the second sort of objective.

Second, it results in substantive change. In order for strategic planning to be transformative, it must affect an institution in ways that go far deeper than slight modifications to existing policies and programs. An effective strategic planning process can cause fundamental priorities to change, and thus the way in which budgets are allocated will necessarily change as well. The essential principle for strategic planning is as follows:

> At institutions with effective strategic planning processes, the budget is guided by the plan. At institutions without effective strategic planning processes, the budget is the plan.

As colleges and universities recreate themselves in order to improve or at least to remain as strong as possible, they need to redirect funding from lower priorities to more significant goals. The strategic plan guides administrators in how to make those changes.

Third, a strategic plan has a well-defined timetable and rationale. An institution that plans to increase its enrollment by 40 percent, double its amount of externally sponsored research, and triple its number of national or international teaching awards has a vision of where it wants to go and may be said to have a plan. But an institution that wants to attain these goals within seven years, has identified why those goals are important to its future, and has constructed a road map by which it will reach those targets in an incremental progress may truly be said to have a strategic plan. When an institution does not set a deadline, understand the reasons for the change, and work out the steps required to achieve the objective, much of its planning remains little more than an optimistic vision for the future. It's the strategic plan that gives the vision a reasonable chance of becoming reality.

What Department Chairs Need to Know About Strategic Planning

Although strategic planning is usually initiated at the level of the governing board or chief executive officer, department chairs need to know how the process works in order to contribute effectively to the institution's overall effort and implement its decisions in their area. There is a great deal of variety in how strategic planning processes function at different institutions, and no single survey of the topic can possibly reflect all the possibilities. But the most complete strategic planning processes in higher education tend to be those that flow seamlessly from the institution's mission and vision through its budgeting and assessment process, feeding the results of the activity back into a revised and expanded vision for the future. In other words, we can think of strategic planning in the following way:

Step 1: Mission. Institutions either develop or clarify and recommit to a statement of their basic identity, goals, and guiding principles.

They decide who their stakeholders are now and are likely to be in the future and determine how they see themselves benefiting these different stakeholders. The product of step 1 is usually a mission statement.

Step 2: Vision. Based on their idea of what they are now, institutions define what they can and should become in the future. They seek to identify new ways of remaining relevant to current stakeholders or explore how they might serve other constituents in the future. The product of step 2 is usually a vision statement.

Step 3: Strategic transformation. Based on their idea of what they can and should become, institutions identify changes that they will need to make in order to attain those goals. Strategic transformation usually involves grouping long-term goals into a number of clusters, such as building a stronger community and expanding a culture of engagement, that do not coincide with existing institutional divisions or the organizational chart. The product of step 3 is usually a macrolevel strategic plan.

Step 4: Strategic implementation. Since transformational goals by their very nature cut across existing organizational structures, implementing these goals requires melding the plan with the way in which the institution actually operates. Frequently this process involves drilling down into the macrolevel strategic plan and assigning responsibilities for its implementation to the vice presidents in charge of different areas of the institution. The product of step 4 is usually an implementation plan.

Step 5: Tactical planning. Since the goals for the various vice-presidential areas of the institution are (in truly effective strategic planning processes) too ambitious to be achieved within a single year, they must be broken down into tactical plans with objectives and targets assigned to deans, directors, and department chairs throughout the institution. Unless a department chair happens to be involved with earlier steps in the process (for example, by being a member of a strategic planning council), it is at step 5 that departments become most directly involved in this effort. The product of step 5 is usually an annual plan.

Step 6: Assessment. In order to determine whether adequate progress is being made and whether the strategies in place have been effective, assessment of the entire strategic planning process

Figure 45.1 Strategic Planning Process

must occur regularly. This goal may be achieved through assessment techniques ("Are the expected outcomes being achieved?"; see Chapter Forty-One), comprehensive program review ("Is this program of high quality, viable, and central to our mission?"; see Chapter Forty-Two), or some combination of the two. The product of step 6 is usually an assessment report.

The assessment report then feeds back into step 2 of the process—"Based on who we have become now because of our progress, what should our next vision be for the future?"—and the cycle continues. Since, except in rare cases of institutions facing imminent disaster or other reasons for extensive change, the mission of the institution will remain unaltered, step 1 occurs only at the beginning of the process and need not become a regular stage in the strategic planning cycle. Step 1 thus occurs infrequently, steps 2 through 4 occur periodically, and steps 5 and 6 occur annually. Figure 45.1 shows how the strategic planning process is structured at many institutions.

The Role of SWOT Analysis in Strategic Planning

Most academic strategic planning processes include a procedure known as SWOT analysis, usually as a prelude to the development of a vision statement or as a part of the institution's strategic transformation. SWOT analysis received its name because it involves the formal identification of the institution's strengths, weaknesses, opportunities, and threats. As illustrated in Figure 45.2, strengths and weaknesses

Figure 45.2 SWOT Analysis

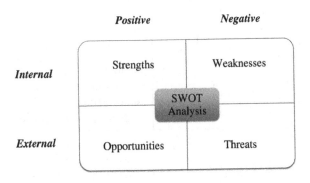

are internal aspects of the institution: the condition of the physical plant, the adequacy of technology and information resources, the distinctiveness of the curriculum, and so on. Opportunities and threats address factors external to the institution: demographic patterns, competition with other colleges and universities, enrollment trends in various disciplines, and so on. By examining the positive and negative factors that exist in each of these categories, institutions can develop a better sense of where they are in terms of their individual growth and development, thus clarifying where they need to go in the future.

The way in which the SWOT analysis is conducted depends a great deal on the needs and nature of the institution. Sometimes it can be completed as a brainstorming exercise conducted at a retreat or with focus groups drawn from the school's constituent groups. At other times, marketing firms or external consultants are brought in to conduct a more intensive examination of the institution's status compared to its peer and aspirational institutions, competitors, and models of best practices. The goal is to come away from the SWOT analysis with a well-defined concept of what long-term strategies are likely to be necessary in light of where the institution is right now in the evolving landscape of higher education.

Although many chairs may prefer to participate in SWOT analysis only as part of the larger institutional strategic planning process, it is also possible to adopt this technique for planning within the discipline itself. For example, a chair could lead a planning discussion for the department that resulted in the following conclusions for the Department of Analogy:

Strengths	95 percent placement rate of departmental graduates in first-choice careers Increasing annual giving by departmental alumni
Weaknesses	Limited research funding available in departmental budget Aging facilities that sometimes dissuade potential majors
Opportunities	Rising enrollment patterns in analogy courses nationwide Strong employment demand for graduates in analogy studies likely to continue
Threats	Declining college-age populations in several of the department's key recruitment areas New Department of Analogy just created at Aspirational State University, less than fifty miles away

On the basis of this SWOT analysis, the department might make a strategic decision to direct some of the external funding contributed by alumni to boosting research support and to recruit future students from new markets with a larger population of college-age students. The new recruitment strategy would focus on the department's established record at placing its graduates in highly desirable positions and the rising interest that programs in this discipline are attracting nationwide, thus reducing the challenge provided by the new program initiated by the other university not far away. In this manner, SWOT analysis frequently ends up suggesting strategies that may not have been as apparent to departments if they had not engaged in this formal exercise.

Moving from Strategic to Tactical Plans

In many ways, department chairs operate at the most important level of the institution for strategic planning because it is in the activities they supervise that plans generally become reality. The goal of strategic implementation and tactical planning is to focus the overall plan in two key areas:

1. *The goal of strategic transformation.* What does the plan mean for what my discipline does?
2. *The goal of tactical planning.* What does the plan mean I must do this year?

As an example, suppose that you work in an institution where the vision is to increase research capacity and double the graduate program within ten years. Strategic transformation helps you clarify how your own area will need to change in light of this goal:

o How would your research facilities need to change in order to support a larger graduate program?

o Which external sources of funding would you need to rely on as you build more research capacity?

o Can you identify graduate degrees in your area that are ripe for expansion because of increasing demand from students to enter the program or from the entities that hire graduates in that discipline?

o Are there current areas of your program that you offer only at the undergraduate level but seem suitable for expanding at the master's or doctoral level?

Once it is clear how your area will need to change over the course of the ten-year plan, what tactical steps do you need to take this year in order to achieve that goal in a decade? If you are still in the initial stages of planning, your tactics for the first year might include conducting a needs assessment, reviewing best practices at peer institutions, and speaking to focus groups about desirable features in the expanded curriculum. The second year might be devoted to curricular development, the third to a pilot project, the fourth to tweaking the program based on the results of the pilot, the fifth to promoting the new endeavor more broadly, and so on. The key factors are that strategic transformation and tactical planning always result in a better understanding of what you need to do and what you need to do right now.

Keep in mind too that not every aspect of a strategic plan is about growth and the addition of new programs. It can be just as important to consolidate or eliminate programs, if that is in the long-term best interest of the institution, as it can be to expand offerings. In fact, consolidation and expansion frequently occur in tandem, as programs that are less successful or no longer in demand are phased out in favor of new endeavors that place the institution in a strong position overall. For this reason, the comprehensive program review procedure explored in Chapter

Forty-Two is a vital component of most effective strategic planning systems. Program review helps determine programs that are low in quality but need to be strengthened strategically, as well as programs that are no longer viable or central to the institution's mission and thus appear to be likely candidates for consolidation.

Assessment and Closing the Loop

The final stage in a thorough strategic planning process should be to assess the effectiveness of the tactics you've chosen and use that information to guide the process as it continues. Assessing a strategic planning process involves many of the same activities that you're probably familiar with from assessing academic programs. (See Chapter Forty-One.) You have to establish outcomes for each action, determine whether the appropriate thresholds or trigger points have been reached, and then use the data that you've gathered to build on or alter the tactic that you adopted.

As an example, let's return to the hypothetical institution we just considered that is trying to expand its graduate programs. If you are in the third year of a ten-year plan at this institution and conducting a pilot program in your discipline, you may have established an outcome that at the end of the first year of the program, 95 percent of the students will be qualified to register for advanced seminars in the discipline, as indicated by grades of 85 percent or above on placement tests, submission of an acceptable thesis proposal, and the recommendation of their academic advisors. Suppose that at the end of your pilot program, you discover that only 53 percent of the students who originally began the program are qualified to continue. Did you fail? Not necessarily. Remember that you were conducting a pilot program and you suspected you'd learn from this experiment about several factors that need to be changed. Since the 53 percent qualification rate fell significantly short of your 95 percent target, you will want to explore the data more completely in order to learn why the rate was so low and what you can do to address the situation—for example:

○ Perhaps students simply dropped out of the program during the first year, suggesting that there was not a good fit between the students you were admitting and the nature of the program you had designed.

○ Perhaps students were not achieving the minimum score of 85 percent on the placement tests, suggesting that introductory courses in the program needed to be revised to address the development of basic knowledge and skills.

- o Perhaps the thesis proposals were not acceptable, indicating that more attention needs to be paid to research skills and the construction of proper proposals early in the program's curriculum.

- o Perhaps advisors were not recommending students in large enough numbers, suggesting a disconnect between the advisors' expectations and what the program has been able to achieve.

- o Perhaps the 95 percent rate was excessively high, and your review of the standards in place for comparable programs at peer institutions suggests that the outcome itself needs to be reexamined.

- o Perhaps the statistic is meaningless since students did not have a clear idea of what the program involved, because it was new, and therefore dropped out or took on more than was reasonable. In this case, you may need to clarify how the program is advertised to prospective students.

Closing the loop then consists of modifying your tactics in light of what you learn from this assessment and feeding that information back into the overall strategic planning process. In other words, although your pilot program's individual experience is unlikely to change the institution's mission, it may well lead to a rethinking of the institution's vision. That ten-year goal of doubling graduate enrollment may not be feasible, or the institution may need to be even more aggressive at building infrastructure and capacity in order to achieve the original goal.

---

o

Although some faculty members regard strategic planning as an unwelcome intrusion from the corporate world into academic life, a comprehensive planning process has the potential to reinforce programs that are already strong, transform institutions that are facing significant challenge, and allow colleges and universities to be intentional, rather than simply reactive, in the changes they implement. Department chairs who develop a good background in strategic planning help their disciplines in the present and open up opportunities for advancement to higher administrative levels if they so desire.

RESOURCES

Dickeson, R. C. (2010). *Prioritizing academic programs and services: Reallocating resources to achieve strategic balance* (Rev. ed.). San Francisco: Jossey-Bass.

Houston, D. (2008, February). Rethinking quality and improvement in higher education. *Quality Assurance in Education, 16*(1), 61–79.

Morrill, R. L. (2007). *Strategic leadership: Integrating strategy and leadership in colleges and universities.* Westport, CT: ACE/Praeger.

Rowley, D. J., Lujan, H. D., & Dolence, M. G. (1997). *Strategic change in colleges and universities: Planning to survive and prosper.* San Francisco: Jossey-Bass.

Sanaghan, P. (2009). *Collaborative strategic planning in higher education.* Washington, DC: NACUBO.

Sweet, C., Blythe, H., Keeley, E. J., & Forsyth, B. (2008). Popes in the pizza: Analyzing activity reports to create and sustain a strategic plan. *Journal of Faculty Development, 22,* 196–208.

46

PLANNING A BUDGET

THE RESPONSIBILITIES THAT DEPARTMENT chairs may be assigned in the area of budgeting vary widely from one institution to the next. Some chairs serve as the primary budgetary authority for their units and take full responsibility for every expenditure. Others, particularly those in smaller departments or at smaller institutions, have little direct authority in this area. They may simply track the expenses incurred by the members of their faculty or, in certain cases, serve as a conduit for budgetary information, with the actual decisions made at other levels of the institution. But no matter what level of budgetary authority you may have as a chair, you will perform your responsibilities better if you understand at least some aspects of how college and university budgeting tends to be done, why decisions are made as they are, and how this knowledge can best serve your individual discipline and its constituents.

It's useful to think of budgeting as having two primary phases: planning and implementation. The planning phase consists of all of those activities—beginning a year or more before the onset of an institution's fiscal year—by which anticipated sources of income are identified and initial strategies for allocation and expenditure are developed. The implementation phase occurs during the fiscal year itself, as actual expenditures are made and allocations are modified as necessary within or among budgetary units, and concludes when the institution's budget is formally audited by an external and (it is hoped) objective agency. Because the chair's role in these two budgetary phases can be significantly different, it is useful to explore each of them individually, with planning addressed in this chapter and implementation discussed in the next chapter.

The Basics of Budget Planning

During the planning phase of budgeting, goals are set for the institution's income and expenditures for a predetermined period, usually a fiscal year—any regular twelve-month period over which an institution plans and tracks the use of its funds. For some institutions, fiscal years are identical to calendar years, but most institutions find that some other twelve-month division—such as July 1 through the following June 30—fits their academic calendars, state legislative cycles, and student enrollment habits better. It is traditional to denote a fiscal year through the abbreviation *FY*, followed by two or four digits indicating the calendar year in which the fiscal year ends. Thus, most institutions use the designation FY16 or FY2016 to indicate a fiscal year that begins in 2015, but concludes on a predetermined date in the year 2016. Most state institutions and many private institutions require that budgets be closed out in each fiscal year, which means that funds and deficits cannot be carried over from one fiscal year to the next. In these systems, on the last day of the fiscal year, all unexpended monies must be spent and all unreconciled deficits must be covered. This practice leads to the possibility of year-end funds, which is addressed in the next chapter. If this requirement does not exist, the funds that may be transferred from one fiscal year to the next are known as *carry-over funding*. The flexibility provided by this funding is highly desirable because it allows small units to plan for major purchases, such as large pieces of equipment, that could not ordinarily be accommodated within their annual budgets.

In planning for the budget of each fiscal year, institutions have several options. They may practice *zero-base budgeting,* in which all budgetary sources and allocations are reestablished every time that a new budget is set, or they may practice some form of *historical budgeting* (sometimes known as *incremental budgeting*), in which a past record of income and expenditures is used to help plan for the future. The advantages of zero-base budgeting are that it is flexible, helps free institutions from budget patterns that no longer make sense, and cause every goal in the budget to be developed with a clear and defensible rationale. The disadvantages to this system are that it is time intensive, can exacerbate divisiveness within an institution, and frequently does not result in budgets that are much different from a more historically based approach. The advantages of historical budgeting are that it is quick to implement, gives institutions an initial plan that they can adjust according to their needs, and has the merit of having been tested by the experience of previous years. The disadvantages of this system result from the practice of having each year's budget based (at least initially) on that which was used the previous year. As a result, it can be extremely difficult to change poor practices that are well entrenched; it is also relatively easy to overlook poor budgetary plans since every category of income and expenditure tends not to be justified each time the budget is set.

Historical or incremental budgeting and zero-based budgeting are by far the most common models that colleges and universities use, but other systems exist. *Performance-based budgeting* is an approach that ties funding to institutional goals and projects rather than traditional units such as departments and colleges. A central component of performance-based budgeting is the identification of key performance indicators (KPI), quantifiable standards that measure the degree of success in attaining a goal. For a department, typical KPIs might include enrollment figures, broken down by upper-division and lower-division courses, as well as number of majors, amount of grant funding received, number of refereed books and articles produced in a year, and other measures appropriate for the discipline. Units that regularly meet or exceed their KPIs are frequently rewarded with increases in funding; those that consistently fail to meet their goals remain level in funding, have their budgets cut, or undergo some type of reorganization.

Responsibility-centered budgeting is an entrepreneurial approach that encourages academic units to generate revenue by allowing them to keep a certain amount of funding they produce in excess of their costs. In a responsibility-centered budgeting model, units are charged by the central administration for certain services but allowed a great deal of autonomy over other areas of the budget on the principle that they'll be better motivated to seek efficiencies if they directly benefit from the costs saved. In addition, units have a far stronger impetus to seek external funding and be innovative in the implementation of fees, since the revenue generated by these mechanisms can be reinvested in the program itself.

Although relatively few institutions use performance-based and responsibility-centered budgeting extensively, department chairs need to know about these approaches because they may be useful in special cases. For example, responsibility-centered budgeting might be proposed as a way of expanding a discipline's summer programming, or performance-based budgeting might be used to justify the continuation of a center or institute.

Finally, *service-level budgeting* is a melding of zero-based and responsibility-based approaches in which budgets are set each year in accordance with the specific services that organizational units are expected to perform. As levels of service change or there is an increase or decrease in the number of people the unit must serve, budgets fluctuate from year to year in a much more flexible manner than in historical or incremental systems.

Regardless of the budgeting system in place at a college or university, the planning process tends to be hierarchical: departments usually submit plans to colleges, colleges to the university, and the university to the university system. Even at small institutions, private colleges, and autonomous state institutions, the budgetary planning process follows a hierarchical design: plans and proposals move from smaller units to larger units (bottom to top), and budgetary decisions are passed from larger units to smaller units (top to bottom).

The precise manner in which your department will be asked to submit its plan to your division, college, or institution is likely to be different from that expected of your colleague at another institution. Some colleges have established formats for budget requests; others do so quite informally ("Get me a list of your most critical needs for the coming year by [date]"). Some institutions have formal budget hearings at which proposals for the coming fiscal year are made, discussed, and debated before the budget is finally set; others leave this process to a committee, the president's cabinet, or even, at certain institutions, the discretion of the chief financial officer.

Principles for Preparing a Budget

Regardless of the specific planning process in place at your institution, keep the following principles in mind as you prepare your budget proposals each year:

Tie all requests to your institution's strategic plan.

The essential principle that we saw in Chapter Forty-Five remains valid throughout the budget planning process: at institutions with effective strategic planning processes, the budget is guided by the plan; at institutions without effective strategic planning processes, the budget *is* the plan. A request for an expenditure that is not supported by planning and data is unlikely to be taken seriously by the individuals making decisions at your college or university. Every budgetary request should be tied convincingly to the fulfillment of the strategic plan. In the best possible scenario, the existence of clear strategic priorities should help guide your priorities in requesting additional funding or, in more difficult fiscal environments, proposing areas for possible reductions. If one of your institution's major strategic goals is to reduce the student-to-faculty ratio, it becomes easier to justify a request for additional faculty (or conversely, to protect current lines) than if the strategic plan emphasizes the expansion of research facilities and the reduction of deferred maintenance. Nevertheless, if your discipline still feels that increasing faculty positions is vital to its continued success despite no obvious connection between this goal and the institution's strategic plan, you'll need to find a convincing rationale for your request. Perhaps the proposed faculty members can play an important role in staffing the new research facilities, or there may be some other strategic goal that lends greater support to what your department is hoping to obtain.

All requests should have a clear priority order based on the institution's mission and plan.

Budgetary requests that are not made in a clear and compelling order based on established institutional values are mere wish lists that will ultimately prove ineffective. If a specific item must appear in a priority order that may initially surprise a reader, then that item should be given more extensive and compelling justification. Making that connection will help even individuals who are unfamiliar with your discipline understand why that item serves to advance the fundamental mission of your college or university. For instance, if you are requesting research equipment at an institution that has just reaffirmed a "teaching-first" philosophy in its mission statement and strategic plan, you may need to explain that the primary purpose of this equipment will be pedagogical, permitting a type of student-directed experiential learning that is not now possible.

Keep in mind that budgets have two components: income as well as expenditure.

Most department chairs are fairly good at recognizing how money needs to be spent in their disciplines; relatively few chairs are equally knowledgeable about how that revenue is to be generated. Chairs weaken their cases considerably when they make budget proposals implying that additional sources of funding will automatically be granted to them if they merely state their needs in sufficiently compelling terms.

All department chairs need to be aware that for every additional dollar allocated in one area, a different need of the institution will receive less funding. The total budget of an institution is a zero-sum game, and so it's important to consider possible sources for the funding that you request, not just the benefits that will result from the expenditure. Is there a way, for instance, for your department to develop a funding source that can generate some or all of the cost associated with an item? Can a fee be established, admission charged for a popular departmental event, external donations be solicited, a foundation be approached for seed money, or existing funds be redirected from a low-priority item in your department to this new higher priority? (As a mental exercise, you might try imagining how you would redirect 5 percent of your current operating budget so as to give more funding to the highest priorities of your discipline. You may be surprised to discover what you can do internally simply by refocusing your priorities.) In most cases, requests for funding are more likely to be approved if you can provide a well-considered plan to pay for them. When planning a budget, the idea that "it's my job to spend the money and their job to raise it" is never appropriate.

Be aware of the difference between one-year expenditures and continuous expenditures.

Not all spending is alike. Purchasing an extra piece of equipment affects a single year's budget. Adding a new faculty line, permanently increasing scholarship aid, or launching a distinguished lecture series requires support year after year. A surprising number of academics confuse these two types of expenditures, saying things like, "Well, we just won't get a new copier next year, so we can use that money to expand our current part-time position into a full-time tenure-track position." As a chair, you can't afford to make this type of mistake. At best, you will undermine your credibility with others at your institution who deal with budgeting on a daily basis. At worst, you may inadvertently commit your department and institution to an ongoing expense that can't be sustained.

———— o ————

The budget planning process should flow smoothly from the mission and vision of the institution that inform the discipline's strategic priorities, through those strategic priorities that inform the department's objectives for the coming year, and through those objectives to actual cost centers, projects to be funded, and annual goals that must be achieved. When departments try to plan their budgets apart from this context, they fall into the trap of becoming too beholden to history (sustaining funding as it is because "it's always been that way") or creating strategic plans that have no realistic hope of being achieved. Along with good interpersonal skills, effective budgeting skills are among the most important abilities chairs can develop. The time invested in learning more about institutional budgeting almost always pays dividends by increasing a chair's effectiveness.

RESOURCES

Barr, M. J., & McClellan, G. S. (2011). *Budgets and financial management in higher education*. San Francisco: Jossey-Bass.

Bryant, P. T. (2005). *Confessions of an habitual administrator: An academic survival manual*. San Francisco: Jossey-Bass/Anker.

Chu, D. (2006). Budget. In *The department chair primer: Leading and managing academic departments* (pp. 43–54). San Francisco: Jossey-Bass/Anker.

Luna, A. L., & Brennan, K. A. (2009). Using regression analysis in departmental budget allocations. *IR Applications, 24*(1), 1–12.

Whalen, E. (1991). *Responsibility center budgeting: An approach to decentralized management for institutions of higher education*. Bloomington: Indiana University Press.

47

IMPLEMENTING A BUDGET

IN THE PREVIOUS CHAPTER, we explored concepts that chairs need to know in order to plan and propose a budget. The focus of this chapter shifts to budget implementation. That change in emphasis is important because once budgets have been set for a fiscal year, the department chair's duties largely shift away from envisioning future budgets to allocating the budget established for the current year.

The two sets of skills are quite different. Planning a budget requires vision, broad institutional knowledge, and excellent rhetorical skills; it is largely a leadership activity. Implementing a budget requires attention to details, accuracy, and an ability to enforce policies effectively; it is largely a management activity. It is not uncommon for chairs to excel in one area of budgeting, while facing significant challenges in the other. Moreover, each institution will have its own system for tracking the budgetary activity of its departments, and so experience in one budgetary environment is not necessarily transferable to another. At most institutions, financial information is available electronically and is updated continually. At some institutions, budgetary statements are still sent in hard copy, with revenue, recent transfers, and expenditures listed according to each major category. So while it's possible to speak in terms of some generally effective practices for implementing departmental budgets, chairs will also need to acquaint themselves with their own institution's individual systems and procedures.

Cost Accounting at the Departmental Level

The most common system used for tracking activity within budgets is to tie each transaction to a specific object code or operational category that indicates the precise location and type of transaction that has occurred. Institutional systems of object codes vary from the relatively simple to the extraordinarily complex, depending on the nature of the institution, its organizational structure, and the manner in which it is following the practices required by the appropriate board of accounting standards. For public institutions, that body is the Governmental Accounting Standards Board (GASB, pronounced "GAS-be"). Private institutions are governed by a similar body, known as the Financial Accounting Standards Board (FASB, pronounced "FASS-be"). In most cases, the object codes are nine or more digits, with each digit or group of digits providing such information as the specific campus on which the transaction took place (in multi-campus systems), the source of funding (education and general, foundation, sponsored programs, and the like), the unit responsible for the transaction (college, division, department, program, and so on), and the precise nature of the income, transfer, or expenditure (which can fall into a vast array of different categories, such as full-time salaries, part-time salaries, casual labor, benefits, postage, telephone: local, telephone: toll, subscriptions, memberships, equipment over a certain amount, equipment under a certain amount, travel, food, lodging, office supplies, and many more).

Since institutions almost always allow at least some types of transfer among these different funds, most chairs find it useful—unless otherwise instructed by their business offices—to tie each transaction as closely as possible to its actual object code, not simply whichever account happens to have a sufficient balance remaining. For instance, in a year when your department's small equipment account has already been depleted, you may be tempted to fund the purchase of an additional item of small equipment through your department's telecommunications account or account for supplies and expenses. Nevertheless, it's preferable—and at many institutions it is required—for you to fund the purchase from the account you would ordinarily use for small equipment, even though it is depleted, and then submit a one-year transfer of funds from the other account to cover that expense.

While this approach may seem like useless paper shuffling to some chairs, it's an effective tool for both keeping accurate records and planning purposes. By charging expenses to the appropriate accounts, it's much easier for departmental accounts to be reconciled and audited later when you may have forgotten how you paid for that piece of equipment purchased several years ago. (Keep in mind, too, that future chairs may need to make sense of the records that were developed during your term, and that task becomes far more difficult when expenses are not charged to the appropriate account.) Furthermore, tying purchases to the correct object code provides a far more realistic picture of your future needs when you review previous fiscal years. For instance, if you notice that you are transferring funds from the operating supplies to the small equipment category several years in a row, you may decide that it is preferable to realign these accounts permanently and request an increase from the general appropriation. In addition, if you are chronically short of funds in one account and must repeatedly cover those expenditures by piecing together remaining bits from several accounts, you can use this as strong additional support for a request that the underfunded account be increased by your institution.

Transfers among certain accounts may not be possible at your institution. In particular, there may be restrictions on transfers between personal services accounts (those used to pay for salaries and benefits) and operating supplies accounts that limit whether you can transfer unexpended salary funding to such accounts as travel, photocopying, and equipment. Other institutions may have restrictions on whether institutional funds (the type of accounts usually known as "Education and General Funds") may be used for such purchases as student travel, entertainment, the purchase of food or alcoholic beverages, and the like. Your institution's business office or chief financial officer can give you an overview of the restrictions in place in your system. Most important, in cases where restrictions on transfers or expenditures exist, be sure to ask about permissible ways to achieve your ultimate goal. Restrictions on institutional funds may not apply, for instance, to funds overseen by a college's foundation; it is possible that the foundation may be willing to cover the cost itself or to swap a cost with you, paying for some item or activity that is permissible for it while you absorb an equivalent expense that it was going to pay but that your institution would allow to be charged to your department. In other cases, it may not be possible to transfer the funds in one direction, while it is perfectly permissible to transfer the cost in the other direction.

A good budget officer will know the most appropriate way to accomplish your general objective. Never assume that there is only one way of fulfilling a budgetary goal. If you are informed that a certain type of purchase or transfer is not allowed, be flexible in your response. Say something like, "Well, this is essentially what I need to do. What are the ways you can explore with me that would allow me to accomplish that same goal within our existing operating procedure?"

Salary Saving and Other Unexpended Funds

Unexpended funds on salary lines, commonly referred to as *salary savings,* occur in a number of different ways. For example, if a faculty member is earning $110,000 and either retires or otherwise leaves the institution, a replacement hired for $70,000 results in a salary savings of $40,000. (The resulting savings in benefits may well make the actual gain somewhat higher.) That $40,000 in savings is of great interest to those at all levels of the institution since it is continuing money—money that would remain in the budget year after year, even increasing in years when raises are allocated—rather than a one-time expenditure. For this reason, it is likely that your institution has standard procedures for how salary savings are allocated. They may revert to the general budget to aid the bottom line, they may be absorbed by the upper administration (presidents, provosts, and deans frequently combine pools of salary savings to create new positions), or they may remain with the units that generated them.

Whenever you are replacing an individual in your department and salary savings are likely to result, always inquire about the institution's plans for those funds. If the amount is large and your department is severely understaffed, you might inquire into the possibility of splitting one faculty line into two or using the savings for an additional lab assistant, student worker, or secretarial support. If the amount is small, you might inquire into the possibility of shifting the savings into a permanent increase for one of your accounts that you frequently deplete early in the fiscal year, such as faculty travel or supplies. You should by no means expect that you will be successful every time that you make one of these requests. Nevertheless, success will be all but impossible if you do not approach each opportunity with a clear and compelling plan.

No matter how much budgetary information your institution provides, most department chairs find it useful to maintain their own shadow budget in an electronic spreadsheet. Items are occasionally coded incorrectly at other levels of an institution, and shadow budgets can help you detect discrepancies when you are either charged for something that should have been charged to a different unit or not credited with funding that should properly be yours. It is often the case, too, that official institutional budget reports lag actual activity by a substantial period; preserving records in a shadow budget prevents you from accidentally spending the same money more than once, resulting in a deficit at the end of the year. Think of your shadow budget as something similar to the check record you keep in your checkbook. Reconciling this record with your bank statement helps you to spot errors and avoid overdrawing your account. It also assists you in identifying funds that you have already encumbered or promised to use for a particular purpose but haven't technically spent yet.

On both your shadow budget and official budget, one figure you will wish to track is the percentage of each account expended versus the percentage of the fiscal year expended. If your institution does not calculate this ratio for you, it is easy to set up a spreadsheet formula that does so:

(Amount expended ÷ original amount) × 100 =
Percentage of account expended to date

(Day within fiscal year ÷ 365) × 100 =
Percentage of fiscal year that has passed to date

Comparing these two figures provides a picture of whether the budget is being expended at a faster rate than might be expected. But the goal isn't quite as simple as to keep the first number smaller than the second. After you have tracked this information for several years, you will learn the particular budgetary patterns and rhythms of your department, thus understanding the red flags to watch for in your budget. Thus, an account that is 98 percent expended with only 35 percent of the academic year gone may or may not be an area of concern. The account could be used for equipment, supporting only one or two purchases each year. Alternatively, the account could cover the type of supplies or services that are regularly needed at the start of the academic year but rarely again afterward. On the other hand, a photocopying account that is depleted too rapidly may leave your department vulnerable when final exams must be copied at the end of the semester. Your own familiarity with the needs of your discipline, coupled with a healthy dose of common sense, will guide you in determining which percentages are problematic and which are not. (You may need to explain your department's spending patterns to budget officers outside your department who may not know your discipline's rhythms as well as you do.)

Year-End Expenditures

One aspect of academic spending patterns that may occur at your institution—and that you may well need to plan for—is the phenomenon of year-end money. Year-end money occurs at institutions that need to zero out their budgets at the end of each fiscal year, covering all deficits and depleting all other accounts. In years when funding remains in an institution's budget at the end of the year, departments may be required to spend it in order to bring the books to a zero balance. There are frequently restrictions on what may be purchased with year-end money—for example, supplies but not equipment, equipment only if it has been priced according to a preexisting contract, and the like—and you will need to know what these limitations are at your institution. But the possibility of year-end funding can, if it is permitted, be an important part of your funding strategy. You may be able to stock up on supplies at the end of a fiscal year, thus transferring funds from operating supplies to another critical area during the new fiscal year. You may be able to purchase a piece of equipment that exceeds the equipment budget of your individual department, pooling your own funds with year-end money from other areas.

One other budgetary item that you may wish to track is your unit's cost in relation to other departments at your institution and similar departments at other institutions. How much does it cost to produce, for instance, one student credit hour of instruction in your discipline at your institution compared with similar programs at other institutions? Frequently the business office of an institution has a system in place to calculate these figures. If your institution does not, you can determine at least a crude approximation of cost by adding all of your department's expenditures in salaries, benefits, and all categories of operating expenses (being sure to include travel funding and other accounts that may not be controlled within your department itself) and dividing that figure by the number of student credit hours your discipline produces in the same fiscal period. The reason that the resulting figure is crude is that it does not account for overhead and other institutional expenses, such as your department's share of the salaries paid to your president, provost, and dean, for instance, not to mention librarians, support staff outside your department, the registrar, and others. These items of overhead are precisely the factors that certain alternative budgeting systems, such as responsibility-centered budgeting and service-level budgeting (both explained in the previous chapter), seek to track more effectively. Yet even with the simple system outlined here, you will get a good general sense of how expensive your program is to maintain, provided that you calculate rates for other departments in exactly the same way. If you discover that it costs significantly less to produce one student credit hour in your department than it does in other departments at your institution or in similar disciplines at other institutions, you may be able to use this information to argue for your program's efficiency and sustainability. If you find that your costs are much higher, you can be proactive in identifying some of the actions that you can take internally to help reduce those costs. In either case, this type of very basic cost accounting can only be to the benefit of your institution. You might even begin using it to determine the cost-benefit ratio of making certain types of equipment purchases.

—————— o ——————

There is certainly no need for every department chair to become an accountant or master every detail of an institution's fiscal procedure. The more you do understand about budgeting, however, the better you will be able to help your program tie resources to priorities and make its most compelling case for institutional support.

RESOURCES

Drew, G. M. (2006). Balancing academic advancement with business effectiveness? The dual role for senior university leaders. *International Journal of Knowledge, Culture and Change Management, 6,* 117–125.

Geoffrion, A. M., Dyer, J. S., & Feinberg, A. (1972). An interactive approach for multi-criterion optimization, with an application to the operation of an academic department. *Management Science, 19,* 357–388. This work presents a now classic mathematical model for departmental decision making and budget planning.

Groccia, J. E., & Miller, J. E. (2005). *On becoming a productive university: Strategies for reducing costs and increasing quality in higher education.* San Francisco: Jossey-Bass/Anker.

Higgerson, M. L., & McCauliff, B. (2009). Managing tight budgets. *Department Chair, 20*(1), 1–3.

Leaming, D. R. (1998). *Academic leadership: A practical guide to chairing the department.* San Francisco: Jossey-Bass/Anker.

48

FUNDRAISING

THE FINANCING OF HIGHER education is so complex that every department chair should have some familiarity with the basic principles of fundraising. Even if there is already a well-established advancement office at your institution—in fact, particularly if there is a well-established advancement office at your institution—there could well be a time when some highly desirable opportunity for your department can be pursued only through external funding. Perhaps there is a special project (such as a scholarship in your discipline, a distinguished lecture series, a conference, or a new or expanded facility) that would help you advance your program's goals but for which your regular, internal sources of funding are insufficient. It is also possible that someday a donor who has a particular interest in making a contribution to your area will approach you about it. Whatever the situation may be, you will need to know at least the basics of fundraising and understand what your role in this process could be. This chapter offers a general primer of fundraising, outlining a few basics that every department chair needs to know.

The Importance of Careful Preparation

Fundraising projects largely fall into two categories: those that originate at the institution and for which external funding is sought and those that arise out of the interest of a donor who approaches the institution with a desire to make a contribution of some kind. The first of these two types is significantly more common than the second, and in order for these projects to be successfully developed and implemented, they require a great deal of planning, research, and preparation. Even in situations that arise out of a donor's interest, however, and in which the donor may feel a great deal of urgency, it is important for the chair to be certain that proper steps are taken and the appropriate plans are made before the project gets too far along. Failure to prepare properly can leave the institution vulnerable to unanticipated costs at a later date, alienate a once enthusiastic donor, and doom what could have been a highly successful project. Careful preparation for every fundraising gift should always include the following components.

Professional Support from the Institution's Advancement Staff

In any fundraising venture, make use of your institutional advancement staff sooner rather than later. These individuals are more likely than most department chairs to understand immediately both the legal and long-term financial implications of a gift proposal. They are likely to understand options that can simultaneously be of greater benefit to both the donor and the department than an outright gift may be. They are likely to have some sense of the larger picture of the institution's financial plans and thus may be able to use your current project to leverage even greater support for your department in the long run. Members of the advancement staff are your strongest and best allies in the area of fundraising for your department; it is always a mistake to exclude them from your discussions, even at an extremely early stage in your planning.

A Case Statement to Guide Your Project and Elicit Contributions

A case statement is a concise summary of your department's mission, whom it serves, its specific need in terms of the project that you are proposing, and its potential to fulfill its mission more effectively, better serve its constituents, and satisfy your established need through the completion of the current project. A good case statement should not be wordy; a reader should be able to digest it quickly and easily. It should represent a clear plan that will seem important to the reader, inspire that person to become part of the solution to the problem you have outlined, and supply a sufficient amount of evidence that the project you are proposing is both realistic and significant. (On best practices in constructing case statements, see Seiler and Aldrich, 2010.)

*Investigation of Ties Between a Prospective Donor and Your
Department and Institution*

One of the fundamental principles of fundraising is that people give
money to people more than they give money to causes. The cause may
seem to you to be the most important thing, and perhaps it is, but a potential donor is unlikely to invest in that cause unless he or she trusts
your ability to steward resources properly and use them in the most effective way possible. For this reason, the more time you are willing to invest
in cultivating a potential donor, making that person feel an important
part of your program and your future, the more successful your project is
likely to be in the long run. Even if it is the prospective donor who made
the initial contact with you and has proposed the project that is being
considered, you should spend as much time as you can learning about
what is important to that person. Try to identify connections between
the values of the potential donor and the unique mission of your department. Listen to the potential donor's story and, when possible, find connections to your department's story. Remember that you are ultimately
not seeking an isolated gift but, wherever possible, a new advocate for
the goals, values, and aspirations of your program.

The Value of Teamwork

Too often department chairs feel that they ought to make their advancement calls all on their own. Either they do not want to distract the other
members of the department from their critical duties in teaching or scholarship, or (more ominous) they are hoping to take full credit for the
entire project. In many cases, however, chairs may choose to go it alone
simply because they do not understand the valuable contributions others
can make to the success of the proposal. Whatever the motivation, attempting to initiate, develop, and close an entire fundraising proposal
alone is rarely successful and deprives the chair of the expertise that the
following individuals might bring to the project.

Advancement Officer

Advancement officers have a great deal of experience in making contacts
with donors, potential donors, and other supporters of the institution.
They are much more likely than the department chair to have detailed
knowledge about the financial and legal implications of different types of
gifts, the vocabulary that tends to motivate or reassure potential donors,

and the often complicated steps that the institution may require in order for a gift to be accepted, recorded, and acknowledged.

Faculty Member

Faculty members may be able to describe the impact of a gift in a manner that is far more eloquent than anything the chair alone might say. Particularly if the potential donor is a graduate of your institution, a cherished faculty member can help remind the donor of the important role that your department played in his or her life and intensify already close emotional ties to the institution.

Student

Students can help make the impact of a potential gift more immediate. The donor will be able to visualize more readily the sort of person that his or her gift may help. A carefully selected—and rehearsed!—student can speak personally about the importance of your program in the lives of students today, its success in improving students' career opportunities, and the type of needs it has if it is to fulfill its vital mission for the future.

Another Donor

Another donor can help the prospective contributor feel part of a larger and important activity. Potential donors may feel more secure when they encounter other donors who are like them or whose opinion they respect. Current donors help keep the purpose of the fundraising call as "pure" as possible; in other words, they are not the ones who will be benefiting from this new gift. Rather, they have been people who have caused similar benefits in the past. Current donors can also say, "Join me in making this important dream a reality," in ways that can be extraordinarily powerful and much more effective than when the same words are spoken by the chair.

The Effectiveness of the Personal Touch

Potential donors respond more effectively to results than they do to any vague statements you may make about your department's outstanding qualities and past achievements. They want to know whom they will be helping and how. They will be interested in understanding why the constituents of your department will not be served as effectively if the project you are proposing does not include their support. Therefore, prepare a clear summary of all the ways in which the project you are proposing will provide a genuine and demonstrable benefit to people.

Try to identify the type of person who is most likely to be helped by the idea that has been developed. Will all the students at the institution be better off because of the new facility, scholarship, or lecture series that you are trying to create? If so, how? How will this endeavor help your institution attract and retain a larger student body or students who are more likely to succeed at your program? Are there underprivileged students who have not been able to benefit from your department's work because of the high cost of tuition, laboratory expenses, or private instruction? Is there a larger need in society that is likely to be filled through the research that will result from this project? Are there external constituents who could benefit from the type of work conducted in your department if only the Web site, library resource, television program, or lecture series that you are proposing were in place? Make these potential beneficiaries of the proposal as vivid as possible in the mind of the donor by finding areas of commonality between those who would gain from the project and either yourself or, even better, the donor. In this way, you will help make the project's importance seem more tangible to the donor by making its benefits seem as personally significant as possible.

The Significance of Strong Departmental Support

Potential donors are much more likely to contribute to your department if you can say something like, "Our program is so important to our faculty members that every single one of them contributes each year to the annual fund." Even better, imagine the impact of being able to say, "All of my faculty have already contributed seed money to this project. That's how much we all believe in it." The individual contributions of the members of your department need not be huge—it is the contribution rate that will matter more than the total amount you have raised—but it should be as broadly based as possible. In the case of the most recalcitrant members of the department (and make no mistake: these individuals exist everywhere), try to point out to them the importance of even a five- or ten-dollar annual gift that could help produce many times that amount in new contributions.

Even before you approach potential donors with a large request, increasing the participation rate among members of your department can begin paying dividends. You can use any improvement in contribution rate that you can document ("We raised our departmental contribution rate by over 35 percent in only one year") in order to help promote similar higher rates of contribution from alumni, parents, and friends of the department. Then, when you are ready to begin cultivating a potential donor for a larger project, you can approach that individual with an established record of fundraising success and a history of effective use of these increased contributions for the benefit of your department.

The Role of Having the Proper Attitude Toward Fundraising

Too often academics feel that the whole process of fundraising is slightly unsavory; seeking external support smacks of asking for charity or implying that one's program has not been receiving its appropriate level of support from the institution and therefore is not seen as important. The fact of the matter is, however, that contributing to an academic department is a form of making a financial investment, not unlike the other types of financial investments that all of us make every day of our lives. Either we make investments because we believe we are likely to receive a greater return or because there is a particular product, service, or experience that we wish to obtain.

A contributor is actually investing in the quality of your program and its future growth. The return that donors will see on their investment is the satisfaction they will derive from knowing that they have played an important role in helping to solve a problem, serve a new generation of students, or improve the lives of others. What we sometimes forget is the amount of satisfaction that people derive from their own generosity. By requesting a gift to your department, you are helping potential donors focus their natural desire for serving others toward a tangible project from which they can derive pleasure and satisfaction. People, particularly those who have amassed a great deal of wealth, are rarely offended when they are asked—appropriately and with the right amount of planning on your part—for a substantial gift. In fact, if your request is too large, they are more likely to be flattered that you considered them capable of making such a sizable contribution than insulted by the size of the gift you are seeking. The important thing to keep in mind, however, is that any contribution you are requesting should be worth the investment the individual is expected to make. Your request should include a clear plan of how the gift will be used, how the impact of the project will be measured, and how the benefit produced by the project will be made known to others. The only time potential donors are likely to be offended by a gift request is when they feel that you have not thought through your proposal sufficiently and thus are wasting their time, insulting their intelligence, and not respecting the effort they exerted in acquiring their assets to begin with. Only in such a case are you better off never to have made any request at all.

Five Fundraising Mistakes and How to Avoid Them

Chairs who have never before given much thought to advancement activities are frequently concerned about precisely where they should begin and anxious about making mistakes in an area where they have little training and even less confidence. As a result, department chairs are likely to make at least one of five common rookie mistakes when they contact external sources about potential contributions to their programs. By avoiding these five common errors, you'll be far more likely to be successful in closing the deal and far less likely to feel out of your depth when meeting with a prospective donor. Here are the five mistakes all chairs should be certain to avoid when raising funds for their departments.

Not Being a Team Player

Since many department chairs don't know precisely where to begin in the area of fundraising, they just begin. The problem with this approach is that they deprive themselves of the help that their institution's advancement office can provide to them and increase the likelihood of stepping on the toes of someone else's prospect. More than one chair has reported to a dean or president the joy in just having been promised a $500,000 gift from an external source only to be severely reprimanded because it will now be all but impossible for the institution to make the $5 million or $50 million ask that it was planning to make of this same person. Forgetting that your department is only part of a much larger enterprise is one of the most serious mistakes that you can make when seeking external funding.

To avoid this mistake: Never go it alone when planning your department's advancement strategies. As soon as you feel that you have the time to begin pursuing some external support for your department, make your desire to become involved in this area known to your dean and your institution's chief advancement officer. Be sure to state the reasons you are developing this interest. In other words, what specifically are you hoping to accomplish through your activity? If your primary interest is career development, your dean and advancement office may be able to assist you in one way; if you are more concerned about resources for your discipline, they may be able to help you in a different way. If it is a particular facility, piece of equipment, or curricular enhancement that you wish to pursue, they will need to guide you in how this project relates to the institution's other priorities.

If you have a list of possible donors, be sure to share them with your advancement office. Find out which potential donors are already active prospects for other endeavors at the institution. Be prepared to back off from others who are being pursued for other or larger purposes. One other aspect of being a team player is remaining flexible about what sort of funding you are willing to pursue. Gifts that are budget relieving for the institution (they free up for other purposes money already being spent) may be particularly desirable for the school's financial officers. Are there ways in which you can combine a proposal that helps raise funds for a new project that is important to your discipline with an opportunity to redirect some money currently being spent by the institution on salaries, supplies, faculty development, or equipment? Is there a way in which your project could be redesigned so as to bring greater benefit to the college as a whole? Could you enlist the support of and help provide assistance to other disciplines or programs?

Not Doing Your Homework

Individuals with the resources to make substantial contributions to your program tend to have extraordinarily busy schedules and limited amounts of time to discuss your pet projects with you. Even those who are retired or appear to have a great deal of leisure time are frequently committed to other time-consuming projects or charitable endeavors. As a result, potential donors will expect your calls to and visits with them to be fully worth the amount of time that they are spending with you. A vague idea that has not yet been fleshed out, a proposal that contradicts the donor's own interests and values (not all of which may be readily apparent to you or that you might immediately expect), or a proposal that has already been presented to this person, unsuccessfully, in a different form can immediately alienate the individual whom you want to cultivate as a supporter of your program. By not doing your homework and thinking through everything you will need to discuss with the donor, questions they may have, and priorities they may address, you are making a serious, and potentially career-threatening, mistake.

To avoid this mistake: Work closely with your college's advancement office long in advance of the donor visit. What do they know about this particular donor's interests, habits, and dislikes? What proposals, if any, were previously presented to this individual? Of those that were received favorably, what aspects of the proposal did the donor particularly like? Of those proposals that were declined, what aspects of the project did the donor find least attractive? If the prospective donor is a graduate of your institution, contact the alumni office for any information about the donor's interests, level of activity at college functions since graduation, and anything else useful that may be in the files. (Alumni offices frequently survey their constituents and maintain records on their activities since graduation. This information, which is of great benefit to the alumni office in planning its events, can also guide you in how best to explain a project to an alumni donor.) If an alumnus or alumna had a particular professor who was a favorite or who served that person as a mentor, perhaps this person will be willing to serve as liaison to the potential donor. If that professor is already deceased or has left the area, perhaps the potential gift can be constructed as a memorial or honor to this individual. Most important, however, never request funding for a project unless you can outline, with a great deal of specificity, how that project will function, when it will begin, what benefits will accrue, and how decisions will be made along the way. Many individuals with a high net worth attained their wealth by paying attention to details of this sort. If you embark on your proposal unable to answer the numerous operational questions that the donor is likely to ask, you are almost certainly not going to be successful in your request. Even worse, you may leave the impression that individuals at your institution don't know what they're doing.

Not Considering All Options

Thinking through all of the details is not precisely the same as developing a proposal so inflexible, narrow, or restrictive that it can function in only one way. Interesting potential donors in departmental projects should never be a take-it-or-leave-it proposition. Nevertheless, it is not at all uncommon for a department chair to be so focused on one highly desirable scenario for an anticipated new program, building, or improvement to facilities that any deviation from that plan seems to betray the project's original purpose. This approach is bound to be counterproductive since prospective donors will almost certainly have their own points of view about how they want their contribution to be used and how your proposal would best be implemented. For instance, several donors may be approached about a new graduate program but be interested only in enhancements to undergraduate education. You may go to them wanting to talk about a new facility, but discover that they have a strong senti-mental attachment to the current facility and strongly resist any plans to replace it. Adhering too strongly to one way in which the goal might be accomplished can turn a likely contribution into a failed opportunity. Even worse, it could sour the potential donor on the institution as a whole, transforming a small but consistent contributor to the annual fund into someone who no longer makes any contribution whatsoever.

To avoid this mistake: Work out multiple game plans with your ad-vancement office as part of your preparation for the visit. Consider possi-ble responses to the proposal that you are making and how you should best address each response. Realize that very rarely are requests granted in the full amount and exactly in the way that the original proposal is made. As a result, be sure to develop clear strategies for various options. How would the proposal develop if the contribution were stretched over a far longer period than you had anticipated? Are there other ways of achieving your goal besides the method you are proposing? What would be the implication if the contribution were given to you in the form of a trust or a challenge grant? It is far better to be able to say, "We've thought of that, and while that could be one avenue toward accomplish-ing our goal, here are the drawbacks that we foresee if we proceed that way . . . ," than, "I never thought of that. I *guess* we could give it a try." Whenever possible, approach the potential donor with a solid and detailed primary proposal in mind, but with several other equally well worked out scenarios just in case the conversation goes in a direction that you do not expect. It often will.

Not Listening Carefully

As advocates for our individual areas, we are sometimes so fixated on our own needs and programs that we fail to listen to the verbal cues that a potential donor is providing to us. We may approach a prospect who graduated with a degree in science from our institution, had a distin-guished career in medicine, and supported a number of smaller science projects before, thinking that the person is a logical candidate to fund a new lab or underwrite a new science center at our institutions. But we may not realize that all the donor wishes to speak about is a spouse's interest in the arts or a new-found commitment to ethical issues. Failure to comprehend that this individual's priorities have changed can lead to a situation where we seem to the potential donor to be bringing the subject back repeatedly to a topic that has already been dealt with and set aside. Not listening carefully enough to a donor can also mean missing the key phrases or issues that motivate this individual. We may be so pre-occupied with the importance of, for example, establishing a speaker series that brings scholars of international prominence to our campuses that we do not hear the potential donor's emphasis on the length of the student's exposure to a scholar over such issues of name recognition or prominence.

To avoid this mistake: Remember that you are meeting with the prospective donor to learn a great deal about his or her interests and help this person accomplish something that would lead to his or her personal satisfaction. Your task is not simply to sell a preconceived product that the potential donor will have no role in shaping and no pride in making succeed. Keep alert to issues that the donor keeps returning to, and make a mental note of what aspects of your discussion he or she tends not to mention, describes rather differently from how you have presented them, or simply seems not to respond to with any enthusiasm. Repeat several of the individual's key phrases and priorities in order to make sure that you understand them, and write them down. If you notice, for example, that the potential donor keeps bringing the subject back to the life-changing nature of the courses that he or she took in an area completely different from your own, this may be a signal that the person's interests have changed and may be more responsive to a proposal advanced by a different discipline. Listen carefully. Try to understand as much as possible of the prospect's concern. Then talk privately and candidly afterward with your advancement office about possibly putting the chair of a more appropriate department in touch with the candidate. Handing off a prospective donor in this way may help you build good relationships with your colleagues elsewhere in the institution, reward you when they know of prospective donors interested in your area, and prevent your institution from alienating an important contact who has developed new interests and areas of philanthropic concern.

Not Following Through

At times when an institution is so excited about receiving a major gift and so focused on the important new activity, building, or scholarship resulting from it that it tends to forget the person who made it all possible: the donor. After having been the center of attention while the institution was trying to obtain the gift, donors sometimes feel forgotten once the contribution has been made. They learn about new developments at the institution only from the newspaper. They fail to receive invitations to important campus events associated with their contribution. And sometimes they become annoyed because after weeks or months of frequent contact, the phone calls and visits simply stop. Not following through adequately after a gift has been made can turn a friend of your institution into one of its most bitter opponents. It can also cost you other fundraising prospects in the future.

To avoid this mistake: Keep in mind that the stewardship of a gift is at least as important as obtaining the gift itself (see Buller, 2008). On a practical level, excellent stewardship of gifts leads to further gifts from either the original donors or their friends and associates. On a moral level, failure to follow through after a gift is made reinforces the worst possible stereotype of the fundraiser as someone who will say anything for the sake of a contribution and then use the gift for whatever the institution wants, even if it has no relationship to the proposal initially made.

As a department chair, you are in a perfect position to steward a gift in the best possible manner. You almost certainly have fewer major contributors to track than do any one of the major gift officers in the advancement office; you can thus work much more personally with a donor—with a visit or an extended phone call—than can many of the professional fundraisers. You have the information at your fingertips to tell the donor what he or she really wants to know: the lasting impact of the gift on the lives of the students and faculty members of your department. It should be your role, every time an activity occurs on campus that is in any way connected to this gift, to be sure that the donor is contacted, informed well in advance of what will occur, and invited to participate in an appropriate way. As a department chair, you are used to being an advocate for your disciple. Part of this advocacy must now include remembering the needs of your donors as well.

Glossary of Fundraising Terms

There are a few terms with specific or technical meaning in fundraising that every department chair ought to know since they are likely to arise in discussions of various kinds of gifts and during donor calls:

> *Bequest*—a legacy or gift of personal property that comes to the institution through the terms of someone's will.
>
> *Book a gift*—the official recording of a gift's receipt and incorporation into the institution's resources. Institutions have very specific accounting rules regarding when a gift may officially be booked (such as, "gifts must never be booked before a formal agreement has been signed by both the donor and institution") and

the way in which the value of the gift must be calculated. The determination of a gift's value will be subject to restrictions set forth by the U.S. Internal Revenue Code and by appropriate accounting standards. (On the boards responsible for these standards, see Chapter Forty-Seven.)

Endowment—the transfer of money or property to an institution for a particular purpose. In most cases, the endowment of a college or university is a corpus of funds, the interest of which (or, in most cases, some portion of that interest, often 4 to 6 percent or the total amount invested) may be used for operating the institution while the principal remains intact.

Gift agreement—a document that sets forth the terms under which a gift is offered by the donor and accepted by the institution. Gift agreements usually specify the donor's charitable intent, what would happen to the gift if the original purpose is no longer to be appropriate for the institution at some point in the future (or, in the worst case, if either the department or institution ceases to exist), who will be responsible for making certain decisions about the gift, and any other operating procedures that may be necessary for the successful completion of the project that has been proposed.

Gift-in-kind—a gift made in some other form than cash. Tangible gifts-in-kind may consist of property or services. Intangible gifts-in-kind may consist of rights (such as patents or copyrights) that have the potential of providing value at some future time.

Lead trust (also referred to as *charitable lead trust*)—a trust in which the income (or some specified portion of the income) created by the corpus is donated for charitable purposes but at some particular time in the future (such as the death of the donor), the corpus reverts to the donor's beneficiaries. Lead trusts are frequently attractive to individuals who want to reduce their tax liability for a set period. They have an added advantage in that the federal government taxes only what they project the likely value of the principal will be at the end of the trust period. If, as is often the case, the value of the principal increases beyond what the Internal Revenue Service has calculated, that additional increase can pass to heirs free of transfer taxes.

Remainder trust (also referred to as *charitable remainder trust*)—in many ways the opposite of a lead trust. A remainder trust occurs when the income of a trust is distributed to beneficiaries until some particular time in the future, after which the trust is donated to the specified charity. Remainder trusts are frequently attractive to donors who wish to reduce the amount of tax that will need to be paid from their estate or wish to provide a guaranteed income to a beneficiary, while also achieving a second charitable goal at a later date.

Trust—a right of property that an individual or institution holds on behalf of (and for the benefit of) another.

For a more extensive glossary of fundraising terms, see Tempel, Seiler, Aldrich, and Rosso (2011).

_____ o _____

Like so many other aspects of departmental administration, fundraising is a skill that gets easier the more that it is practiced. Very few academic administrators come to their profession with formal academic training in philanthropy. As a result, fundraising is something that most of us learn on the job. If you have not yet had any significant exposure to fundraising, contact your advancement office and ask if it offers any formal training to those who want to do more for the institution. Offer to tag along with a more experienced fundraiser on a call to a prospective donor in order to see how it is done. Ask the alumni office for the names of graduates who may have expressed an interest in remaining involved with your area; check with the advancement office to make sure that these individuals are not already being cultivated elsewhere at your institution and, if not, make some phone calls and talk with them about how they may be able to assist your department in a way that they will find personally satisfying. Understand that many people will volunteer their time before they consider contributing their money. Start out small, and avoid the five common mistakes outlined in this chapter, and you will already be on your way to successful fundraising both for your institution and for your department.

REFERENCES

Buller, J. L. (2008, Spring). Stewardship in fundraising. *Department Chair, 18*(4), 1–3.

Seiler, T. L., & Aldrich, E. E. (2010). The case for support. In A. Sargeant & J. Shang, *Fundraising principles and practice*. San Francisco: Jossey-Bass.

Tempel, E. R., Seiler, T. L., Aldrich, E. E., & Rosso, H. A. (2011). *Achieving excellence in fundraising*. San Francisco: Jossey-Bass.

RESOURCES

Buchanan, P.M.E. (2000). *Handbook of institutional advancement* (3rd ed.). Washington, DC: CASE.

Buller, J. L. (2011, Winter). Fundraising 201: What to do after you've learned the basics. *Department Chair, 21*(3), 6–9.

Elliott, D. (1995). *The ethics of asking: Dilemmas in higher education fund raising.* Baltimore: Johns Hopkins University Press.

Hopkins, K. B., Friedman, C. S., & Friedman, C. S. (1997). *Successful fundraising for arts and cultural organizations.* Westport, CT: Oryx Press.

Panas, J. (2007). *Asking: A 59-minute guide to everything board members, volunteers, and staff must know to secure the gift.* Medfield, MA: Emerson & Church.

Rhodes, F.H.T. (1997). *Successful fund raising for higher education: The advancement of learning.* Westport, CT: Oryx Press.

Tromble, W. W. (1998). *Excellence in advancement: Applications for higher education and nonprofit organizations.* Gaithersburg, MD: Aspen.

Worth, M.J.E. (1993). *Educational fund raising: Principles and practice.* Westport, CT: ACE/Oryx Press.

Worth, M.J.E. (2002). *New strategies for educational fund raising.* Westport, CT: Oryx.

49

ACCOUNTING FOR
SPONSORED RESEARCH

THE TERM *SPONSORED RESEARCH* refers to all scholarly and creative activities that make use of institutional resources but are funded by outside agencies. While most people may tend to think of sponsored research as the sort of scientific experiments that are conducted in laboratories or the type of social science investigation that is conducted by means of surveys and the analysis of data, sponsored research can include many other activities typically pursued at a college or university. For example, creative activities—such as a sculpture commissioned by a local business or the script of a play underwritten by a local historical society—could, in certain institutional environments, fall within the category of sponsored research. For the purposes of this chapter, however, we'll focus primarily on activities that meet at least one of the following criteria:

○ They involve proposals in which the institution's office or division of research, sponsored research, or external programs would ordinarily take a special interest.

○ They deal with grants or contracts that produce indirect costs (sometimes known as facility and administrative costs), which consist of overhead and administrative fees imposed by the institution for the use of its resources.

○ They result in the accumulation of property, including intellectual property, about which rights of ownership must be defined in advance of the project.

In fact, most types of sponsored research conducted at a college or university meet all of these criteria simultaneously. Sponsored research thus differs from fundraising, institutional advancement, or development in that for these activities, contributions are made without the expectation that ownership of a specific product (whether tangible or intellectual) will be retained by the donor once the project is completed. While the office of institutional advancement may charge the unit receiving the donation a gift fee, these charges are usually far lower than the indirect costs associated with sponsored research and tend to be applied to the overhead of the advancement operation itself rather than that of the institution as a whole.

Sponsored research typically occurs in two forms: grants and contracts. The two forms have a great deal in common with one another, and it's not uncommon for people in higher education to use the two terms interchangeably. Both grants and contracts may be of any size or duration, and both may involve relationships of a specific term between the institution and a corporation, organization, foundation, individual, or other entity. The distinction largely involves the end product that is sought. Grants are given for research or scholarly projects with the expectation that reasonable and serious effort will be made to pursue a specified result. Contracts are made for projects in which the institution commits itself to attain a specific result. So if an institution receives a grant to investigate possible cures for a particular disease, makes a reasonable and serious effort to investigate the causes of and treatments for that disease, but is unable to find a cure by the end of the grant, it has still met its full obligation to the granting agency. But if an institution enters into a contract to conduct a survey of potential voters in order to determine which candidate is most likely to win an upcoming election, makes a reasonable and serious effort, but is unable to analyze the data sufficiently to identify a likely winner of the election, it has violated the terms of its contract. It has bound itself contractually to provide a product that it ended up not providing, and so hasn't met its full obligation to the funding agency. (Of course, no contract would ever be written or enforceable if the promise was to predict the actual winner of an election; the most that institutions can do is to determine likely winners. It was that obligation that went unmet in the example.)

The Research Strategy

Regardless of whether grants or contracts are involved, many departments discover that they are more successful in obtaining external funding for scholarly projects if they adopt a formal research strategy. The concept of a research strategy is a bit like a strategic plan that is focused on research, particularly the type of research that is likely to attract outside sponsorship. Perhaps one of the best definitions of a departmental statement of research may be found on the Web site of the Department of Communication Technology at Denmark's Aalborg University (2003):

> A strategy is a guiding vision of the future, flexible and adaptive to the changes in the environment. It is not an action plan telling us what to do tomorrow, more a rough outline telling the outside world what we are interested and competent in, and also an internal guide for decision making, when choices have to be made. Especially in a research environment it is important to keep the strategy open ended. The strategy is of course also dependent on the environment, influenced by trends in the research community and by the needs of the industrial community. By negation it also tells what we are not interested in. A common strategy can help give a sense of working together for a general purpose, although the "lone wolf" is also an acceptable actor on the scene.

In light of this definition, it's important for chairs to keep in mind that effective departmental research strategies are simultaneously

- Visionary but flexible
- Focused on areas of expertise shared by several faculty members but not designed so that they exclude support of individual faculty members
- Written primarily for an external audience
- Responsive to international research trends

Based on these principles, Aalborg's Department of Communication Technology developed a research strategy that can be expressed in three words when appropriate ("the wireless world"), although the department's Web site also provides an 881-word elaboration of that theme, further defining its focus and interests to potential research sponsors.

Some chairs may find that a single research strategy like "the wireless world" does not adequately embrace the diversity of scholarly expertise in their disciplines. In this case, a statement of research strategy that identifies a small, related cluster of interests or addresses a more comprehensive research philosophy may be the most useful approach. For example, the Department of History at Sheffield University (2009) has adopted a statement of research strategy that deals with how the scholarly interests of individual faculty members will be reviewed periodically in order to maintain a record of achievement for the discipline that helps preserve the institution's reputation at the academic forefront:

The Department's research strengths lie in the research energies and commitments of all its research practitioners, especially its individual full-time academic members of staff. Each member of staff has a clearly identified research agenda over the medium term (c. five years). The individual research strategy covers the following aspects: a statement of expected research engagements, an identification of anticipated research applications, clarifying the objectives and benefits for periods of research leave, a notification of particular research resource needs, a review of disciplinary and interdisciplinary research activity in the university and in the wider research community. This will be reviewed each year in a meeting with the Department Research Committee chair or Head of Department. These research review discussions provide the basis for the statements of Departmental research strategy in its presentations to the Faculty and University.

A practical way for chairs to begin the development of a disciplinary statement of research strategy is to encourage members of the discipline to select one of these three major approaches—single area of focus, small cluster of related areas of focus, or fundamental research philosophy—and draft a statement, intended for external constituents, that clarifies what scholarship in the discipline means and why it should matter to the broader community.

Preaward Concerns

In the period before the application for a grant or contract is submitted to the funding agency, departments should be in close contact with their institution's division of research, office of sponsored programs, or whichever other unit is responsible for the administration of external funding. One reason is that certain foundations and agencies have limits to the number of proposals an institution may submit during any given cycle. A centralized office at the institution should be aware of who else intends to prepare a proposal for that program and may recommend staggering the institution's submissions to take advantage of multiple cycles, combining proposals to create a stronger overall application, or conducting an internal competition to ensure that the institution includes its best current proposals in the next available cycle. Another reason is that research offices frequently have grant writers or facilitators on their staff who are familiar with the sometimes arcane requirements of different granting agencies, the necessary steps for constructing an acceptable budget, and best practices in aligning the goals of the researcher with the interests of the funding agency. In addition, certain grants and contracts, particularly those involving the government, have strict legal requirements that must be met, and staff members from a research office can provide advice on how proposals can be constructed to meet those requirements.

During the preaward period, the person who will be in charge of the grant or contract once it is funded—the principal investigator (PI)—along with the department chair, dean, and appropriate representatives of the university, need to come to terms with what commitment to the project the college or university is willing to make:

- If the institution is to be responsible for matching funds, what form will that funding take, and what will be its source? For instance, although most people tend to think of the institutional match or cost sharing in terms of actual dollars, it may also be possible for the institution to provide a certain value of goods or services as a way of meeting any requirement for an institutional match.

- If the grant or contract will require the PI to be released from other duties to the institution, how will those duties be covered? Does the grant or contract allow for a buyout of the PI's time, or is the institution expected to provide that contribution as part of its participation in the project? From the perspective of the chair and dean, this question usually takes the form of, "How will I be able to cover the classes I would ordinarily be assigning this faculty member?"

- Are there any compliance issues that need to be addressed before this proposal can be submitted? For instance, has the project been appropriately evaluated by the Institutional Review Board if the project involves human subjects or the Institutional Animal Care and Use Committee if it involves animal subjects? If hazardous materials will be used, have the proper steps been followed to ensure their safe use, storage, and disposal?

- What agreements are in place governing any intellectual property or profit resulting from the grant or contract? If patent rights are involved, who will hold them? Who will hold the right to publish the findings of the research or other project?

- What steps need to be followed to make sure that there are no conflicts of interest? For instance, if vendors must be selected for purchase of equipment or supplies, what assurances can be given the funding agency that no one involved with the project will profit from these exchanges?

○ If the same project is being proposed to several funding sources, when will notification occur about the proposal's success? If word comes from one source that the project has been approved, how will other potential sources be notified and the proposal withdrawn?

One of the most important roles that a chair can play in the pre-award phase of a grant or contract is to insist that the proposal be drafted well in advance of the deadlines. Many funding agencies have program directors who, while they can't directly help authors with the drafting of their proposals, can provide useful advice on the types of projects that have recently been funded and areas of emphasis that may make an application stronger. The institutional office of research also will need lead time to review the budget, polish the proposal, and provide other kinds of assistance that will not be possible if a proposal reaches them on the day it's due at the funding agency. Finally, any impact a chair might have in promoting institutional policies that reward a faculty member simply for the submission of a properly constructed proposal (itself a time-consuming and highly educational process) will make a major contribution toward creating a culture in which more proposals, and ultimately more successful ones, are developed at the college or university.

Postaward Concerns

Just as in departmental budgeting, the focus of a chair shifts significantly when the process changes from planning to implementation, so in sponsored research is the postaward role of the chair rather different from that played during the preaward process. Once a grant or contract has been made, the chair has a responsibility to ensure that the institution properly administers the funding it receives, meets all of the obligations it has agreed to, and follows scrupulously both its internal procedures and any relevant policies that apply from the funding agency. Failure to achieve any of these goals not only jeopardizes the current project but puts at risk the institution's ability to secure additional grants and contracts in the future. Among the issues that the chair needs to consider are these:

○ Is the PI appropriately supervising the day-to-day activities of the grant so that obligations are being met in a timely manner and expenditures are charged appropriately? Since it will be necessary in an audit to verify that all fees, subcontracting charges, and other expenses are genuine and not in violation of the conflict-of-interest policy, it is beneficial (and often required) that expenses be reviewed by someone other than the PI. If you don't have a budget director in the department or a suitable staff member in the research office, who has the technical knowledge to fill this function?

○ If progress reports are periodically due to the funding source, what provisions have been made to ensure their accuracy and completion? If the institution committed itself to cost sharing or providing matching funds through contributions of goods or services, are these responsibilities being met and duly reported to the funding source?

○ Since travel expenses must often meet both institutional policies and the terms of the agreement with the funding source, what will be the procedure to meet this dual set of requirements? Faculty members, particularly those who have not worked extensively with sponsored research before, may feel that as long as their travel expenses are acceptable to the granting agency, they don't need any other approval. But certain types of travel (such as research trips abroad, travel involving undergraduate students, or periods in which teaching duties cannot be met) require advance approval, frequently at high administrative levels. There is often a difficult learning process before the full complexities of reimbursement by external sources are understood, and department chairs can provide valuable assistance in this process.

○ When equipment is purchased on the grant or contract, how does the institutional property management policy affect these items? Must the equipment be tagged or bar-coded, as it would if it were purchased through institutional funds, or do some other procedures apply?

○ If hiring occurs as a result of the grant, what legal and institutional requirements must be met? Many institutions require that all personnel, even those hired through grants and contract, be hired through a centralized office of human resources and receive orientation training. In addition, special categories of employees— foreign residents on a visa, people who will be working in a school or with minors, temporary employees with access to hazardous materials—may well fall under requirements imposed by federal, state, or local laws. The chair can assist the PI in addressing those obligations.

In addition, although it isn't really a requirement, it can be extremely useful to convey word of the new grant or contract to any funding sources that earlier provided seed money, planning grants, or preliminary studies that made this new research possible. These agencies and individuals are always glad to hear that their initial investment is paying lasting dividends, and good communication may increase the likelihood that they'll provide additional funding to your area in the future.

o

Many colleges and universities provide training programs on such topics as identifying funding sources, grant writing, contract management, and the specific requirements of individual funding agencies. Both online and in-class training programs exist in a variety of formats. A few good examples of what is possible in a well-designed training program may be seen at Princeton University (n.d.), University of North Carolina (2011), and University of Florida (n.d.). In addition, an excellent summary of preaward and postaward expectations, which provided a great deal of structure and content for this chapter, may be found at Florida Atlantic University (n.d.).

REFERENCES

Aalborg University. (2003). *Research strategy for Department of Communication Technology*. Retrieved from http://kom.aau.dk/ADM/research/strategy.htm

Florida Atlantic University. (n.d.). *Grant management: Responsibilities of principal investigators*. Retrieved from http://www.fau.edu/research/osr/files/PI-Responsibilities.pdf

Princeton University. (n.d.). *Sponsored research training for department administrators*. Retrieved from http://www.princeton.edu/orpa/da_training/01_01.html

Sheffield University. (2009). *Department of History, research and innovation strategy 2009–2013*. Retrieved from http://www.shef.ac.uk/content/1/c6/02/47/55/Research%20Strategy%20-%202009.pdf

University of Florida. (n.d.). *Office of Research*. Retrieved from http://apps.research.ufl.edu/research/training/

University of North Carolina at Chapel Hill. (2011). *Office of Sponsored Research*. Retrieved from http://research.unc.edu/offices/sponsored-research/training/DATA_RES_OSR_TRAININGARCHIVES#PastTraining

RESOURCES

Bauer, D. G. (2007). *The "how to" grants manual: Successful grantseeking techniques for obtaining public and private grants.* Westport, CT: Praeger.

Donaldson, C. (1991, December 7). Developing a successful sponsored research program at a "teaching" college. *SRA: Journal of the Society of Research Administrators, 23*(2), 35–40.

Mishler, J. M. (1988, December 1). Enhancing the prospects for acquisition of sponsored funds at small to mid-level colleges and universities: A guide for program development. *Research Management Review, 2*(2), 17–31.

50

A SCENARIO ANALYSIS
ON STRATEGIC BUDGETING
AND PLANNING

FOR A DISCUSSION OF how scenario analyses are structured and suggestions on how to use this exercise most productively, see Chapter Nine.

Case Studies

Past Practice Versus the Strategic Plan

You chair the Department of Aeronautics and Aerobics, a department that contains two largely independent subdisciplines. Each departmental subdivision, Aeronautics and Aerobics, includes roughly the same number of faculty members, majors, and student credit hour production. Neither area has been particularly active in securing external funding, and as a result, both areas depend almost exclusively on the annual budget assigned by your central administration.

Before your arrival as chair, Aeronautics and Aerobics were once independent departments, with the Aerobics program funded at a significantly higher level than the Aeronautics program. After reviewing the budget, you have come to believe that as a result of these historical factors, Aerobics has long been overfunded while Aeronautics has been underfunded. Your attempts to provide greater equity in funding have met with resistance from faculty members in Aerobics, who have come to expect high levels of institutional support for travel and equipment. Recently, however, your institution's new strategic plan has declared that Aerobics will be a major focal point for the university, while you can find no direct and obvious tie of Aeronautics to the strategic plan. The budget looks good this year, and your dean tells you that for the first time in recent memory, your non–personal services budget will be increased. You may even receive one or two new faculty lines.

Based on all of these competing considerations, what do you do?

The Midyear Budget Cut

You chair an academic department at a university that's part of a state system. It's now February, and the system chancellor has announced an unexpected round of midyear budget cuts. At your institution, these budget cuts are being implemented as a freeze on all hiring and new equipment purchases. All of these restrictions are frustrating, of course, but your real problem is that departmental supply and travel budgets are also being reduced from your original allocation. In the past, you have been able to fund the first thousand dollars of a faculty member's travel; occasionally you were able to help even more by transferring supply money to travel. Because of the reduction and freeze, these transfers are now no longer possible. At a faculty meeting, you announce that from now until the end of the year, you cannot fund any more than the first five hundred dollars of any faculty member's travel. You apologize for taking this action because you've already promised some faculty members a larger amount, and they've committed to their trips. But due to the budget freeze and reduction, you say you have no alternative.

There's an immediate outcry. Faculty members whose major conferences are still to come claim that your announcement is unfair since it's not their fault that they didn't travel before the cuts were announced. Faculty members who already have traveled, however, say that the travel money they received has already been spent and that there is no alternative to your plan.

What do you do?

Transfers in a Tight Budget

The fiscal year has just begun, and you, as department chair, are meeting with your dean to discuss priorities for the coming year. Your dean has asked you whether you might want to transfer funds among your existing accounts in order to meet your department's needs more efficiently. You know that any one of your non–personal services accounts could use help, but you're not sure where to get it. For instance, you could transfer funds out of your equipment account and hope to buy new equipment with funding that may become available at the end of the year when the budget is closed out. But relying on year-end funding is rather risky, and you are badly in need of several major equipment upgrades. You could transfer funds out of your travel account, but you have a large number of younger faculty members who desperately need to travel for professional development. You could transfer money out of your supplies account, but you barely made it through last year because of the high cost of toner, paper, and other routine expenses.

How might you proceed?

Just Haggling over the Price

Your department works with a long-term donor whose generosity has made possible many scholarships in your department as well as a much-appreciated supplement to your faculty development fund. Many students are majoring in your discipline who could not do so if it weren't for the scholarship opportunities. Many of your area's most successful research projects would have to be discontinued if the donor were to cease these generous contributions. You have often thought that the funding received from this donor has kept your department going when others at the institution have been pressing for it to be phased out.

The good news is that this donor wants to make a major new contribution to your area. The bad news is that the funding is restricted to support of a new academic emphasis in your area, and all of your faculty members (yourself included) believe the area that the donor wants to fund is unnecessary and unrelated to your department's mission. The consensus among the faculty is, in fact, that the area the donor wishes to fund is really just a pseudoscience, and you will have a difficult time justifying it to your peers outside your institution.

You've had a number of meetings with the donor and representatives from your institution's advancement office. You've talked about more pressing needs in your area. You've diplomatically tried to dissuade the donor from restricting the funds so narrowly. You've provided data indicating that a much greater impact could be made if the donor targeted the funds toward a different goal of your department. Nothing seems to have dissuaded the donor from the original plan. In fact, despite your best efforts at tact and negotiation, you can sense that the donor is becoming increasingly frustrated.

"Look," the donor finally says, "it's very simple: either you want my money or you don't. Add the emphasis that I want, and then staffing, equipment, whatever it takes . . . I'll cover it. And I'll increase my contribution to your scholarships and research fund. Heck, I'll even take care of some of those other needs you told me are so critical to you. But if you don't take on this project exactly as I've outlined it, I'll pull everything: no more scholarships, no more faculty development funding, nothing. Now, take it or leave it."

As you are pondering this unpalatable choice, you are reminded of the old story (probably an urban legend) about Winston Churchill offering one million pounds sterling if a woman would sleep with him. When she agreed, he lowered his offer to five pounds sterling. The woman became indignant and asked, "What do you think I am?" Churchill's answer, so the story goes, was, "We've already established what you are, madam. Now we're just haggling over the price."

Your repeated attempts to satisfy the concerns of the donor make you feel as though that particular constituent has already established what *you* are, and now you, too, are just haggling over the price.

How do you reply?

Considerations

1. Answer the following questions as you reflect on "Past Practice Versus the Strategic Plan":

   a. Do you tell the dean that based on the priorities set by the strategic plan, you want to apply these increases to Aerobics even though you personally believe that the greater needs are in Aeronautics?

   b. At what point do you involve faculty members in the decision-making process? Do you inform them only when a decision is made, or do you include wider representation in your budgetary planning?

   c. If you accept additional funding for Aerobics, how do you justify what appears to be a sudden shift in your funding priorities?

   d. If you prefer to argue for additional funding for Aeronautics, how do you justify this in light of institutional strategic priorities?

2. Consider the following questions in connection with "The Midyear Budget Cut":

   a. Is there anything you might have done earlier in the budgeting process to make this unfortunate situation any fairer?

b. If you stick to your original plan for allocating funds and imposing the required cuts, how do you justify your decision to the angry faculty members in a way that they will best accept?

c. If you modify your original plan, how do you do so in a manner that is most equitable to all concerned and best preserves faculty morale?

3. With regard to the "Transfers in a Tight Budget," consider these questions:

a. What additional information do you need in order to clarify your priorities?

b. Since you seem to be stretched thin in every category, can you think of a reason that you might still want to transfer funding and thus strain one of your accounts even further?

c. How do you go about getting your faculty members to be more proactive in controlling costs and thus making better use of the budget that you have?

d. Does it ever make sense to defer equipment purchases or faculty travel from one year to the next?

e. What strategies can you suggest for not "just making it through the year" but for making your department stronger for the future?

4. In "Just Haggling over the Price," would your response be any different if the project that the donor wished to fund

a. Involved an area of your discipline that, while certainly regarded as quirky by most members of your profession, was nevertheless represented by several panels each year at your national conference?

b. Was so far beyond the limits of acceptability in your discipline that it would probably make your department a laughingstock?

c. Was in an area that may well be ridiculed in the short term but is likely to be vindicated as farsighted in a decade?

d. Involved creationism (or, depending on the nature of your institution, a scientific approach limited solely to a secular model of evolution)?

e. Was associated with a view of the world that was widely, though perhaps unjustly, regarded as racist?

Suggestions

Past Practice Versus the Strategic Plan

In this case, the subdiscipline of Aerobics has been advantaged by two factors: the historically greater funding it had received when it existed as an independent department and the emphasis placed on it in the institution's strategic plan. At the same time, the subdiscipline of Aeronautics has, from one perspective at least, outproduced Aerobics by serving the same number of majors and generating the same number of student credit hours with less funding.

In order for you to make a well-informed decision about what to propose to the dean, begin by gathering some information. For instance, is Aerobics given priority in the strategic plan because it is demonstrably more central to your institution's overall mission and measurably higher in quality that the Aeronautics program? Your program review procedure can give you insights into both of these considerations. (See Chapter Forty-Two.) Or might the higher funding received by the Aerobics program have made it more visible as a likely pillar of excellence when the strategic plan was being developed? If the former is true and you can demonstrate the greater centrality of Aerobics to mission and higher quality than the Aeronautics program, you may be well advised to use this opportunity to continue investing in an area that is so clearly important to your institution's future. But if your review of the data indicates that Aerobics' prominence is largely the result of historical factors, a better strategy might be to present these findings to the dean and use the opportunity to address the equity issues you've identified.

In either case, you'll need good, solid information in order to justify your decision in the face of the resistance you'll inevitably receive from at least some faculty members in your department (and possibly from your dean as well).

The Midyear Budget Cut

This case illustrates the dilemma that chairs can face in trying to develop consistent plans during inconsistent budgetary environments. Even if you try to do your best budgetary stewardship by having faculty members submit all of their research and travel needs before any amount is allocated, that process can still suddenly unravel when midyear reductions, or givebacks, arise. One strategy in the current situation is to work out an acceptable compromise with your faculty (or with faculty representatives if your department is extremely large) that takes the new fiscal reality into account. This approach has the advantage of providing the faculty with some excellent hands-on training in academic leadership at the same time that it may result in a solution with which they have greater buy-in since they helped to develop it.

If the department is too fragmented or politicized to make this type of consensus approach possible, an alternative strategy—although it would have been better to begin in this way than to announce a finalized plan, as occurred in the case study—is to develop two or three genuine alternatives for meeting the reduction goal, share them with the faculty, and proceed with the plan that receives the majority vote. If you decide to adopt this second alternative, it's probably advisable to identify as clearly as you can the pros and cons of each approach in order to present all the possibilities in a fair and objective manner. Remember to examine all unexpended funds in the budget to see whether you have any flexibility to offset the limitations that have been imposed on you. While salary savings pools or excess maintenance funds can't address the challenges you're facing with the hiring freeze—as discussed in connection with the difference between one-year expenditures and continuous expenditures in Chapter Forty-Six—it may be possible to offset some of your reductions in supply and travel funding with these sources.

Transfers in a Tight Budget

This case provides a useful exercise in decision making. Various paths are possible, depending on circumstances that are not specifically outlined in the scenario. Yet as you make your decision, it may be helpful to keep the following principles in mind.

It's not necessarily wise to take advantage of an opportunity to pursue a course of action simply because you have that opportunity. In other words, the dean has given you a chance this year to implement a number of transfers among accounts. But you may well decide that since the budget is so tight and so many of your needs are already underfunded, it is not the right moment to pursue this course of action. You may be better off spending your time considering how you could enhance your area's revenue rather than building a false cushion in one area by unnecessarily depleting another.

Certain decisions must be based on your personal tolerance for risk. For instance, the case study says that "year-end funding is rather risky," but not all risks are alike. In your own situation, it may even be the case that although year-end funding can never be guaranteed, it tends to be available in nine out of every ten years, in which case the overall risk will be extremely small.

All budgetary decisions, even temporary ones, must occur within the context of the strategic plan. Thus, under "Considerations" you're asked, "Does it ever make sense to defer equipment purchases or faculty travel from one year to the next?" One of the times in which such a decision would make sense is when one or the other is centrally connected to your department's mission and highest strategic goals. If you place a strong emphasis on teaching, what is the equipment for? Is it pedagogical in nature or related to research needs that affect teaching only indirectly? If research is your primary focus, what is the faculty travel for? Is it for presentation of scholarly results and examination of documents unavailable elsewhere, or is it primarily intended for student recruitment and trips related to course work?

Just Haggling over the Price

Your decision in this case is likely to depend entirely on just how unacceptable the proposed emphasis is to members of your discipline. In light of the donor's offer to fund the entire program, increase current areas of support, and even address some of your other unmet needs, it would probably be extremely shortsighted to turn down an offer simply because the new program didn't fit your department's anticipated trajectory or was considered slightly idiosyncratic in your field. After all, it's not unheard of in academia for today's slightly unusual program to become tomorrow's cutting-edge leader. But if it's truly the case that what the donor proposes could subject your department to ridicule or scorn, then no amount of funding can counterbalance that cost. The likely impact a gift of the latter sort will have on your enrollment, accreditation, and ability to secure funding from other donors could potentially be so severe that it is in your program's long-term best interests to decline (politely) the donation that's being offered. One of your duties as a department chair is to serve as a strong advocate for the highest professional standards in your discipline. Accepting a gift that compromised those standards is simply not worth the short-term benefit.

EPILOGUE: A CHECKLIST FOR THE ESSENTIAL DEPARTMENT CHAIR

THE SKILLS REQUIRED FOR success as a department chair are many and varied. Moreover, the factors that lead to a high level of achievement in one environment are not always transferable to different types of departments, institutions, or cultures. Nevertheless, effective department chairs often share many qualities, among the most important of which are the following.

○

The essential department chair combines excellent interpersonal skills with effectiveness in seeing projects through.

One of the biggest surprises for many new department chairs is how much of their time is required for mediating conflicts, hearing complaints, and counseling members of the faculty and staff. Good interpersonal skills are a key component of most chairs' success, and the ability to work well with others tends to become at least as important as the capacity to be visionary, plan schedules and course rotations efficiently, and prepare budgetary documents. But a chair who gets along with everyone while letting important details slip through the cracks isn't likely to be successful either. Effective department chairs usually realize that they have to move back and forth between being people oriented and task oriented, and so they look for ways to improve their skills in both areas.

○

The essential department chair is always learning.

As a result of this recognition that continual development of skills is important for success, effective department chairs relish opportunities to learn and improve the abilities they already have. It's certainly a difficult balance to remain current with research developments in your field, advances in pedagogical technology, and strategic trends at your college or university while at the same time learning as much as you can about becoming better as an administrator. But even if you still see your role more as a faculty member than as an entry-level administrator (and that's precisely how many of the most effective department chairs view themselves), it's still important to recognize that administrative duties are a major part of your job right now. Your discipline needs you to read what other chairs are saying in journals and newsletters for academic leaders, go to conferences and workshops where you can develop your own academic leadership, and build a valuable library of resources that you can turn to for advice, ideas, and even comfort. The Resources section at the end of most chapters is a good place to start, and excellent new books, articles, and Web sites appear all the time.

○

The essential department chair understands that it's important to get out of the office on a regular basis.

Academic leadership requires administrators to be proactive in addressing the needs of their programs, not merely to be reactive in solving the problems that are brought to them. For this reason, a regular part of the day for a department chair is to walk through the areas of campus where their faculty members hold classes, conduct research, or meet to share ideas. An impromptu conversation with a student can alert you to a problem before it becomes too severe—or provide you with a success story to share with a potential donor. Going on rounds periodically can even save you a great deal of time. People who make appointments with you to discuss an issue or even just drop into your office when they decide that they need action immediately will usually occupy a larger part of your day than if they mention their concern when they happen to see you as you're walking across campus. Be sure to carry a small note pad or make a record of the issue on your cell phone and then follow up when you return to the office. The only thing worse than having a chair not act because he or she is unaware of a problem is having a chair who has been fully informed of the problem yet fails to act.

○

The essential department chair recognizes when to advocate for those in the discipline, when to hold them to higher standards, and when to give them some space.

Successful academic leadership requires administrators to be consistent about their core principles, fundamental vision for the discipline, willingness to do more than what's outlined in the official job description, and much more. But good department chairs also recognize that different faculty members and students in their programs often have different needs. And they have different needs at different points in their development too. For this reason, department chairs who are consistently demanding and accept nothing less than absolute perfection in everything people do are no more likely to be effective over the long term than chairs who simply want to get along with everyone, approve exceptions to every policy, and consistently tell people what they want to hear, not what they need to hear. Truly effective administrators realize that their job consists of both seeking what they need others to do and providing an environment in which others can receive what they need. In fact, the very best department chairs spend roughly ten times the amount of energy in a day determining and addressing the needs of others than they do pursuing their own agendas, and they develop a reliable sense of knowing when people need to be pushed a bit harder and when they need to be left on their own.

The essential department chair realizes that preparation is at least as important as planning.
My final essential principle is perhaps the most important of all:

> You can't plan everything. But you can prepare for almost anything.

With the amount of emphasis colleges and universities place on strategic planning, it becomes easy for administrators to lapse into the planning fallacy: the misconception that organizations develop in a predictable manner, that variables as complex as those affecting an institution of higher education can all be known and controlled, and that the context in which organizations operate today will be largely similar to the context in which they will operate five or more years in the future. To the contrary, the sheer number of circumstances that make up the environment of higher education—demographic trends, the local and international economy, enrollment trends in disciplines that can be affected by factors as diverse as the job market and fads in popular entertainment, political changes, technological advancements, shifts in research priorities, and on and on—make it impossible to develop a model of the future of higher education that allows highly detailed planning. The strategic plans for most institutions often provide a rather detailed road map for a year or two but then begin to be accurate only in large and general terms (at best) once five or ten years have passed since they were drafted. Yet this doesn't mean that planning is worthless. What it means is that a plan is not so much a guide to the future as it is a source of insight into how best to prepare for a variety of potential futures. Your own personal planning must be very similar. You can't predict every opportunity and challenge that will come your way, but careful preparation can position you so that you'll be ready for whatever occurs.

o

The essential department chair does not send veiled messages but states openly what he or she means.

One sign of a dysfunctional department is that faculty members gather in small groups after a meeting and ask, "What did the chair mean by saying . . . ?" or "What message do you think the chair was trying to convey by implying . . . ?" Highly politicized environments lead to indirect, veiled, and coded speech, such as occurs when diplomats try to untangle the message hidden in a foreign ruler's speech or when investors try to decipher the implications of remarks by the chairman of the federal reserve. That type of indirect communication can be disastrous in an academic department. Effective chairs say what they mean and mean what they say. If they're dissatisfied with someone's work, they send that message clearly and distinctly through regular procedures as well as through candid, constructive, and private conversations with the faculty member. They never try to communicate indirectly through body language, by how warmly (or not) they acknowledge different members of the department, or by offering and withholding special favors.

o

The essential department chair maintains a healthy work-life balance.

Chairing a department is a hard job. It can consume your life and leave you with little time for your family, friends, hobbies and other interests, or any of the other components that make up a rich, well-balanced life. The most effective department chairs do work very hard on behalf of their disciplines and institutions, but they also keep their professional responsibilities in perspective. Serving as a department chair is what they do; being a department chair isn't who they are. They're able to cope with professional setbacks because there's more to their lives than work alone; they're able to keep their personal problems from undermining their effectiveness at work because they're aware of where one part of their responsibilities ends and another begins. Your department not only needs you as chair to be decisive, supportive, and attentive; it also needs you to be happy, because the attitude that you bring to the office will affect how others view and approach their own responsibilities.

If there is one final insight that every reader should take away from this book, it's that being effective and focusing on the essential activities that make the best use of your time at work can also free up more of your day for all of those other activities that make you a better person as well.

INDEX

Page references followed by *fig* indicate an illustration; followed by *t* indicate a table.